ASA
C42-1941

American Standard
DEFINITIONS
of
ELECTRICAL TERMS

APPROVED
American Standards Association
August 12, 1941

Canadian Engineering Standards Association
March 2, 1942

SPONSOR
American Institute of Electrical Engineers

Price

$1.00 in the United States
$1.25 outside the United States
($1.00 in Canada if ordered from CESA)

Published by
American Institute of Electrical Engineers
33 West Thirty-Ninth Street, New York

Printed in the United States of America

INTRODUCTION

Organization

The American Standards Association approved the initiation of this definitions project in 1928 on the recommendation of the Standards Committee of the American Institute of Electrical Engineers, the scope being outlined as follows:

"Definitions of technical terms used in electrical engineering, including correlation of definitions and terms in existing standards."

Under this authorization, the Sectional Committee on Definitions of Electrical Terms was organized under the sponsorship of the AIEE. This sectional committee has forty-three members representing thirty-three organizations, including national engineering, scientific and professional societies, trade associations, government departments and miscellaneous groups. Eighteen subcommittees were appointed to whom divisions of the work were allotted. These subcommittees, with a total personnel of about 120, have called freely upon non-member experts, so that, in all, over 300 men in all fields have aided in the work. The complete list of the sectional committee and subcommittee personnel follows this introduction.

The reports prepared by the subcommittees were widely publicized and circulated for comment, first in typed form and, after revision, in printed form. From these circulations the sectional committee obtained extensive constructive criticism both from fellow members of the committee and interested experts outside the committee and subcommittee personnel. Three thousand copies of the complete printed report of 1932 were distributed in this country and abroad. As a result of the further wide publicity thus obtained, many additional changes were suggested and considered. The entire report then, in accordance with ASA procedure, was sent in 1937 to letter ballot of the sectional committee. As a result of further criticisms, additional changes were made and a supplemental ballot taken early in 1941. The final report then received official approval by the AIEE and ASA.

The Definitions

The primary aim in compiling this glossary has been to express for each term the meaning which is generally associated with it in electrical engineering work in this country. When possible, the definitions have been generalized so as not to preclude the different specific interpretations which may be attached to the term in particular applications, the greatest weight naturally being given to the strictly engineering applications. Also, it was agreed that the preferred definition is a simple one and the tendency has been toward the simple statement of function rather than to the explicit description of all properties included and excluded.

Arrangement of Glossary

In this glossary the field of electrical engineering is divided into various groups and subsidiary sections, and the terms arranged accordingly so as to permit ready comparison of closely related terms. Where a term occurs in more than one group or section, the definition, if identical, is usually given but once and elsewhere the term alone is given with cross-reference. Where more than one term is in use for the same concept, one term is given first in bold-face type and the synonyms are given in light-face type. Deprecated synonyms are so indicated by a footnote.

The numbering system used to identify terms is based on a system proposed for use by the International Electrotechnical Commission. The numbers consist of three parts separated by periods. The first part, of two digits, identifies the GROUP; the second, also of two digits, denotes the SECTION within the GROUP; and the third, of three digits, designates the TERM. With certain exceptions the group, section and term numbers use at present only the multiples of five so as to permit future interpolations. Groups and sections 05 and 95 have been set aside in all cases for "General" terms and "Not Otherwise Classified," respectively.

The alphabetical index refers to the terms by number. In this index synonyms are given and terms consisting of more than one word may be entered under several.

Acknowledgment

On behalf of the American Institute of Electrical Engineers and the American Standards Association, appreciation and acknowledgment of indebtedness are extended to all those organizations and individuals who have given so freely of their time and experience. The assistance obtained from the definitions and glossaries issued by various technical organizations and national standards associations, particularly the British and the experience of the Secretariat on Nomenclature of the International Electrotechnical Commission, has been very valuable.

Comments Solicited

It is recognized that the glossary in its present state does not include all terms which might be considered pertinent to the electrical field. This statement applies particularly to fundamental and specialized terms. The main efforts of the committees have been devoted to obtaining general agreement on the definitions of terms in greatest use in the electrical standardization field. Although some cases presented difficulties owing to the widely varying views of the interested specialists, they were eventually solved by the adoption of the most generally acceptable wording. If after a period of time following issuance of this publication it proves desirable that certain definitions be revised, such action may be taken in future editions.

Comments and suggestions are requested. Communications should be addressed to H. E. Farrer, Secretary of the Sectional Committee on Definitions of Electrical Terms, AIEE, 33 West 39th Street, New York, N. Y.

SECTIONAL COMMITTEE ON DEFINITIONS OF ELECTRICAL TERMS

Name	Affiliation	Representing
C. H. Sanderson, *Chairman*	Consolidated Edison Co. of N. Y., Inc.	American Institute of Electrical Engineers
H. E. Farrer, *Secretary*	American Institute of Electrical Engineers	
A. W. Baker	American Transit Association	American Transit Association
		Association of American Railroads (Alternate)
E. W. Barnes	Chicago & North Western Rwy. Co.	Association of American Railroads
E. Bennett	University of Wisconsin	Society for Promotion of Engineering Education
C. H. Berry	Harvard University	American Society of Mechanical Engineers
E. M. Bouton	Westinghouse Electric Elevator Co.	Elevator Manufacturers Association
E. D. Brown	McCleary-Harmon Co.	National Electrical Contractors Assn.
C. V. Christie	McGill University	Canadian Engineering Standards Assn.
L. W. Chubb	Westinghouse Elec. & Mfg. Co.	National Electrical Manufacturers Assn.
R. W. Clark	General Electric Co.	American Welding Society
E. C. Crittenden	National Bureau of Standards	Illuminating Engineering Society
H. L. Curtis	National Bureau of Standards	American Society for Testing Materials
J. H. Davis	Baltimore & Ohio Railroad	Association of American Railroads
F. M. Farmer	Electrical Testing Laboratories	American Welding Society
H. Fletcher	Bell Telephone Laboratories, Inc.	National Academy of Sciences
W. J. Foster	General Electric Co.	American Institute of Electrical Engineers
J. C. Frey	National Electric Products	National Electrical Contractors Association (Alternate)
G. H. Garcelon	Westinghouse Elec. & Mfg. Co.	American Institute of Electrical Engineers
R. A. Hentz	Philadelphia Electric Co.	Edison Electric Institute
E. V. Huntington	Harvard University	American Mathematical Society
		Mathematical Association of America
L. C. Ilsley	Bureau of Mines, Experiment Station	United States Bureau of Mines
B. M. Leece	Leece-Neville Co.	Society of Automotive Engineers
O. K. Marti	Allis-Chalmers Mfg. Co.	National Electrical Manufacturers Assn.
W. H. Martin	Bell Telephone Laboratories, Inc.	ASA Telephone Group
A. Maxwell	Edison Electric Institute	Edison Electric Institute (Alternate)
J. Franklin Meyer	National Bureau of Standards	United States National Committee, IEC
L. B. Morse	College of the City of New York	American Physical Society
Officer in Charge, Spec. Sec.	Design Division, Bureau of Engineering, Navy Department	Bureau of Engineering, Navy Department
E. B. Paxton	General Electric Co.	American Institute of Electrical Engineers
H. Pratt	Mackay Radio & Telegraph Co.	Institute of Radio Engineers
W. J. Quinn	Third Avenue Railway System	American Transit Association
H. E. Ruggles	Westinghouse Elec. & Mfg. Co.	National Electrical Manufacturers Assn.
M. R. Scharff	285 Madison Ave., New York, N. Y.	American Institute of Consulting Engineers
W. J. Shackelton	Bell Telephone Laboratories, Inc.	American Society for Testing Materials
C. H. Sharp	294 Fisher Ave., White Plains, N. Y.	Association Edison Illuminating Companies
A. R. Small	Underwriters Laboratories, Inc.	National Fire Protection Association
A. B. Smith	Associated Electric Laboratories, Inc.	United States Independent Telephone Association
V. L. Smithers	National Battery Manufacturers Assn.	National Battery Manufacturers Assn.
R. C. Sogge	General Electric Co.	National Electrical Manufacturers Assn.
J. B. Taylor	General Electric Co.	American Institute of Electrical Engineers
G. W. Vinal	National Bureau of Standards	American Electrochemical Society
C. Wagner	Westinghouse Elec. & Mfg. Co.	American Institute of Electrical Engineers
J. B. Whitehead	Johns Hopkins University	Division of Engineering & Industrial Research, National Research Council
S. E. Whiting	Liberty Mutual Insurance Co.	National Safety Council
W. Wilson	Bell Telephone Laboratories, Inc.	American Institute of Electrical Engineers

SUBCOMMITTEES

of

SECTIONAL COMMITTEE ON DEFINITIONS OF ELECTRICAL TERMS

Subcommittee No. 1

GENERAL (FUNDAMENTAL AND DERIVED) TERMS

H. L. Curtis, *Chairman*
National Bureau of Standards
Washington, D. C.

A. A. Bennett
Brown University
Providence, R. I.

C. V. Christie
McGill University
Montreal, Que., Canada

L. B. Morse
College of the City of New York
New York, N. Y.

W. J. Shackelton
Bell Telephone Laboratories, Inc.
New York, N. Y.

J. B. Whitehead
Johns Hopkins University
Baltimore, Md.

Subcommittee No. 2

ROTATING MACHINERY

C. V. Christie, *Chairman*
McGill University
Montreal, Que., Canada

S. L. Henderson
Westinghouse Elec. & Mfg. Co.
E. Pittsburgh, Pa.

E. B. Paxton
General Electric Co.
Schenectady, N. Y.

O. E. Shirley
General Electric Co.
Schenectady, N. Y.

W. F. Sims
Commonwealth Edison Co.
Chicago, Ill.

Subcommittee No. 3

TRANSFORMERS, REGULATORS, REACTORS AND RECTIFIERS

R. C. Sogge, *Chairman*
General Electric Co.
Schenectady, N. Y.

A. C. Farmer
Westinghouse Elec. & Mfg. Co.
Sharon, Pa.

O. K. Marti
Allis-Chalmers Mfg. Co.
Milwaukee, Wis.

V. M. Montsinger
General Electric Co.
Pittsfield, Mass.

C. H. Sanderson
Consolidated Edison Co. of N. Y., Inc.
New York, N. Y.

6

Subcommittee No. 4

SWITCHING EQUIPMENT

H. E. Ruggles, *Chairman*
Westinghouse Elec. & Mfg. Co.
E. Pittsburgh, Pa.

H. C. Fitch
West Penn Power Co.
Pittsburgh, Pa.

W. T. O'Connell
General Electric Co.
Philadelphia, Pa.

H. P. Sleeper
Public Service Gas & Electric Co.
Newark, N. J.

Subcommittee No. 5

CONTROL EQUIPMENT

G. H. Garcelon, *Chairman*
Westinghouse Elec. & Mfg. Co.
E. Pittsburgh, Pa.

T. E. Barnum
Cutler-Hammer, Inc.
Milwaukee, Wis.

E. M. Bouton
Westinghouse Electric Elevator Co.
Chicago, Ill.

*M. G. Lloyd
National Bureau of Standards
Washington, D. C.

R. N. Shepard
Underwriters' Laboratories, Inc.
New York, N. Y.

W. C. Yates
General Electric Co.
Schenectady, N. Y.

Subcommittee No. 6

INSTRUMENTS, METERS AND METER TESTING

J. Franklin Meyer, *Chairman*
National Bureau of Standards
Washington, D. C.

A. S. Albright
Detroit Edison Co.
Detroit, Mich.

C. H. Berry
Harvard University
Cambridge, Mass.

*O. J. Bushnell
Commonwealth Edison Co.
Chicago, Ill.

H. B. Brooks
National Bureau of Standards
Washington, D. C.

G. H. Garcelon
Westinghouse Elec. & Mfg. Co.
E. Pittsburgh, Pa.

E. S. Lee
General Electric Co.
Schenectady, N. Y.

F. V. Magalhaes
Consolidated Edison Co. of N. Y., Inc.
New York, N. Y.

W. H. Pratt
General Electric Co.
W. Lynn, Mass.

G. Thompson
Electrical Testing Laboratories
New York, N. Y.

Subcommittee No. 7

GENERATION, TRANSMISSION AND DISTRIBUTION

C. H. Sanderson, *Chairman*
Consolidated Edison Co. of N. Y., Inc.
New York, N. Y.

F. M. Farmer
Electrical Testing Laboratories
New York, N. Y.

*M. G. Lloyd
National Bureau of Standards
Washington, D. C.

R. G. McCurdy
American Tel. & Tel. Co.
New York, N. Y.

W. J. Quinn
Third Avenue Railway System
New York, N. Y.

R. C. Sogge
General Electric Co.
Schenectady, N. Y.

C. Wagner
Westinghouse Elec. & Mfg. Co.
E. Pittsburgh, Pa.

* Deceased.

7

Subcommittee No. 8

TRANSPORTATION

J. H. Davis, *Chairman*
Baltimore & Ohio Railroad
Baltimore, Md.

A. H. Candee
Westinghouse Elec. & Mfg. Co.
E. Pittsburgh, Pa.

*F. E. Case
General Electric Co.
Erie, Pa.

W. E. Goodman
Goodman Mfg. Co.
Chicago, Ill.

W. J. Quinn
Third Avenue Railway System
New York, N. Y.

W. E. Thau
Westinghouse Elec. & Mfg. Co.
New York, N. Y.

W. D. Tipton
Curtis-Wright Flying Service
Baltimore, Md.

Subcommittee No. 9

ELECTROMECHANICAL APPLICATIONS

E. B. Paxton, *Chairman*
General Electric Co.
Schenectady, N. Y.

F. A. Annett
McGraw-Hill Publishing Co.
New York, N. Y.

C. H. Berry
Harvard University
Cambridge, Mass.

*M. H. Christopherson
New York State Department of Labor
New York, N. Y.

G. A. Dawson
Westinghouse Electric Elevator Co.
New York, N. Y.

J. A. Dickinson
National Bureau of Standards
Washington, D. C.

H. D. James
Commonwealth Annex
Pittsburgh, Pa.

D. Lindquist
Otis Elevator Co.
New York, N. Y.

J. J. Matson
General Electric Co.
Schenectady, N. Y.

G. H. Reppert
Otis Elevator Co.
New York, N. Y.

R. H. Rogers
General Electric Co.
Schenectady, N. Y.

W. Sykes
Inland Steel Co.
Chicago, Ill.

F. Thornton, Jr.
Westinghouse Elec. & Mfg. Co.
E. Pittsburgh, Pa.

Subcommittee No. 10

ELECTRIC WELDING AND CUTTING

F. M. Farmer, *Chairman*
Electrical Testing Laboratories
New York, N. Y.

A. M. Candy
Hollup Corp.
Chicago, Ill.

R. W. Clark
General Electric Co.
Schenectady, N. Y.

J. W. Owens
Fairbanks, Morse & Co.
Beloit, Wis.

*A. Churchward
Wilson Welder & Metals, Inc.
Hoboken, N. J.

*D. H. Deyoe
General Electric Co.
Schenectady, N. Y.

---

* Deceased.

8

Subcommittee No. 11

ILLUMINATING ENGINEERING

C. H. Sharp, *Chairman*
294 Fisher Avenue
White Plains, N. Y.

E. C. Crittenden
National Bureau of Standards
Washington, D. C.

F. Benford
General Electric Co.
Schenectady, N. Y.

W. E. Forsythe
General Electric Co.
Cleveland, Ohio

H. P. Gage
Corning Glass Works
Corning, N. Y.

D. R. Grandy
General Electric Vapor Lamp Co.
Hoboken, N. J.

*G. A. Hoadley
The Franklin Institute
Philadelphia, Pa.

*A. E. Kennelly
Harvard University
Cambridge, Mass.

M. Luckiesh
General Electric Co.
Cleveland, Ohio

*C. O. Mailloux
Consulting Engineer
New York, N. Y.

A. S. McAllister
National Bureau of Standards
Washington, D. C.

*I. G. Priest
National Bureau of Standards
Washington, D. C.

W. J. Serrill
Haverford, Pa.

G. H. Stickney
Box 5056, Sea Breeze
Daytona Beach, Fla.

G. Thompson
Electrical Testing Laboratories
New York, N. Y.

A. G. Worthing
University of Pittsburgh,
Pittsburgh, Pa.

Subcommittee No. 12

ELECTROCHEMISTRY AND ELECTROMETALLURGY

G. W. Vinal, *Chairman*
National Bureau of Standards
Washington, D. C.

F. M. Becket
Electrometallurgical Co.
New York, N. Y.

W. Blum
National Bureau of Standards
Washington, D. C.

J. D. Edwards
Aluminum Company of America
New Kensington, Pa.

H. W. Gillett
Battelle Memorial Institute
Columbus, Ohio

C. A. Gillingham
National Carbon Co.
Cleveland, Ohio

L. O. Grondahl
Union Switch & Signal Co.
Swissvale, Pa.

D. A. MacInnes
Rockefeller Institute for Medical Research
New York, N. Y.

W. E. Moore
W. E. Moore & Co.
Pittsburgh, Pa.

D. A. Prichard
Canadian Industries, Ltd.
Montreal, Que., Canada

O. C. Ralston
Bureau of Mines, Experiment Station
College Park, Md.

S. Skowronski
Anaconda Copper Co.
Perth Amboy, N. J.

J. L. Woodbridge
Electric Storage Battery Co.
Philadelphia, Pa.

---

* Deceased.

Subcommittee No. 13

WIRE COMMUNICATION

W. H. Martin, *Chairman*
Bell Telephone Laboratories, Inc.
New York, N. Y.

*W. H. Capen
International Tel. & Tel. Co.
New York, N. Y.

L. J. Prendergast
Southern Railway System
Washington, D. C.

A. B. Smith
Associated Electric Laboratories, Inc.
Chicago, Ill.

F. A. Wolff
National Bureau of Standards
Washington, D. C.

Subcommittee No. 14

RADIO COMMUNICATION

Haraden Pratt, *Chairman*
Mackay Radio & Telegraph Co.
New York, N. Y.

H. E. Hallborg
RCA Communications, Inc.
New York, N. Y.

A. F. Van Dyck
Radio Corporation of America
New York, N. Y.

L. E. Wittemore
American Tel. & Tel. Co.
New York, N. Y.

Subcommittee No. 15

ELECTRONICS

W. Wilson, *Chairman*
Bell Telephone Laboratories, Inc.
New York, N. Y.

K. Henney
McGraw-Hill Publishing Co.
New York, N. Y.

O. W. Pike
General Electric Co.
Schenectady, N. Y.

G. A. Randall
Western Union Telegraph Co.
New York, N. Y.

B. E. Shackelford
Radio Corporation of America
New York, N. Y.

W. F. Snyder
National Bureau of Standards
Washington, D. C.

D. Ulrey
Westinghouse Elec. & Mfg. Co.
E. Pittsburgh, Pa.

C. M. Wheeler
Federal Telegraph Co.
Newark, N. J.

Subcommittee No. 16

RADIOLOGY

*M. G. Lloyd, *Chairman*
National Bureau of Standards
Washington, D. C.

A. C. Christie
1835 Eye Street
Washington, D. C.

A. U. Desjardins
Mayo Clinic
Rochester, Minn.

G. Failla
Memorial Hospital
New York, N. Y.

L. J. Menville
1201 Maison Blanche Bldg.
New Orleans, La.

M. Morrison
Westinghouse X-Ray Co., Inc.
Long Island City, N. Y.

R. R. Newell
Stanford University Hospital
San Francisco, Calif.

H. K. Pancoast
University Hospital
Philadelphia, Pa.

* Deceased.

Subcommittee No. 17

ELECTROBIOLOGY, INCLUDING ELECTROTHERAPEUTICS

*M. G. Lloyd, *Chairman*
National Bureau of Standards
Washington, D. C.

A. U. Desjardins
Mayo Clinic
Rochester, Minn.

G. M. MacKee
200 West 59th Street
New York, N. Y.

M. Morrison
Westinghouse X-Ray Co., Inc.
Long Island City, N. Y.

R. B. Osgood
372 Marlborough St.
Boston, Mass.

Subcommittee No. 18

MISCELLANEOUS

*M. G. Lloyd, *Chairman*
National Bureau of Standards
Washington, D. C.

A. Coggeshall
Hatzel & Buehler, Inc.
New York, N. Y.

D. S. Cole
Leece-Neville Co.
Cleveland, Ohio

C. H. Sanderson
Consolidated Edison Co. of N. Y., Inc.
New York, N. Y.

A. R. Small
Underwriters' Laboratories, Inc.
Chicago, Ill.

S. E. Whiting
Liberty Mutual Insurance Co.
Boston, Mass.

* Deceased.

TABLE OF CONTENTS

DEFINITIONS OF ELECTRICAL TERMS

GROUP 05—GENERAL (FUNDAMENTAL AND DERIVED) TERMS

SECTIONS

05   General Mathematical and Physical Terms
10   Matter and Electricity
15   Electrostatics
20   Electrokinetics (Electrodynamics)
21   Power and Related Quantities in Alternating-Current Circuits

25   Magnetics
30   Electrical Properties of Materials
35   Units and Systems of Measurement
40   Laws and Effects
45   Apparatus and Accessories
50   General Engineering Terms

Section 05—General Mathematical and Physical Terms

Magnitude of a Physical Quantity   05.05.005

The magnitude of a physical quantity is the absolute value of the number (either real or complex) used to represent the relationship between the physical quantity and the unit used in measuring it.

The absolute value of a number, x, is denoted by the symbol $|x|$.

Examples of absolute numbers: If $x = 5$, $|x| = 5$; if $x = -5$, $|x| = 5$; if $x = 3 + 4\sqrt{-1}$, $|x| = \sqrt{9 + 16} = 5$.

Scalar Quantity   05.05.010

(Scalar)

A scalar quantity is any quantity which has magnitude only. The relationship between any physical quantity and the unit used to measure it is completely described by a real number.

Examples of scalar quantities for which the relationship to the unit can be represented by a positive number: Mass, energy, electric resistance. Examples of scalar quantities for which the relationship can be represented by either a positive or a negative number: Time, temperature, quantity of electricity.

Vector Quantity   05.05.015

(Vector)

A vector quantity is a quantity which has both magnitude and direction.

Examples of physical quantities that are vectors: Displacement, velocity, force, magnetic intensity.

The most common methods of describing a vector quantity are by means of the projections on a system of rectangular coordinates, or by stating the magnitude and direction by means of spherical coordinates. In rectangular coordinates, if i, j, k represent unit vectors along the X, Y, Z axes, respectively, and if V_x, V_y and V_z are the scalar values of the projections of the vector V on the axes, then $V = i\,V_x + j\,V_y + k\,V_z$ where the + sign denotes vector addition. If R, θ and ϕ are the spherical coordinates of V (as in the accompanying figure) then

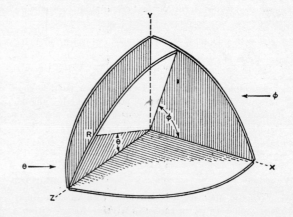

$$V_x = R \sin \theta \cos \phi$$
$$V_y = R \sin \theta \sin \phi$$
$$V_z = R \cos \theta$$

Here a right-handed system of coordinates must be used; that is, a system in which a right-handed screw advancing along the positive Z axis will make the X axis coincide with the Y axis by a rotation of 90 degrees.

A vector that is confined to a plane can be represented by a complex number.

Scalar Product   05.05.020

(Dot Product) (Inner Product)*

The scalar product of two vectors is the scalar quantity obtained by multiplying the product of the magnitudes of the two vectors by the cosine of the angle between them. The scalar product of two vectors A and B may be indicated by means of a dot, A·B. Another common method is to enclose A and B in parentheses, (A B). If the values of the two vectors are given in terms of their rectangular components, then

$$A \cdot B = (A\,B) = A_x\,B_x + A_y\,B_y + A_z\,B_z$$

Example: Work is the scalar product of force times displacement.

----
* Deprecated.

Vector Product   05.05.025

(Cross Product) (Outer Product)*

The vector product of vector **A** times vector **B** is a vector **C** which has a magnitude obtained by multiplying the product of the magnitudes of **A** and **B** by the sine of the angle between them; the positive direction of **C** is that traveled by a right-handed screw turning about an axis perpendicular to the plane of **A** and **B**, in the sense in which **A** would move into **B** by a rotation of less than 180 degrees; it is assumed that **A** and **B** are drawn from the same point.

The vector product of two vectors **A** and **B** may be indicated by using a small multiplication sign, $A \times B$. Another common method is to enclose **A** and **B** in brackets, [**A B**]. The direction of the vector product depends on the order in which the vectors are multiplied so that [**A B**] = − [**B A**]. If the values of the two vectors are given in terms of their rectangular components, then

$$A \times B = [AB] = \begin{vmatrix} i & j & k \\ A_x & A_y & A_z \\ B_x & B_y & B_z \end{vmatrix} = \begin{array}{l} i\,(A_y B_z - A_z B_y) \\ + j\,(A_z B_x - A_x B_z) \\ + k\,(A_x B_y - A_y B_x) \end{array}$$

Example: The linear velocity **V** of a particle in a rotating body is the vector product of the angular velocity, ω, and the radius vector, **r**, from any point on the axis to the point in question, or

$$V = [\omega\,r] = \omega \times r$$
$$= -[r\,\omega] = -r \times \omega$$

Function   05.05.030

When a quantity u is so related to a variable quantity x that to every choice of a value for x (within a given range of values for x) there correspond one or more definite values of u, then u is said to be a function of x, written u = f (x). The independent variable x is called the argument of the function. In general, u is a variable, but may be a constant or zero.

When a quantity u depends on two or more variable quantities, x, y, z . . ., so that for any set of values of x, y, z . . . (within a given range for each of the variables) there corresponds one or more definite values of u, then u is a function of the several variables, written

$$u = f\,(x, y, z \ldots)$$

If x and u are real numbers, the functional relation u = f (x) may be represented in a limited range of values of x by a curve, x being the abscissa and u the ordinate. The slope of the curve at any point is the derivative of the function at that point.

Single-Valued Function   05.05.035

If a quantity u has only one value for each value of x, or for each set of values of x, y, z . . ., then u is a single-valued function.

Example: The temperature at any point of a room is a single-valued function of the position of the point. As three variables determine the position, the temperature of a room cannot be represented by a curve.

* Deprecated.

Multiple-Valued Function   05.05.036

If a quantity u has two or more values for some or all values of x or for some or all sets of values of x, y, z . . ., then u is a multiple-valued function.

Example: The angle, u, having a cosine x (written u = cos⁻¹ x) is a multiple-valued function of x. Before any such multiple-valued function is used in computation, it is necessary to specify which "branch" of the function is intended. For example, the function cos⁻¹ x is ordinarily used only for an angle between 0 degree and 180 degrees.

Scalar Function   05.05.040

A scalar function of a variable scalar quantity is a scalar quantity which has one or more definite values for every value, within assigned limits, of the independent variable.

Examples: The kinetic energy of a body is a scalar function of its velocity (velocity is a vector). The resistance of a given conductor is a scalar function of the temperature of the conductor.

Vector Function   05.05.045

A vector function of a variable quantity is a vector quantity which has a definite value for every value within assigned limits of the independent variable.

Example: The magnetic intensity at a point near an electric circuit is a vector function of the current in the circuit.

Scalar Field   05.05.050

A scalar field in a given region of space is the totality of values of some scalar quantity which has a definite value at each point of the region.

Examples: The distribution of the electric potential in a region surrounding a system of charged bodies is a single-valued scalar field. The distribution of the magnetic potential in a region surrounding a conductor carrying an electric current is a multiple-valued scalar field.

Vector Field   05.05.055

A vector field in a given region of space is the totality of values of some vector quantity which has a definite value at each point of the region.

Example: The distribution of magnetic intensity in a region surrounding a conductor carrying a current is a vector field.

Field Intensity   05.05.060

(Field Strength)

The field intensity at any point in the region occupied by a vector field is the value of the vector at that point.

Uniform Field   05.05.065

A uniform scalar (or vector) field is a field in which, at the instant under consideration, the scalar (or vector) has the same value at every point in the region under consideration.

Non-Uniform Field   05.05.070

A non-uniform scalar (or vector) field is a field in which at the instant under consideration the scalar (or vector) does not have the same value at every point in the region under consideration.

Stationary Field   05.05.075

(Constant Field)*

A stationary scalar (or vector) field is a field in which the scalar (or vector) at any point does not change during the time interval under consideration.

Variable Field   05.05.080

A variable scalar (or vector) field is a field in which the scalar (or vector) at any point changes during the time under consideration, *i. e.*, the scalar (or vector) at any point is a non-constant function of the time.

Rotating Field   05.05.085

A rotating field is a vector field in which the vector at each point rotates in a plane, the planes of rotation being parallel. All vectors in one plane must be in phase, but there may be a change in phase from one plane to another.

Examples: The rotating magnetic field of an induction motor; the electric and the magnetic vectors in circularly and elliptically polarized light.

Sinusoidal Field   05.05.090

A sinusoidal field of either a scalar or a vector quantity is a field in which the magnitude of the quantity at any point varies as the sine or cosine of an independent variable, such as time, displacement or temperature.

Line Integral   05.05.095

The line integral between two points on a given straight or curved line in the region occupied by a vector field is the definite integral of the product of a line element by the component of the vector which is tangent to that element. Thus

$$I = \int_a^b V \cos \theta \; ds = \int_a^b \mathbf{V} \cdot d\mathbf{s}$$
$$= \int_a^b (V_x \; dx + V_y \; dy + V_z \; dz)$$

where $\mathbf{V}$ is the vector having a magnitude V, d$\mathbf{s}$ the element of the line, and θ the angle between $\mathbf{V}$ and d$\mathbf{s}$.

Example: The magnetomotive force along a line connecting two points in a magnetic field is the line integral of the magnetic intensity, *i. e.*, the definite integral between the two points of the product of an element of the line by the tangential component of the magnetic intensity at the element.

Circuitation   05.05.100

(Circulation)*

The circuitation of a closed path in a vector field is the line integral of the vector around the closed path.

* Deprecated.

Flux (in a vector field)   05.05.105

The flux through a surface in any vector field is the integral over the surface of the product of a surface element by the normal component of the vector at that element. Thus

$$\phi = \int\int V \cos \theta \; dS = \int\int \mathbf{V} \cdot d\mathbf{S}$$

where ϕ is the flux, V is the magnitude of the vector $\mathbf{V}$ at an element of surface d$\mathbf{S}$, and θ is the angle between $\mathbf{V}$ and the normal to dS.

Example: The flux of velocity through any surface in a stream of fluid is the surface integral over that surface of the normal component of the velocity. If the velocity field is uniform over a plane surface of area S, then the flux ϕ is given by the equation

$$\phi = V S \cos \theta$$

where V is the magnitude of the velocity (constant over the area) and θ is the angle between the direction of the velocity and the normal to the surface. If the velocity field is a stationary field, the product of the velocity flux by a time gives the volume of fluid which passes through the surface in the given time.

Line of a Vector (in a vector field)   05.05.106

[Characteristic Line (of a vector field)]

A line of a vector in a vector field is a straight or curved line such that, at each point of the path, the vector at that point is tangent to the line.

Examples: Lines of magnetic induction, lines of flow.

Tube (in a vector field)   05.05.110

(Field Tube)

A tube in a vector field is the space which is bounded by the lines of the vector passing through the points of a closed contour.

Gradient (of a scalar field)   05.05.115

The gradient of a scalar field at a point is a vector, the magnitude of which is equal to the space rate of variation of the scalar field in the direction of greatest increase, and the direction of which is in the direction of greatest increase.

If a scalar field U is expressed as a function of the three coordinates X, Y, Z, the three components of the gradient (abbreviated grad U or ∇ U, the latter read nabla U or del U) are the partial derivatives of U with respect to X, Y, Z; or grad U $\equiv \nabla$ U = i D_x U + j D_y U + k D_z U, where i, j and k are unit vectors along X, Y and Z, respectively; D_x, D_y and D_z represent partial derivatives with respect to the subscript; and the + sign indicates vector addition.

Examples: Temperature gradient. Gradient of electric potential, which is electric intensity.

Divergence   05.05.120

The divergence of a vector field at a point is a scalar equal to the limit of the quotient of the outward flux through a closed surface which surrounds the point by the volume within the surface, as the volume approaches zero.

ELECTRICAL DEFINITIONS

If the vector, **A**, of a vector field is expressed in terms of its three rectangular components A_x, A_y, A_z, so that the values of A_x, A_y, A_z are each given as a function of X, Y and Z, the divergence of the vector field **A** (abbreviated div **A**) is the sum of the three scalars obtained by taking the derivatives of each component in the direction of its axis, or

$$\text{div } \mathbf{A} \equiv \nabla \cdot \mathbf{A} \equiv (\nabla \mathbf{A}) = D_x A_x + D_y A_y + D_z A_z$$

Examples: The divergence of the flow of heat at a point in a body is equal to the rate of generation of heat per unit volume at the point. The divergence of the electric intensity at a point is proportional to the volume density of charge at the point.

Curl   05.05.125

(Spin)* (Rotation)*

The curl of a vector field at a point is a vector which has a magnitude equal to the limit of the quotient of the circulation around a surface element on which the point is located by the area of the surface, as the area approaches zero, provided the surface is oriented to give a maximum value of the circulation; the positive direction of this vector is that traveled by a right-handed screw turning about an axis normal to the surface element when an integration around the element in the direction of the turning of the screw gives a positive value to the circulation.

If the vector, A, of a vector field is expressed in terms of its three rectangular components A_x, A_y and A_z, so that the values of A_x, A_y and A_z are each given as a function of X, Y and Z, the curl of the vector field (abbreviated curl **A**) is the vector sum of the partial derivatives of each component with respect to the axes that are perpendicular to it, or

$$\text{curl } \mathbf{A} \equiv \nabla \times \mathbf{A} \equiv [\nabla \mathbf{A}] = \begin{vmatrix} i & j & k \\ D_x & D_y & D_z \\ A_x & A_y & A_z \end{vmatrix} =$$
$$i\,(D_y A_z - D_z A_y) + j\,(D_z A_x - D_x A_z) + k\,(D_x A_y - D_y A_x)$$

where i, j and k are unit vectors along the X, Y and Z axes, respectively.

Examples: The curl of the linear velocity of points in a rotating body is equal to twice the angular velocity. The curl of the magnetic intensity at a point within an electric conductor is equal to 4π times the current density at the point.

Tubular Vector Field   05.05.130

(Solenoidal Field)

A vector field is tubular when the divergence is zero at every point. A tubular vector field can be represented by closed tubes closed on themselves.

Examples: Velocity in a liquid; field of magnetic induction.

Circuital Vector Field   05.05.135

(Rotational Field)* (Cyclical Field)*

---

* Deprecated.

A circuital vector field is a vector field in which there are closed paths within the field for which the circuitation does not vanish.

Example: The field of magnetic intensity associated with an electric current.

Non-Circuital Vector Field   05.05.140

(Lamellar Field) (Irrotational Field)* (Non-Cyclical Field)*

A non-circuital vector field is a vector field for which the circuitation vanishes around every closed path. The curl of a non-circuital vector field is zero at every point.

Example: The field of electric intensity in the neighborhood of stationary electric charges.

Scalar Potential Field   05.05.145

The scalar potential field of a non-circuital vector field is a scalar field which had the property that at every point the negative of its gradient is the value of the vector field at that point.

Example: The electric potential in the region surrounding electric charges has the property that the negative of its gradient is the electric intensity.

Vector Potential Field   05.05.150

A vector potential field of a tubular vector field is a vector field which has the property that its curl is the tubular vector field.

Example: The vector potential field of the current density in an electric circuit is the field of magnetic intensity in the region occupied by the current.

NOTE: Any vector field can be expressed as the gradient of a scalar potential field plus the curl of a vector potential field, either of which may be zero.

Equipotential Line, Surface or Space   05.05.155

An equipotential line, surface or space in a scalar potential field is a line, surface or space in which no potential difference exists between any two points of the line, surface or space.

Monotonic Quantity   05.05.160

A monotonic quantity is a quantity which, as a function of some independent variable (such as time), has the property that, as the independent variable increases, the function either never decreases or never increases.

A monotonic function has no maxima or minima, so that its derivative does not change sign.

Example: The discharge current from a condenser through a non-inductive resistance is a monotonic quantity in which time is the independent variable.

Exponential Quantity   05.05.161

An exponential quantity is a monotonic quantity in which the rate of increase (or decrease) of the quantity is proportional to the quantity itself.

The quantity, y, is an exponential quantity with respect to an independent variable, x, if

$$y = b\,\epsilon^{\alpha x}$$

---

* Deprecated.

where α and b are real constants, and ϵ is the base of the natural logarithms. By differentiation of the equation

$$\frac{dy}{dx} = \alpha \, b \, \epsilon^{\alpha x} = \alpha \, y$$

Hence,

$$y = \frac{1}{\alpha} \frac{dy}{dx}$$

Example: The discharge current of a capacitor through a non-inductive resistance, given as an example of a monotonic quantity, is also an exponential quantity.

Time Constant of an Exponential Quantity   05.05.162

The time constant of an exponential quantity which decreases as the independent variable increases is the factor by which the rate of increase of the quantity must be multiplied to give the quantity itself.

Time constant is the reciprocal of α when the equation for the exponential quantity is written

$$y = b \, \epsilon^{-\alpha x}$$

This reciprocal is called the time constant because the independent variable, x, is most often a time. Numerous statements have been prepared to give a concrete picture of the meaning of time constant. The one most commonly used is that the time constant is the time required for the exponential quantity to change by an amount equal to 0.6321206 times the total change that will occur [$0.6321206 = (\epsilon - 1)/\epsilon$ where ϵ is the base of the natural logarithms].

The time constant of an electric circuit or of a piece of electric apparatus is the same as the time constant of a current in the circuit or in the apparatus.

Examples: The time constant of an inductor which has an inductance L and a resistance R is L/R; of a capacitor which has a resistance, r, in series with its capacitance, C, is r C.

Oscillating Quantity   05.05.165

An oscillating quantity is a quantity which, as a function of some independent variable (such as time), alternately increases and decreases in value, always remaining within finite limits.

Example: The discharge current from a condenser through an inductive resistance (provided the inductance is greater than the product of the capacitance times the square of the resistance).

Periodic Quantity   05.05.170

(Harmonic Quantity)*

A periodic quantity is an oscillating quantity the values of which recur for equal increments of the independent variable. If a periodic quantity, y, is a function of x, then y has the property that $y = f(x) = f(x + k)$, where k, a constant, is *a period* of y. The smallest positive value of k is the primitive period of y, generally called simply *the period* of y.

In general a periodic function can be expanded into a series of that form.

_____
* Deprecated.

$$y = f(x) = A_0 + A_1 \sin(\omega x + \alpha_1)$$
$$+ A_2 \sin(2\omega x + \alpha_2) + \ldots$$

where ω, a positive constant, equals 2π divided by the period k, and the A's and α's are constants which may be positive, negative or zero. This is called a Fourier series.

Period   05.05.175

(Primitive Period)

The period of a periodic quantity is the smallest value of the increment of the independent variable which separates recurring values of the quantity.

If the periodic quantity is expressed by the Fourier series given in its definition, then the period k is given by the equation

$$k = \frac{2\pi}{\omega}$$

In case the independent variable is time, the letter T is often used to designate the period.

Frequency   05.05.180

The frequency of a periodic quantity, in which time is the independent variable, is the number of periods occurring in unit time.

If a periodic quantity, y, is a function of the time, t, such that

$$y = f(t) = A_0 + A_1 \sin(\omega t + \alpha_1)$$
$$+ A_2 \sin(2\omega t + \alpha_2) + \ldots$$

then the frequency is $\omega/2\pi$

Angular Velocity   05.05.185

The angular velocity of a periodic quantity is the frequency multiplied by 2π. If a periodic quantity is expressed as above, the angular velocity is ω.

If the periodic quantity can be considered as resulting from the uniform rotation of a vector, the angular velocity is the number of radians per second passed over by the rotating vector.

Cycle   05.05.190

A cycle is the complete series of values of a periodic quantity which occur during a period.

Alternating Quantity   05.05.195

(Balanced Periodic Quantity)

An alternating quantity is a periodic quantity which has an average value of zero over a complete period.

The equation for an alternating quantity is the same as for a periodic quantity except that $I_0 = 0$.

Symmetrical Alternating Quantity   05.05.200

A symmetrical alternating quantity is an alternating quantity of which all values separated by a half period have the same magnitude but opposite sign. A symmetrical alternating quantity, y, can be represented by the equation

$$y = A_1 \sin(\omega x + \alpha_1) + A_3 \sin(3\omega x + \alpha_3) + A_5 \sin(5\omega x + \alpha_5) + \ldots$$

This equation has the characteristic that it contains only odd terms.

Also $y = f(x) = -f(x + T/2)$ where T is the period.

Generalized Sinusoidal Quantity 05.05.205

A generalized sinusoidal quantity is a quantity which can be represented by a function of the form

$$y = f_0(x) \sin(\omega x + \alpha)$$

where $f_0(x)$, called the modifying function, is a given function of x, and ω and α are constants.

Damped Sinusoidal Quantity 05.05.210

A damped sinusoidal quantity is a generalized sinusodial quantity in which $|f_0(x)|$ is some decreasing function of the independent variable.

Exponentially Damped Sinusoidal Quantity 05.05.215

An exponentially damped sinusoidal quantity is a damped sinusoidal quantity in which the decreasing function is a negative exponential of the independent variable. Thus

$$y = A \epsilon^{-\beta x} \sin(\omega x + \alpha)$$

where A and α are constants, and β and ω are positive constants.

Example: The current when a capacitor is discharged through an inductive resistance, provided the inductance is greater than the product of the capacitance times the square of the resistance.

Simple Sinusoidal Quantity 05.05.220

(Sinusoidal Quantity) (Simple Harmonic Quantity)

A simple sinusoidal quantity is a quantity which is the product of a constant and the sine or cosine of an angle having values varying linearly with the values of the independent variable. Thus $y = A \sin(\omega x + \alpha)$ and $y = A \cos(\omega x + \alpha)$ are simple sinusoidal quantities, where A, ω and α are constants.

NOTE: Any quantity that can be represented by a sine function can also be represented by a cosine function.

Complex Sinusoidal Quantity 05.05.221

(Complex Harmonic Quantity)

The complex sinusoidal quantity corresponding to a given simple sinusoidal quantity is that quantity which is obtained from the simple sinusoidal quantity by replacing the sine or cosine of the angle by the sum of the cosine of the angle and $\sqrt{-1}$ times the sine of the angle. Thus if

$y = A \cos(\omega x + \alpha)$ or $y' = A \sin(\omega x + \alpha)$
$\bar{y} = A[\cos(\omega x + \alpha) + j \sin(\omega x + \alpha)]$

where y (or y') is a simple harmonic quantity, $\bar{y}$ is the corresponding complex harmonic quantity, and $j = \sqrt{-1}$.
But

$$\cos(\omega x + \alpha) + j \sin(\omega x + \alpha) = \epsilon^{j(\omega x + \alpha)}$$

Hence

$y = $ real part of $A \epsilon^{j(\omega x + \alpha)}$
$y' = $ imaginary part of $A \epsilon^{j(\omega x + \alpha)}$

The geometric representation of a complex harmonic quantity is a vector of length A which rotates counterclockwise in the complex plane with an angular velocity ω. For any value of x a complex quantity can be represented by a vector which has a length, A, and makes an angle $(\omega x + \alpha)$ with the real axis.

NOTE: Since the complex harmonic quantity is represented by a line in a complex plane, it is often called a **plane vector**. However, the multiplication and division of plane vectors is very different from that of vectors in space.

Conjugate of a Complex Sinusoidal Quantity 05.05.222

The conjugate of a complex sinusoidal quantity is another complex sinusoidal quantity; the two differing only by having opposite signs before their imaginary portions. Thus if $\bar{y}$ represents the complex sinusoidal quantity and $\hat{y}$ its conjugate

$\bar{y} = A[\cos(\omega x + \alpha) + j \sin(\omega x + \alpha)] = A \epsilon^{j(\omega x + \alpha)}$

$\hat{y} = A[\cos(\omega x + \alpha) - j \sin(\omega x + \alpha)] = A \epsilon^{-j(\omega x + \alpha)}$

In the geometrical representation of these quantities, the direction of rotation of the conjugate is opposite to that of the complex sinusoidal quantity.

NOTE: The conjugate is sometimes represented as y*.
Ed. Note: The use of the asterisk in this case does not signify that this term is deprecated as is the case in other parts of this book.

Vector Representation of a Simple Sinusoidal Quantity 05.05.223

(Complex Representation of the Instantaneous Value of a Sinusoidal Quantity)

A simple sinusoidal quantity can be represented by the vector which represents the corresponding complex sinusoidal quantity. The vector may be considered as rotating or as stationary corresponding to some chosen instant of time.

Modulated Quantity 05.05.225

A modulated quantity is a combination of two or more oscillating quantities which result in the production of new frequency components not present in the original oscillating quantities.

Example: In communication, one of the oscillating quantities of a modulated quantity is called a carrier and the other a signal.

Pulsating Quantity 05.05.230

A pulsating quantity is a periodic quantity which can be considered as the sum of a continuous component and an alternating component of the quantity. The expression for a pulsating quantity is the same as for a periodic quantity; viz.,

$$y = A_0 + A_1 \sin(\omega x + \alpha_1) + A_2 \sin(2\omega x + \alpha_2) + \ldots$$

but with the limitation that $A_0 \neq 0$.

Ripple Quantity 05.05.235

A ripple quantity is the alternating component of a pulsating quantity when this component is small relative to the continuous component.

Harmonic Component   05.05.236

A harmonic component of a periodic quantity is any one of the simple sinusoidal quantities of the Fourier series into which the periodic quantity may be resolved.

Fundamental Harmonic   05.05.237

The fundamental harmonic of a periodic quantity is the harmonic component having the lowest frequency.

Harmonics   05.05.238

The harmonics of a periodic quantity are all of the harmonic components except the fundamental.

Effective Value of a Periodic Quantity   05.05.240

(Root-Mean-Square Value)

The effective value of a periodic quantity is the square root of the average of the squares of the values of the quantity taken throughout one period. Thus, if y is a periodic function of t

$$Y_{eff} = \left[\frac{1}{T} \int_0^T y^2 \, dt \right]^{\frac{1}{2}}$$

where Y_{eff} is the effective value of y, and T is the period.

If a periodic quantity is represented by the Fourier series given in its definition,

$$Y_{eff} = \frac{1}{\sqrt{2}} \sqrt{2 A_0^2 + A_1^2 + A_2^2 + \ldots}$$

Average Value of a Periodic Quantity   05.05.245

The average value of a periodic quantity is the average of the values of the quantity taken throughout one period. If y is a periodic function of t

$$Y_{ave} = \frac{1}{T} \int_0^T y \, dt$$

where Y_{ave} is the average value of y, and T is the period.

If a periodic quantity is represented by the Fourier series given in its definition

$$Y_{ave} = A_0$$

Half-Period Average Value of a Symmetrical Alternating Quantity   05.05.255

(Average Value)* (Mean Value)*

The half-period average value of a symmetrical alternating quantity is the absolute value of the average of the values of the quantity taken throughout a half period, beginning with a zero value. If the quantity has more than two zeros during a cycle, that zero shall be taken which gives the largest half-period average value. Thus if y = f (t) is a symmetrical alternating quantity having a period T, the half-period average value, Y_{ha}, is

$$Y_{ha} = \left| \frac{2}{T} \int_0^{T/2} y \, dt \right| = \left| \frac{2}{T} \int_{T/2}^T y \, dt \right|$$

* Deprecated.

provided the integral is the largest that can be obtained by choosing t = 0 when y = 0.

Rectified Value of an Alternating Quantity   05.05.256

The rectified value of an alternating quantity is the average of all the positive (or negative) values of the quantity during an integral number of periods.

Since the positive values of a quantity, y, are represented by the expression

$$\tfrac{1}{2} \, [y + |\, y \,|]$$

the positive rectified value, Y_r, of the variable quantity y is

$$Y_r = \frac{1}{T} \int_0^T \tfrac{1}{2} \, [\, y + |\, y \,| \,] \, dt$$

where $|\, y \,|$ is the absolute value of y, *i. e.*, the value is always taken as positive, even though the actual value is negative.

Form Factor of a Symmetrical Alternating Quantity   05.05.260

The form factor of a symmetrical alternating quantity is the ratio of the effective value of the quantity to its half-period average value.

Crest Value   05.05.265

(Peak Value)

The crest value of any quantity which varies with the time is the maximum value which the quantity attains during the time interval under consideration. The crest value of a periodic quantity is the maximum value which the quantity attains at any time during a period.

Crest Factor of a Periodic Quantity   05.05.266

The crest factor of a periodic quantity is the ratio of the crest value to the effective value of the quantity.

Amplitude of a Generalized Sinusoidal Quantity   05.05.270

The amplitude of a generalized sinusoidal quantity for any value of the independent variable is the value of the modifying function for that particular value of the independent variable. If $y = f_0 (x) \sin (\omega x + \alpha)$, the amplitude y_1 of y for $x = x_1$ is $y_1 = f_0 (x_1)$.

Amplitude of a Simple Sinusoidal Quantity   05.05.275

The amplitude of a simple sinusoidal quantity is the largest value that the quantity attains. If

$$y = A \sin (\omega x + \alpha),$$

A is the amplitude.

Phase   05.05.280

The phase of a periodic quantity, for a particular value of the independent variable, is the fractional part of a period through which the independent variable has advanced measured from an arbitrary origin. In the case of a simple sinusoidal quantity, the origin is usually taken as the last previous passage through zero from the negative to positive direction. The origin is generally so chosen that the fraction is less than unity.

Phase Angle 05.05.285

The phase angle of a periodic quantity, for a particular value of the independent variable, is the angle obtained by multiplying the phase by 2π if the angle is to be expressed in radians, or by 360 degrees if the angle is to be expressed in degrees.

Phase Difference 05.05.290

The phase difference between two sinusoidal quantities which have the same period is the fractional part of a period (not greater than one-half) through which the independent variable must be assumed to be advanced with respect to only one of the quantities in order that similar values of the fundamental components of the two quantities shall coincide.

Angular Phase Difference 05.05.295

The angular phase difference between two periodic quantities which have the same period is 2π radians (or 360 deg) times the phase difference.

Angle of Lead 05.05.296

The angle of lead of one sinusoidal quantity with respect to a second sinusoidal quantity having the same period is the angular phase difference by which the *second* quantity must be assumed to be *advanced* to coincide with the *first*.

Angle of Lag 05.05.297

The angle of lag of one sinusoidal quantity with respect to a second sinusoidal quantity having the same period is the angular phase difference by which the *second* quantity must be assumed to be *retarded* to coincide with the *first*.

Synchronism 05.05.300

Synchronism expresses the phase relationship between two or more periodic quantities of the same period when the phase difference between them is zero.

Quadrature 05.05.305

Quadrature expresses the phase relationship between two periodic quantities of the same period when the phase difference between them is one-fourth of a period.

Opposition 05.05.310

Opposition expresses the phase relationship between two periodic quantities of the same period when the phase difference between them is one-half of a period.

Ripple Ratio 05.05.315

The ripple ratio of a ripple quantity is the ratio of the difference between the maximum and minimum values of the quantity to the average value.

Oscillation 05.05.320

(Vibration)

Oscillation is applied to the state of a physical quantity when, in the time interval under consideration, the value of the quantity is continually changing in such a manner that it passes through maxima and minima.

Examples: Oscillating pendulum, oscillating electric current, oscillating electromotive force.

NOTE: Vibration is sometimes used synonymously with oscillation, but is more properly applied to the motion of a mechanical system in which the motion is in part determined by the elastic properties of the body.

Free Oscillation 05.05.325

(Free Vibration)

The free oscillation of a system is the oscillation of some physical quantity connected with the system under the influence either of internal forces or of a constant force having its origin outside the system, or of both.

Examples: The electricity in an electric circuit executes free oscillations under the influence of internal forces only. A pendulum executes free oscillations under the influence of the constant force arising from gravity. A magnet suspended horizontally by an elastic wire executes free torsional oscillations (or vibrations) under the combined influence of internal forces (torsion of suspension) and of a constant external force (earth's magnetic field).

Forced Oscillation 05.05.330

(Forced Vibration)

The forced oscillation of a system is the oscillation when periodic forces outside the body or system determine the period of the oscillations.

Sustained Oscillation 05.05.335

(Sustained Vibration)

The sustained oscillation of a system is the oscillation when forces outside the system, but controlled by the system, maintain a periodic oscillation of the system with a period which is nearly the natural period of the system.

Example: Pendulum actuated by a clock mechanism.

Damped Oscillation 05.05.336

(Damped Vibration)

The damped oscillation of a system is the oscillation when the amplitude of the oscillating quantity decreases with time. If the rate of decrease can be expressed by means of a mathematical function, the name of the function may be used to describe the damping. Thus if the rate of decrease is expressed as a negative exponential, the system is said to be an exponentially damped system.

Natural Period 05.05.340

The natural period of a body or system is the period of the free oscillation of the body or system.

When the period varies with amplitude, the natural period is the period when the amplitude approaches zero.

Damped Harmonic System 05.05.345

(Linear System with One Degree of Freedom)

A damped harmonic system is a physical system in which the internal forces, when the system is in motion, can be represented by the terms of a linear differential equation with constant coefficients, the order of the equation being higher than the first.

When the constants of a damped harmonic system are such that the system is capable of executing free oscillations, the period of the free oscillation is independent of amplitude, so that the natural period can be measured at any amplitude of oscillation.

Example: The differential equation of a damped harmonic system is often of the form

$$M \frac{d^2x}{dt^2} + F \frac{dx}{dt} + S x = f (t)$$

where M, F and S are positive constants of the system; x is the variable of the system (displacement in mechanics, quantity in electricity, etc.); and f (t) is some function of the time, or some constant (including zero).

Examples: A tuning fork is a damped harmonic system in which case M represents a mass; F a coefficient of damping; S a coefficient of restitution; and x a displacement. Also an electric circuit containing inductance, resistance and capacitance is, when a current is flowing, a damped harmonic system, in which case M represents the self inductance of the circuit; F the resistance of the circuit; S the reciprocal of the capacitance; and x the quantity of electricity which has passed through a cross-section of the circuit.

Damping   05.05.350

The damping of the motion of a body or system (including electric charges) which has those characteristics necessary to develop oscillations or vibrations is the effect on the system of those continuously applied agencies, either external or internal, which hinder or prevent the execution of vibrations or oscillations.

Underdamping   05.05.355

(Periodic Damping)*

Underdamping describes the condition of a system when the amount of damping is sufficiently small so that, when the system is subjected to a single disturbance, either constant or instantaneous, one or more oscillations are executed by the system. A damped harmonic system is underdamped if $F^2 < 4 M S$.

Aperiodic Damping   05.05.360

Aperiodic damping describes the condition of a system when the amount of damping is so large that, when the system is subjected to a single disturbance, either constant or instantaneous, the system comes to a position of rest without passing through this position. While an aperiodically damped system is not strictly an oscillating system, it has such properties that it would become an oscillating system if the damping were sufficiently reduced. A damped harmonic system is aperiodically damped if $F^2 \gtrless 4 M S$.

Critical Damping   05.05.365

Critical damping is the limiting case of aperiodic damping such that any decrease in the amount of damp-

* Deprecated.

ing will change the damping from aperiodic damping to underdamping. A damped harmonic system is critically damped if $F^2 = 4 M S$.

Overdamping   05.05.370

Overdamping is any case of aperiodic damping in which the amount of damping is greater than that required for critical damping. A damped harmonic system is overdamped if $F^2 > 4 M S$.

Logarithmic Decrement   05.05.375

The logarithmic decrement of an underdamped harmonic system is the natural logarithm of the ratio of the excursions during two successive oscillations when no external forces are applied to maintain the oscillations. The logarithmic decrement of an underdamped harmonic system is:

$$\ln (X_1/X_2) = \frac{2 \pi F}{\sqrt{4 M S - F^2}}$$

where X_1 and X_2 are the maximum amplitudes in two successive cycles.

Damping Factor   05.05.380

The damping factor of any underdamped motion is, during any complete oscillation, the quotient obtained by dividing the logarithmic decrement by the time required for the oscillation.

The damping factor of a damped harmonic system represented by the equation of 05.05.345 is $F/2 M$.

Resonance   05.05.385

Resonance exists between one coordinate of a system which is executing oscillations or vibrations and a periodic agency which maintains the oscillations or vibrations when a small amplitude of the periodic agency produces in the system a relatively large amplitude of oscillation or vibration.

Amplitude Resonance   05.05.390

Amplitude resonance exists when the resonance is such that any change in the period of the periodic agency without changing its amplitude produces a decrease in the amplitude of the oscillation or vibration of the system.

Period Resonance   05.05.395

(Natural Resonance)

Period resonance exists when the resonance is such that the period of the applied agency is the same as the natural period of oscillation or vibration of the system.

Phase Resonance   05.05.400

(Velocity Resonance) (Resonance)

Phase resonance exists when the resonance is such that the angular phase difference between the fundamental components of the oscillation or vibration and of the applied agency is 90 degrees ($\pi/2$ rad).

With phase resonance, the time derivative of the coordinate which is in resonance is a maximum.

Resonance in an Electric Circuit 05.05.401

Resonance may exist in an electric circuit possessing inductance, resistance and capacitance between the quantity of electricity which oscillates and a periodically applied electromotive force which sustains the oscillations. Any one of the three kinds of resonance, *viz.*, amplitude resonance, period resonance or phase resonance, may exist depending on the constants of the circuit.

Example: In a circuit possessing inductance L, resistance R, and capacitance C connected in series with an impressed electromotive force $E \sin \omega t$, causing a quantity of electricity q to oscillate, the differential equation connecting potential differences and the electromotive force is

$$L \frac{d^2q}{dt^2} + R \frac{dq}{dt} + \frac{q}{C} = E \sin \omega t$$

where L is the inductance of the circuit in which a quantity of electricity dq passes any cross-section in time dt, R is its resistance, and C its series capacitance. The applied electromotive force has a maximum value E and a period equal to $2 \pi/\omega$. Solving and neglecting terms which rapidly vanish with the time,

$$q = \frac{E \sin (\omega t - \alpha)}{\sqrt{R^2 \omega^2 + \left(\frac{1}{C} - L \omega^2\right)^2}}$$

where $\alpha = \tan^{-1} \dfrac{R \omega}{\dfrac{1}{C} - L \omega^2}$

Applying to this value of q the conditions for the different kinds of resonance, the values of the amplitude, period and phase difference are as given in the following table:

Wave 05.05.405

A wave is a disturbance which is propagated in a medium in such a manner that at any point in the medium the displacement is a function of the time, while at any instant the displacement at a point is a function of the position of the point.

Any physical quantity which has the same relationship to some independent variable (usually time) that a propagated disturbance has, at a particular instant, with respect to space, may be called a wave.

NOTE: In this and following definitions displacement is used as a general term, indicating not only mechanical displacement, but also electric displacement, temperature displacement, etc.

Pulse 05.05.410

A pulse is a wave in which the displacement at each point of the medium is an aperiodic function of the time. A pulse produces at any point a single displacement subsequent to which the medium returns to a state of passive equilibrium.

Periodic Wave 05.05.415

A periodic wave is a wave in which the displacement at each point of the medium is a periodic function of the time.

Periodic waves are classified in the same manner as periodic quantities.

Stationary Wave 05.05.420

(Standing Wave)

A stationary wave is a periodic wave in which the amplitude of the displacement of the medium is a periodic function of the distance in the direction of any line of propagation of the wave.

A stationary wave results from the combination of two or more waves of the same period. The equation of a simple sinusoidal stationary wave when the two

Kind of resonance	Amplitude of oscillation	Period of oscillation	Tangent of angular phase difference between applied electromotive force and oscillations of q
Amplitude[1]	$\dfrac{E \sqrt{L C}}{R \sqrt{1 - \dfrac{R^2 C}{4 L}}}$	$\dfrac{2 \pi \sqrt{L C}}{\sqrt{1 - \dfrac{R^2 C}{2 L}}}$	$\dfrac{2 L \omega}{R} = \sqrt{\dfrac{4 L}{R^2 C} - 2}$
Period[2] (natural)	$\dfrac{E \sqrt{L C}}{R \sqrt{1 - \dfrac{3 R^2 C}{16 L}}}$	$\dfrac{2 \pi \sqrt{L C}}{\sqrt{1 - \dfrac{R^2 C}{4 L}}}$	$\dfrac{4 L \omega}{R} = 2 \sqrt{\dfrac{4 L}{R^2 C} - 1}$
Phase[3]	$\dfrac{E \sqrt{L C}}{R}$	$2 \pi \sqrt{C L}$	∞

Requirements for resonance:
1. Amplitude of oscillation of quantity of electricity is a maximum.
2. Period of applied electromotive force same as natural period of oscillation of quantity of electricity.
3. Angular phase difference between the applied electromotive force and the resulting oscillation of quantity of electricity is $\pi/2$ radians (90 deg) or the amplitude of the current is a maximum.

If the resistance of the circuit is small, there is little difference between the three kinds of resonance.

waves have opposite directions and the same amplitude is

$$y = A \left[\cos \omega \left(t + c\,x\right) + \cos \omega \left(t - c\,x\right)\right]$$
$$= 2\,A \cos \omega\,t \cos \omega\,c\,x$$

Node   05.05.421

A node of a stationary wave is a point in a line of propagation at which the amplitude is a minimum.

Anti-Node   05.05.422

An anti-node of a stationary wave is a point in a line of propagation at which the amplitude is a maximum.

Wave Front   05.05.425

The wave front of a wave in space is a continuous surface at every point of which the displacement from zero in the positive (or negative) direction has at any instant the same value. If the wave is periodic, the displacements of the points on a wave front are in the same phase.

The wave front of a surface wave is a continuous line, the points of which have the same properties as those in the wave front of a wave in space.

See 35.90.105.

Direction of Propagation   05.05.430

The direction of propagation of a wave at any point in an isotropic medium is the normal to the wave front, the positive direction being away from the source of the wave.

Wavelength   05.05.435

The wavelength of a periodic wave in an isotropic medium is the perpendicular distance between two wave fronts in which the displacements have a difference in phase of one complete period.

Attenuation of a Wave   05.05.440

The attenuation of a periodic wave is the decrease in amplitude with distance in the direction of wave propagation when the amplitude at any given place is constant in time or the decrease in amplitude with time at a given place.

Undistorted Wave   05.05.445

An undistorted wave is a periodic wave in which both the attenuation and velocity of propagation are the same for all sinusoidal components and in which no sinusoidal component is present at one point that is not present at all points.

Signal Wave   05.05.450

A signal wave is a wave the characteristics of which permit some intelligence, message or effect to be conveyed.

Modulated Wave   05.05.455

A modulated wave is a combination of two or more waves which results in the production of frequencies not present in the original waves, these new frequencies being ordinarily made up of sums and differences of integral multiples of the frequencies present in the original waves. As an example a modulated wave which is a combination of a carrier wave and a signal wave is employed to transmit signals or speech through a particular physical system. In this case the frequency of the modulated wave is usually taken as the frequency of the carrier wave.

Carrier Wave   05.05.460

A carrier wave is a wave having those characteristics which are essential in order that the modulated wave may be transmitted through a particular physical system.

Damped Wave   05.05.465

A damped wave is a wave in which, at every point, the amplitude of each sinusoidal component is a decreasing function of the time.

Wave Train   05.05.470

A wave train is a limited series of wave cycles caused by a periodic disturbance of short duration.

Longitudinal Wave   05.05.475

A longitudinal wave is a wave in which the direction of displacement at each point of the medium is the same as the direction of propagation.

Transverse Wave   05.05.480

A transverse wave is a wave in which the direction of displacement at each point of the medium is perpendicular to the direction of propagation.

NOTE: In those cases where the displacement makes an acute angle with the direction of propagation, the wave is considered to have longitudinal and transverse components.

Plane Polarized Wave   05.05.485

(Linearly Polarized Wave)

A plane polarized wave is a transverse wave in which the displacements at all points along a line in the direction of propagation lie in a plane passing through this line.

The above definition is equivalent to stating that, in a plane polarized wave, the displacement vector at any point lies in a straight line passing through the point.

Elliptically Polarized Wave   05.05.490

An elliptically polarized wave is a transverse wave in which the displacement vector at any point rotates about the point, and has a magnitude which varies as the radius vector of an ellipse.

An elliptically polarized wave is equivalent to two superimposed plane polarized waves of simple sinusoidal form in which the displacements lie in perpendicular planes and are in quadrature.

Circularly Polarized Wave   05.05.495

A circularly polarized wave is an elliptically polarized wave in which the displacement at any point rotates about the point with constant angular velocity and has a constant magnitude.

A circularly polarized wave is equivalent to two superimposed plane polarized waves of sinusoidal form in which the displacements have the same amplitude, lie in perpendicular planes, and are in quadrature.

Force   05.05.500

A force is any physical cause which is capable of modifying the motion of a body.

The vector sum of the forces acting on a body at rest or in uniform rectilinear motion is zero.

Mass   05.05.505

The mass of a body is that property which determines the acceleration the body will have when acted upon by a given force.

Work   05.05.510

The mechanical work which is done by a force acting on a body is the scalar product of the force by the linear distance through which the point of application moves.

Energy   05.05.515

Energy of a system is measured by the amount of mechanical work which the system is capable of doing.

Kinetic Energy   05.05.520

Kinetic energy is the energy which a mechanical system possesses by virtue of its motion.

The kinetic energy of a particle at any instant is $m v^2/2$, where m is the mass of the particle and v is its path velocity at that instant. The kinetic energy of a body at any instant is the sum of the kinetic energies of its several particles.

Potential Energy   05.05.525

The potential energy of a body or of a system of bodies in a given configuration is the work required to bring the system from an arbitrarily chosen reference configuration to the given configuration without change in the kinetic energy of the system.

Power   05.05.530

Power is the time rate of transferring or transforming energy.

GROUP 05—GENERAL (FUNDAMENTAL AND DERIVED) TERMS

Section 10—Matter and Electricity

Matter   05.10.005

Matter is any physical entity which possesses mass.

Body   05.10.010

A body is a definite portion of matter considered separately from other matter.

Isotropic Body   05.10.011

An isotropic body is a body in which the value of any given property is independent of the direction of measurement.

NOTE: A body may be isotropic with regard to one or more physical properties when it is not isotropic for others.

Electricity   05.10.015

Electricity is a physical agent pervading the atomic structure of matter and characterized by being separable, by the expenditure of energy, into two components designated as positive and negative electricity, in which state the electricity possesses recoverable energy.

Electrification   05.10.020

Electrification of a body is the process of establishing an excess of positive electricity or negative electricity in a body.

Negative Electricity   05.10.025

Negative electricity is the kind of electricity which predominates in a body composed of resin after it has undergone electrification by rubbing with wool.

Positive Electricity   05.10.030

Positive electricity is the kind of electricity which predominates in a body composed of glass after it has undergone electrification by rubbing with silk.

Quantity of Electricity   05.10.035

(Electric Charge) (Charge)

The quantity of electricity on (or in) a body is the excess of one kind of electricity over the other kind.

A plus sign indicates that the positive electricity is in excess, a minus sign indicates that the negative electricity is in excess.

Electron   05.10.040

An electron is the natural, elementary quantity of negative electricity.

The quantity of electricity on an electron is 1.592×10^{-19} coulomb, or 4.774×10^{-10} electrostatic unit. The mass of an electron at rest is 9.00×10^{-28} gram.

Proton   05.10.045

A proton is the natural, elementary quantity of positive electricity when associated with a mass of atomic magnitude.

The mass of the proton is 1847 times the mass of the electron; i. e., 1.662×10^{-24} gram.

The quantity of positive electricity on the proton is numerically equal to the quantity of negative electricity on the electron.

Positron   05.10.046

The positron is the natural elemental quantity of positive electricity when associated with a mass of electronic magnitude.

See Note under 05.10.047.

Neutron   05.10.047

A neutron is an electrically neutral particle having about the mass of a proton.

NOTE: The positron and neutron have been so recently discovered and are of so rare occurrence as isolated entities that their properties are not well known.

Ion 05.10.050

An ion is an electrified portion of matter of subatomic, atomic or molecular dimensions.

Ionization 05.10.055

Ionization is the process of producing ions.

Electron Volt 05.10.060

(Equivalent Volt)*

An electron volt is the amount of energy gained by an electron in passing from one point to another when the potential of the second point is one volt higher than the first.

One electron volt $= 1.592 \times 10^{-12}$ erg.

GROUP 05—GENERAL (FUNDAMENTAL AND DERIVED) TERMS

Section 15—Electrostatics

Electrostatics 05.15.005

Electrostatics is that branch of science which deals with the laws of electricity at rest.

Electric Intensity 05.15.010

(Electric Field Strength) (Electric Force)*

The electric intensity at a point is a vector which has the direction of the force that would be exerted on a charged particle placed at the point and a magnitude equal to the quotient of the force divided by the quantity of electricity on the particle. It is assumed that the quantity of electricity on the particle does not affect the electric field.

Electric Flux 05.15.015

The electric flux through a surface is the integral over the surface of the normal component of the electric intensity. Thus

$$N = \int \int \mathcal{E} \cos \theta \, dS = \int \int (\mathcal{E} \, dS)$$

where N is the flux through the surface, $\mathcal{E}$ the electric intensity at the surface element dS and θ is the angle between $\mathcal{E}$ and a normal to the surface element.

Electric flux is a scalar, the sign of which depends on the assumption made concerning the positive direction of the normal. With a closed surface, the outward normal is taken as positive.

Electric Field 05.15.020

An electric field is a vector field in which the vector is the electric intensity. An electric field in which there are no electric charges can be quantitatively represented by vector tubes, called tubes of electric intensity, so that such an electric field is a tubular field.

Electric Potential Difference 05.15.025

(Potential Difference)

The electric potential difference between two points is equal to the work associated with the transfer of unit quantity of positive electricity from one point to the other. If outside energy is required to transfer unit positive quantity from a to b, b is at a higher potential than a.

From the definition of electric intensity, it follows that the potential difference between two points is equal to the line integral, along any line connecting the points, of the electric intensity. Thus

$$V_a - V_b = \int_a^b \mathcal{E} \, ds \cos \theta = \int_a^b (\mathcal{E} \cdot ds)$$

where $V_a - V_b$ is the potential difference between a and b; $\mathcal{E}$ is the electric intensity (of magnitude $\mathcal{E}$) at an element of the line ds; θ is the angle between $\mathcal{E}$ and ds.

Electric Potential 05.15.030

The electric potential of a point is the potential difference between the point and some equipotential surface, usually the surface of the earth, which is arbitrarily chosen as having zero potential. A point which has a higher potential than a zero surface is said to have a positive potential; one having a lower potential has a negative potential.

Coefficients of Potential 05.15.035

The coefficients of potential in a system, consisting of one or more insulated conductors, surrounded by a conducting shell maintained at zero potential, or located on one side of an infinite conducting plane, are the coefficients by which the charges on the different conductors must be multiplied in order to give equations for expressing the potential, relative to the shell or plane, of each conductor when the charges on the conductor are known. In the equations

$$V_1 = p_{11} Q_1 + p_{12} Q_2 + \ldots$$
$$V_2 = p_{21} Q_1 + p_{22} Q_2 + \ldots$$
$$\text{etc.}$$

the p's are the coefficients of potential when the V's represent the potentials of the different conductors and the Q's the charges on them. It follows that p_{11} is the potential of conductor 1 when there is unit charge on conductor 1 and zero charge on all other conductors; p_{12} is the potential of conductor 1 when there is unit charge on conductor 2 and zero charge on all other conductors, with similar meanings for the other p's. On account of the equality of reciprocal coefficients, i. e., $p_{12} = p_{21}$, etc., the total number of independent coefficients of potential for n conductors is $(n + 1) n/2$.

---

* Deprecated.

* Deprecated.

Coefficients of Electrostatic Induction 05.15.040

The coefficients of electrostatic induction in a system consisting of two or more conductors surrounded by a conducting shell, or located on one side of an infinite conducting plane, are the coefficients by which the potentials of the different conductors must be multiplied in order to give the charge induced on a conductor which is maintained at zero potential.

Coefficient of Capacitance 05.15.045

The coefficient of capacitance of one conductor in a system of insulated conductors surrounded by a conducting shell maintained at zero potential, or located on one side of an infinite conducting plane, is the quantity of electricity required to raise the potential of the conductor to unity if all the other conductors of the system are kept at the potential of the shell or plane. If there is but one conductor inside the shell, or adjacent to the plane, then the coefficient of capacitance of this conductor is the capacitance between the conductor and shell or between the conductor and plane.

If q_{11} is the coefficient of capacitance of conductor 1, q_{22} of conductor 2, etc., and if q_{12} is the coefficient of induction between conductors 1 and 2, q_{13} between 1 and 3, etc., then the total charge Q_1, Q_2, etc., on each of the conductors at potentials V_1, V_2, etc., is given by the equation

$$Q_1 = q_{11} V_1 + q_{12} V_2 + q_{13} V_3 + \ldots$$
$$Q_2 = q_{21} V_1 + q_{22} V_2 + q_{23} V_3 + \ldots$$
$$\text{etc.}$$

Since $q_{12} = q_{21}$, $q_{13} = q_{31}$, etc., the number of coefficients of capacitance is n and of induction is $(n - 1) n/2$.

Capacitance 05.15.050

(Capacity)

Capacitance is that property of a system of conductors and dielectrics which permits the storage of electricity when potential differences exist between the conductors.

Its value is expressed as the ratio of a quantity of electricity to a potential difference. A capacitance value is always positive.

See 05.20.215.

Capacitance Between Two Conductors 05.15.060

The capacitance between two conductors is equal to the ratio of the charge placed on either conductor to the resulting change in potential difference, provided the conductors have received equal and opposite charges.

Capacitances of a Multiple-Conductor System 05.15.065

The capacitances of a multiple-conductor system are all related to the capacitances between the conductors taken in pairs as defined above, so that in an n-conductor system there are $\frac{1}{2} n (n - 1)$ independent capacitances, each of which is a direct capacitance as defined below. As defined below, total, grounded, direct, mutual and plenary are used to indicate different groupings of the

n conductors, and the names are used even if, in addition to the n conductors constituting the working system, there are additional conductors which, either intentionally, or because they are inaccessible, are not counted. Two or more conductors when connected conductively together are regarded as one conductor.

Ignored Conductor 05.15.066

An ignored conductor in a multiple-conductor system is a conductor either accessible or inaccessible, the charge of which is not changed and to which no connection is made in the course of the determination of any one of the capacitances of the remaining conductors of the system.

Total Capacitance 05.15.070

The total capacitance of a conductor in a multiple-conductor system is the capacitance between this conductor and the other $(n-1)$ conductors connected together.

Note: The total capacitance of a conductor equals the sum of its $(n-1)$ direct capacitances to the other $(n-1)$ conductors.

Grounded Capacitance 05.15.075

The grounded capacitance of a conductor in a multiple-conductor system is the capacitance between this conductor and the other $(n-1)$ conductors when they are connected together and connected to ground.

Direct Capacitance 05.15.080

The direct capacitance between two conductors in a multiple-conductor system is the part of the total capacitance of each conductor which is not a part of the total capacitance of the two conductors connected together.

The direct capacitance is equal to one-half of the excess of the sum of the total capacitances of the two conductors considered separately over the total capacitance of the two connected together.

Note: Direct capacitance equals the ratio of the charge placed on either conductor to its resulting change in potential above the other conductor when all remaining $(n-2)$ conductors are at the potential of the first conductor, the charge placed on the second conductor being equal to the sum of the charges placed on all the other conductors. It is the negative of Maxwell's "Coefficient of Induction."

For any n-conductor system there is an electrically "equivalent direct capacitance network" made up of the $\frac{1}{2} n (n-1)$ direct capacitances connecting in pairs the n terminals of the network.

Plenary Capacitance 05.15.085

The plenary capacitance between two conductors is the capacitance between them when each of the other $(n-2)$ conductors including ground is regarded as an ignored conductor.

Mutual Capacitance 05.15.090

The mutual capacitance between two conductors is the capacitance between them when the other $(n-2)$ conductors, including ground, are connected together and then regarded as an ignored conductor.

Capacitance Diagram for Multiple Conductors   05.15.091

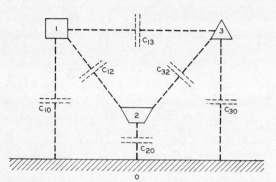

Capacitance Diagram—Showing the equivalent direct capacitance network of a 4-conductor system, when one of the conductors is the ground.

Capacitance Relationships for Multiple Conductors   05.15.092

The relationships of the direct capacitances in a four-conductor system to the other defined capacitances and to the coefficients of capacitance and electrostatic induction are given in the following table. As in the diagram, the direct capacitances between the conductors of the system, including ground, are indicated as C_{10}, C_{12}, C_{13}, etc. In order to arrange in a cyclic order, the direct capacitance between conductors 1 and 2 is written either as C_{12} or C_{21}, and similarly for the other conductors.

lent to a system consisting of two infinite charges of opposite sign at an infinitesimal distance apart.

Dipole   05.15.120

A dipole is a molecule which has an electric moment. For a molecule to be a dipole, the centroid or effective center of the positive charges must be at a different point from the centroid of the negative charges.

Gauss' Theorem   05.15.125

Gauss' theorem states that the integral over any closed surface of the normal component of the electric displacement is equal to the electric charge within the surface. Thus

$$(\smallint\smallint)\,(\mathbf{D}\cdot d\mathbf{S}) = \frac{K}{4\pi}\,(\smallint\smallint)\,(\mathbf{E}\cdot d\mathbf{S}) = Q$$

where $(\smallint\smallint)$ means integration over a closed surface, $\mathbf{D}$ is the displacement, and $\mathbf{E}$ the electric intensity at an element of surface $d\mathbf{S}$, Q is an electric charge within the surface, and K is the dielectric constant of the material within the surface.

Poisson's Equation   05.15.130

Poisson's equation states that, at any point in an isotropic medium, the divergence of the electric displacement is proportional to the density of the electric charge. If all quantities are measured in cgs electrostatic units, the equation is

$$K\,\nabla^2 V = -4\pi\rho$$

where K, V and ρ represent the dielectric constant, the

Conductor	Total capacitance	Grounded capacitance	Coefficient of capacitance
1	$C_{10} + C_{12} + C_{13}$	$C_{10} + C_{12} + C_{13}$	$q_{11} = C_{10} + C_{12} + C_{13}$
2	$C_{20} + C_{21} + C_{23}$	$C_{20} + C_{21} + C_{23}$	$q_{22} = C_{20} + C_{21} + C_{23}$
3	$C_{30} + C_{31} + C_{32}$	$C_{30} + C_{31} + C_{32}$	$q_{33} = C_{30} + C_{31} + C_{32}$

Pairs of conductors	Plenary capacitance	Mutual capacitance	Coefficient of induction
1–2	$C_{12} + \dfrac{C_{30}(C_{10}+C_{13})(C_{20}+C_{23})+C_{10}C_{20}(C_{31}+C_{32})+C_{31}C_{32}(C_{10}+C_{20})}{C_{30}(C_{10}+C_{13}+C_{20}+C_{23})+(C_{10}+C_{20})(C_{31}+C_{32})}$	$C_{12} + \dfrac{(C_{13}+C_{10})(C_{23}+C_{20})}{C_{13}+C_{10}+C_{23}+C_{20}}$	$q_{12} = -C_{12}$
2–3	$C_{23} + \dfrac{C_{10}(C_{20}+C_{21})(C_{30}+C_{31})+C_{20}C_{30}(C_{31}+C_{21})+C_{31}C_{21}(C_{20}+C_{30})}{C_{10}(C_{20}+C_{21}+C_{30}+C_{31})+(C_{20}+C_{30})(C_{31}+C_{21})}$	$C_{23} + \dfrac{(C_{21}+C_{20})(C_{31}+C_{30})}{C_{21}+C_{20}+C_{31}+C_{30}}$	$q_{23} = -C_{23}$
3–1	$C_{31} + \dfrac{C_{20}(C_{10}+C_{12})(C_{30}+C_{32})+C_{10}C_{30}(C_{32}+C_{12})+C_{12}C_{32}(C_{10}+C_{30})}{C_{20}(C_{10}+C_{12}+C_{30}+C_{32})+(C_{10}+C_{30})(C_{12}+C_{32})}$	$C_{31} + \dfrac{(C_{32}+C_{30})(C_{12}+C_{10})}{C_{32}+C_{30}+C_{12}+C_{10}}$	$q_{31} = -C_{31}$

Electric Moment   05.15.110

The electric moment of two charges of equal magnitude and opposite sign is a vector which has magnitude equal to the product of the magnitude of each charge by the distance between the centers of the charges. The direction of the vector is from the negative to the positive charge.

NOTE: The electric moment is not analogous to a mechanical moment, since the direction of an electric moment is the same as the direction of the line joining the charges, whereas the direction of a mechanical moment is perpendicular to the plane in which the forces are acting.

Electric Doublet   05.15.115

An electric doublet is a system which has a finite electric moment, and which is mathematically equiva-

potential, and the charge density, respectively. In rectangular coordinates this is written

$$K\left(\frac{\partial^2 V}{\partial X^2} + \frac{\partial^2 V}{\partial Y^2} + \frac{\partial^2 V}{\partial Z^2}\right) = -4\pi\rho$$

Laplace's Equation   05.15.135

Laplace's equation states that, at any point in an isotropic medium, which is devoid of electric charges, the divergence of the electric displacement is zero. Expressed as an equation

$$\nabla^2 V = 0$$

or in rectangular coordinates

$$\frac{\partial^2 V}{\partial X^2} + \frac{\partial^2 V}{\partial Y^2} + \frac{\partial^2 V}{\partial Z^2} = 0$$

GROUP 05—GENERAL (FUNDAMENTAL AND DERIVED) TERMS

Section 20—Electrokinetics (Electrodynamics)

Electrokinetics   05.20.005

Electrokinetics is that branch of science which deals with the laws of electricity in motion.

Electric Current   05.20.010

An electric current through a surface is the time rate at which positive or negative electricity passes through the surface. If both positive and negative electricity simultaneously pass through the surface, it is the time rate of passage of the algebraic sum of the two.

Direction of Current   05.20.015

The direction of a current through a surface is, by agreement, taken as the direction of the movement of the positive electricity when it is the predominating component in motion and as the direction opposite to the direction of movement of the negative electricity when the latter is the predominating component in motion.

Conduction Current   05.20.020

A conduction current is a current comprising the movement of negative electricity (electrons) exclusive of any movement due to the transportation of negative electricity by masses larger than electrons.

Convection Current   05.20.025

A convection current is a current in which the electricity is carried by moving masses heavier than electrons.

Cathode-Ray Current   05.20.030

A cathode-ray current is a current in a vacuum or in a rarefied gas comprising the movement of negatively charged subatomic particles, usually electrons.

Anode-Ray Current   05.20.035

(Positive-Ray Current)

An anode-ray current is a current in a rarefied gas comprising the movement of positively charged particles.

Current Density   05.20.045

Current density at a point is a vector having the same direction as the current and having a magnitude equal to the quotient of the current flowing through an infinitesimal area surrounding the point and perpendicular to the direction of the current divided by the area.

In media which obey Ohm's law the current density is proportional to the gradient of the electric potential.

Electric Circuit   05.20.050

An electric circuit is a path or a group of interconnected paths capable of carrying electric currents.

Closed Electric Circuit   05.20.051

A closed electric circuit is a continuous path in the form of a loop or a group of interconnected loops in which each loop is capable of carrying an electric current.

Electromotive Force   05.20.055

Electromotive force is the property of a physical device which tends to produce an electric current in a circuit.

Unidirectional Current   05.20.056

A unidirectional current is a current which has either all positive or all negative values.

Direct Current   05.20.057

(Continuous Current)

A direct current is a unidirectional current in which the changes in value are either zero or so small that they may be neglected. A given current would be considered a direct current in some applications, but would not necessarily be so considered in other applications.

Bidirectional Current   05.20.058

A bidirectional current is a current which has both positive and negative values.

Oscillating Current   05.20.060

An oscillating current is a current which alternately increases and decreases in magnitude with respect to time according to some definite law.

Periodic Current   05.20.065

A periodic current is an oscillating current the values of which recur at equal intervals of time. Thus

$$i = I_0 + I_1 \sin(\omega t + a_1) + I_2 \sin(2\omega t + a_2) + \ldots$$

where

i = the instantaneous value of a periodic current at time t

I_0, I_1, I_2, a_1, a_2 = constants (positive, negative or zero)

$\omega = \dfrac{2\pi}{T}$ (T being the period)

Alternating Current   05.20.070

An alternating current is a periodic current the average value of which over a period is zero. The equation for an alternating current is the same as that for periodic current except that $I_0 = 0$.

Symmetrical Alternating Current   05.20.075

A symmetrical alternating current is an alternating current of which all pairs of values that are separated by a half period have the same magnitude but opposite sign.

A symmetrical alternating current is represented by an equation such as shown under "Periodic Current" in which the constants I_0, I_2, I_4, etc., are all zero.

Simple Sinusoidal Current   05.20.080

(Simple Harmonic Current) (Sinusoidal Current)

A simple sinusoidal current is a symmetrical alternating current the instantaneous values of which are equal to the products of a constant, and the sine or cosine of an angle having values varying linearly with time. Thus

$$i = I_m \sin (\omega t + \alpha)$$
$$\text{or } i = I_m \cos (\omega t + \alpha)$$

where I_m is the maximum value of the current.

Complex Sinusoidal Current   05.20.081

(Vector Current)

A complex sinusoidal current corresponding to a given simple sinusoidal current is that current which is obtained from the simple sinusoidal current by replacing the sine or cosine of the angle by the sum of the cosine of the angle and the $\sqrt{-1}$ times the sine of the angle. Thus if

$$i = I_m \cos (\omega t + \alpha) \text{ or } i' = I_m \sin (\omega t + \alpha)$$

the corresponding complex harmonic current is

$$\bar{i} = I_m \left[\cos (\omega t + \alpha) + j \sin (\omega t + \alpha) \right] = I_m \, \epsilon^{j(\omega t + \alpha)}$$

where i or i' is the simple harmonic current, $\bar{i}$ is a complex harmonic current, and $j = \sqrt{-1}$. Hence

$$i = \text{real part of } I_m \, \epsilon^{j(\omega t + \alpha)}$$
$$\text{and} \qquad i' = \text{imaginary part of } I_m \, \epsilon^{j(\omega t + \alpha)}$$

NOTE: See **05.05.221** for the geometric representation of any complex sinusoidal quantity.

Conjugate of a Complex Sinusoidal Current   05.20.082

(Conjugate Current)*

The conjugate of a complex sinusoidal current is another complex sinusoidal current, the two differing by having opposite signs before their imaginary portions. Thus if $\bar{i}$ represents the complex sinusoidal current and $\hat{i}$ represents its conjugate,

$$\bar{i} = I \left[\cos (\omega t + \alpha) + j \sin (\omega t + \alpha) \right] = I \, \epsilon^{j(\omega t + \alpha)}$$
$$\hat{i} = I \left[\cos (\omega t + \alpha) - j \sin (\omega t + \alpha) \right] = I \, \epsilon^{-j(\omega t + \alpha)}$$

NOTE: See **05.05.221** and **05.05.222** for geometrical representation and vector properties of these quantities.

Vector Representation of a Simple Sinusoidal Current

See **05.05.223**.

Pulsating Current   05.20.085

A pulsating current is a periodic current which is the sum of a direct current and an alternating current.

The equation for a pulsating current is the same as for a periodic current, but $I_0 \neq 0$.

NOTE: A pulsating current is sometimes defined as a unidirectional periodic current so that its values are always positive or always negative.

For this definition the equation is the same as in the preceding case, but there is the added condition that $| I_0 |$ is always greater than the maximum value of the remainder of the equation for a periodic current.

Ripple Current   05.20.090

A ripple current is the alternating-current component

of a pulsating current when this component is small relative to the direct-current component.

The equation for a ripple current is the same as for an alternating current but with the condition that, in the pulsating current of which this is a component,

$$I_0 \gg \sqrt{I_1^2 + I_2^2 + I_3^2 + \dots}$$

NOTE: A ripple current is sometimes defined as a pulsating current in which the alternating-current component is small. In this definition a ripple current is a variety of pulsating current, whereas the preceding definition includes only the alternating-current component of the pulsating current.

Effective Value of a Periodic Current   05.20.095

(Effective Current) (Root-Mean-Square Current)

The effective value of a periodic current is the square root of the average of the squares of the instantaneous values of the current taken throughout one period.

If I is the effective value of a periodic current having a value i at any time t, represented by the equation

$$i = I_0 + I_{1m} \sin (\omega t + \alpha_1) + I_{2m} \sin (2 \omega t + \alpha_2) + \dots$$

then

$$I = \left[\frac{1}{T} \int_0^T i^2 \, dt \right]^{1/2} = \frac{1}{\sqrt{2}} \sqrt{2 \, I_0^2 + I_{1m}^2 + I_{2m}^2 + \dots}$$

If the effective values of the sinusoidal components are I_1, I_2, etc., then

$$I = \sqrt{I_0^2 + I_1^2 + I_2^2 + \dots}$$

Average Value of a Periodic Current   05.20.100

(Average Current)

The average value of a periodic current is the algebraic average of the values of the current taken throughout one period.

If I_{ave} is the average value of a current having a value i at any instant t represented by a Fourier series, then

$$I_{ave} = \frac{1}{T} \int_0^T i \, dt = I_0$$

Half-Period Average Value of a Symmetrical Alternating Current   05.20.105

(Half-Period Average Current) (Average Current)*

The half-period average value of a symmetrical alternating current is the algebraic average of the values of the current taken throughout a half period beginning with a zero value of the current. If the current has more than two zeros during a cycle, that zero shall be taken which gives the largest half-period average value. If

$$i = I_{1m} \sin (\omega t + \alpha_1) + I_{3m} \sin (3 \omega t + \alpha_3) + \dots$$

is a symmetrical alternating current, then if $t = 0$ when $i = 0$, the half-period average value I_{ha} is

---

$$I_{ha} = \left| \frac{2}{T} \int_0^{T/2} i \, dt \right|$$

$$= \frac{2}{\pi} \left[I_{1m} \cos \alpha_1 + \frac{I_{3m}}{3} \cos \alpha_3 + \ldots \right]$$

provided the integral is the largest that can be obtained by choosing $t = 0$ when $i = 0$.

Rectified Value of an Alternating Current 05.20.106

The rectified value of an alternating current is the average of all the positive (or negative) values of the current during an integral number of periods. See 05.05.256 for the mathematical expression.

Direct Electromotive Force (or Voltage) (or Potential Difference)† 05.20.110

Oscillating Electromotive Force (or Voltage) (or Potential Difference)† 05.20.115

Periodic Electromotive Force (or Voltage) (or Potential Difference)† 05.20.120

Alternating Electromotive Force (or Voltage) (or Potential Difference)† 05.20.125

Symmetrical Alternating Electromotive Force (or Voltage) (or Potential Difference)† 05.20.130

Simple Sinusoidal Electromotive Force (or Voltage) (or Potential Difference)† 05.20.135

Complex Harmonic Electromotive Force (or Voltage) (or Potential Difference)† 05.20.136

Conjugate of a Complex Harmonic Electromotive Force (or Voltage) (or Potential Difference)† 05.20.137

Pulsating Electromotive Force (or Voltage) (or Potential Difference)† 05.20.140

Ripple Electromotive Force (or Voltage) (or Potential Difference)† 05.20.145

Effective Value of a Periodic Electromotive Force (or Voltage) (or Potential Difference)† 05.20.146

Average Value of a Periodic Electromotive Force (or Voltage) (or Potential Difference)† 05.20.147

Half Period of a Symmetrical Alternating Electromotive Force (or Voltage) (or Potential Difference)† 05.20.148

† Definitions for the above terms (05.20.110 through 05.20.148) are obtained by substituting the words "electromotive force" (or "voltage") (or "potential difference") for "current" wherever the latter occurs in the definitions of the corresponding types of current.

The equations contained in the definitions of types of current are applicable to definitions of corresponding types of electromotive force (or voltage) (or potential difference) when the symbols for currents, —i, I_0, I_1, etc.—are changed to the symbols for electromotive force—e, E_0, E_1, etc. (or voltage—v, V_0, V_1, etc.) (or potential difference—v, V_0, V_1, etc.).

Resistance 05.20.150

Resistance is the (scalar) property of an electric circuit or of any body that may be used as part of an electric circuit which determines for a given current the rate at which electric energy is converted into heat or radiant energy and which has a value such that the product of the resistance and the square of the current gives the rate of conversion of energy.

In the general case, resistance is a function of the current, but the term is most commonly used in connection with circuits where the resistance is independent of the current.

Direct-Current Resistance 05.20.155

(Resistance)

Direct-current resistance (ordinarily indicated simply as resistance) is the resistance for an unvarying current.

Effective Resistance 05.20.160

Effective resistance is the resistance to a periodic current. It is measured as the quotient of the average rate of dissipation of electric energy during a cycle divided by the square of the effective current.

Inductance 05.20.165

Inductance is the (scalar) property of an electric circuit, or of two neighboring circuits, which determines the electromotive force induced in one of the circuits by a change of current in either of them.

Self Inductance 05.20.170

Self inductance is the property of an electric circuit which determines, for a given rate of change of current in the circuit, the electromotive force induced in the same circuit. Thus

$$e_1 = - L \frac{di_1}{dt}$$

where e_1 and i_1 are in the same circuit and L is the coefficient of self inductance.

Mutual Inductance 05.20.175

Mutual inductance is the common property of two associated electric circuits which determines, for a given rate of change of current in one of the circuits, the electromotive force induced in the other. Thus

$$e_1 = M \frac{di_2}{dt}$$

and

$$e_2 = M \frac{di_1}{dt}$$

where e_1 and i_1 are in circuit 1, e_2 and i_2 are in circuit 2, and M is the coefficient of mutual inductance.

Conductance 05.20.180

Conductance is the property of an electric circuit, or of a body that may be used as a part of an electric circuit, which determines for a given electromotive force in the circuit or for a given potential difference between the terminals of a part of a circuit, the rate at which electric energy is converted into heat or radiant energy, and which has a value such that the product of the conductance and the square of the electromotive force, or potential difference, gives the rate of conversion of energy.

In the general case, conductance is a function of the potential difference, but the term is most generally used in connection with circuits where the conductance is independent of the potential difference.

Direct-Current Conductance   05.20.185

(Conductance)

Direct-current conductance (usually called simply conductance) is the conductance for an unvarying potential difference.

Direct-current conductance is the reciprocal of direct-current resistance.

Effective Conductance   05.20.190

Effective conductance is the conductance for a periodic potential difference. It is measured as the quotient of the average rate of transforming electric energy into heat during a cycle divided by the square of the effective potential difference.

Impedance   05.20.195

The impedance of a portion of an electric circuit to a completely specified periodic current and potential difference is the ratio of the effective value of the potential difference between the terminals to the effective value of the current, there being no source of power in the portion under consideration.

The impedance of a portion of a circuit is

$$Z = \frac{E}{I} = \frac{\sqrt{2\,E_0^2 + E_{1m}^2 + E_{2m}^2 + \ldots}}{\sqrt{2\,I_0^2 + I_{1m}^2 + I_{2m}^2 + \ldots}} =$$

$$\frac{\sqrt{E_0^2 + E_1^2 + E_2^2 + \ldots}}{\sqrt{I_0^2 + I_1^2 + I_2^2 + \ldots}}$$

where E, I, E_1, I_1, etc., represent effective values and E_{1m}, I_{1m}, etc., represent maximum values.

Vector Impedance   05.20.196

(Complex Impedance of a Simple Sinusoidal Current and Potential Difference)

The vector impedance of a portion of an electric circuit for a simple sinusoidal current and potential difference is the ratio of the corresponding complex harmonic potential difference to the corresponding complex current. If

$e = E \cos (\omega t + \alpha)$ is the sinusoidal potential difference
$\bar{e} = E \, \epsilon^{j(\omega t + \alpha)}$ is the corresponding complex potential difference
$i = I \cos (\omega t + \beta)$ is the sinusoidal current
$\bar{i} = I \, \epsilon^{j(\omega t + \beta)}$ is the corresponding complex current
$\bar{z}$ = vector impedance
$Z = E/I$ = scalar impedance
$\bar{z} = \bar{e}/\bar{i} = \dfrac{E}{I} \, \epsilon^{j(\alpha - \beta)} = Z \,[\cos (\alpha - \beta) + j \sin (\alpha - \beta)]$

The vector impedance $\bar{z}$ has the magnitude Z and makes an angle $(\alpha - \beta)$ with the real axis.

Admittance   05.20.200

Admittance is the reciprocal of the impedance.

Vector Admittance   05.20.201

The vector admittance of a portion of an electric circuit for a simple sinusoidal current and potential difference is the ratio of the corresponding complex harmonic current to the corresponding complex potential difference. If

$$\bar{z} = Z \, \epsilon^{j(\alpha - \beta)}; \text{ then } \bar{y} = Y \, \epsilon^{j(\beta - \alpha)}$$

where $\bar{z}$ and $\bar{y}$ are the vector impedance and vector admittance, respectively, of a portion of a circuit, and Z and Y are the corresponding scalar impedance and scalar admittance so that

$$Y = 1/Z$$

Reactance   05.20.205

The reactance of a portion of a circuit for a sinusoidal current and potential difference of the same frequency is the product of the sine of the angular phase difference between the current and potential difference times the ratio of the effective potential difference to the effective current, there being no source of power in the portion of the circuit under consideration. The reactance of a circuit is different for each component of an alternating current. If

$$e = E_{1m} \sin (\omega t + \alpha_1) + E_{2m} \sin (2\,\omega t + \alpha_2) + \ldots$$

and

$$i = I_{1m} \sin (\omega t + \beta_1) + I_{2m} \sin (2\,\omega t + \beta_2) + \ldots$$

then the reactances, X_1, X_2, etc., for the different components are

$$X_1 = \frac{E_{1m} \sin (\alpha_1 - \beta_1)}{I_{1m}} = \frac{E_1 \sin (\alpha_1 - \beta_1)}{I_1}$$

$$X_2 = \frac{E_{2m} \sin (\alpha_2 - \beta_2)}{I_{2m}} = \frac{E_2 \sin (\alpha_2 - \beta_2)}{I_2}$$

etc.

NOTE: The reactance for the entire periodic current is *not* the sum of the reactances of the components. A definition of reactance for a periodic current has not yet been agreed upon.

Susceptance   05.20.210

The susceptance of a portion of a circuit for a sinusoidal current and potential difference of the same frequency is the product of the sine of the angular phase difference between the current and potential difference times the ratio of the effective current to the effective potential difference, there being no source of power in the portion of the circuit under consideration. The susceptance of a circuit is different for each component of an alternating current.

If the current and potential difference are represented by the equations of the preceding definition, then the susceptances B_1, B_2, etc., of the components are

$$B_1 = \frac{I_1 \sin (\alpha_1 - \beta_1)}{E_1}$$

$$B_2 = \frac{I_2 \sin (\alpha_2 - \beta_2)}{E_2}$$

etc.

NOTE: The susceptance for the entire periodic potential difference is *not* the sum of the susceptances of the components. A definition of the susceptance for a periodic current has not yet been agreed upon.

Capacitance   05.20.215

Capacitance from the viewpoint of electrokinetics is the property of an electric system comprising insulated conductors and associated dielectrics which determines for a given time rate of change of potential difference between the conductors, the displacement currents in the system. Thus in a system of two conductors only

$$i = C \frac{de}{dt}$$

where C is the capacitance, i the displacement current and e the potential difference between the conductors.

That the electrostatic and electrokinetic definitions lead to identical values is evident from the following:

The electrostatic definition is $Q = Ce$. Since $Q = \int i \, dt$, it follows that

$$\int i \, dt = C e$$

By differentiation

$$i = C \frac{de}{dt}$$

the kinetic definition.

See 05.15.050.

Capacitance in Multiple-Conductor Systems   05.20.220

In a system of more than two conductors, the general definition of capacitance does not suffice to give a definite value to the capacitance relative to any two selected conductors. In such systems, the following definite values are of importance. Corresponding and identical values are defined in Section 05.15. As in Section 05.15, the terms are used to indicate different groupings of n selected conductors of the system and the names are used even if there are any number of additionally ignored conductors, which may be either concealed or intentionally neglected. Ignored conductors are treated, for the purpose of these definitions as though non-existent.

Direct Capacitance   05.20.225

The direct capacitance between any two conductors is the value of C obtained from the equation

$$i = C \frac{de}{dt}$$

when the displacement current i has the value of the current between the conductors which flows as a result of connecting to the conductors, the varying electromotive force e, and which is not a part of the current from either conductor to any other of the n conductors.

Total Capacitance   05.20.230

The total capacitance of a conductor in a multiple-conductor system is the sum of the direct capacitance of the conductor to all of the remaining $(n-1)$ conductors of the system.

Grounded Capacitance   05.20.235

The grounded capacitance of a conductor is its total capacitance when the remaining connected conductors of the system include ground.

Plenary Capacitance   05.20.240

The plenary capacitance between any two conductors is the value of C obtained from the equation

$$i = C \frac{de}{dt}$$

when the displacement current i has the value of the whole current flowing between the two conductors as a result of connecting to them the varying electromotive force e, when each of the other conductors, including ground, is regarded as an ignored conductor.

Under these conditions equal currents flow onto each of the conductors; that is, no current enters or leaves the system at any of the other conductors.

Mutual Capacitance   05.20.245

The mutual capacitance between any two conductors is the value of C obtained from the equation

$$i = C \frac{de}{dt}$$

when the displacement current i is the value of the whole current flowing between the two conductors as a result of connecting to them the varying electromotive force e, when all the other conductors including ground are connected together and then ignored.

Under these conditions, equal currents flow onto each of the conductors, that is, no current enters or leaves the system at any of the other conductors.

GROUP 05—GENERAL (FUNDAMENTAL AND DERIVED) TERMS
Section 21—Power and Related Quantities in Alternating-Current Circuits

Delimited Region for Electric Power Measurements   05.21.005

A delimited region for electric power measurements is a space from which, or into which, electric energy is transmitted and of which the bounding surface cuts each conductor that brings power into or out of a region, in a cross-section that is an equipotential surface.

Examples of regions that may be delimited for power measurement purposes: A generating station, a manufacturing establishment, a transformer station, a generator, a motor, a lamp, etc.

Point of Entry   05.21.006
(Terminal)

A point of entry for a conductor entering a delimited region is that equipotential cross-section of the conductor which coincides with the bounding surface of the region.

In a conventional circuit, each point of entry is a plane perpendicular to the axis of the conductor.

It follows from this definition that the algebraic sum of the instantaneous currents through the points of entry of a delimited region is zero at every instant.

NOTE: The term "point of entry" has been introduced because of the need in precise definitions of indicating the equipotential surfaces between which potential differences are measured. The term "surface of entry" is more logical, but is lacking in euphony. The terms "terminal" and "phase (or neutral) conductor" refer to a portion of a conductor rather than to an equipotential surface and hence are somewhat indefinite, although they may be considered by a practical engineer as representing a portion throughout which the variation in potential is negligibly small. Hence, the engineer may consider each of these terms synonymous with point of entry.

Sign of Potential Difference   05.21.010

The sign of the potential difference between two points, one of which is taken as a reference point, is positive if work must be expended to transfer positive electricity from the reference point to the other point.

Equation for an Alternating Potential Difference   05.21.015

If the instantaneous potential difference, e, of one point with respect to a reference point is an alternating function of the time, t, measured from some particular instant, the equation connecting e and t is

$$e = E_{1m} \cos (\omega t + \alpha_1) + E_{2m} \cos (2 \omega t + \alpha_2) + \ldots$$
where
$$\omega = 2 \pi \text{ times the frequency}$$
$E_{1m}, E_{2m},$ etc. = the maximum values of the harmonic components of the potential difference
$\alpha_1, \alpha_2,$ etc. = the phase angles of the harmonic components

The coefficients $E_{1m}, E_{2m},$ etc., have definite numerical values, but may be changed from positive to negative or, *vice versa*, by adding, to the phase angle of the corresponding harmonic component, the product obtained by multiplying π radians (180 deg) by an odd integer.

The values of the phase angles $\alpha_1, \alpha_2,$ etc., depend on the instant chosen from which to measure the time, t, which is generally so chosen that α lies between $-\pi$ and $+\pi$ radians (-180 deg and $+180$ deg) with E_{1m} positive.

Sign of Current   05.21.020

The sign (positive or negative) of a current through a surface is a matter of convention. In the following definitions, the direction into the delimited region is taken as positive. The current through a point of entry is positive when positive electricity is flowing through it into the delimited region, or when negative electricity is flowing through it out of the delimited region.

Equation for an Alternating Current   05.21.025

If the instantaneous current, i, through a point of entry is an alternating function of the time, t, measured from some particular instant, the equation connecting i and t is

$$i = I_{1m} \cos (\omega t + \beta_1) + I_{2m} \cos (2 \omega t + \beta_2) + \ldots$$
where
$$\omega = 2 \pi \text{ times the frequency}$$
$I_{1m}, I_{2m},$ etc. = the maximum values of the harmonic components of the current
$\beta_1, \beta_2,$ etc. = the phase angles of the harmonic components

The coefficients $I_{1m}, I_{2m},$ etc., have definite numerical values, but their sign depends both on the convention as to sign through a surface and on the instant chosen from which to measure the time, t. The instant from which t is measured is generally so chosen that β_1 lies between $-\pi$ and $+\pi$ radians (-180 deg and $+180$ deg), although it is often more convenient to change the instant of zero time by a half period, in which case β_1 is changed by π radians (180 deg) and the sign of I_{1m} is also changed.

Instantaneous Power   05.21.030

Instantaneous power at the points of entry of an electric circuit into a region is the rate at which electric energy is being transmitted by the circuit into the region.

Single-Phase Circuit   05.21.035

A single-phase circuit is either an alternating-current circuit which has only two points of entry or one which, having more than two points of entry, is intended to be so energized that the potential differences between all pairs of points of entry are either in phase or differ in phase by 180 degrees.

A single-phase circuit with only two points of entry is called a single-phase, two-wire circuit.

Instantaneous Power of a Single-Phase, Two-Wire Circuit   05.21.040

The instantaneous power at the two points of entry of a single-phase, two-wire circuit is equal to the product obtained by multiplying the instantaneous current through one point of entry by the instantaneous potential difference between that point of entry and the second point which is taken as the reference point.

If both the potential difference and the current are sinusoidal, the instantaneous power, p, at any instant, t, is given by the equation

$$\begin{aligned}
p = ei &= [E_m \cos (\omega t + \alpha)] [I_m \cos (\omega t + \beta)] \\
&= E_m I_m \cos (\omega t + \alpha) \cos (\omega t + \beta) \\
&= \tfrac{1}{2} E_m I_m [\cos (2 \omega t + \alpha + \beta) + \cos (\beta - \alpha)] \\
&= E I [\cos (2 \omega t + \alpha + \beta) + \cos (\beta - \alpha)]
\end{aligned}$$

where E_m and I_m represent the maximum values of the potential difference and current, respectively, and E and I the corresponding effective values.

With alternating current in which both the potential difference and current have harmonics, the instantaneous power is given by the equation

$$\begin{aligned}
p = e i = &\tfrac{1}{2} E_{1m} I_{1m} [\cos (2 \omega t + \alpha_1 + \beta_1) + \cos (\beta_1 - \alpha_1)] \\
&+ \tfrac{1}{2} E_{1m} I_{2m} [\cos (3 \omega t + \alpha_1 + \beta_2) + \cos (\omega t + \beta_2 - \alpha_1)] \\
&+ \tfrac{1}{2} E_{2m} I_{1m} [\cos (3 \omega t + \alpha_2 + \beta_1) + \cos (\omega t + \alpha_2 - \beta_1)] \\
&+ \tfrac{1}{2} E_{2m} I_{2m} [\cos (4 \omega t + \alpha_2 + \beta_2) + \cos (\beta_2 - \alpha_2)] \\
&+ \ldots
\end{aligned}$$

where

$E_{1m}, E_{2m} \ldots = $ the maximum values of the harmonic components of the potential difference

$I_{1m}, I_{2m} \ldots = $ the maximum values of the harmonic components of the current

$\alpha_1, \alpha_2 \ldots = $ the phase angles of the harmonic components of the potential difference

$\beta_1, \beta_2 \ldots = $ the phase angles of the harmonic components of the current

All the phase angles are determined relative to the same zero of time. The *effective* values of the potential differences E_1, E_2, etc., and of the currents I_1, I_2, etc., can be substituted for the maximum values provided the fraction $\tfrac{1}{2}$ is omitted from each term.

The equation for instantaneous power can be conveniently written as a double summation by using a general expression for the amplitude and phase of each harmonic component of potential difference and current.

$I_q = $ the effective value of the current of the q*th* harmonic component

$E_r = $ the effective value of the potential difference of the r*th* harmonic component

Then

$$p = e i = \sum_{q=1}^{\infty} \sum_{r=1}^{\infty} I_q E_r \{ \cos [(r + q) \omega t + \beta_q + \alpha_r] + \cos [(r - q) \omega t + \beta_q - \alpha_r] \}$$

From the conventions here assumed for the sign of the potential difference between two points of entry and for the sign of the current through a point of entry,

instantaneous power is positive when the flow of energy is into the delimited region.

The value of instantaneous power is given in watts when the instantaneous current is in amperes and the instantaneous potential difference is in volts.

Active Power of a Single-Phase, Two-Wire Circuit   05.21.045

(Power) (Actual Power)

Active power at the points of entry of a single-phase, two-wire circuit is the time average of the values of the instantaneous power when the average is taken over a cycle of the alternating current.

The active power, P, in a single-phase, two-wire circuit in which both the potential difference and the current are sinusoidal is given by the equation

$$P = \frac{1}{T} \int_0^T p \, dt = \tfrac{1}{2} E_m I_m \cos (\beta - \alpha) = E I \cos (\beta - \alpha)$$

where T is the period of the alternating current.

The active power in a circuit in which both potential difference and current are sinusoidal is equal to one-half of the real part of the product of the corresponding complex sinusoidal potential difference and the conjugate of the corresponding complex sinusoidal current. Also the active power is equal to $\tfrac{1}{2}$ the real part of the product of the corresponding complex sinusoidal current and the conjugate of the complex sinusoidal potential difference. In the above statements the effective potential difference and the effective current can be used with the omission of the factor $\tfrac{1}{2}$.

If

$$e = E_m \cos (\omega t + \alpha); \quad \bar{e} = E_m \epsilon^{j (\omega t + \alpha)};$$
$$\hat{e} = E_m \epsilon^{-j (\omega t + \alpha)}$$

and

$$i = I_m \cos (\omega t + \beta); \quad \bar{i} = I_m \epsilon^{j (\omega t + \beta)};$$
$$\hat{i} = I_m \epsilon^{-j (\omega t + \beta)}$$

$$\begin{aligned}
P &= \tfrac{1}{2} \text{ real part of } \bar{e} \, \hat{i} = \tfrac{1}{2} \text{ real part of } E_m I_m \epsilon^{j (\alpha - \beta)} \\
&= E I \cos (\alpha - \beta) = E I \cos (\beta - \alpha)
\end{aligned}$$

Also

$$\begin{aligned}
P &= \tfrac{1}{2} \text{ real part of } \hat{e} \, \bar{i} = \tfrac{1}{2} \text{ real part of } E_m I_m \epsilon^{-j(\beta - \alpha)} \\
&= E I \cos (\beta - \alpha)
\end{aligned}$$

In these equations E_m and I_m represent the maximum values of the potential difference and current, and E and I, the effective values.

If both the potential difference and current have harmonics, the equation for the active power can be written in any of the following forms:

$$\begin{aligned}
P = \frac{1}{T} \int_0^T p \, dt &= \tfrac{1}{2} E_{1m} I_{1m} \cos (\beta_1 - \alpha_1) \\
&\quad + \tfrac{1}{2} E_{2m} I_{2m} \cos (\beta_2 - \alpha_2) + \ldots \\
&= \tfrac{1}{2} \sum_{r=1}^{\infty} E_{rm} I_{rm} \cos (\beta_r - \alpha_r) \\
&= \sum_{r=1}^{\infty} E_r I_r \cos (\beta_r - \alpha_r)
\end{aligned}$$

in which E_{rm} and I_{rm} are the maximum values of the rth harmonic component of the potential difference and the current, respectively, and the remaining symbols have the same significance as in the preceding definition.

From the convention here assumed for the sign of a current through a point of entry, active power is positive when the flow of energy is into the delimited region though the portion contributed by some of the individual harmonic components may be negative.

The value of active power is given in watts when the effective current is in amperes and the effective potential difference is in volts.

Reactive Power of a Single-Phase, Two-Wire Circuit   05.21.050

Reactive power at the two points of entry of a single-phase, two-wire circuit, for the special case of a sinusoidal current and a sinusoidal potential difference of the same frequency, is equal to the product obtained by multiplying the effective value of the current by the effective value of the potential difference, and by the sine of the angular phase difference by which the current leads the potential difference.

The equation for the reactive power, Q, of a sinusoidal current and the potential difference is

$$Q = \tfrac{1}{2} E_m I_m \sin (\beta - \alpha) = E I \sin (\beta - \alpha)$$

where the symbols have the same meaning as in 05.21.045.

The reactive power in a circuit in which both the potential difference and current are sinusoidal is equal to one-half of the imaginary part of the product of the conjugate of the corresponding complex sinusoidal potential difference by the corresponding complex sinusoidal current. Also the reactive power is the negative of $\tfrac{1}{2}$ the product of the corresponding complex sinusoidal potential difference and the conjugate of the corresponding complex current. In the above statements the effective potential difference and the effective current can be used with the omission of the factor $\tfrac{1}{2}$. Thus

$$Q = \tfrac{1}{2} \text{ imaginary part of } \hat{e}\,\bar{\imath} = \tfrac{1}{2} \text{ imaginary part of}$$
$$E_m I_m \,\epsilon^{j\,(\beta - \alpha)}$$
$$= E I \sin (\beta - \alpha)$$
$$= - \tfrac{1}{2} \text{ imaginary part of } \bar{e}\,\hat{\imath} = - \tfrac{1}{2} \text{ imaginary part of}$$
$$E_m I_m \,\epsilon^{j\,(\alpha - \beta)}$$
$$= - E I \sin (\alpha - \beta)$$
$$= E I \sin (\beta - \alpha)$$

In these equations E_m and I_m represent the maximum values of the potential difference and current, and E and I the effective values.

The reactive power for the general case of an alternating current and an alternating potential difference where both have harmonics is the algebraic sum of the reactive powers corresponding to the sinusoidal harmonic components.

For this case, the reactive power, Q, is given by the equation

$$Q = \tfrac{1}{2} E_{1m} I_{1m} \sin (\beta_1 - \alpha_1) + \tfrac{1}{2} E_{2m} I_{2m} \sin(\beta_2 - \alpha_2) + \ldots$$
$$= \tfrac{1}{2} \sum_{r=1}^{\infty} E_{rm} I_{rm} \sin (\beta_r - \alpha_r)$$
$$= \sum_{r=1}^{\infty} E_r I_r \sin (\beta_r - \alpha_r)$$

Reactive power may be either positive or negative, and the different components may have different signs. With the convention here used for the sign of a current through a point of entry, a component of reactive power such as the rth, resulting from the rth harmonic components of current and potential difference is positive if, when the phase angles of the current and potential difference have been so chosen that E_{rm} and I_{rm} are both positive, α_r must be increased by less than π radians (180 deg) to make it equal to β_r (current leading potential difference).

The value of reactive power is given in vars when the effective current is in amperes and the effective potential difference is in volts.

NOTE 1: The name var for the unit of reactive power was adopted at the Stockholm meeting of the International Electrotechnical Commission in 1930.

NOTE 2: Under sinusoidal conditions, the definition gives a positive sign to reactive power, if the current leads the potential difference as in the case of the reactive power supplied to a capacitive circuit. Positive reactive power is often called *capacitive reactive power*; negative reactive power is called *inductive reactive power*. This designation of positive sign to capacitive reactive power corresponds to the decision reached in 1935 by the International Electrotechnical Commission.

Vector Power of a Single-Phase, Two-Wire Circuit   05.21.055

(Combined Power) (Vector Volt-Amperes)

Vector power at the points of entry of a single-phase, two-wire circuit is equal, in magnitude, to the square root of the sum of the squares of the active power and the reactive power.

Vector power when both the current and potential difference are sinusoidal is equal to one-half of the product of the corresponding complex sinusoidal current and the conjugate of the complex sinusoidal potential difference. In the above statements the effective potential difference and the effective current can be used with the omission of the factor $\tfrac{1}{2}$. If

$$i = I_m \cos (\omega t + \beta); \ \ \bar{\imath} = I_m \,\epsilon^{j\,(\omega t + \beta)}$$
$$e = E_m \cos (\omega t + \alpha); \hat{e} = E_m \,\epsilon^{-j\,(\omega t + \alpha)}$$

the vector power, $\overline{V}$, is given in both magnitude and direction in a complex plane by the equation

$$\overline{V} = \hat{e}\,\bar{\imath} = \tfrac{1}{2} I_m E_m \,\epsilon^{j\,(\beta - \alpha)} = I E \,[\cos (\beta - \alpha) +$$
$$j \sin (\beta - \alpha)]$$
$$= P + jQ$$

In these equations E_m and I_m represent the maximum values of the potential difference and current, and E and I the effective values.

NOTE: The product $\bar{e}\,\hat{\imath}$ gives the conjugate of the vector power.

The vector power when both the current and potential difference have harmonics is the vector sum of the vector powers of the harmonic components. If $\overline{V}$ is the total vector power and $\overline{V}_1$, $\overline{V}_2$, etc., the vector powers of the harmonic components

$$\overline{V} = \overline{V}_1 + \overline{V}_2 + \ldots$$
$$= E_1 I_1 [\cos (\beta_1 - \alpha_1) + j \sin (\beta_1 - \alpha_1)]$$
$$+ E_2 I_2 [\cos (\beta_2 - \alpha_2) + j \sin (\beta_2 - \alpha_2)] + \ldots$$

If V is the magnitude of $\overline{V}$, P the total active power, P_1, P_2, etc., the active powers of the harmonic components; Q the total reactive power and Q_1, Q_2, etc., the reactive powers of the harmonic components, it follows from the above equation that

$$V = \sqrt{(P_1 + P_2 + \ldots)^2 + (Q_1 + Q_2 + \ldots)^2}$$
$$= \sqrt{P^2 + Q^2}$$

Also if θ is the direction that $\overline{V}$ makes with the real axis,

$$\tan \theta = (Q_1 + Q_2 + \ldots)/(P_1 + P_2 + \ldots) = Q/P$$

For definition of Average Vector Power, see **05.21.175.**

Apparent Power of a Single-Phase, Two-Wire Circuit   05.21.060

Apparent power at the two points of entry of a single-phase, two-wire circuit is equal to the product of the effective current in one conductor multiplied by the effective potential difference between the two points of entry.

The apparent power, U, when both the potential difference and the current are sinusoidal is given by the equation

$$U = E I$$

so that in this case the apparent power is the same as the magnitude of vector power.

The apparent power, U, when either the potential difference, or the current, or both, have harmonics is given by the equation

$$U = E I = \sqrt{(E_1^2 + E_2^2 + \ldots)(I_1^2 + I_2^2 + \ldots)}$$

where

E and I are the effective potential difference and effective current, respectively

E_r is the effective value of the rth harmonic component of the potential difference

I_q is the effective value of the qth harmonic component of the current

If harmonics are present, the apparent power is not identical with vector power.

The unit of apparent power is the volt-ampere.

NOTE: The term volt-ampere, without a qualifying adjective is used as the unit of apparent power because it can be directly measured by means of a voltmeter and an ammeter. Also, it has historical significance.

Distortion Power of a Single-Phase, Two-Wire Circuit   05.21.065

Distortion power is equal to the square root of the difference of the squares of the apparent power and the vector power.

The distortion power, D, is given by the equation

$$D = \sqrt{U^2 - V^2}$$
$$= \sqrt{\sum_{r=1}^{\infty} \sum_{q=1}^{\infty} \{E_r^2 I_q^2 - E_r E_q I_r I_q \cos [(\beta_r - \alpha_r) - (\beta_q - \alpha_q)]\}}$$

where the symbols are those of the preceding definitions.

NOTE: The distortion power is zero if $\beta_r - \alpha_r = \beta_q - \alpha_q$ and if, at the same time, $E_r / E_q = I_r / I_q$; since under these conditions every term of the summation is zero. These conditions are always fulfilled if the circuit between the points of entry consists only of a resistance or if both current and potential difference are sinusoidal.

The unit of distortion power is the distortion volt-ampere.

Fictitious Power of a Single-Phase, Two-Wire Circuit   05.21.070

Fictitious power is equal to the square root of the difference of the squares of the apparent power and the active power. If both the current and potential difference are sinusoidal, or if both have the same wave form (distortion power equal to zero), fictitious power is the same as reactive power.

The fictitious power, F, when either the potential difference or the current contain harmonics, is given by the equation

$$F = \sqrt{U^2 - P^2} = \sqrt{Q^2 + D^2}$$
$$= \sqrt{\sum_{r=1}^{\infty} \sum_{q=1}^{\infty} \{E_r^2 I_q^2 - E_r E_q I_r I_q \cos (\beta_r - \alpha_r) \cos (\beta_q - \alpha_q)\}}$$

where the symbols are those of the preceding definitions.

The unit of fictitious power is the fictitious volt-ampere.

Non-Reactive Power of a Single-Phase, Two-Wire Circuit   05.21.075

Non-reactive power is equal to the square root of the difference of the squares of the apparent power and the reactive power. If both current and potential difference are sinusoidal, or if both have the same wave form (distortion power equal to zero), non-reactive power is the same as active power.

The non-reactive power, N, when either the potential difference or the current contains harmonics, is given by the equation

$$N = \sqrt{U^2 - Q^2} = \sqrt{P^2 + D^2}$$
$$= \sqrt{\sum_{r=1}^{\infty} \sum_{q=1}^{\infty} \{E_r^2 I_q^2 - E_r E_q I_r I_q \sin (\beta_r - \alpha_r) \sin (\beta_q - \alpha_q)\}}$$

where the symbols are those of the preceding definitions.

The unit of non-reactive power is the non-reactive volt-ampere.

Geometric Power Diagram for a Single-Phase, Two-Wire Circuit 05.21.080

The geometric power diagram shows the relationships between the different types of power arranged as vectors in space. In this diagram, active power, reactive power and distortion power are represented in the directions of three rectangular axes. The first two may be either positive or negative, but distortion power is always considered as positive. The accompanying diagram corresponds to a case in which all three are positive.

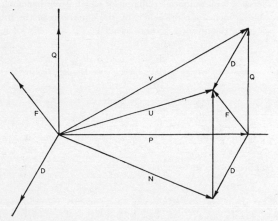

Geometric Power Diagram For a Single-Phase, Two-Wire Circuit

NOMENCLATURE

P = Active power
Q = Reactive power
V = Vector power
U = Apparent power
D = Distortion power
F = Fictitious power
N = Non-reactive power

Single-Phase, Three-Wire Circuit, Definitions of Power Quantities in a 05.21.085

The definitions of the power quantities for a single-phase circuit of more than two wires are the same as those given below for a polyphase circuit.

Polyphase Circuit 05.21.090

A polyphase circuit is a group of alternating-current circuits (usually interconnected) which enter (or leave) a delimited region at more than two points of entry and which are intended to be so energized that in the steady state the alternating currents through the points of entry and the alternating potential differences between them all have exactly equal periods but have differences in phase and may have differences in wave form.

Neutral Conductor 05.21.095

The neutral conductor (when one exists) of a polyphase circuit, or of a single-phase, three-wire circuit, is that conductor which is intended to have a potential such that the potential differences between it and each of the other conductors are approximately equal in magnitude and are also equally spaced in phase.

NOTE: The neutral conductor in a three-wire, direct-current system meets only the magnitude requirement of the above definition.

Phase Conductor 05.21.100

The phase conductors of a polyphase circuit are those conductors other than the neutral conductor.

Star-Connected Circuit 05.21.105

A star-connected circuit is a polyphase circuit in which all the current paths within the region that delimits the circuit extend from each of the points of entry of the phase conductors to a common conductor (which may be the neutral conductor).

Y-Connected Circuit 05.21.106

A Y-connected circuit is a three-phase circuit which is star-connected.

Mesh-Connected Circuit 05.21.109

A mesh-connected circuit is a polyphase circuit in which, within the region which delimits the circuit, current paths extend between the various points of entry in such a manner that one or more closed paths may be traced out, each touching three or more points of entry. A mesh-connected circuit is usually used to designate a circuit within a region when the flow of electric energy is either all into the region or all out of the region.

Completely Mesh-Connected Circuit 05.21.110

A completely mesh-connected circuit is a polyphase circuit in which, within the region that delimits the circuit, a current path extends directly from each point of entry to every other point of entry.

Simply Mesh-Connected Circuit 05.21.115

A simply mesh-connected circuit is a polyphase circuit in which, within the region that delimits the circuit, a current path extends from the point of entry of each phase conductor only to the points of entry of those other two phase conductors which are nearest to *it* in effective potential.

Delta-Connected Circuit (Δ-Connected) 05.21.116

A delta-connected circuit is a three-phase circuit which is simply mesh-connected.

Polyphase Set of Potential Differences 05.21.120

A polyphase set of potential differences is a group of interrelated alternating potential differences all of which have the same fundamental frequency, but each of which differs from every other in phase and may differ in effective value and wave form.

The equations for a polyphase set of n potential differences when each one is sinusoidal are as follows:

$$e_a = E_{am} \cos (\omega t + \alpha_a)$$
$$e_b = E_{bm} \cos (\omega t + \alpha_b)$$
$$e_c = E_{cm} \cos (\omega t + \alpha_c)$$
$$\cdot$$
$$\cdot$$
$$\cdot$$
$$e_n = E_{nm} \cos (\omega t + \alpha_n)$$

where the symbols have the same meaning as for the general case given below.

The equations of a polyphase set of n potential differences each of which has an infinite number of harmonics, one of which is the r*th*, and for each of which the potential difference may be measured from a different base point, are

$$e_a = E_{a1m} \cos (\omega t + \alpha_{a1}) + E_{a2m} \cos (2 \omega t + \alpha_{a2}) + \ldots + E_{arm} \cos (r \omega t + \alpha_{ar}) + \ldots$$
$$e_b = E_{b1m} \cos (\omega t + \alpha_{b1}) + E_{b2m} \cos (2 \omega t + \alpha_{b2}) + \ldots + E_{brm} \cos (r \omega t + \alpha_{br}) + \ldots$$
.
.
.
$$e_n = E_{n1m} \cos (\omega t + \alpha_{n1}) + E_{n2m} \cos (2 \omega t + \alpha_{n2}) + \ldots + E_{nrm} \cos (r \omega t + \alpha_{nr}) + \ldots$$

where

e_a, e_b, . . . e_n = the instantaneous values of the potential differences

E_{a1m} . . . E_{nrm} = the maximum values of the harmonic components of the individual potential differences. The first character of the subscript (a letter between a and n) distinguishes the individual potential difference from other members of the set and the second character of the subscript (a number except as r is used for a generalized number) indicates the number of the harmonic component of the potential difference. The subscript m is added to indicate that the maximum value is used

α_{a1} . . . α_{nr} = the phase angles, each corresponding to the potential difference with the same subscript except that the letter m is dropped, all of which are determined relative to the same zero time

$\omega = 2 \pi$ times the frequency of the fundamental

t = the time measured from an arbitrary origin

Symmetrical Polyphase Set of Potential Differences   05.21.125

A symmetrical polyphase set of n potential differences is a set in which each potential difference has the same effective value and the same wave form as each other potential difference and in which the members of the set can be arranged in a sequence such that, for the fundamental component, the phase difference between each member and the one following it, and between the first and last members, is $2\pi/n$ radians or an integral multiple of this quantity.

In a three-phase circuit in which the potential dif-

ferences are sinusoidal, the potential differences form a symmetrical set if their maximum (or effective) values are equal and if the phase angles can be arranged in a sequence having a difference of $2\pi/3$ radians (or 120 deg), or twice or three times this value.

A set of potential differences which are all sinusoidal are symmetrical if the maximum potential differences are all equal; and if there is the same phase difference between each potential difference and the succeeding one in the set, and between the last and first members of the set.

A set of potential differences which have harmonics and which are represented by the equations of the preceding definition is symmetrical if

$$E_{a1m} = E_{b1m} = \ldots = E_{n1m}$$
$$E_{a2m} = E_{b2m} = \ldots = E_{n2m}$$
.
.
$$E_{arm} = E_{brm} = \ldots = E_{nrm}$$

and

$$\alpha_{b1} - \alpha_{a1} = \alpha_{c1} - \alpha_{b1} = \ldots = \alpha_{a1} - \alpha_{n1} = k \left(\frac{2 \pi}{n} \right)$$

$$\alpha_{b2} - \alpha_{a2} = \alpha_{c2} - \alpha_{b2} = \ldots = \alpha_{a2} - \alpha_{n2} = k \left(\frac{4 \pi}{n} \right)$$
.
.
.
$$\alpha_{br} - \alpha_{ar} = \alpha_{cr} - \alpha_{br} = \ldots = \alpha_{ar} - \alpha_{nr} = k \left(\frac{2 r \pi}{n} \right)$$

Polyphase Set of Alternating Currents   05.21.130

A polyphase set of alternating currents, each in a separate conductor, is a group of interrelated alternating currents all of which have the same fundamental frequency, but may differ in effective value, phase, and wave form.

NOTE: In a star-connected circuit, which has a neutral, the current in the neutral is not generally considered as a separate current of the set, but as the sum of all the other currents.

The equations of a polyphase set of n currents when each one is sinusoidal are as follows:

$$i_a = I_{am} \cos (\omega t + \beta_a)$$
$$i_b = I_{bm} \cos (\omega t + \beta_b)$$
.
.
.
$$i_n = I_{nm} \cos (\omega t + \beta_n)$$

where the symbols are the same as in the general case given below.

The equations of a polyphase set of n currents, each of which has an infinite number of harmonics, one of which is the r*th*, are

$$i_a = I_{a1m} \cos(\omega t + \beta_{a1}) + I_{a2m} \cos(2\omega t + \beta_{a2}) + \ldots + I_{arm} \cos(r\omega t + \beta_{ar}) + \ldots$$

$$i_b = I_{b1m} \cos(\omega t + \beta_{b1}) + I_{b2m} \cos(2\omega t + \beta_{b2}) + \ldots + I_{brm} \cos(r\omega t + \beta_{br}) + \ldots$$

.

.

.

$$i_n = I_{n1m} \cos(\omega t + \beta_{n1}) + I_{n2m} \cos(2\omega t + \beta_{n2}) + \ldots + I_{nrm} \cos(r\omega t + \beta_{nr}) + \ldots$$

where

$i_a, i_b, \ldots i_n$ = the instantaneous values of the currents (considered positive when directed into the delimited region)

$I_{a1m}, \ldots I_{nrm}$ = the maximum values of the harmonic components of the individual currents. The first character of the subscript (a letter between a and n) distinguishes the individual current from other members of the set and the second character of the subscript (a number except as r is used for a generalized number) indicates the number of the harmonic component of the current. The subscript m is added to indicate that the maximum value is used

$\beta_{a1} \ldots \beta_{nr}$ = the phase angles, each corresponding to the current with the same subscript except that the letter m is dropped, all of which are determined relative to the same zero time

$\omega = 2\pi$ times the frequency of the fundamental

t = the time measured from an arbitrary origin

NOTE: These equations have the same form as those for a polyphase set of potential differences.

Symmetrical Polyphase Set of Currents   05.21.135

This definition is obtained from the definition of a symmetrical set of polyphase potential differences by substituting the word "current" for "potential difference." In the mathematical expression "I" replaces "E" and "β" replaces "α"; the subscripts remaining unchanged.

Characteristic Angular Phase Difference   05.21.140

The characteristic angular phase difference of a symmetrical polyphase set of potential differences or currents is the angular phase difference between adjacent members of the sequence.

In a symmetrical polyphase set of n potential differences, the characteristic angular phase difference is $k(2\pi/n)$ radians or $k(360/n)$ degrees.

Symmetrical Components of a Polyphase Set of Potential Differences   05.21.145

The symmetrical components of an unsymmetrical polyphase set of n sinusoidal potential differences are the n symmetrical polyphase sets into which the unsymmetrical set may be uniquely resolved, each component set consisting of n potential differences, and each having a characteristic angular phase difference which increases from set to set by $2\pi/n$ radians.

In the more general case of an unsymmetrical polyphase set of n alternating potential differences, each of which has harmonics, each potential difference is resolved into its harmonic components; then the harmonic components of all the potential differences are grouped to form unsymmetrical sinusoidal sets that are resolved into symmetrical components.

There is only one possible set of symmetrical components for a given set of unsymmetrical sinusoidal potential differences. Since an alternating potential difference has only one possible set of harmonic components, it follows that the symmetrical components of an unsymmetrical set of alternating potential differences are uniquely determined.

The symmetrical components of the fundamental frequency and of each harmonic component have the characteristic angles $2k\pi/n$, $2(2k\pi/n) \ldots n(2k\pi/n)$ radians where k is an integer (usually unity) and n is the number of potential differences of the polyphase set. The symmetrical components obtained when k is a factor in each of the characteristic angles are called the k-sequence symmetrical components of an unsymmetrical set of potential differences.

Positive-Sequence Symmetrical Component   05.21.146

The positive-sequence symmetrical component of an unsymmetrical three-phase set of potential differences (or currents) is that component which has the characteristic angular phase difference of $2\pi/3$ radians or 120 degrees.

Negative-Sequence Symmetrical Component   05.21.147

The negative-sequence symmetrical component of an unsymmetrical three-phase set of potential differences (or currents) is that component which has the characteristic angular phase difference of $4\pi/3$ radians or 240 degrees.

Zero-Sequence Symmetrical Component   05.21.148

The zero-sequence symmetrical component of an unsymmetrical set of potential differences (or currents) is that component which has a characteristic angular phase difference of 2π radians or 360 degrees.

Symmetrical Components of a Polyphase Set of Currents   05.21.150

The definition for symmetrical components of a polyphase set of currents is obtained by substituting the word "current" for "potential difference" in the corresponding definition relating to potential differences (05.21.145). Likewise the definitions for the positive, negative and zero sequences of the currents in a three-phase circuit can be obtained by substituting "current" for "potential difference" in the corresponding definitions.

Instantaneous Power of a Polyphase Circuit   05.21.155

The instantaneous power at the points of entry of a polyphase circuit is equal to the algebraic sum of the products obtained by multiplying the instantaneous current at each point of entry by the potential difference between that point of entry and some arbitrarily selected reference point (which may be the neutral point of entry) from which all the potential differences are measured.

From the convention here used that a current is positive when its direction is into a delimited region, it follows that instantaneous power is positive when the instantaneous transmission of electric energy is into the region delimited by the points of entry.

The instantaneous power, p, at the four points of entry of a three-phase circuit when both the currents and potential differences are sinusoidal and the potential differences are measured from the neutral is given by the equation

$$
\begin{aligned}
p = {} & E_1 I_1 \left\{ \cos (2 \omega t + \alpha_1 + \beta_1) + \cos (\alpha_1 - \beta_1) \right\} \\
+ {} & E_2 I_2 \left\{ \cos (2 \omega t + \alpha_2 + \beta_2) + \cos (\alpha_2 - \beta_2) \right\} \\
+ {} & E_3 I_3 \left\{ \cos (2 \omega t + \alpha_3 + \beta_3) + \cos (\alpha_3 - \beta_3) \right\}
\end{aligned}
$$

If there are only three points of entry and the potential differences are measured from one of them, one of the terms in the equation is zero.

If both the potential differences and currents constitute symmetrical sets (a balanced system—see 35.20.065) then

$$ p = 3 E_1 I_1 \cos (\alpha_1 - \beta_1) $$

This shows that the instantaneous power under this condition is constant throughout the cycle.

The instantaneous power, p, at the $(n + 1)$ points of entry of a polyphase circuit when both the currents and potential differences have harmonics and the potential differences are measured from one point of entry is expressed by the equation

$$
\begin{aligned}
p &= \sum_{s=1}^{n} i_s e_s \\
&= \sum_{s=1}^{n} \sum_{q=1}^{\infty} \sum_{r=1}^{\infty} I_{sq} E_{sr} \left\{ \cos [(r + q) \omega t + \beta_{sq} + \alpha_{sr}] \right. \\
&\qquad\qquad \left. + \cos [(r - q) \omega t + \alpha_{sr} - \beta_{sq}] \right\}
\end{aligned}
$$

where

  i_s = the instantaneous current through the sth point of entry

  e_s = the instantaneous potential difference between the sth point of entry and the arbitrarily selected reference point

  I_{sq} = the effective value of the qth harmonic component of the current at the sth point of entry

  = the maximum value divided by $\sqrt{2}$

  E_{sr} = the effective value of the rth harmonic component of the potential of the sth point of entry

  = the maximum value divided by $\sqrt{2}$

  β_{sq} = the phase angle of the qth harmonic component of the current at the sth point of entry, where this phase angle and all others of both current and potential difference are determined from the same zero of time

  α_{sr} = the phase angle of the qth harmonic component of the potential difference between the sth point of entry and the reference point, where this phase angle and all the others of both current and potential difference are determined from the same zero of time

One of the $(n + 1)$ points of entry may be an equipotential cross-section of the neutral conductor, or may be a point chosen solely as a reference from which to measure potential differences. In special cases this reference may be an equipotential surface of one of the phase conductors.

The value of the instantaneous power is given in watts when the currents are in amperes and the potential differences in volts.

Active Power of a Polyphase Circuit   05.21.160
(Power) (Actual Power)

The active power at the points of entry of a polyphase circuit is the time average of the values of the instantaneous power at the points of entry, the average being taken over a complete cycle of the alternating current.

The active power, P, at any set of points of entry of a polyphase circuit, at which the instantaneous power is p, is given by the equation

$$ P = \frac{1}{T} \int_0^T p \, dt $$

where T is the period of the alternating current.

The active power, P, in a three-phase circuit having four points of entry when both potential differences and currents are sinusoidal and when the potential differences are measured from the neutral is given by the equation

$$
\begin{aligned}
P &= E_1 I_1 \cos (\beta_1 - \alpha_1) + E_2 I_2 \cos (\beta_2 - \alpha_2) + \\
&\qquad\qquad E_3 I_3 \cos (\beta_3 - \alpha_3) \\
&= \sum_{s=1}^{3} E_s I_s \cos (\beta_s - \alpha_s)
\end{aligned}
$$

where E_s and I_s are the effective values of the potential differences and currents, respectively, and α_s and β_s their respective phase angles. If there are only three points of entry and if the potential differences are measured from one of these, one of the terms in the equation is zero.

The active power at the points of entry of a polyphase circuit is equal to the algebraic sum of the active powers for the individual points of entry when the potential differences are all determined with respect to the same arbitrarily selected reference point (which may be the neutral point of entry).

Hence the active power, P, for $(n + 1)$ points of entry, one of which is the point from which all potential differences are measured, is, when both the potential differences and the currents contain harmonics, **given by** the equation

$$P = \sum_{s=1}^{n} \sum_{r=1}^{\infty} E_{sr} I_{sr} \cos (\beta_{sr} - \alpha_{sr})$$

The symbols have the same meaning as in **05.21.155.**

The active power can also be stated in terms of the effective values of the symmetrical components of the currents and potential differences as

$$P = n \sum_{k=1}^{n} \sum_{r=1}^{\infty} I_{kr} E_{kr} \cos (\beta_{kr} - \alpha_{kr})$$

where k is the number of the symmetrical component, and r is the number of the harmonic component.

The convention for direction of current which is used in these definitions makes active power positive when the electric energy is transmitted into the delimited region and negative when out of this region.

The value of active power is given in watts when the effective currents are in amperes and the effective potential differences are in volts.

Reactive Power of a Polyphase Circuit   05.21.165

The reactive power at the points of entry of a polyphase circuit is the algebraic sum of the reactive powers for the individual points of entry when the potential differences are all determined with respect to the same arbitrarily selected reference point (which may be the neutral point of entry).

The reactive power, Q, at the four points of entry of a three-phase circuit when both the currents and potential differences are sinusoidal and when all the potential differences are measured from the neutral is given by the equation

$$Q = E_1 I_1 \sin (\beta_1 - \alpha_1) + E_2 I_2 \sin (\beta_2 - \alpha_2) + E_3 I_3 \sin (\beta_3 - \alpha_3)$$

$$= \sum_{s=1}^{3} E_s I_s \sin (\beta_s - \alpha_s)$$

The reactive power, Q, at the $(n + 1)$ points of entry when both the currents and the potential differences have harmonics and when all potential differences are measured from one point of entry is expressed by the equation

$$Q = \sum_{s=1}^{n} \sum_{r=1}^{\infty} I_{sr} E_{sr} \sin (\beta_{sr} - \alpha_{sr})$$

where the symbols have the same meaning as in **05.21.155.**

In terms of the effective values of the symmetrical components of the currents and potential differences,

$$Q = n \sum_{k=1}^{n} \sum_{r=1}^{\infty} I_{kr} E_{kr} \sin (\beta_{kr} - \alpha_{kr})$$

where k is the number of the symmetrical component and r is the number of the harmonic component.

The magnitude and sign of the reactive power of a

polyphase circuit is independent of the point that is chosen as the reference point provided the same convention as regards sign is used for all points of entry. The convention used in these definitions gives a positive sign to the reactive power of a harmonic component at any point of entry when the phase relation of current and potential difference is that which would exist if, within the delimited region, a capacitive circuit connected the point of entry to the reference point.

The value of reactive power is given in vars when the effective currents are in amperes and the effective potential differences are in volts.

NOTE: Even a set of ideal wattmeters, connected in the most favorable manner, does not measure the reactive power unless the voltages or the currents are sinusoidal and either the voltages or the currents are symmetrical.

The most favorable method of connecting n wattmeters to indicate the reactive power of a polyphase circuit is to connect the current coil of each wattmeter in series with one conductor, and its voltage coil between a pair of terminals or points of entry that are symmetrically located with respect to the phase conductor in which the current coil is connected. If the phase conductors are numbered in their normal sequence, and if the wattmeter, which has its current coil in the s*th* phase conductor, has its voltage coil connected between the symmetrical terminals $(s + x)$ and $(n + s - x)$, where $x < n / 2$, so that the voltage coil spans $(n - 2 x)$ phases, the algebraic sum of the wattmeter readings, Q', is given by the equation

$$Q' = n \sum_{k=1}^{n} \sum_{r=1}^{\infty} \frac{\sin 2 \pi k x / n}{\sin 2 \pi x / n} I_{kr} E_{kr} \sin (\beta_{kr} - \alpha_{kr})$$

Vector Power of a Polyphase Circuit   05.21.170

(Combined Power) (Vector Volt-Amperes)

Vector power at the points of entry of a polyphase circuit is equal in magnitude to the square root of the sum of the squares of the active power and the reactive power.

Vector power in a polyphase circuit is conveniently treated as a vector in a complex plane. The components of vector power are active power and reactive power. Since both the active power and the reactive power are definite constants of the system and hence are independent of the way that the circuit may be divided, the vector power of a circuit is the vector sum of the vector powers of all its parts. The vector power of a polyphase circuit has a magnitude, V, given by the equation

$$V = \sqrt{P^2 + Q^2}$$
$$= \sqrt{(P_{12} + P_{23} + \ldots)^2 + (Q_{12} + Q_{23} + \ldots)^2}$$

and a direction such that the angle θ which it makes with the P-axis is determined by the relationship

$$\tan \theta = Q / P = (Q_{12} + Q_{23} + \ldots) / (P_{12} + P_{23} + \ldots)$$

In these equations P represents the total active power and Q the total reactive power. P_{12}, P_{23}, etc., represent the active power as measured at the points of entry designated by the subscripts; and Q_{12}, Q_{23}, etc., the corresponding reactive powers. In each case P_{12}, Q_{12}, etc., include the active or reactive powers of the harmonics as well as of the fundamental, so that V_{12}, V_{23}, etc., may each be treated as the vector sum of the vector powers of all the harmonic components of the separate phases. If the angle which the vector power makes with the P-axis has the same value in each phase, the magnitude of vector power is the sum of the magnitudes of vector powers of the different phases. Expressed mathematically, if

$$\tan \theta = Q / P = Q_{12} / P_{12} = Q_{23} / P_{23} = \ldots,$$
$$V = V_{12} + V_{23} + \ldots$$

In the special case where either the potential differences or the currents are sinusoidal, and where they both form symmetrical sets

$$V = n V_{01} = nEI$$

In this equation V_{01} signifies the vector power corresponding to the neutral and any phase conductor such as No. 1, E is the effective value of the potential differences between the neutral and a phase conductor, and I the effective value of the current in each phase conductor.

The unit of vector power is the vector volt-ampere.

Average Vector Power   05.21.175

The average vector power at the points of entry of any electric circuit, averaged over a time interval which contains a large number of periods of the alternating current, is equal to the square root of the sum of the squares of the average active power during the interval and of the average reactive power during the same interval.

The average vector power, V_a, is given by the equation

$$V_a = \sqrt{P_a^2 + Q_a^2}$$

where P_a and Q_a are average active and reactive powers, respectively. This method is equivalent to taking the average vector power as the quotient of the vector sum of the vector powers of the successive cycles of the alternating current divided by the number of cycles.

NOTE: This definition extends the concepts of reactive power and vector power to circuits in which the amplitudes either of the potential differences or of the currents, or of both, may be slowly changing from cycle to cycle.

Arithmetic Apparent Power of a Polyphase
Circuit   05.21.180

The arithmetic apparent power at the points of entry of a polyphase circuit is the arithmetic sum of the apparent powers (05.21.060) of all points of entry when each is associated with the neutral point of entry, or, if one does not exist, with an artificial neutral point, the potential of which is established by joining it to each of the points of entry by a star of equal resistances.

If both the currents and potential differences are sinusoidal and if both form symmetrical sets, then the arithmetic apparent power is identical in magnitude with vector power.

The unit of arithmetic apparent power is the volt-ampere.

Algebraic Apparent Power of a Polyphase Circuit 05.21.185

The algebraic apparent power at the points of entry of a polyphase circuit is the largest of a group of values, each of which is the algebraic sum of the apparent powers (05.21.060) of all points of entry when each is associated with an artificial neutral point, the potential of which is established by a "proportionality star" of resistances. Each proportionality star has, in each branch, such a resistance (positive or negative) that the ratio of the effective current in a resistance to the effective current in the point of entry to which it is connected is the same for all branches. The apparent power at a point of entry to which a negative resistance is connected is taken as negative in forming the algebraic sum.

The algebraic apparent power is numerically equal to the maximum value of the active power which could be transmitted through the points of entry without changing either the effective currents in them or the effective potential differences between them.

If both the currents and potential differences are sinusoidal and if both form symmetrical sets, then the algebraic apparent power is identical with arithmetic apparent power and with the magnitude of vector power.

The unit of algebraic apparent power is the volt-ampere.

NOTE: This is the Lyon-Lienard definition. It appears to have been developed to correspond to the definition in a single-phase, two-wire circuit, by considering only the fact that, in the single-phase case, the apparent power is the maximum power that can be obtained with a given effective current and effective potential difference. The value of the algebraic apparent power is very difficult to deduce from ammeter and voltmeter readings.

Limiting Apparent Power of a Polyphase Circuit   05.21.190

Limiting apparent power of a polyphase circuit at the points of entry at which it is intended that the currents and potential differences shall form symmetrical sets, is equal to the result obtained by multiplying the largest effective value of current in any phase conductor, by the largest effective value of potential difference between any two adjacent phase conductors, and by the number of phase conductors, and dividing this product by twice the sine of one-half of the characteristic angular phase difference of the symmetrical set of potential differences.

The limiting apparent power, U_l, is given by

$$U_l = \frac{n E_x I_y}{2 \sin (\pi / n)}$$

where

n = the number of phase conductors
E_x = largest effective value of potential difference between any two points of entry which are adjacent in the sense that they are intended to be energized by successive members of the symmetrical set of potential differences
I_y = largest effective value of current in any phase conductor

The unit of limiting apparent power is the volt-ampere.

Distortion Power of a Polyphase Circuit   05.21.195

Distortion power at the points of entry of a polyphase circuit is equal to the sum of the distortion powers of the group of single-phase circuits into which the polyphase circuit may be considered to be divided.

A convenient method of division is to choose a reference point from which to measure the potentials of the points of entry, and to consider the single-phase circuit corresponding to each point of entry as having the current in the conductor at the point of entry and the potential difference between the point of entry and the reference point. Since in a single-phase circuit, the distortion power is zero if both the current and potential differences are sinusoidal, it follows that the distortion power in a polyphase circuit is zero if both the currents in the conductors are all sinusoidal and the potential differences between conductors are also sinusoidal.

The value of distortion power depends on the choice of reference point as well as on the circuit.

The unit of distortion power is the distortion volt-ampere.

Mesh Power of a Polyphase Circuit   05.21.200

Mesh power at the points of entry of a polyphase circuit is equal to the square root of the result obtained by subtracting from the square of the apparent power the sum of the squares of the vector power and the distortion power; the same origin being chosen for measuring potentials in determining distortion power as in determining apparent power.

It follows that mesh power must be designated as arithmetic or algebraic corresponding to arithmetic or algebraic apparent power.

The mesh power, M, is given by the equation

$$M = \sqrt{U^2 - (V^2 + D^2)} = \sqrt{U^2 - (P^2 + Q^2 + D^2)}$$

where

U = apparent power (either arithmetic or algebraic)
P = active power
Q = reactive power
V = vector power
D = distortion power

If both the currents and potential differences are sinusoidal and if both form symmetrical sets, then the mesh power is zero.

The unit of mesh power is the mesh volt-ampere.

Fictitious Power of a Polyphase Circuit   05.21.205

Fictitious power at the points of entry of a polyphase circuit is the square root of the difference of the squares of the apparent power and the active power.

It follows that fictitious power must be designated as arithmetic or algebraic corresponding to arithmetic or algebraic apparent power.

The fictitious power, F, is given by the equation

$$F = \sqrt{U^2 - P^2} = \sqrt{Q^2 + D^2 + M^2}$$

where the symbols have the same meaning as in **05.21.-200.**

If both the currents and potential differences are sinusoidal and if both form symmetrical sets, then the fictitious power is the same as the reactive power.

The unit of fictitious power is the fictitious volt-ampere.

k-Sequence Active Power of a Polyphase Circuit   05.21.210

The k-sequence active power at the $(n + 1)$ points of entry (one of which is the neutral) of a polyphase circuit, is n times the sum of the products obtained by multiplying, for each harmonic component, the k-sequence symmetrical component of the potential difference to neutral, the k-sequence symmetrical component of the current, and the cosine of the angular phase difference between them.

The k-sequence active power is given by the equation

$$P_k = n \sum_{r=1}^{\infty} I_{kr} E_{kr} \cos (\beta_{kr} - \alpha_{kr})$$

where I_{kr} and E_{kr} are the effective values of the k*th* symmetrical component of the r*th* harmonic component of the currents and potential differences, respectively. Also, β_{kr} and α_{kr} are the phase angles of the corresponding currents and potential differences.

Fundamental k-Sequence Active Power of a Polyphase Circuit   05.21.215

The fundamental k-sequence active power is the k-sequence active power for the fundamental component.

The equation for the fundamental k-sequence active power, P_{k1}, is

$$P_{k1} = n I_{k1} E_{k1} \cos (\beta_{k1} - \alpha_{k1})$$

k-Sequence Reactive Power of a Polyphase Circuit   05.21.220

The k-sequence reactive power at the $(n + 1)$ terminals (one of which is the neutral) of a polyphase circuit, is n times the sum of the products obtained by multiplying, for each harmonic component, the k-sequence component of the potential difference to neutral, the k-sequence component of the current, and the sine of the angular phase difference between them.

The k-sequence reactive power, Q_k, is given by the equation

$$Q_k = n \sum_{r=1}^{\infty} I_{kr} E_{kr} \sin (\beta_{kr} - \alpha_{kr})$$

where I_{kr} and E_{kr} are the effective values of the currents and potential differences, respectively, of the k*th* symmetrical component of the r*th* harmonic component. Also β_{kr} and α_{kr} are the phase angles of the corresponding currents and potential differences.

Fundamental k-Sequence Reactive Power of a Polyphase Circuit   05.21.225

The fundamental k-sequence reactive power is the k-sequence reactive power for the fundamental component.

The equation for the fundamental k-sequence reactive power, Q_{k1}, is

$$Q_{k1} = n\, I_{k1}\, E_{k1} \sin (\beta_{k1} - \alpha_{k1})$$

Positive-Sequence Active Power†	05.21.230
Negative-Sequence Active Power†	05.21.235
Zero-Sequence Active Power†	05.21.240
Positive-Sequence Reactive Power†	05.21.245
Negative-Sequence Reactive Power†	05.21.250
Zero-Sequence Reactive Power†	05.21.255
Fundamental Positive-Sequence Active (or Reactive) Power†	05.21.260
Fundamental Negative-Sequence Active (or Reactive) Power†	05.21.265
Fundamental Zero-Sequence Active (or Reactive) Power†	05.21.270

† The definitions of the above terms (05.21.230 through 05.21.270), which are especially applicable to three-phase circuits, are formed by placing the appropriate adjective in the general definitions given in 05.21.210 through 05.21.225. Also, the terms given can be logically extended to include a large number of terms, such as: the k-sequence vector power, the k-sequence power factor, the fundamental zero-sequence power factor, etc.

Power Factor   05.21.275

Power factor is the ratio of active power to apparent power.

The power factor, Λ (Greek lambda), is given by the equation

$$\Lambda = P\,/\,U$$

It follows that the power factor of a polyphase circuit must be designated as arithmetic or algebraic to indicate whether arithmetic or algebraic apparent power is used in the denominator. If both the currents and potential differences are sinusoidal and if both form symmetrical sets, then

$$\Lambda = \cos(\beta - \alpha)$$

Vector Power Factor   05.21.280

Vector power factor is the ratio of the active power to the vector power.

The vector power factor, Λ_v, is given by the equation

$$\Lambda_v = P\,/\,V$$

If both the currents and potential differences are sinusoidal and if both form symmetrical sets, then the vector power factor is the same as the power factor.

Reactive Factor   05.21.285

Reactive factor is the ratio of reactive power to apparent power. It follows that the reactive factor of a polyphase circuit must be designated as arithmetic or algebraic to indicate whether arithmetic or algebraic apparent power is used in the denominator.

If both the currents and potential differences are sinusoidal and if both form symmetrical sets, then the reactive factor is $\sin(\beta - \alpha)$.

GROUP 05—GENERAL (FUNDAMENTAL AND DERIVED) TERMS

Section 25—Magnetics

Magnetics   05.25.005

Magnetics is that branch of science which deals with the laws of magnetic phenomena.

Magnetizing Force—Symbol H   05.25.010

(Magnetic Intensity) (Magnetic Force)

Magnetizing force is a vector magnetic quantity which arises from magnetized bodies and from electric currents. When arising only from currents its value at a point in a continuous isotropic medium is independent of the properties of the surrounding medium and depends only on the position of the point relative to the currents and on their magnitudes.

The magnetizing force at a point which results from magnetized bodies depends on the position of the point relative to the bodies and on the intensity of magnetization of the bodies so that in general its computation requires a knowledge of values which are not readily measurable.

The magnetizing force which results from a combination of known currents and magnetized bodies (whether they be permanent magnets or magnets resulting from the currents) is the vector sum of the magnetizing forces from all of the individual sources.

The magnetizing force $\mathbf{H}_i$ at a point P arising from a current I in an electric circuit is given by the equation

$$\mathbf{H}_i = I \oint \frac{[\mathbf{r} \times d\mathbf{s}]}{r^3}$$

where $\mathbf{r}$ is a vector of magnitude r extending from an element $d\mathbf{s}$ of the circuit to the point P; $[\mathbf{r} \times d\mathbf{s}]$ is the vector product of $\mathbf{r}$ and $d\mathbf{s}$; and the integral is taken completely around the circuit.

The magnetizing force $\mathbf{H}$ at a point P arising from a magnetized body is given by the equation

$$\mathbf{H} = \nabla \int \int \int \left(\mathbf{M} \cdot \nabla \frac{1}{r} \right) dV$$

where r is the distance from a volume element dV of the body to the point P; $\mathbf{M}$ is the intensity of magnetization of dV, and the integral is taken over the entire volume of the magnetized body. This equation holds whether the point is within or without the body.

NOTE: Magnetizing force at a point is also defined as the vector quantity which is measured by the force (mechanical) which is exerted on a unit magnetic pole placed at the point, when the point under consideration is in a vacuum.

Polarizing Magnetizing Force—Symbol H_d 05.25.011

The polarizing magnetizing force at a point is the algebraic mean of the maximum and minimum values of a periodic magnetizing force which exists at the point during a cycle.

NOTE: If the periodic magnetizing force is produced by a periodic current of which the alternating component is symmetrical, the polarizing magnetizing force may be considered as produced by the direct-current component of the periodic current, so that the reading of a D'Arsonval type ammeter in the circuit of the periodic current is directly proportional to the polarizing magnetizing force.

Incremental Magnetizing Force—Symbol H_Δ 05.25.012

The incremental magnetizing force at a point is one-half the algebraic difference of the maximum and minimum values of the periodic magnetizing force at that point during a cycle.

Magnetic Field   05.25.015

A magnetic field is a vector field of magnetizing force.

At every point the divergence of the magnetic intensity of a current is zero, so that the magnetic field of a current is a tubular field.

NOTE: As generally used a magnetic field indicates the region throughout which the magnetizing force values are of significant magnitude with respect to the conditions under consideration.

Magnetic Potential Difference   05.25.020

The magnetic potential difference between two points in a magnetic field is the line integral of magnetizing force between the two points.

Since the magnetic field of a current is a tubular field, the magnetic potential difference in such a field is a multiple-valued function.

Magnetomotive Force—Symbol $\mathfrak{F}$ 05.25.025

The magnetomotive force acting in any closed path in a magnetic field is the line integral of the magnetizing force around the path.

In any closed path, the magnetomotive force resulting from a current is directly proportional to the current which links the path. The magnetomotive force $\mathfrak{F}$ around any path is given in gilberts by the equation

$$\mathfrak{F} = \frac{4 \pi N I}{10}$$

where N is the number of times the electric circuit links the path, and I is the current in amperes.

Magnetic Induction—Symbol B   05.25.030

(Magnetic Flux Density)

Magnetic induction at any point in a magnetic field is a vector quantity which determines the electromotive force induced in an elementary conductor that is moving through the field at that point.

The value of the electromotive force is proportional to the component of the magnetic induction which is perpendicular to the plane in which the conductor moves, as well as to the product of the length of the conductor, its velocity, and the sine of the angle between the direction of the conductor and the direction of motion. In a vacuum, magnetic induction at a point has the same direction as, and is proportional in magnitude to, the magnetizing force at the point. In material media, magnetic induction is a function of the configurations of the electrons and atoms of the material.

The vector equation connecting magnetic induction and electromotive force is

$$e = [V \times 1] \cdot B$$

where 1 is the length of a conductor moving with velocity V across a uniform field of magnetic induction B, and e is the electromotive force produced. The quantities in the above equation may all be measured either in the cgs electromagnetic system of units or in the cgs electrostatic system. In some other systems a proportionality factor is required.

NOTE: In an isotropic material which has been magnetized by a unidirectional magnetizing force the magnetic induction has the same (or opposite) direction as the magnetizing force. In anisotropic materials (such as single crystals and some annealed metals) the direction of the induction is a function of the magnitude of the magnetizing force, the orientation of the crystal axes of the material and its previous condition of magnetization.

NOTE: Among American writers, the term "magnetic induction" appears to be used more often than "magnetic flux density", while the reverse is the case among English writers. Some writers in England use magnetic induction in a different sense, viz., as the total flux of a magnetic circuit.

Polarized Induction—Symbol B_d 05.25.031

The polarized induction in a magnetic material at a point at which it is subjected to a polarizing magnetizing force is the algebraic mean of maximum and minimum values of the magnetic induction at the point during a cycle.

Incremental Induction—Symbol B_Δ 05.25.032

The incremental induction in a magnetic material at a point at which it is subjected to a polarizing magnetizing force is one-half the algebraic difference of the maximum and minimum values of the magnetic induction at the point during a cycle. Twice the incremental induction is indicated by ΔB, so that

$$\Delta B = 2 B_\Delta$$

Magnetic Flux—Symbol ϕ 05.25.035

Magnetic flux through an area is the surface integral of the normal component of the magnetic induction over the area.

Thus

$$\phi = \int \int B \cos \theta \, dS = \int \int (B \cdot dS)$$

where ϕ is the magnetic flux through area S, B is the induction at the surface element dS and $(B \cdot dS)$ is the scalar product of B and dS.

Permeability—Symbol μ 05.25.040

Permeability is the property of an isotropic medium which determines, under specified conditions, the magnitude relation between magnetic induction and magnetizing force in the medium.

Under the specified conditions, permeability is measured as the ratio of the magnetic induction to the magnetizing force.

Space Permeability—Symbol μ_v 05.25.045

Space permeability is the factor that expresses the ratio of magnetic induction to magnetizing force in vacuum.

In the cgs electromagnetic system of units, the permeability of a vacuum is arbitrarily taken as unity.

Reluctivity   05.25.050

Reluctivity of a medium is the reciprocal of its permeability.

Diamagnetic Material   05.25.055

A diamagnetic material is a material having a permeability less than that of a vacuum.

Ferromagnetic Material   05.25.060

A ferromagnetic material is a material having a permeability that varies with the magnetizing force and that is considerably greater than the permeability of a vacuum.

NOTE: Three different principles might be used to distinguish a ferromagnetic material; viz., magnitude of permeability, existence of saturation induction or presence of hysteresis. Magneticians are not agreed concerning the property that should be used in defining ferromagnetism. Hence, at present a strictly quantitative definition is not feasible.

Paramagnetic Material   05.25.065

A paramagnetic material is a material having a permeability which is slightly greater than that of a vacuum and which is approximately independent of the magnetizing force.

Magnetic Circuit   05.25.070

A magnetic circuit is a closed path of magnetic flux, the path having the direction of the magnetic induction at every point.

Permeance—Symbol P   05.25.075

The permeance of a portion of a magnetic circuit, bounded by two equipotential surfaces and by a third surface at every point of which there is a tangent having the direction of the magnetic induction, is the ratio of the flux through any cross-section to the magnetic potential difference between the surfaces when taken within the portion under consideration.

The equation for the permeance of a region defined as above is

$$P = \frac{\phi}{\mathfrak{F}}$$

Reluctance—Symbol $\mathfrak{R}$ 05.25.080

Reluctance is the reciprocal of permeance.

Cyclicly Magnetized Condition   05.25.081

A magnetic material is in a cyclicly magnetized condition when it has been under the influence of a magnetizing force varying between two specific limits until, for each increasing (or decreasing) value of the magnetizing force, the magnetic induction has the same value in successive cycles.

Symmetrically Cyclicly Magnetized Condition   05.25.082

A magnetic material is in a symmetrically cyclicly magnetized condition when it is cyclicly magnetized and the limits of the applied magnetizing forces are equal and of opposite sign, so that the limits of induction are equal and of opposite sign.

Normal Induction in a Magnetic Material   05.25.085

The normal induction in a magnetic material is the limiting induction either positive or negative in a material which is in a symmetrically cyclicly magnetized condition.

Intrinsic Induction—Symbol B_i 05.25.090

(Ferric Induction)*

Intrinsic induction in a magnetic material for a given value of the magnetizing force is the excess of the normal induction over the induction in vacuum.

The equation for intrinsic induction is

$$B_i = B - \mu_v H$$

Intensity of Magnetization—Symbol J   05.25.091

The intensity of magnetization of a magnetic material is the intrinsic induction divided by 4π.
Hence

$$J = \frac{B - \mu_v H}{4\pi}$$

Saturation Induction—Symbol B_s 05.25.095

Saturation induction is the maximum intrinsic induction possible in a material.

Normal Permeability   05.25.100

(Cyclic Permeability)

Normal permeability is the ratio of the normal induction to the corresponding magnetic intensity.

Initial Permeability—Symbol μ_0 05.25.105

Initial permeability is the normal permeability when both the magnetizing force and induction are vanishingly small.

Differential Permeability   05.25.110

Differential permeability is the ratio of the positive increase of normal induction to the positive increase of magnetizing force when these increases are vanishingly small.

Incremental Permeability   05.25.115

Incremental permeability is the ratio of the cyclic change in magnetic induction to the corresponding cyclic change in magnetizing force when the mean induction differs from zero.

Reversible Permeability   05.25.120

Reversible permeability is the incremental permeability when the change in induction is vanishingly small.

* Deprecated.

Intrinsic Permeability   05.25.125

Intrinsic permeability is the ratio of intrinsic induction to the corresponding magnetizing force.

Susceptibility—Symbol κ 05.25.126

The susceptibility of a material for a given value of the magnetizing force is the intensity of magnetization divided by 4π times the product of the permeability of a vacuum and the magnetizing force.
Hence

$$\kappa = \frac{J}{\mu_v H} = \frac{B - \mu_v H}{4\pi \mu_v H} = \frac{\mu - \mu_v}{4\pi \mu_v}$$

In the cgs electromagnetic system of units $\mu_v = 1$, so that in this system $\kappa = \dfrac{\mu - 1}{4\pi}$. However, the value of κ is independent of the system of units.

Remanence   05.25.130

Remanence is the magnetic induction which remains in a magnetic circuit after the removal of an applied magnetomotive force.

Residual Induction   05.25.135

Residual induction in a magnetic material is the magnetic induction at which the magnetizing force is zero when the material is in a symmetrically cyclicly magnetized condition.

Retentivity   05.25.140

Retentivity is the property of a material which is measured by the residual induction corresponding to the saturation induction for the material.

Coercive Force   05.25.145

Coercive force for a magnetic material is the magnetizing force at which the magnetic induction is zero when the material is in a symmetrically cyclicly magnetized condition.

Coercivity   05.25.150

Coercivity is the property of a magnetic material measured by the coercive force corresponding to the saturation induction for the material.

Magnetic Hysteresis   05.25.151

Magnetic hysteresis is the property of a magnetic material by virtue of which the magnetic induction for a given magnetizing force depends upon the previous conditions of magnetization.

Magnetic Hysteresis Loss   05.25.152

Magnetic hysteresis loss in a material for a specified cycle of magnetizing force is the energy converted into heat as a result of magnetic hysteresis when the magnetic induction is also cyclic.

Incremental Hysteresis Loss   05.25.153

Incremental hysteresis loss in a magnetic material is the hysteresis loss when the material is subjected to a pulsating magnetizing force.

Hysteresis Loop   05.25.154

A hysteresis loop for a magnetic material in a cyclicly magnetized condition is a curve (usually with rectangular coordinates) showing, for each value of the magnetizing force, two values of the magnetic induction, one when the magnetizing force is increasing, the other when it is decreasing.

Magnet   05.25.155

A magnet is a body which produces a magnetic field external to itself.

Magnetic Pole   05.25.160

The magnetic poles of a magnet are those portions of the magnet toward which the external magnetizing force tends to converge or diverge.

The size and position of the poles of a magnet depend upon its shape and characteristics. For a long, thin magnet, the poles occupy small regions near the ends, so that for many purposes the poles of such a magnet may be considered as concentrated at points.

Strength of Magnetic Pole   05.25.165

The strength of a magnetic pole which can be considered as concentrated at a point is measured by the force which is exerted on the pole when placed in a magnetic field of known intensity in a vacuum.

Unit Magnetic Pole   05.25.170

A unit magnetic pole is a magnetic pole which is concentrated at a point and which has such strength, that, when it is placed at unit distance from an exactly similar pole, the two poles will repel each other with unit force.

GROUP 05—GENERAL (FUNDAMENTAL AND DERIVED) TERMS

Section 30—Electrical Properties of Materials

Conducting Material   05.30.004

A conducting material is any material having the property that, when a potential difference exists between any two points on, or in, a body constructed from the material, there will be, between the two points, a current which is appreciable for the application under consideration.

Materials like metals and strong electrolytes are considered conductors in all applications, while materials like wood and distilled water are considered conductors in some applications and insulators in others.

Conductivity   05.30.005

The conductivity of a material is the direct-current conductance between the opposite, parallel faces of a portion of the material having unit length and unit cross-section.

Effective Conductivity   05.30.010

The effective conductivity of a material to a periodic current is the effective conductance between the opposite, parallel faces of a portion of the material having unit length and unit cross-section.

Resistivity   05.30.015

The resistivity of a material is the reciprocal of its conductivity.

Effective Resistivity   05.30.020

The effective resistivity of a material to a periodic current is the effective resistance between the opposite, parallel faces of a portion of the material having unit length and unit cross-section.

Insulator   05.30.021

An insulator is a material of such low conductivity that the flow of current through it can usually be neglected.

Surface Leakage   05.30.025

Surface leakage is the passage of current over the boundary surfaces of an insulator rather than through its volume.

Surface Resistivity   05.30.030

Surface resistivity of a material is the resistance between two opposite sides of a unit square of its surface. Surface resistivity may vary widely with the conditions of measurement.

Dielectric   05.30.035

A dielectric is a medium having the property that the energy required to establish an electric field is recoverable, in whole or in part, as electric energy.

A vacuum is a dielectric.

Perfect Dielectric   05.30.040

(Ideal Dielectric)

A perfect dielectric is a dielectric in which all the energy required to establish an electric field in the dielectric is returned to the electric system when the field is removed.

From the definitions, a perfect dielectric must have zero conductivity. Also, all absorption phenomena must be lacking. A vacuum is the only known perfect dielectric.

Imperfect Dielectric   05.30.045

An imperfect dielectric is a dielectric in which a part of the energy required to establish an electric field in the dielectric is not returned to the electric system when the field is removed. The energy which is not returned is converted into heat in the dielectric.

Dielectric Constant   05.30.050

(Specific Inductive Capacity) (Permittivity)

The dielectric constant of a dielectric is that property which determines the electrostatic energy stored per unit volume for unit potential gradient.

The dielectric constant K is proportional to W / g^2,

where W is the energy per unit volume, and g the potential gradient.

The electrostatic energy of a capacitor is proportional to the product of the capacitance and the square of the potential difference between the plates, so that the dielectric constant of the dielectric of a capacitor is proportional to its capacitance.

If a capacitor has a measured capacitance C_s when filled with a standard dielectric having a dielectric constant K_s, and if the same capacitor has a measured capacitance C_x when filled with a dielectric having an unknown dielectric constant K_x, then

$$K_x = K_s C_x / C_s$$

In the electrostatic system of units, the dielectric constant of a vacuum is unity, so that the dielectric constant of a dielectric is measured as the ratio of capacitance with the dielectric to the capacitance with a vacuum.

In the electromagnetic system of units, the dielectric constant of a vacuum is

$$1.1127 \times 10^{-21} \frac{\text{ergs / cm}^3}{(\text{abvolts / cm})^2}$$

In the practical system of units, the dielectric constant of a vacuum is

$$1.1127 \times 10^{-12} \frac{\text{joules / cm}^3}{(\text{volts / cm})^2}$$

Electric Induction   05.30.051

(Dielectric Flux Density)

The electric induction at any point in an isotropic dielectric is a vector which has the same direction as the electric intensity and a magnitude equal in electrostatic units to the product of the electric intensity and the dielectric constant. Thus

$$N = K E$$

where N is the electric induction, K is the dielectric constant and E is the electric intensity.

The electric induction is a solenoidal vector in all regions containing no free charge.

Polarization in a Dielectric   05.30.052

Polarization at a point in an isotropic dielectric is a vector which has the direction of the electric intensity at a point and a magnitude in electrostatic units given by the equation

$$P = \frac{(K - 1) E}{4 \pi}$$

where P is the polarization.

From the above definitions

$$N = 4 \pi P + E$$

Displacement   05.30.053

The displacement at any point in an isotropic dielectric is a vector which has the same direction as the electric intensity and a magnitude in electrostatic units given by the equation

$$D = \frac{K\,E}{4\,\pi}$$

where **D** is the displacement.

The electric displacement is a solenoidal vector in all regions containing no free charge.

Displacement Flux   05.30.054

The displacement flux through a surface in a dielectric is the integral over the surface of the normal component of the displacement. Thus

$$Q_D = \int\int D \cos\theta \, ds = \int\int (\mathbf{D} \cdot \mathbf{ds})$$

where Q_D is the displacement flux.

Dielectric Susceptibility   05.30.055

The dielectric susceptibility of a material is the polarization per unit electric intensity. Thus

$$k = \frac{P}{E}$$

where k is the susceptibility.

From the equation for polarization it follows that the relation between the dielectric constant K and the dielectric susceptibility k is

$$K = 1 + 4\,\pi\,k$$

Dielectric Absorption   05.30.056

Dielectric absorption is that property of an imperfect dielectric whereby there is an accumulation of electric charges within the body of the material when it is placed in an electric field.

Dielectric Current   05.30.060

The dielectric current flowing at any instant through any surface in an isotropic dielectric, which is in a changing electric field, can usually be considered as having four components, namely,

1. Displacement current
2. Absorption current
3. Conduction current
4. Decaying conduction current

Of these currents, the displacement current is the only one that is present in every dielectric.

Displacement Current   05.30.065

The displacement current I_D through any surface in an isotropic dielectric is proportional to the time rate of change of displacement flux through the surface.

If the displacement vector **D** is changing at every surface element d**A** of an area, the displacement current I_D through the area is

$$I_D = \frac{d}{dt}\int\int (\mathbf{D} \cdot \mathbf{dA})$$

where the integration is taken over the entire area. In case the surface of area A is perpendicular to the displacement vector which at any instant is constant over the surface, the displacement is proportional to the dielectric constant K times the electric intensity (potential gradient) E,

$$I_D = A\,\frac{dD}{dt} = \frac{K\,A}{4\,\pi}\,\frac{dE}{dt}$$

Absorption Current   05.30.070

(Reversible Absorption Current)

The absorption current I_a in an imperfect, isotropic dielectric is a current proportional to the rate of accumulation of electric charges within the dielectric. The rate of accumulation, and hence the absorption current, decreases with time after any change of the potential gradient, and occurs with both an increase and a decrease of potential gradient, so that the absorption current is reversible.

The absorption current I_a resulting from any change of the potential gradient is a function of the time, f (t), which has elapsed since the change occurred. The absorption current through a plane surface of the area A which is perpendicular to the potential gradient is

$$I_a = \frac{K\,A}{4\,\pi}\,f\,(t)\,\frac{dE}{dt}$$

where f (t) must be experimentally determined for each dielectric.

Conduction Current in a Dielectric   05.30.075

The conduction current I_c through a surface in an imperfect, isotropic dielectric is the current which is proportional to the potential gradient. The conduction current is not dependent on the time that the electric field has been applied to the dielectric, and hence is measured after the electric field has remained unchanged for so long a time that the current has become constant. The general equation for the conduction current is

$$I_c = \frac{1}{\rho}\int\int (\mathcal{E} \cdot \mathbf{dA})$$

where ρ is the resistivity of the dielectric, $\mathcal{E}$ is the electric intensity at an element of surface **A** and the integral of the scalar product is taken over the entire surface. In the particular case where the surface is a plane of area A, perpendicular to the electric intensity $\mathcal{E}$,

$$I_c = \frac{A\,\mathcal{E}}{\rho} = -\frac{A}{\rho}\,\frac{dV}{ds}$$

where

$-\dfrac{dV}{ds}$ is the potential gradient and hence equal to $\mathcal{E}$.

Decaying Conduction Current   05.30.080

(Irreversible Absorption Current)

The decaying conduction current I_k in an imperfect, isotropic dielectric is a current which is related to the conduction current by a decreasing function of the time, which function must be experimentally determined for each dielectric. Thus

$$I_k = I_c \, \phi \, (t)$$

where ϕ (t) is a decreasing function of the time which is zero when t is infinite.

Dielectric Loss   05.30.085

Dielectric loss is the time rate at which electric energy is transformed into heat in a dielectric when it is subjected to a changing electric field.

Dielectric Phase Angle   05.30.090

Dielectric phase angle is the angular difference in phase between the sinusoidal alternating potential difference applied to a dielectric and the component of the resulting alternating current having the same period as the potential difference.

Dielectric Loss Angle   05.30.095

(Dielectric Phase Difference)

Dielectric loss angle is the difference between ninety degrees (90°) and the dielectric phase angle.

Dielectric Power Factor   05.30.100

The dielectric power factor of a material is the cosine

of the dielectric phase angle (or sine of the dielectric loss angle).

Dielectric Loss Factor   05.30.101

(Dielectric Loss Index)

The dielectric loss factor of a material is the product of its dielectric constant and the tangent of its dielectric loss angle.

Dielectric Tests   05.30.102

Dielectric tests are tests which consist of the application of a voltage higher than the rated voltage for a specified time for the purpose of determining the adequacy against breakdown of insulating materials and spacings under normal conditions.

Electric Strength   05.30.105

(Dielectric Strength) (Critical Gradient)* (Disruptive Gradient)*

The electric strength of a dielectric material is the maximum potential gradient that the material can withstand without rupture.

The value obtained for the electric strength will depend on the thickness of the material and on the method and conditions of test.

---

* Deprecated.

GROUP 05—GENERAL (FUNDAMENTAL AND DERIVED) TERMS

Section 35—Units and Systems of Measurement

System of Units   05.35.005

A system of units is an assemblage of units for measuring physical quantities.

A system of units is complete if it is applicable to the measurement of all known physical quantities.

Absolute System of Units   05.35.010

An absolute system of units is a system of units in which a small number of units are chosen as fundamental and all other units are derived from them by taking a definite proportionality factor in each of those laws which are chosen as the basic laws for expressing the relationships between the physical quantities.

The proportionality factor is generally taken as unity.

Fundamental Units   05.35.015

The fundamental units of an absolute system of units are those units which are selected to serve as the basis of the system. Fundamental units are, of necessity, arbitrarily chosen.

Derived Units   05.35.020

The derived units of a system are those which are derived from the fundamental units by the application of physical laws.

CGS System of Units   05.35.025

The cgs system of units is an absolute system for measuring physical quantities in which the fundamental units are the centimeter, gram and second.

This system is primarily applicable only to mechanical units. It is extended to other fields of physical science

by accepting the doctrine of the conservation of energy and by introducing a fourth unit or a property of a material. For example, in the theory of heat, the degree centigrade is taken as an additional unit.

CGS Electrostatic System of Units   05.35.030

The cgs electrostatic system of units is an absolute system of units for measuring electrical and magnetic quantities based on the cgs system of units, on the assignment of the value of unity to the constants in the equation for the force between point charges in a vacuum, and on the measurement of potential difference as the quotient of unit energy divided by unit charge. This is equivalent to assigning the value of unity to the dielectric constant of a vacuum, and to measuring electric energy in mechanical units.

The unit quantity q is determined by the equation $F = q \, q' \, / \, r^2$, where F is the force in dynes exerted between two equal charges, q and q', when in a vacuum, and r is the distance in centimeters between the charges. The unit of potential difference is determined by the equation V q = W where the work W in ergs is required to transfer a charge q between two points having a potential difference V.

The extension of the electrostatic system to magnetic units is made by the use of the law

$$H_s = I_s \oint \frac{[\mathbf{r} \times d\mathbf{s}]}{r^3}$$

where $\mathbf{H}_s$ is the magnetic intensity at a point P in electrostatic units; I_s is the current in a circuit in electrostatic units, ds is an element of the circuit through which I_s flows; r is the distance in centimeters from P to ds; [r $\times$ ds] is the vector product of r and ds; and $\oint$ is the line integral around the circuit.

Heaviside-Lorentz Electromagnetic System of Units   05.35.040

(Rational Electrical Units)

The Heaviside-Lorentz electromagnetic system of units is so devised that, in the magnetic laws and in the corresponding electrical laws, the same constants appear. The fundamental laws may be expressed by the equations

$$F = \frac{m\,m'}{4\,\pi\,r^2} \qquad\qquad E = \frac{W}{q}$$

$$F = \frac{q\,q'}{4\,\pi\,r^2} \qquad\qquad E = \frac{W}{m}$$

where F is the force in dynes between two equal magnetic poles m and m', or between two equal electric charges q and q' when the measurements are made in a vacuum; r is the distance between the poles or charges; E is the electric or magnetic potential difference between two points when the work W is required to transfer a charge q or a pole m from one point to the other.

The Heaviside-Lorentz units are frequently used in electromagnetic theory, but are seldom used in measurements.

CGS Electromagnetic System of Units   05.35.045

The cgs electromagnetic system of units is an absolute system for measuring electrical and magnetic quantities based on the cgs system of units, on the assignment of the value of unity to the strength of each of two equal magnetic poles which repel each other in a vacuum with a force of one dyne at a distance of one centimeter, on the measurement of current by means of its magnetic effect (see definition of current for the law), and on the measurement of potential difference as the quotient of power divided by current. This is equivalent to assigning the value of unity to the permeability of a vacuum and to measuring electric energy in mechanical units.

The cgs electromagnetic system has been more widely applied than any of the previously defined systems. Many of the magnetic units of this system have been given names by international bodies, but the electrical units have not been named though they are frequently designated by the prefix "ab" attached to the units of the practical system. The names herein used for the magnetic units were adopted by the International Electrotechnical Commission in 1930.

Unit Magnetic Pole   05.35.050

Two equal magnetic poles of the same sign have unit value when they repel each other with a force of one dyne if placed one centimeter apart in a vacuum.

Oersted—The CGS Electromagnetic Unit of Magnetic Intensity   05.35.055

The oersted is the unit of magnetic intensity (mag-netizing force) in the cgs electromagnetic system. At any point in a vacuum the value of the magnetic intensity in oersteds is equal to the force in dynes exerted on a unit magnetic pole placed at the point.

Gilbert—The CGS Electromagnetic Unit of Magnetomotive Force   05.35.060

The gilbert is the unit of magnetomotive force in the cgs electromagnetic system such that the value of the magnetomotive force in gilberts in any magnetic circuit is equal to the line integral around the circuit of the magnetic intensity when the magnetic intensity is expressed in oersteds and the length in centimeters.

Abampere—The CGS Electromagnetic Unit of Current   05.35.065

The cgs electromagnetic unit of electric current is defined by means of the law connecting the current in an electric circuit with the magnetic intensity at any point in its magnetic field.

The law is given by the equation

$$\mathbf{H} = k\,I \oint \frac{[\mathbf{r} \times d\mathbf{s}]}{r^3}$$

When this equation is used to define the cgs electromagnetic unit of current, the symbols have the following meanings:

H is the magnetic intensity in oersteds at any point P in the magnetic field of a circuit carrying a current I; k is a proportionality factor which is given the value of unity to establish the cgs unit of current; r is the magnitude of the vector r, representing the distance in centimeters from the point P to an element ds of the electric circuit; and the line integral of the vector product of r and ds is taken completely around the electric circuit.

Example: If one centimeter of a circuit is bent into an arc of one centimeter radius, the current is one abampere if the magnetic field intensity at the center is one oersted, provided the remainder of the circuit produces no magnetic field at the center of the arc.

Abcoulomb—The CGS Electromagnetic Unit of Quantity   05.35.070

The cgs electromagnetic unit of quantity is the quantity of electricity which passes any section of an electric circuit in one second when the current is one abampere.

Abvolt—The CGS Electromagnetic Unit of Electromotive Force   05.35.075

The cgs electromagnetic unit of electromotive force is the electromotive force in a circuit when, with one abampere of current flowing, electric energy is converted to other kinds of energy at the rate of one erg per second.

Abvolt—The CGS Electromagnetic Unit of Potential Difference   05.35.080

The cgs electromagnetic unit of potential difference is the potential difference between two points when one erg of work is required to transfer one abcoulomb of positive electricity from the point of lower potential to the point of higher potential.

Abfarad—The CGS Electromagnetic Unit of Capacitance 05.35.085

The cgs electromagnetic unit of capacitance is the capacitance of a condenser when a charge of one abcoulomb produces a difference of potential between the terminals of one abvolt.

Abohm—The CGS Electromagnetic Unit of Resistance 05.35.090

The cgs unit of resistance is the resistance of a conductor when, with an unvarying current of one abampere flowing through it, the potential difference between the ends of the conductor is one abvolt.

Abmho—The CGS Electromagnetic Unit of Conductance 05.35.091

The cgs unit of conductance is the conductance of a conductor when, with an unvarying potential difference of an abvolt between its ends, the current in the conductor is one abampere.

Abhenry—The CGS Electromagnetic Unit of Inductance (Centimeter)* 05.35.095

The cgs unit of inductance is the inductance in a circuit in which an electromotive force of one abvolt is induced by a current changing at the rate of one abampere per second.

Gauss—The CGS Electromagnetic Unit of Magnetic Induction 05.35.100

The cgs unit of magnetic induction is obtained from the law connecting magnetic induction with the electromotive force induced in a conductor which is moving through a magnetic field.

The law is

$$[V \times l] \cdot B = k\,E$$

When this equation is used to define the gauss, the symbols have the following meanings: V is the velocity in centimeters per second with which a conductor of length l in centimeters is moving through a magnetic field where the magnetic induction in gausses is B. The electromotive force in abvolts induced in the conductor is E, and k is a proportionality factor which is taken as unity to establish the gauss. In the simplest case V, l and B are mutually perpendicular, under which condition the indicated product of the three vectors is equal to the numerical product of their magnitudes.

Maxwell—The CGS Electromagnetic Unit of Magnetic Flux 05.35.105

The cgs unit of magnetic flux is obtained from the law connecting magnetic flux and magnetic induction.

The law is

$$\phi = k \int \int (B \cdot dA)$$

When this equation is used to define the maxwell, the symbols have the following meanings: ϕ is the

*Deprecated.

magnetic flux in maxwells through an area measured in square centimeters, the magnetic induction in gausses is B at each surface element dA. The proportionality factor, k, is taken as unity to establish the maxwell. The integration of the scalar product is taken over the entire area.

"Practical" System of Electrical Units 05.35.110

The "practical" system of electrical units is a system in which the units are the multiples or submultiples of the units of the cgs electromagnetic system which are given below. The units of this system were so selected that, at the time of its establishment, the more important units would be of convenient size, and that, in the most common electrical equations, the proportionality factor would be unity.

The important electrical units of this system have received the names given below. They are sometimes called the absolute ampere, absolute coulomb, etc., to distinguish them from the international ampere, international coulomb, etc.

Ampere 05.35.115

An ampere is one-tenth of an abampere.

Coulomb 05.35.120

A coulomb is one-tenth of an abcoulomb.

Volt 05.35.125

A volt is equal to one hundred million (10^8) abvolts.

Ohm 05.35.130

An ohm is equal to one billion (10^9) abohms.

Mho 05.35.131

A mho is equal to one billion (10^9) abmhos

Henry 05.35.135

A henry is equal to one billion (10^9) abhenrys.

Farad 05.35.140

A farad is one-billionth part (10^{-9}) of an abfarad.

Joule 05.35.145

A joule is ten million (10^7) ergs.†

† The erg is the work done by a force of one dyne when its point of application is moved through one centimeter in the direction of the force.

The dyne is the force which produces an acceleration of one centimeter per second per second when applied to a mass of one gram.

Watt 05.35.150

A watt is ten million (10^7) ergs per second.

Watthour 05.35.155

A watthour is 3,600 joules.

Relationships Between the "Practical" Electrical Units 05.35.160

The relationships between the "practical" units can be expressed by equations in which the proportionality

ELECTRICAL DEFINITIONS

factor is unity. The important equations are: $E = I R$; $Q = I t$; $E = - L dI / dt$; $Q = C E$; $P = E I = I^2 R$; $W = E I t$. The symbols in these equations are:

E is electromotive force in volts
I is current in amperes
R is resistance in ohms
Q is quantity in coulombs
L is inductance in henries
C is capacitance in farads
P is power in watts
W is energy in joules
t is time in seconds

International System of Electrical and Magnetic Units   05.35.165

The international system of electrical and magnetic units is a system for electrical and magnetic quantities which takes as the four fundamental quantities resistance, current, length and time.

The units of resistance and current are arbitrary values that approximately correspond to the absolute ohm and the absolute ampere, and the units of length and time are the centimeter and second.

The international units were defined by the International Electrical Congress at Chicago in 1893 and slightly modified by the London Electrical Conference in 1908. The International Committee of Weights and Measures has decided to discard these units in the near future.

International Ampere   05.35.170

The international ampere is defined as the current which will deposit silver at the rate of 0.00111800 gram per second.

Experimental results show that one international ampere equals 0.99985 absolute ampere.

International Coulomb   05.35.175

An international coulomb is the quantity of electricity which passes any section of an electric circuit in one second, when the current in the circuit is one international ampere.

One international coulomb equals 0.99985 absolute coulomb.

International Ohm   05.35.180

The international ohm is defined as the resistance at zero degree centigrade of a column of mercury of uniform cross-section, having a length of 106.300 centimeters and a mass of 14.4521 grams.

Experimental results show that one international ohm equals 1.00048 absolute ohms.

International Volt   05.35.185

The international volt is the voltage that will produce a current of one international ampere through a resistance of one international ohm.

One international volt equals 1.00033 absolute volts.

International Henry   05.35.190

The international henry is the inductance which produces an electromotive force of one international

volt when the current is changing at the rate of one international ampere per second.

One international henry equals 1.00048 absolute henrys.

International Farad   05.35.195

The international farad is the capacitance of a capacitor if a charge of one international coulomb produces a potential difference between the terminals of one international volt.

One international farad equals 0.99952 absolute farad.

International Joule   05.35.200

The international joule is the energy required to transfer one international coulomb between two points having a potential difference of one international volt.

One international joule equals 1.00018 absolute joules.

International Watt   05.35.205

The international watt is the power expended when one international ampere flows between two points having a potential difference of one international volt.

One international watt equals 1.00018 absolute watts.

MKS Electromagnetic System of Units   05.35.210
(Giorgi System)

The mks system of units is an absolute system of units which is based on the meter, kilogram and second, and which is extended to the electrical units by the measurement of current by its magnetic effects and of potential difference by the power per unit current.

The mechanical units of the system are developed by means of the recognized equations of mechanics using unity as the proportionality factor in each equation, and inserting a new unit of force for which the name newton has been proposed. In this system, the joule is the unit of energy, and the watt the unit of power.

In extending this system to the practical electromagnetic units, the permeability of a vacuum is taken as 10^{-7}. For example, the equation for determining the current, I, from the force of magnetic repulsion, F, between the two parallel conductors of a return circuit (length of each, b; distance between them, a; and vacuum surrounding the entire circuit), is

$$I = \sqrt{\frac{F a}{2 \mu_v b}}$$

If F is in newtons, if μ_v is 10^{-7} and if b is in the same units as a, then I is in amperes. (NOTE: In the cgs system, F is in dynes, μ_v is unity, and I is in abamperes.) Each of the electrical units of the mks system has the same name and the same value as the corresponding unit of the practical system of electrical units (05.35.110).

There is lack of agreement concerning the extension of the mks system to the magnetic units. This arises from the interrelations among the magnetic quantities which requires a proportionality factor of 4π in some of the magnetic equations. For example, if the force, F, of attraction or repulsion between two magnetic poles is $F = - m m' / \mu r^2$, then the magnetizing force, H, within a long solenoid is H = 4 π N I. The magnetic units established by these equations are called the unrationalized units. However if units are so changed that the equation for the magnetizing force within a solenoid has unity for its proportionality factor, *i. e.*, H = N I, then the equation for the force between the magnetic poles becomes

$$F = \frac{m\,m'}{4\,\pi\,\mu\,r^2}$$

The magnetic units established by these equations are called the rationalized units.

There is the same lack of agreement in extending the mks system to the electrostatic units.

The International Electrotechnical Commission approved the use of the mks system in 1935 (except as to the question of rationalization) and sanctioned the name of the system as the Giorgi system in compliment to its original proponent.

GROUP 05—GENERAL (FUNDAMENTAL AND DERIVED) TERMS

Section 40—Laws and Effects

Law of Electrostatic Attraction   05.40.005

(Coulomb's Law)

The force of attraction or repulsion between two charges of electricity concentrated at two points in an isotropic medium is proportional to the product of their magnitudes and is inversely proportional to the square of the distance between them.

The force between unlike charges is an attraction; between like charges a repulsion.

Law of Electromagnetic Induction   05.40.010

(Faraday's Law)

The electromotive force induced in a circuit is proportional to the time rate of change of the flux of magnetic induction linked with the circuit.

When the change in flux linkages is caused by the motion, relative to a magnetic field, of a conductor forming part of an electric circuit, the electromotive force induced in the circuit is proportional to the rate at which the conductor cuts the flux of magnetic induction.

This law is often associated with the name of Faraday, but was not enunciated by him.

Dynamic Equilibrium of an Electromagnetic
System   05.40.015

(a) Any two circuits carrying current tend so to dispose themselves that the flux of magnetic induction linking the two will be a maximum.

(b) Every electromagnetic system tends to change its configuration so that the flux of magnetic induction will be a maximum.

Direction of an Induced Current   05.40.020

(Lenz's Law)

The current induced in a circuit as a result of its motion in a magnetic field is in such a direction as to exert a mechanical force opposing the motion.

Ohm's Law   05.40.025

Ohm's law states that the current in an electric circuit is directly proportional to the electromotive force in the circuit.

Ohm's law does not apply to all circuits. It is applicable to all metallic circuits and to many circuits containing an electrolytic resistance.

Ohm's law was first enunciated for a circuit in which there is a constant electromotive force and an unvarying

current. It is applicable to varying currents if account is taken of the induced electromotive force resulting from the self inductance of the circuit and of the distribution of current in the cross-section of the circuit.

Heating Effect of a Current   05.40.030

(Joule's Law)

The rate at which heat is produced in an electric circuit of constant resistance is proportional to the square of the current.

Laws of Electric Networks   05.40.035

(Kirchoff's Laws)

1. The algebraic sum of the currents flowing toward any point in a network is zero.

2. The algebraic sum of the products of the current and resistance in each of the conductors in any closed path in a network is equal to the algebraic sum of the electromotive forces in that path.

These laws apply to the *instantaneous* values of currents and electromotive forces, but may be extended to the *effective* values of sinusoidal currents and electromotive forces by replacing "algebraic sum" by "vector sum" and by replacing "resistance" by "impedance."

Contact Potential   05.40.045

(Volta Effect)

When two dissimilar uncharged metals are placed in contact with each other, one becomes positively charged and the other negatively charged, and a difference of potential, depending on the nature of the metals, is set up between them.

Peltier Effect   05.40.050

When a current flows across the junction of two dissimilar metals, it causes either an absorption or liberation of heat, depending on the direction of the current, at a rate proportional to the first power of the current.

Thermoelectric Effect   05.40.055

(Seebeck Effect)

An electromotive force results from a difference of temperature between two junctions of dissimilar metals in the same circuit.

Thomson Effect   05.40.060

When a current flows from a hotter to a colder portion of a conductor, heat is liberated or absorbed depending on the material of which the conductor is made.

A more general statement is: The heat liberated by a current in a conductor in which there is a temperature gradient depends on the direction of the current with respect to the direction of the temperature gradient. The equation giving the rate at which electric energy is transformed into heat at a given point is

$$Q = b \ (\mathbf{J} \cdot \mathbf{q}) + \rho \ \mathbf{J}^2$$

where Q is the rate of energy transformation per unit volume, ρ the resistivity of the material, $\mathbf{J}$ the current density, $\mathbf{q}$ the temperature gradient and b the Thomson energy coefficient of the material (which may be either positive or negative).

Hall Effect   05.40.065

When a thin rectangular sheet of metal carrying an electric current in the direction of its length is subjected to a magnetic field normal to the sheet, an electromotive force is developed which is at right angles both to the direction of the current and to the magnetic field.

A general statement of the Hall effect is: "When a conductor in which a current is flowing is placed in a magnetic field, a potential gradient is developed which is, at each point, a function, f, of the vector product of the magnetic intensity and the current density." Thus

$$\mathbf{g} = f[\mathbf{J} \times \mathbf{H}]$$

where $\mathbf{g}$ is the potential gradient developed, $\mathbf{J}$ is the current density, and $\mathbf{H}$ is the magnetic intensity. In the simplest case, the potential gradient is proportional to the vector product, so that

$$\mathbf{g} = R[\mathbf{J} \times \mathbf{H}]$$

In this case, R is the Hall coefficient.

Thermionic Emission   05.40.070

(Edison Effect) (Richardson Effect)

Electrons are emitted from hot bodies, the rate of emission increasing rapidly with temperature.

Photoelectric Effect   05.40.075

Electromagnetic radiation (light) incident on the surface of a body may cause the emission of electrons.

For a body of a given material, the emission occurs only for a particular band of wavelengths of the incident radiation; and for a given wavelength, the rate of emission of electrons is proportional to the incident radiant flux.

Piezoelectric Effect   05.40.080

A crystalline dielectric, which is anisotropic and has no center of symmetry, becomes electrically polarized when it is mechanically strained. The direction and magnitude of the polarization depend upon the nature and amount of the strain, and upon the direction of the strain with reference to the axes of the crystal.

On such crystals the converse effect is observed; viz., that a strain results from the application of an electric field.

Electro-Optical Effect in Dielectrics   05.40.085

(Kerr Electrostatic Effect)

Certain transparent dielectrics when placed in a strong electrostatic field become doubly refracting.

The strength of the electro-optical effect for unit thickness of the dielectric varies directly as the square of the electric intensity.

Magnetic Rotation of Polarized Light   05.40.090

(Faraday Effect)

When a plane polarized beam of light passes through certain transparent substances along the lines of a strong magnetic field, the plane of polarization of the emergent light is different from that of the incident light. On looking from north to south along a line of magnetic intensity, the rotation is clockwise.

Magnetic Transition Temperature   05.40.095

(Curie Point)

The magnetic transition temperature of a ferromagnetic material is the temperature at which, with increasing temperature, the transition from ferromagnetic to paramagnetic properties appears to be complete.

The change in magnetic properties with temperature extends over an appreciable temperature interval, so that the value obtained for the *magnetic transition* temperature depends upon experimental conditions.

Magnetic Intensity Produced by an Electric Current   05.40.100

(Biot-Savart Law) (Ampere's Law)

The magnetic intensity at any point in the neighborhood of a circuit in which an electric current, i, is flowing can be computed on the assumption that every infinitesimal length of circuit produces at the point an infinitesimal magnetic intensity and the resulting magnetic intensity at the point is the vector sum of the contributions of all the elements of the circuit.

The contribution, d$\mathbf{H}$, to the magnetic intensity at a point P caused by the current i in an element ds of a circuit which is at a distance r from P, has a direction which is perpendicular to both ds and r and a magnitude equal to

$$\frac{i \ ds \ \sin \theta}{r^2}$$

where θ is the angle between the element ds and the line $\mathbf{r}$. In vector notation

$$d\mathbf{H} = \frac{i \ [\mathbf{r} \times d\mathbf{s}]}{r^3}$$

This law is sometimes attributed to Biot-Savart, sometimes to Ampere, but neither gave it in its differential form.

Poynting's Vector   05.40.105

If there is a flow of electromagnetic energy into or out of a closed region, the rate of flow of this energy is, at any instant, proportional to the surface integral of the vector product of the electric and magnetic intensities. This vector product is called Poynting's vector.

If, in electromagnetic units, the electric intensity is **E** and the magnetic intensity is **H**, then Poynting's vector **U**, in ergs per second per square centimeter is given by the equation

$$U = \frac{[E \times H]}{4\pi} = \frac{E\,H\,\sin\alpha}{4\pi}$$

where α is the angle between **E** and **H**.

Poynting's vector is seldom employed in connection with ordinary electric circuits, but has important applications in electric waves.

Skin Effect in a Conductor   05.40.110

Skin effect is the phenomenon of non-uniform current distribution over the cross-section of a conductor caused by the variation of the current in the conductor itself.

Proximity Effect   05.40.115

Proximity effect is the phenomenon of non-uniform current distribution over the cross-section of a conductor caused by the variation of the current in a neighboring conductor.

Eddy Currents   05.40.120

(Foucault Currents)

Eddy currents are those currents which are induced in the body of a conducting mass by a variation of magnetic flux.

NOTE: The variation of magnetic flux may be the result of a varying magnetic field or of a relative motion of the mass with respect to the magnetic field.

GROUP 05—GENERAL (FUNDAMENTAL AND DERIVED) TERMS

Section 45—Apparatus and Accessories

Conductor   05.45.005

A conductor is a body so constructed from conducting material that it may be used as a carrier of electric current.

Coil   05.45.010

A coil is a compact assemblage of successive convolutions of a conductor.

Resistor   05.45.015

(Resistance)*

A resistor is a device, the primary purpose of which is to introduce resistance into an electric circuit.

Adjustable Resistor   05.45.020

An adjustable resistor is a resistor so constructed that its resistance can be readily changed.

Rheostat   05.45.025

A rheostat is an adjustable resistor so constructed that its resistance may be changed without opening the circuit in which it may be connected.

Resistance Box   05.45.030

A resistance box is a rheostat consisting of an assembly of resistors of definite values so arranged that the resistance of the circuit in which it is connected may be changed by known amounts.

Continuously Adjustable Resistor   05.45.035

(Variable Resistor)

A continuously adjustable resistor is an adjustable resistor in which the resistance can have every possible value within its range.

Capacitor   05.45.040

(Condenser)

A capacitor is a device, the primary purpose of which is to introduce capacitance into an electric circuit.

Capacitors are usually classified, according to their dielectrics, as air capacitors, mica capacitors, paper capacitors, etc.

Subdivided Capacitor   05.45.045

(Condenser Box)*

A subdivided capacitor is a capacitor in which several capacitors known as sections are so mounted that they may be used individually or in combination.

Adjustable Capacitor   05.45.050

An adjustable capacitor is a capacitor the capacitance of which can be readily changed.

Continuously Adjustable Capacitor   05.45.055

(Variable Capacitor)

A continuously adjustable capacitor is an adjustable capacitor in which the capacitance can have every possible value within its range.

Inductor   05.45.060

(Inductance Coil)*

An inductor is a device, the primary purpose of which is to introduce inductance into an electric circuit.

Self Inductor   05.45.065

A self inductor is an inductor for changing the self inductance of a circuit.

Mutual Inductor   05.45.070

A mutual inductor is an inductor for changing the mutual inductance between two circuits.

Adjustable Inductor   05.45.075

An adjustable inductor is an inductor in which the self or mutual inductance can be readily changed.

* Deprecated.

* Deprecated.

Continuously Adjustable Inductor   05.45.080
(Variable Inductor)

A continuously adjustable inductor is an adjustable inductor in which the inductance can have every possible value within its range.

Reactor   05.45.085
(Reactance)*

A reactor is a device, the primary purpose of which is to introduce reactance into a circuit.

Network   05.45.089

An electric network is a system of interconnected admittances.

The point at which three or more admittances meet is called a junction point of the network. An admittance connecting any two junction points is called an arm or branch of the network. A mesh within a network is a closed path through three or more junction points.

Bridge Circuit   05.45.090

A bridge circuit is a network which is so arranged that, when an electromotive force is present in one branch, the response of a suitable detecting device in another branch may be made zero by a suitable adjustment of the electrical constants of still other branches; and which is characterized by the fact that, if the electromotive force and the detecting device are interchanged, after completing an adjustment, the response of the detecting device is still zero.

See 30.40.010.

Potentiometer Circuit   05.45.095

A potentiometer circuit is a network which is so arranged that, when two or more electromotive forces (or potential differences) are present in as many different branches, the response of a suitable detecting device in one of these branches may be made zero by a suitable adjustment of the electrical constants of the network; and which is characterized by the fact that the detecting device and the electromotive force (or potential difference) under measurement are in the same branch.

Galvanometer
See 30.40.050.

Electrodynamometer   05.45.105

An electrodynamometer is an instrument in which the mechanical reactions between two parts of the same circuit are used for detecting or measuring an electric current.

Electrometer   05.45.110

An electrometer is an instrument for detecting or measuring a potential difference by means of the mechanical forces exerted between electrically charged bodies.

See also 30.40.025.

* Deprecated.

Spark Gap   05.45.115

A spark gap is an arrangement of two electrodes between which a disruptive discharge of electricity may take place, and such that the insulation is self-restoring after the passage of a discharge.

Sphere Gap   05.45.120

A sphere gap is a spark gap in which the electrodes are spheres.

Needle Gap   05.45.125

A needle gap is a spark gap in which the electrodes are needle points.

Rod Gap   05.45.126

A rod gap is a spark gap in which the electrodes are two coaxial rods with the ends between which the discharge takes place cut perpendicular to the axis.

NOTE: Specifications usually require square rods.

Pole Piece   05.45.130

A pole piece is a piece of ferromagnetic material forming one end of a magnet, and so shaped as to control the distribution of the magnetic flux in the adjacent medium.

Armature of a Magnet   05.45.135

The armature of a magnet is a piece of ferromagnetic material connecting or placed between the pole pieces of a magnet in such a manner that it may have motion relative to the pole pieces or may be detached from them.

Yoke   05.45.140

A yoke is a piece of ferromagnetic material, without windings, which permanently connects two or more magnet cores.

Amplifier   05.45.155

An amplifier is a device for increasing the power associated with a phenomenon without appreciably altering its quality, through control by the amplifier input of a larger amount of power supplied by a local source to the amplifier output.

Oscillator   05.45.160

An oscillator is an apparatus for setting up and maintaining oscillations of a frequency determined by the physical constants of the system.

Resonator   05.45.165

A resonator is an apparatus or system in which some physical quantity is capable of being put into a state of oscillation by oscillations in another system.

Solenoid   05.45.170

A solenoid is an electric conductor wound as a helix with a small pitch, or as two or more coaxial helices.

ELECTRICAL DEFINITIONS

GROUP 05—GENERAL (FUNDAMENTAL AND DERIVED) TERMS
Section 50—General Engineering Terms

Load   05.50.005

(1) The load on a machine or apparatus is the power which it delivers.

(2) The load on an alternating-current machine or apparatus is the product of the effective current through the machine or apparatus and the effective potential difference between its terminals.

Duty   05.50.010

Duty is a requirement of service which defines the degree of regularity of the load.

Continuous Duty   05.50.015

Continuous duty is a requirement of service that demands operation at a substantially constant load for an indefinitely long time.

Short-Time Duty   05.50.020

Short-time duty is a requirement of service that demands operation at a substantially constant load for a short and definitely specified time.

Intermittent Duty   05.50.025

Intermittent duty is a requirement of service that demands operation for alternate intervals of (1) load and no-load; or (2) load and rest; or (3) load, no-load and rest; such alternate intervals being definitely specified.

Periodic Duty   05.50.030

Periodic duty is a type of intermittent duty in which the load conditions are regularly recurrent.

Varying Duty   05.50.035

Varying duty is a requirement of service that demands operation at loads, and for intervals of time, both of which may be subject to wide variation.

Rating   05.50.040

A rating of a machine, apparatus or device is a designated limit of operating characteristics based on definite conditions.

NOTE: Such operating characteristics as load, voltage, frequency, etc., may be given in the rating.

Continuous Rating   05.50.045

Continuous rating is the rating that defines the load which can be carried for an indefinitely long time.

Short-Time Rating   05.50.050

The short-time rating is the rating that defines the load which can be carried for a short and definitely specified time, the machine, apparatus or device being at approximately room temperature at the time the load is applied.

Capacity   05.50.055

(a) The capacity of a machine, apparatus or device is the rated load.

(b) The capacity of a machine, apparatus or device is the maximum load of which it is capable under existing service conditions.

Efficiency   05.50.060

The efficiency of a device with respect to a physical quantity which may be stored, transferred or transformed by the device is the ratio of the useful output of the quantity to its total input. Unless specifically stated otherwise, the term *efficiency* means efficiency with respect to power.

Temperature Detector   05.50.065

A temperature detector is any instrument which may be used to measure the temperature of a body or of some particular part of a body.

A temperature detector may employ any physical property that is dependent on temperature. The most commonly used properties are: differential expansion of two bodies, thermoelectromotive force at the junction of two metals, change of resistance of a metal, and radiation from a hot body.

Thermocouple Thermometer   05.50.080

(Thermocouple)

A thermocouple thermometer is a device for measuring temperature which depends upon the variation of the contact electromotive force between two different metals or alloys with temperature.

A thermocouple consists of a conductor of one metal or alloy which has attached to each end a conductor of a second metal or alloy for connecting to a measuring instrument, the arrangement being such that one of the junctions between the metals can be placed at the point where the temperature is to be measured and the second junction kept at a known temperature.

Resistance Thermometer   05.50.090

A resistance thermometer is an instrument for measuring temperature, which depends for its operation upon the variation of electric resistance with temperature.

A resistance thermometer consists of a conductor of some metal having a large change of resistance with temperature, the conductor being of such form that it can be placed in the region where the temperature is to be measured, and that its resistance can be measured independently of the resistance of the leads.

ELECTRICAL DEFINITIONS

GROUP 10—ROTATING MACHINERY

SECTIONS

10 Machines
15 Machine Parts
20 Speed Classification of Motors
25 Enclosure and Ventilation of Machines
30 Protection of Machines

35 Synchronous Machine Quantities
40 Kinds of Torque
50 Duty Classification
95 Not Otherwise Classified

Section 10—Machines

Direct-Current Commutating Machine   10.10.010

A direct-current commutating machine comprises a magnetic field excited from a direct-current source or formed of permanent magnets, an armature and a commutator connected therewith. Specific types of direct-current commutating machines are: direct-current generators, motors, synchronous converters, boosters, balancers and dynamotors.

Armature-Reaction Excited Machine   10.10.015

An armature-reaction excited machine is a machine having a rotatable armature, provided with windings and a commutator, whose load-circuit voltage is generated by flux that is produced primarily by the magnetomotive force of currents in the armature winding. By providing the stationary member of the machine with various types of windings different characteristics may be obtained, such as a constant-current characteristic or a constant-voltage characteristic.

The machine is normally provided with two sets of brushes, displaced around the commutator from one another, so as to provide primary and secondary circuits through the armature. The primary circuit carrying the excitation armature current may be completed externally by a short-circuit connection, or through some other external circuit, such as a field winding or a source of power supply; and the secondary circuit is adapted for connection to an external load.

Synchronous Machine   10.10.020

A synchronous machine is one in which the average speed of normal operation is exactly proportional to the frequency of the system to which it is connected.

Asynchronous Machine   10.10.030

An asynchronous machine is one in which the speed of operation is not proportional to the frequency of the system to which it is connected.

Induction Machine   10.10.035

An induction machine is an asynchronous alternating-current machine which comprises a magnetic circuit interlinked with two electric circuits, or sets of circuits, rotating with respect to each other and in which power is transferred from one circuit to another by electromagnetic induction. Examples of induction machines are induction motors, induction generators and certain types of frequency converters and phase converters.

Acyclic Machine   10.10.040

(Unipolar Machine)* (Homopolar Machine)*

An acyclic machine is a direct-current machine, in which the voltage generated in the active conductors maintains the same direction with respect to those conductors.

Electric Generator   10.10.050

An electric generator is a machine which transforms mechanical power into electric power.

Magnetoelectric Generator   10.10.060

A magnetoelectric generator is an electric generator, the field poles of which are permanent magnets.

Exciter   10.10.070

An exciter is an auxiliary generator which supplies energy for the field excitation of another electric machine.

Main Exciter   10.10.075

A main exciter is an exciter which supplies energy for the field excitation of a principal electric machine.

Pilot Exciter   10.10.080

A pilot exciter is an exciter which supplies energy for the field excitation of another exciter.

Double-Current Generator   10.10.090

A double-current generator is a machine which supplies both direct and alternating currents from the same armature winding.

Synchronous Generator   10.10.100

(Alternator)*

A synchronous generator is a synchronous alternating-current machine which transforms mechanical power into electric power.

Single-Phase Synchronous Generator   10.10.110

A single-phase synchronous generator is one which produces a single alternating electromotive force at its terminals. It delivers electric power which pulsates at double frequency.

Polyphase Synchronous Generator   10.10.120

A polyphase synchronous generator is one whose alternating-current circuits are so arranged that two or more symmetrical alternating electromotive forces with

* Deprecated.

definite phase relationships are produced at its terminals. Polyphase synchronous generators are usually two-phase, producing two electromotive forces displaced 90 electrical degrees with respect to one another or three-phase, with three electromotive forces, displaced 120 electrical degrees with respect to each other.

Double-Winding Synchronous Generator 10.10.130

A double-winding synchronous generator is one which has two similar windings, in phase with one another, mounted on the same magnetic structure but not connected electrically, designed to supply power to two independent external circuits.

Inductor Type Synchronous Generator 10.10.140

An inductor type synchronous generator is one in which the field coils are fixed in magnetic position relative to the armature conductors, the electromotive forces being produced by the movement of masses of magnetic material.

Induction Generator 10.10.150

An induction generator is an induction machine, driven above synchronous speed by an external source of mechanical power.

Booster 10.10.160

A booster is a generator inserted in series in a circuit to change its voltage.

Reversible Booster 10.10.170

A reversible booster is a booster capable of adding to and subtracting from the voltage of a circuit.

Negative Booster 10.10.180

A negative booster is a booster used in connection with a ground-return system for the purpose of reducing the difference of potential between two points on the grounded return. It is connected in series with a supplementary insulated feeder extending from the negative bus of the generating station or substation to a distant point on the grounded return.

Electric Motor 10.10.200

An electric motor is a machine which transforms electric energy into mechanical energy.

Universal Motor 10.10.210

A universal motor is a series-wound or a compensated series-wound motor which may be operated either on direct current or single-phase alternating current at approximately the same speed and output. These conditions must be met when the direct-current and alternating-current voltages are approximately the same and the frequency of the alternating current is not greater than 60 cycles per second.

General Purpose Motor 10.10.220

A general purpose motor is any motor of 200 hp or less and 450 rpm or more, having a continuous rating, and designed, listed or offered in standard ratings for use without restriction to a particular application.

Special Purpose Motor 10.10.230

A special purpose motor is an industrial power motor specifically designated and listed for a particular power application where the load requirements and duty cycle are definitely known.

Fractional Horsepower Motor 10.10.240

A fractional horsepower motor is a motor built in a frame smaller than that having a continuous rating of 1 hp open type, at 1,700–1,800 rpm.

Large Power Motor 10.10.250

A large power motor is a motor built in a frame having a continuous rating of 1 hp, open type, at 1,700–1,800 rpm, or in a larger frame.

Induction Motor 10.10.260

An induction motor is an induction machine which converts electric power delivered to the primary circuit into mechanical power. The secondary circuit is short-circuited or closed through a suitable circuit.

Wound-Rotor Induction Motor 10.10.270

(Slip-Ring Induction Motor)*

A wound-rotor induction motor is an induction motor in which the secondary circuit consists of a polyphase winding or coils whose terminals are either short-circuited or closed through suitable circuits.

Squirrel Cage Induction Motor 10.10.280

A squirrel cage induction motor is one in which the secondary circuit consists of a squirrel cage winding suitably disposed in slots in the secondary core.

Synchronous Motor 10.10.300

A synchronous motor is a synchronous machine which transforms electric power from an alternating-current system into mechanical power. Synchronous motors usually have direct-current field excitation.

Reluctance Motor 10.10.305

A reluctance motor is a synchronous motor similar in construction to an induction motor, in which the member carrying the secondary circuit has salient poles, without direct-current excitation. It starts as an induction motor, but operates normally at synchronous speed.

Subsynchronous Reluctance Motor 10.10.310

A subsynchronous reluctance motor is a form of reluctance motor, which has the number of salient poles greater than the number of electrical poles of the primary winding, thus causing the motor to operate at a constant average speed, which is a submultiple of its apparent synchronous speed.

Hysteresis Motor 10.10.315

A hysteresis motor is a synchronous motor without salient poles and without direct-current excitation, which starts by virtue of the hysteresis losses induced in its hardened steel secondary member by the revolving field

---

* Deprecated.

of the primary and operates normally at synchronous speed due to the retentivity of the secondary core.

Synchronous Induction Motor 10.10.320

A synchronous induction motor is a wound rotor induction motor to which direct-current excitation is supplied when it approaches rated speed, enabling it to start as an induction motor and operate as a synchronous motor.

Shunt-Wound Motor 10.10.330

A shunt-wound motor is a direct-current motor in which the field circuit and armature circuit are connected in parallel.

Stabilized Shunt-Wound Motor 10.10.335

A stabilized shunt-wound motor is a shunt-wound motor having a light series winding added to prevent a rise in speed or to obtain a slight reduction in speed, with increase of load.

Series-Wound Motor 10.10.340

A series-wound motor is a commutator motor in which the field circuit and armature circuit are connected in series.

Compound-Wound Motor 10.10.350

A compound-wound motor is a direct-current motor which has two separate field windings—one, usually the predominating field, connected in parallel with the armature circuit, and the other connected in series with the armature circuit.

Shaded-Pole Motor 10.10.355

A shaded-pole motor is a single-phase induction motor provided with an auxiliary short-circuited winding or windings displaced in magnetic position from the main winding.

Split-Phase Motor 10.10.360

A split-phase motor is a single-phase induction motor equipped with an auxiliary winding, displaced in magnetic position from, and connected in parallel with, the main winding.

NOTE: Unless otherwise specified, the auxiliary circuit is assumed to be opened when the motor has attained a predetermined speed. The term split-phase motor, used without qualification, describes a motor to be used without impedance, other than that offered by the motor windings themselves, other types being separately defined.

Resistance-Start Motor 10.10.370

A resistance-start motor is a form of split-phase motor having a resistance connected in series with the auxiliary winding. The auxiliary circuit is opened when the motor has attained a predetermined speed.

Reactor-Start Motor 10.10.380

A reactor-start motor is a form of split-phase motor designed for starting with a reactor in series with the main winding. The reactor is short-circuited, or otherwise made ineffective and the auxiliary circuit is opened when the motor has attained a predetermined speed.

Capacitor-Start Motor 10.10.390

A capacitor-start motor is a form of split-phase motor having a capacitor connected in series with the auxiliary winding. The auxiliary circuit is opened when the motor has attained a predetermined speed.

NOTE: The capacitor may be connected into the circuit through a transformer.

Capacitor Motor 10.10.400

A capacitor motor is a single-phase induction motor with a main winding arranged for direct connection to a source of power and an auxiliary winding connected in series with a capacitor.

NOTE: The capacitor may be connected into the circuit through a transformer and its value may be varied between starting and running.

Repulsion Motor 10.10.410

A repulsion motor is a single-phase motor which has a stator winding arranged for connection to the source of power and a rotor winding connected to a commutator. Brushes on the commutator are short-circuited and are so placed that the magnetic axis of the rotor winding is inclined to the magnetic axis of the stator winding. This type of motor has a varying-speed characteristic.

Compensated Repulsion Motor 10.10.415

A compensated repulsion motor is a repulsion motor with an added winding to improve the power factor. This type of motor may have constant or varying-speed characteristics.

Repulsion-Start Induction Motor 10.10.420

A repulsion-start induction motor is a single-phase motor having the same windings as a repulsion motor but at a predetermined speed the rotor winding is short-circuited or otherwise connected to give the equivalent of a squirrel-cage winding. This type of motor starts as a repulsion motor but operates as an induction motor with constant-speed characteristics.

Repulsion Induction Motor 10.10.430

A repulsion induction motor is a form of repulsion motor which has a squirrel-cage winding in the rotor in addition to the repulsion motor winding. A motor of this type may have either a constant-speed or varying-speed characteristic.

Shell Type Motor 10.10.435

A shell type motor consists of a stator and rotor without shaft, end shields, bearings or conventional frame. Separate fans or fans larger than the rotor are not included.

Motor Reduction Unit 10.10.440

A motor reduction unit is a motor with an integral mechanical means of obtaining a speed differing from the speed of the motor.

NOTE: Motor reduction units are usually designed to obtain a speed lower than that of the motor, but may also be built to obtain a speed higher than that of the motor.

Dynamotor   10.10.450

A dynamotor is a machine which combines both motor and generator action in one magnetic field, either with two armatures or with one armature having two separate windings.

Motor-Generator Set   10.10.460

A motor-generator set is a machine which consists of one or more motors mechanically coupled to one or more generators.

Synchronous Converter   10.10.470

(Rotary Converter)

A synchronous converter is a synchronous machine which converts alternating current to direct current, or *vice versa*. The armature winding is connected to collector rings and commutator.

Motor Converter   10.10.480

(Cascade Converter)*

A motor converter consists of an induction motor and a synchronous converter with their rotors mounted on the same shaft and with their rotor windings connected in series. Such a converter operates synchronously at a speed corresponding to the sum of the numbers of poles of the two machines. Voltage control with a motor converter is obtained by the same methods as are used with a synchronous converter.

Synchronous Booster Converter   10.10.490

A synchronous booster converter is a synchronous converter having an alternating-current generator mounted on the same shaft and connected in series with it for the purpose of adjusting the voltage at the commutator of the converter.

Frequency Changer   10.10.500

A frequency changer is a machine which converts the power of an alternating-current system from one frequency to another, with or without a change in the number of phases, or in the voltage.

Frequency Converter   10.10.510

A frequency converter is a frequency changer in which the windings carrying the currents of different frequency are in the same magnetic field.

Induction Frequency Converter   10.10.520

An induction frequency converter is a slip-ring induction machine, which is driven by an external source of mechanical power and whose primary circuits are connected to a source of electric energy having a fixed frequency.

The secondary circuits deliver energy at a frequency proportional to the relative speed of the primary magnetic field and the secondary member.

Rotary Phase Converter   10.10.530

A rotary phase converter is a machine which converts power from an alternating-current system of one or more phases to an alternating-current system of a different number of phases, but of the same frequency.

Phase Modifier   10.10.540

A phase modifier is a machine the chief purpose of which is to supply leading or lagging reactive volt-amperes to the system to which it is connected. Phase modifiers may be either synchronous or asynchronous.

Phase Advancer   10.10.550

A phase advancer is a phase modifier which supplies leading reactive volt-amperes to the system to which it is connected. Phase advancers may be either synchronous or asynchronous.

Synchronous Condenser   10.10.560

A synchronous condenser is a synchronous phase modifier running without mechanical load, the field excitation of which may be varied so as to modify the power factor of the system, or through such modification to influence the load voltage.

Direct-Current Balancer   10.10.570

(Direct-Current Compensator)*

A direct-current balancer is a machine which comprises two or more similar direct-current machines (usually with shunt or compound excitation) directly coupled to each other and connected in series across the outer conductors of a multiple-wire system of distribution, for the purpose of maintaining the potentials of the intermediate conductors of the system, which are connected to the junction points between the machines.

GROUP 10—ROTATING MACHINERY

Section 15—Machine Parts

Front of a Motor or Generator   10.15.010

The front of a normal motor or generator is the end opposite the coupling or driving pulley.

Back of a Motor or Generator   10.15.020

The back of a normal motor or generator is the end which carries the coupling or driving pulley.

Frame   10.15.030

A frame is the supporting structure for the stator parts.

In a direct-current machine the frame usually forms a part of the magnetic circuit; it includes the poles only when they form an integral part of it.

Field Pole   10.15.040

A field pole is a structure of magnetic material on which a field coil may be mounted.

Salient Pole   10.15.045

A salient pole is that type of field pole which projects toward the armature.

---

* Deprecated.

* Deprecated.

Commutating Pole   10.15.050

(Interpole)

A commutating pole is an auxiliary pole placed between the main poles of a commutating machine. Its exciting winding carries a current proportional to the load current and produces a flux in such a direction and phase as to assist the reversal of the current in the short-circuited coil.

Pole Shoe   10.15.060

A pole shoe is the portion of a field pole facing the armature of the machine. It may be separable from the body of the pole.

Field Coil   10.15.070

A field coil is a suitably insulated winding to be mounted on a field pole to magnetize it.

Rotor   10.15.080

A rotor is the rotating member of a machine.

Stator   10.15.090

The stator is the portion of a machine which contains the stationary parts of the magnetic circuit with their associated windings.

Armature   10.15.100

The armature is the part of a machine which includes the main current-carrying winding.

In direct-current machines and in alternating-current commutator machines, the armature winding is connected to the commutator and the armature is the rotating member.

In alternating-current machines without commutators the armature may be either the rotating member or the stationary member.

NOTE: In some types of alternating-current machines the use of the term armature is apt to be misleading and should be avoided.

Armature Core   10.15.110

An armature core consists of the assembled armature laminations without the slot insulation or windings.

Armature Quill   10.15.120

An armature quill is a ventilated or unventilated structure upon which an armature and commutator are assembled and which in turn may be mounted on the armature shaft.

Armature Sleeve   10.15.130

An armature sleeve is an unventilated support on which armature laminations are or may be mounted and which in turn is mounted on the armature shaft.

Armature Spider   10.15.140

An armature spider is a ventilated support upon which armature laminations are mounted and which in turn is mounted on the armature shaft.

Commutator   10.15.150

A commutator is a cylindrical ring or disk assembly of conducting members, individually insulated in a supporting structure with an exposed surface for contact with current-collecting brushes and ready for mounting on an armature shaft, quill or spider. The end opposite to the armature core is known as the front end.

Commutator Bars   10.15.160

(Commutator Segments)

Commutator bars are the metal current-carrying members of a commutator which make contact with the brushes.

Commutator Insulating Strips   10.15.170

(Commutator Insulating Segments)*

Commutator insulating strips are the insulating members between adjacent commutator bars.

Commutator Insulating Rings   10.15.180

Commutator insulating rings are rings which constitute all the insulation between the ends of the assembled commutator bars and the supporting structure.

Commutator Shell Insulation   10.15.190

Commutator shell insulation is the insulation between the under (or in the case of a disk commutator, the back) side of the assembled commutator bars and the adjacent supporting structure.

Commutator Bar Assembly   10.15.200

A commutator bar assembly consists of the complete set of commutator bars assembled with the commutator insulating strips bound and ready for installation on the commutator shell, but this term does not include the commutator insulating rings or the commutator shell insulation.

Commutator Shell   10.15.210

A commutator shell is the support on which the commutator bar assembly, commutator insulating rings and metal support rings, and the commutator shell insulation are mounted.

Brush Yoke   10.15.220

A brush yoke is a rocker arm, ring, quadrant or other adjustable support for maintaining the brush holders or brush holder studs in their relative positions.

Brush Holder   10.15.230

A brush holder is a device which holds the brush in position.

Brush Holder Stud   10.15.240

A brush holder stud is an intermediate support between the brush holder and the brush yoke.

Brush   10.15.245

A brush is a conductor serving to maintain electric contact between stationary and moving parts of a machine or other apparatus.

Collector Rings   10.15.250

(Slip Rings)

Collector rings are metal rings suitably mounted

---

* Deprecated.

on an electric machine serving, through stationary brushes bearing thereon, to conduct current into or out of the rotating member.

End Shield 10.15.260

An end shield is a shield secured to the frame and adapted to protect the windings and to support the bearing, but including no part thereof.

Winding Shield 10.15.270

A winding shield is a shield secured to the frame and adapted to protect the windings but not to support the bearing.

Bearing Bracket 10.15.280

A bearing bracket is a bracket secured to the frame to support the bearing but including no part thereof, and not designed specifically to protect the windings.

End Shield Assembly 10.15.285

An end shield assembly is an end shield together with its bearing sleeve and all parts associated therewith.

Bearing Bracket Assembly 10.15.290

(End Shield Assembly)

A bearing bracket assembly is a bearing bracket with its bearing sleeve and all parts associated therewith.

Bearing Sleeve 10.15.300

A bearing sleeve is a bushing, sleeve, box or shell within which the shaft rotates.

Bearing Pedestal 10.15.310

A bearing pedestal is a bearing support, mounted on or constructed as a part of the base plate, but not including the bearing or any part thereof.

Bearing Pedestal Assembly 10.15.320

A bearing pedestal assembly is a bearing pedestal together with its bearing and all parts associated therewith.

Centrifugal Starting Switch 10.15.330

A centrifugal starting switch is a centrifugally operated automatic mechanism usually used in connection with split-phase induction motors to open or disconnect the starting winding after the rotor has attained a predetermined speed, and to close or reconnect it prior to the time the rotor comes to rest.

Automatic Short-Circuiter 10.15.340

An automatic short-circuiter is a device designed to automatically short-circuit the commutator bars in some forms of single-phase commutator motors.

Embedded Temperature Detector 10.15.350

An embedded temperature detector is a resistance thermometer or thermocouple built into a machine for the purpose of measuring the temperature.

Amortisseur Winding 10.15.360

(Damper Winding)

An amortisseur winding is a permanently short-circuited winding, usually uninsulated, so arranged as to oppose rotation or pulsation of the magnetic field with respect to the pole shoes.

NOTE: The term "amortisseur" is commonly limited to forms having the conductors arranged in individually short-circuited groups with bolted or otherwise separable connections between groups. Two other forms are the open amortisseur winding and the squirrel cage winding which are defined separately.

Squirrel Cage Winding 10.15.370

A squirrel cage winding is a permanently short-circuited winding, usually uninsulated (chiefly used in induction machines), having its conductors uniformly distributed around the periphery of the machine and joined by continuous end rings.

Open Amortisseur Winding 10.15.380

An open amortisseur winding is a form of amortisseur winding having its conductors arranged in individually short-circuited groups that are not interconnected.

GROUP 10—ROTATING MACHINERY
Section 20—Speed Classification of Motors

Constant-Speed Motor 10.20.010

A constant-speed motor is one the speed of normal operation of which is constant or practically constant. For example, a synchronous motor, an induction motor with small slip or an ordinary direct-current shunt-wound motor.

Multispeed Motor 10.20.020

A multispeed motor is one which can be operated at any one of two or more definite speeds, each being practically independent of the load. For example, a direct-current motor with two armature windings, or an induction motor with windings capable of various pole groupings.

Single-Winding Multispeed Motor 10.20.030

A single-winding multispeed motor is a type of multispeed motor having a single winding capable of reconnection in two or more pole groupings.

Adjustable-Speed Motor 10.20.040

An adjustable-speed motor is one the speed of which can be varied gradually over a considerable range, but when once adjusted remains practically unaffected by the load, such as a shunt motor with field resistance control designed for a considerable range of speed adjustment.

Base Speed of an Adjustable-Speed Motor 10.20.050

The base speed of an adjustable-speed motor is the

lowest speed obtained at rated load and rated voltage at the temperature rise specified in the rating.

Varying-Speed Motor   10.20.060

A varying-speed motor is one the speed of which varies with the load, ordinarily decreasing when the load increases; such as a series motor or an induction motor with large slip.

Adjustable Varying-Speed Motor   10.20.070

An adjustable varying-speed motor is one the speed of which can be adjusted gradually, but when once adjusted for a given load will vary in considerable degree with change in load; such as a compound-wound direct-current motor adjusted by field control or a slip-ring induction motor with rheostatic speed control.

GROUP 10—ROTATING MACHINERY

Section 25—Enclosure and Ventilation of Machines

Self-Ventilated Machine   10.25.010

A self-ventilated machine is one which has its ventilating air circulated by means integral with the machine.

Separately Ventilated Machine   10.25.020

A separately ventilated machine is one which has its ventilating air supplied by an independent fan or blower external to the machine.

Enclosed Self-Ventilated Machine   10.25.030

An enclosed self-ventilated machine is a machine having openings for the admission and discharge of the ventilating air, which is circulated by means integral with the machine, the machine being otherwise totally enclosed. These openings are so arranged that inlet and outlet ducts or pipes may be connected to them.

NOTE: Such ducts or pipes, if used, must have ample section and be so arranged as to furnish the specified volume of air to the machine, otherwise the ventilation will not be sufficient.

Enclosed Separately Ventilated Machine   10.25.040

An enclosed separately ventilated machine is a machine having openings for the admission and discharge of the ventilating air, which is circulated by means external to and not a part of the machine, the machine being otherwise totally enclosed. These openings are so arranged that inlet and outlet duct pipes may be connected to them.

Open Machine   10.25.050

An open machine is a self-ventilated machine having no restriction to ventilation other than that necessitated by mechanical construction.

NOTE: In the sense of this definition an open machine, when the term is used without qualification, is understood not to be splashproof or drip-proof.

Totally Enclosed Machine   10.25.060

A totally enclosed machine is one so enclosed as to prevent exchange of air between the inside and the outside of the case, but not sufficiently enclosed to be termed airtight.

See 95.90.220

Totally Enclosed Fan-Cooled Machine   10.25.070

A totally enclosed fan-cooled machine is a totally enclosed machine equipped for exterior cooling by means of a fan or fans, integral with the machine but external to the enclosing parts.

GROUP 10—ROTATING MACHINERY

Section 30—Protection of Machines

Protected Machine   10.30.010

(Formerly called semi-enclosed machine)

A protected machine is one in which all ventilating openings in the frame are protected with wire screen, expanded metal or perforated covers.

NOTE: A common form of specification for "protected machine" is: "The openings shall not exceed ½ square inch (323 sq mm) in area and shall be of such shape as not to permit the passage of a rod larger than ½ inch (12.7 mm) in diameter, except where the distance of exposed live parts from the guard is more than 4 inches (101.7 mm) the openings may be ¾ square inch (484 sq mm) in area and must be of such shape as not to permit the passage of a rod larger than ¾ inch (19 mm) in diameter.

Semi-Protected Machine   10.30.020

A semi-protected machine is one in which part of the ventilating openings in the frame, usually in the top half, are protected as in the case of a "protected machine" but the others are left open.

Drip-Proof Machine   10.30.030

A drip-proof machine is one in which the ventilating openings are so constructed that drops of liquid or solid particles falling on the machine at any angle not greater than 15 degrees from the vertical, cannot enter the machine either directly or by striking and running along a horizontal or inwardly inclined surface.

Splashproof Machine   10.30.040

A splashproof machine is one in which the ventilating openings are so constructed that drops of liquid or solid particles falling on the machine or coming toward it in a straight line at any angle not greater than 100 degrees from the vertical cannot enter the machine either directly or by striking and running along a surface.

Explosion-Proof Machine   10.30.050

An explosion-proof machine is one in an enclosing

case which is designed and constructed to withstand an explosion of a specified gas or dust which may occur within it, and to prevent the ignition of the specified gas or dust surrounding the machine by sparks, flashes or explosions of the specified gas or dust, which may occur within the machine casing.

Watertight Machine   10.30.060

A watertight machine is a totally enclosed machine so constructed that it will exclude water applied in the form of a stream from a hose.

NOTE: A common form of specification for a totally enclosed machine is: "A stream of water from a hose (not less than 1 inch in diameter) under a head of 35 feet and from a distance of about

10 feet can be played on the machine without leakage, except that leakage which may occur around the shaft may be considered permissible, provided it is prevented from entering the oil reservoir and provision is made for automatically draining the machine."

The machine may be provided with a check valve for drainage or a tapped hole at the lowest part of the frame which will serve for application of drain pipe or drain plug.

Dust-Tight Machine
See 95.90.130.

Resistant (as a suffix)
See 95.90.020.

Submersible Machine
See 95.90.195.

GROUP 10—ROTATING MACHINERY

Section 35—Synchronous Machine Quantities

Synchronous machine quantities are used in studies of machine characteristics, short-circuit currents and system stability. There are variations of the quantities with saturation of the magnetic circuits. In some cases definitions are based on the rated current values, and in other cases definitions are based on both rated current and rated voltage values.

Three-phase, short-circuit oscillograms are required for the determination of a number of the machine quantities. These tests may result in one or no symmetrical wave and two or three asymmetrical waves. The asymmetrical waves may be analyzed from their envelopes by drawing curves through the peaks of the asymmetrical waves, a median line between these two curves, and then plotting the distance between the median line and the curves. This distance represents the magnitude of the alternating-current component, and the distance from the median line to the zero-current axis is the asymmetrical component of the asymmetrical wave. The curves for the alternating-current components of the three current waves for each test are derived and the values of reactances and time constants are the averages of the values determined from the three waves.[†]

A machine has only one negative sequence and one zero sequence reactance; the other reactances defined are all positive sequence reactances.

List of Symbols

In the following list of symbols, all voltage quantities except terminal voltage refer to line-to-neutral and all current quantities are per line. When the machine is connected delta, the line-to-neutral voltage is the voltage between lines divided by $\sqrt{3}$, and does not represent a voltage actually generated in the machine. The phases a, b, c for delta-connected machines represent the phases of an equivalent Y connection, and not the actual phase windings of the machine. The direct-axis and quadrature-axis quantities are indicated by the subscripts "d" and "q", respectively, and the transient and subtransient quantities are indicated by the superscripts "prime" and "double prime", respectively. The absence of superscripts indicates sustained quantities.

Voltage of Phase a, b, c	E_a, E_b, E_c e_a, e_b, e_c
Terminal Voltage (between lines)	E e
Direct-Axis Synchronous Internal Voltage	E_d e_d
Direct-Axis Transient Internal Voltage	E'_d e'_d
Direct-Axis Subtransient Internal Voltage	E''_d e''_d
Quadrature-Axis Synchronous Internal Voltage	E_q e_q
Quadrature-Axis Transient Internal Voltage	E'_q e'_q
Quadrature-Axis Subtransient Internal Voltage	E''_q e''_q
Synchronous Internal Voltage	E_i e_i
Transient Internal Voltage	E'_i e'_i
Subtransient Internal Voltage	E''_i e''_i
Exciter Voltage	E_{ex} e_{ex}
Synchronous Machine Field Voltage	E_f e_f
Current in Line a, b, c	I_a, I_b, I_c i_a, i_b, i_c
Armature Current	I i
Transient Armature Current	I' i'
Subtransient Armature Current	I'' i''
Direct-Axis Component of Armature Current	I_d i_d

[†] A very close approximation for the reactances and time constants may be obtained by plotting the points for the three alternating-current component curves on one sheet, and then analyzing the average curve.

ELECTRICAL DEFINITIONS

Direct-Axis Component of Transient Armature Current	I'_d i'_d
Direct-Axis Component of Subtransient Armature Current	I''_d i''_d
Quadrature-Axis Component of Armature Current	I_q i_q
Quadrature-Axis Component of Transient Armature Current	I'_q i'_q
Quadrature-Axis Component of Subtransient Armature Current	I''_q i''_q
Field Current	I_f i_f
Impedance Angle	θ
Power-Factor Angle	ϕ
Load Angle (Displacement due to load between the direct-axis voltage and the terminal voltage)	δ
Direct-Current Armature Resistance	r_a
Alternating-Current Armature Resistance	r
Field Resistance	r_f

Direct Axis   10.35.020

The direct axis is the axis of magnetization of the main field winding usually coinciding with the polar axis.

Quadrature Axis   10.35.025

The quadrature axis is the interpolar axis.

Direct-Axis Voltage   10.35.030

A direct-axis voltage is a voltage generated by a flux in the direct axis.

Quadrature-Axis Voltage   10.35.035

A quadrature-axis voltage is a voltage generated by a flux in the quadrature axis.

Direct-Axis Component of Armature Current   10.35.040

A direct-axis component of armature current is one which magnetizes in the direct axis.

Quadrature-Axis Component of Armature Current   10.35.045

A quadrature-axis component of armature current is one which magnetizes in the quadrature axis.

Air-Gap Line   10.35.050

The air-gap line is the extended straight line part of the no-load saturation curve.

Short-Circuit Ratio (SCR)   10.35.100

The short-circuit ratio is the ratio of the field current for rated open-circuit armature voltage and rated frequency to the field current for rated armature current on sustained symmetrical short-circuit at rated frequency.

Direct-Axis Synchronous Reactance (x_d)   10.35.110

The direct-axis synchronous reactance is the ratio of the fundamental component of reactive armature voltage, due to the fundamental direct-axis component of armature current, to this component of current under balanced steady-state conditions and at rated frequency.

Unless otherwise specified the value of synchronous reactance will be that corresponding to the rated armature current.

Synchronous Impedance   10.35.115

The per unit direct-axis synchronous impedance equals the ratio of the field current at rated armature current on sustained symmetrical short-circuit to the field current at normal open-circuit voltage on the air-gap line.

NOTE: This definition of synchronous impedance is used to a great extent in electrical literature and corresponds to the definition of direct-axis synchronous reactance as determined from open-circuit and sustained short-circuit tests.

Direct-Axis Transient Reactance (x'_d)   10.35.120

The direct-axis transient reactance is the ratio of the fundamental component of reactive armature voltage, due to the fundamental direct-axis alternating-current component of the armature current, to this component of current under suddenly applied load conditions and at rated frequency, the value of current to be determined by the extrapolation of the envelope of the alternating-current component of the current wave to the instant of the sudden application of load, neglecting the high-decrement currents during the first few cycles.

The rated current value of the direct-axis transient reactance will be that obtained from a three-phase sudden short-circuit test at the terminals of the machine at no-load and rated speed, and with an initial voltage such as to give a transient value of short-circuit current plus the sustained value equal to the rated current, neglecting the high-decrement current during the first few cycles. This requirement means that the test voltage (per unit) is equal to the rated current value of transient reactance (per unit). In actual practice the test voltages will seldom result in transient currents of exactly the rated value, and it will usually be necessary to determine the rated current value of transient reactance from a curve of reactances plotted against voltage.

The rated voltage value of the direct-axis transient reactance will be that obtained from a three-phase sudden short-circuit test at the terminals of the machine at no-load and rated armature voltage.

Direct-Axis Subtransient Reactance (x''_d)   10.35.130

The direct-axis subtransient reactance is the ratio of the fundamental component of reactive armature voltage, due to the initial value of the fundamental direct-axis component of the alternating-current component of the armature current, to this component of current under suddenly applied load conditions and at rated frequency.

The rated current value of direct-axis subtransient reactance will be that obtained from the tests for the rated current value of direct-axis transient reactance.

The rated voltage value of direct-axis subtransient reactance will be that obtained from a short-circuit test at the terminals of the machine at no-load and rated speed and at rated armature voltage.

Quadrature-Axis Synchronous Reactance (x_q)   10.35.140

The quadrature-axis synchronous reactance is the ratio of the fundamental component of reactive armature voltage, due to the fundamental quadrature-axis component of armature current, to this component of current under steady-state conditions and at rated frequency.

Unless otherwise specified, the value of quadrature-axis synchronous reactance will be that corresponding to rated armature current.

Quadrature-Axis Transient Reactance (x'_q)   10.35.150

The quadrature-axis transient reactance is the ratio of the fundamental component of reactive armature voltage, due to the fundamental quadrature-axis component of the alternating-current component of the armature current, to this component of current under suddenly applied load conditions and at rated frequency, the value of current to be determined by the extrapolation of the envelope of the alternating-current component of the current wave to the instant of the sudden application of load, *neglecting the high-decrement currents during the first few cycles:*

NOTE: The quadrature-axis transient reactance usually equals the quadrature-axis synchronous reactance except in solid-rotor machines, since in general there is no really effective field current in the quadrature axis.

Quadrature-Axis Subtransient Reactance (x''_q)   10.35.160

The quadrature-axis subtransient reactance is the ratio of the fundamental component of reactive armature voltage, due to the *initial* value of the fundamental quadrature-axis component of the alternating-current component of the armature current, to this component of current under suddenly applied balanced load conditions and at rated frequency.

Unless otherwise specified, the quadrature-axis subtransient reactance will be that corresponding to rated armature current.

Negative-Sequence Reactance (x_2)   10.35.170

The negative-sequence reactance is the ratio of the fundamental component of reactive armature voltage, due to the fundamental negative-sequence component of armature current, to this component of armature current at rated frequency.

The rated current value of negative-sequence reactance is the value obtained from a test with a current equal to rated armature current.

The rated voltage value of negative-sequence reactance is the value obtained from a line-to-line short-circuit test at two terminals of the machine at no-load and rated speed, and at rated armature voltage.

Negative-Sequence Resistance (r_2)   10.35.180

The negative-sequence resistance is the ratio of the fundamental component of in-phase armature voltage, due to the fundamental negative-sequence component of armature current, to this component of current at rated frequency.

NOTE: This resistance, which forms a part of the negative-sequence impedance for use in circuit calculations to establish relationships between voltages and currents, *is not directly applicable in the calculations of the total loss in the machine caused by the flow of negative-sequence currents.* This loss is the product of the square of the fundamental component of the negative-sequence current and the difference between twice the negative-sequence resistance and the positive-sequence resistance, *i. e.,* $I_2^2 (2r_2 - r)$.

Zero-Sequence Reactance (x_0)   10.35.190

The zero-sequence reactance is the ratio of the fundamental component of reactive armature voltage, due to the fundamental zero-sequence component of armature current, to this component at rated frequency.

Unless otherwise specified, the value of zero-sequence reactance will be that corresponding to a zero-sequence current equal to rated armature current.

Potier Reactance (x_p)   10.35.200

Potier reactance is a synchronous machine quantity determined from a no-load saturation curve, and a zero power factor (over excited) excitation. It is useful for the calculation of excitation of the machine at other loads and power factors.† The height of a Potier reactance triangle determines the reactance drop, and the reactance x_p is equal to the reactance drop divided by the current.

Unless otherwise specified, the value of Potier reactance shall be that obtained from the no-load normal frequency saturation curve; and the excitation for rated voltage and current at zero power factor (over excited), and at rated frequency.

Approximate values of Potier reactance may be obtained from test-load excitations at loads differing from rated load, and at power factors other than zero.

Direct-Axis Transient Open-Circuit Time Constant (T'_{do})   10.35.210

The direct-axis open-circuit time constant is the time in seconds required for the rms alternating-current value of the slowly decreasing component present in the direct-axis component of symmetrical armature voltage on open-circuit to decrease to $1/\epsilon$ or 0.368 of its initial value when the field winding is suddenly short-circuited with the machine running at rated speed.

Direct-Axis Transient Short-Circuit Time Constant (T'_d)   10.35.220

The direct-axis transient short-circuit time constant is the time in seconds required for the rms value of the *slowly decreasing* component present in the direct-axis component of the alternating-current component of the armature current under suddenly applied symmetrical short-circuit conditions with the machine running at rated speed, to decrease to $1/\epsilon$ or 0.368 of its initial value.

† The excitation results in the range from zero power factor over excited to unity power factor are close enough to the test values for most practical applications.

The rated current value of the direct-axis transient short-circuit time constant will be that obtained from the test for the rated current value of the direct-axis transient reactance.

The rated voltage value of the direct-axis transient short-circuit time constant will be that obtained from the test for the rated voltage value of the direct-axis transient reactance.

Direct-Axis Subtransient Open-Circuit Time Constant (T''_{do})   10.35.230

The direct-axis subtransient open-circuit time constant is the time in seconds required for the *rapidly decreasing* component (negative) present during the first few cycles in the direct-axis component of symmetrical armature voltage under suddenly removed symmetrical short-circuit conditions, with the machine running at rated speed, to decrease to $1/\epsilon$ or 0.368 of its initial value.

Direct-Axis Subtransient Short-Circuit Time Constant (T''_d)   10.35.240

The direct-axis subtransient short-circuit time constant is the time in seconds required for the *rapidly decreasing* component present during the first few cycles in the direct-axis component of the alternating-current component of the armature current under suddenly applied short-circuit conditions, with the machine running at rated speed to decrease to $1/\epsilon$ or 0.368 of its initial value.

The rated current value of the direct-axis subtransient short-circuit time constant will be that obtained from the test for the rated current value of the direct-axis transient reactance.

The rated voltage of the direct-axis subtransient short-circuit time constant will be that obtained from the test for the rated voltage value of the direct-axis transient reactance.

Quadrature-Axis Transient Open-Circuit Time Constant (T'_{qo})   10.35.250

The quadrature-axis open-circuit time constant is the time in seconds required for the rms alternating-current value of the *slowly decreasing* component present in the quadrature-axis component of symmetrical armature voltage on open-circuit to decrease to $1/\epsilon$ or 0.368 of its initial value when the quadrature field winding (if any) is suddenly short-circuited with the machine running at rated speed.

NOTE: This time constant is important only in turbine generators.

Quadrature-Axis Transient Short-Circuit Time Constant (T'_q)   10.35.260

The quadrature-axis transient short-circuit time constant is the time in seconds required for the rms alternating-current value of the *slowly decreasing* component present in the quadrature-axis component of the alter-nating-current component of the armature current under suddenly applied short-circuit conditions with the machine running at rated speed to decrease $1/\epsilon$ or 0.368 of its initial value.

Quadrature-Axis Subtransient Open-Circuit Time Constant (T''_{qo})   10.35.270

The quadrature-axis subtransient open-circuit time constant is the time in seconds required for the *rapidly decreasing* component (negative) present during the first few cycles in the quadrature-axis component of symmetrical armature voltage under suddenly removed symmetrical short-circuit conditions with the machine running at rated speed, to decrease $1/\epsilon$ or 0.368 of its initial value.

Quadrature-Axis Subtransient Short-Circuit Time Constant (T''_q)   10.35.280

The quadrature-axis subtransient short-circuit time constant is the time in seconds required for the *rapidly decreasing* component present during the first few cycles in the quadrature-axis component of the alternating-current component of the armature current under suddenly applied symmetrical short-circuit conditions, with the machine running at rated speed, to decrease to $1/\epsilon$ or 0.368 of its initial value.

Short-Circuit Time Constant of Armature Winding (T_a)   10.35.290

The short-circuit time constant of the armature winding is the time in seconds for the asymmetrical (direct-current) component of armature current under suddenly applied short-circuit conditions, with the machine running at rated speed, to decrease to $1/\epsilon$ or 0.368 of its initial value.

The rated current value of the short-circuit time constant of the armature winding will be that obtained from the test specified for the rated current value of direct-axis transient reactance.

The rated voltage value of the short-circuit time constant of the armature winding will be that obtained from a short-circuit test at the terminals of the machine at no-load and rated speed and at rated armature voltage.

Inertia Constant   10.35.300

The inertia constant is the energy stored in the rotor of a machine when operating at rated speed expressed as kilowattseconds per kva rating of the machine.

The inertia constant is

$$H = \frac{0.231 \times W R^2 \times n^2 \times 10^{-6}}{kva}$$

where
H = inertia constant in kilowattseconds/kva
$W R^2$ = moment of inertia in lb-ft^2
n = speed in revolutions per minute
kva = rating of machine

GROUP 10—ROTATING MACHINERY

Section 40—Kinds of Torque

Locked Rotor Torque   10.40.020

(Static Torque)

The locked rotor torque of a motor is the minimum torque which it will develop at rest for all angular positions of the rotor, with rated voltage applied at rated frequency.

Pull-Up Torque   10.40.030

The pull-up torque of an alternating-current motor is the minimum external torque developed by the motor during the period of acceleration from rest to the speed at which breakdown torque occurs. For motors which do not have a definite breakdown torque, the pull-up torque is the minimum torque developed up to rated speed.

Switching Torque   10.40.035

The switching torque of a motor having an automatic connection change during the starting period is the minimum external torque developed by the motor as it accelerates through switch operating speed.

NOTE: It should be noted that if the torque on the starting connection is never less than the switching torque, the pull-up torque is identical with the switching torque; however, if the torque on the starting connection falls below the switching torque at some speed below switch operating speed, the pull-up and switching torques are not identical.

Pull-In Torque   10.40.040

The pull-in torque of a synchronous motor is the maximum constant torque under which the motor will pull its connected inertia load into synchronism, at rated voltage and frequency, when its field excitation is applied.

The speed to which a motor will bring its load depends on the power required to drive it and whether the motor can pull the load into step from this speed depends on the inertia of the revolving parts, so that the pull-in torque cannot be determined without having the $W R^2$ as well as the torque of the load.

Nominal Pull-In Torque   10.40.050

The nominal pull-in torque of a synchronous motor is the torque it develops as an induction motor when operating at 95 percent of synchronous speed with rated voltage applied at rated frequency.

NOTE: This quantity is useful for comparative purposes when the inertia of the load is not known.

Pull-Out Torque   10.40.060

The pull-out torque of a synchronous motor is the maximum sustained torque which the motor will develop at synchronous speed for one minute, with rated voltage applied at rated frequency and with normal excitation.

Breakdown Torque   10.40.070

The breakdown torque of a motor is the maximum torque which it will develop with rated voltage applied at rated frequency, without an abrupt drop in speed.

GROUP 10—ROTATING MACHINERY

Section 50—Duty Classification

Duty of a Machine   10.50.010

The duty of a machine is a requirement of service which defines the degree of regularity of the load.

Continuous Duty

See 05.50.015.

Short-Time Duty

See 05.50.020.

Intermittent Duty

See 05.50.025.

Periodic Duty

See 05.50.030.

Varying Duty

See 05.50.035.

Rating

See 05.50.040.

Service Factor of an Electric Machine   10.50.080

The service factor of an electric machine is a multiplier which, applied to the rated output, indicates a permissible loading which may be carried continuously under the conditions specified for that service factor.

GROUP 10—ROTATING MACHINERY

Section 95—Not Otherwise Classified

Voltage Regulation of a Synchronous Generator   10.95.100

The voltage regulation of a synchronous generator is the rise in voltage with constant field current, when, with the synchronous generator operated at rated voltage and rated speed, the specified load at the specified power factor is reduced to zero, expressed as a percent of rated voltage.

Voltage Regulation of a Direct-Current Generator   10.95.120

The voltage regulation of a direct-current generator

is the final change in voltage with constant field rheostat setting when the specified load is reduced gradually to zero, expressed as a percent of rated load voltage, the speed being kept constant.

NOTE: In practice it is often desirable to specify the overall regulation of the generator and its driving machine thus taking into account the speed regulation of the driving machine.

Speed Regulation of a Constant-Speed Direct-Current Motor   10.95.150

The speed regulation of a constant-speed direct-current motor is the change in speed when the load is reduced gradually from the rated value to zero with constant applied voltage and field rheostat setting, expressed as a percent of speed at rated load.

Angular Variation in Synchronous Generators   10.95.200

The angular variation in synchronous generators, or alternating-current circuits in general, is the maximum angular displacement, expressed in electrical degrees, of corresponding ordinates of the voltage wave and of a wave of absolutely constant frequency, equal to the average frequency of the synchronous generator in question.

Slip   10.95.250

The slip of an induction machine is the difference between its synchronous speed and its operating speed and may be expressed in the following ways:

    (a)   As a percent of synchronous speed
    (b)   As a decimal fraction of synchronous speed
    (c)   Directly in revolutions per minute

Electrical Degree   10.95.300

An electrical degree is the 360th part of the angle subtended, at the axis of a machine, by two consecutive field poles of like polarity. One mechanical degree is thus equal to as many electrical degrees as there are pairs of poles in the machine.

Saturation Factor of a Machine   10.95.400

The saturation factor of a machine is the ratio of a small percentage increase in field excitation to the corresponding percentage increase in voltage thereby produced. Unless otherwise specified, the saturation factor of a machine refers to the no-load excitation required at rated speed and voltage. It is determined from measurements of saturation made on open-circuit at rated speed.

Deviation Factor of a Wave   10.95.420

The deviation factor of a wave is the ratio of the maximum difference between corresponding ordinates of the wave and of the equivalent sine wave to the maximum ordinate of the equivalent sine wave when the waves are superposed in such a way as to make this maximum difference as small as possible.

Distortion Factor of a Wave   10.95.430

The distortion factor of a voltage wave is the ratio of the effective value of the residue after the elimination of the fundamental to the effective value of the original wave.

Exciter Response   10.95.440

Exciter response is the rate of increase or decrease of the main exciter voltage when resistance is suddenly removed from or inserted in the main exciter field circuit.

NOTE: The response of an exciter may be expressed in volts per second or may be represented by the numerical value obtained by dividing the volts per second by some designated value of voltage, such as the nominal collector ring voltage.

Nominal Exciter Response   10.95.450

The nominal exciter response is defined as the numerical value obtained when the nominal collector ring voltage is divided into the slope, expressed in volts per second, of that straight line voltage–time curve, which begins at nominal collector ring voltage and continues for one-half second, under which the area is the same as the area under the no-load voltage increase–time curve of the exciter starting at the same initial voltage, and continuing for the same length of time.

Nominal Collector Ring Voltage   10.95.460

Nominal collector ring voltage is the voltage required across the collector rings to generate rated kilovolt amperes in the main machine, at rated voltage, speed, frequency and power factor, with the field winding at a temperature of 75 degrees centigrade.

GROUP 15—TRANSFORMERS, REGULATORS, REACTORS AND RECTIFIERS

SECTIONS

10 General	40 Reactors
20 Transformers	50 Rectifiers
30 Regulators	

Section 10—General

Rated Circuit Voltage 15.10.100

In systems employing transformers, the rated voltage of the circuit is the highest rated voltage of the secondaries of transformers supplying the circuit.

NOTE: By "circuit voltage" is meant the voltage from line-to-line as distinguished from line-to-neutral. This voltage rating applies to all parts of the circuit. In the case of transformers having series-multiple secondary connections, the circuit voltage is determined by the series or the multiple connection as used.

Dielectric Tests

See 05.30.102.

Grounded

See 35.15.010.

Equipment Ground

See 35.15.230.

Solidly Grounded

(Directly Grounded)
See 35.15.200.

Effectively Grounded

See 35.15.205.

Resistance Grounded

See 35.15.210.

Reactance Grounded

See 35.15.215.

GROUP 15—TRANSFORMERS, REGULATORS, REACTORS AND RECTIFIERS

Section 20—Transformers

Transformer 15.20.010

A transformer is an electric device, without continuously moving parts, which by electromagnetic induction transforms electric energy from one or more circuits to one or more other circuits at the same frequency, usually with changed values of voltage and current.

Autotransformer 15.20.015

An autotransformer is a transformer in which part of of the winding is common to both the primary and the secondary circuits.

Step-Down Transformer 15.20.020

A step-down transformer is a transformer in which the energy transfer is from a high-voltage winding to a low-voltage winding or windings.

Step-Up Transformer 15.20.025

A step-up transformer is a transformer in which the energy transfer is from a low-voltage winding to a high-voltage winding or windings.

Main Transformer 15.20.030

The main transformer, as applied to two single-phase T-connected units for three-phase to two-phase or two-phase to three-phase operation, is the transformer which is connected directly across one phase of the three-phase lines. A tap is provided at the mid-point for connection to the teaser transformer.

Teaser Transformer 15.20.035

The teaser transformer is that transformer, of two T-connected single-phase units for three-phase to two-phase or two-phase to three-phase operation, which is connected between the mid-point of the main transformer and the third wire of the three-phase system.

Regulating Transformer 15.20.040

A regulating transformer is a transformer having one or more windings excited from the system circuit or a separate source and one or more windings connected in series with the system circuit for adjusting the voltage or the phase relation or both in steps, usually without interrupting the load.

Constant-Current Transformer 15.20.042

A constant-current transformer is a transformer that automatically maintains a constant current in its secondary circuit under varying conditions of load impedance, when supplied from a constant-potential source.

Grounding Transformer 15.20.045

(Ground Transformer)
A grounding transformer is a transformer intended primarily for the purpose of providing a neutral point for grounding purposes.

Rectifier Transformer 15.20.050

A rectifier transformer is a transformer the secondary of which supplies energy to the main anodes of the rectifier.

Interphase Transformer 15.20.055

An interphase transformer is an autotransformer, or a set of mutually coupled reactors, used in conjunction with rectifier transformers to modify current relations in the rectifier so as to increase the number of anodes of different phase relations which carry current at any instant.

Air-Cooled Transformer 15.20.065

An air-cooled transformer is a transformer cooled by the natural circulation of air over the core and coils.

Air-Blast Transformer 15.20.070

An air-blast transformer is a transformer cooled by a forced circulation of air through the core and coils.

Oil-Immersed Self-Cooled Transformer 15.20.075

An oil-immersed self-cooled transformer is a transformer, the core and coils of which are immersed in oil, the cooling being effected by natural circulation of air over the cooling surface.

Oil-Immersed Water-Cooled Transformer 15.20.080

An oil-immersed water-cooled transformer is a transformer, the core and coils of which are immersed in oil, the cooling being effected by the circulation of water through a coil installed in the transformer tank and immersed in the oil.

Oil-Immersed Forced Air-Cooled Transformer 15.20.085

An oil-immersed forced air-cooled transformer is a transformer, the core and coils of which are immersed in oil, and the cooling of which is increased by forced circulation of air over the cooling surface.

Oil-Immersed Forced Oil-Cooled Transformer 15.20.090

An oil-immersed forced oil-cooled transformer is a transformer, the core and coils of which are immersed in oil, and the cooling of which is effected principally by forced circulation of oil through some external cooling means.

Indoor Transformer 15.20.095

An indoor transformer is a transformer which, because of its construction, must be protected from the weather.

Outdoor Transformer 15.20.100

An outdoor transformer is a transformer of weatherproof construction.

Pole Type Transformer 15.20.105

A pole type transformer is a transformer suitable for mounting on a pole or similar structure.

Vault Type Transformer 15.20.115

A vault type transformer is a non-submersible transformer designed for installation in vaults not subject to flooding.

Subway Type Transformer 15.20.120

A subway type transformer is a transformer of submersible construction.

High-Voltage and Low-Voltage Windings 15.20.140

(High-Tension and Low-Tension Windings)

The terms *high voltage* and *low voltage*, as applied to two-winding transformers, are used to distinguish the winding having the greater from that having the lesser voltage rating.

Primary Winding 15.20.145

The primary winding is the winding on the input side.

Secondary Winding 15.20.150

The secondary winding is the winding on the output side.

Stabilizing Winding 15.20.155

(Tertiary Winding)*

A stabilizing winding is an auxiliary winding used particularly in star-connected transformers for such purposes as the following:

(a) To stabilize the neutral point of the fundamental frequency voltages

(b) To protect the transformer and the system from excessive third-harmonic voltages

(c) To prevent telephone interference due to third-harmonic currents and voltages in the lines and earth

Regulating Winding 15.20.160

A regulating winding of a transformer is a supplementary winding which is connected in series with one of the main windings for the purpose of changing the ratio of transformation or the phase relation between circuits or both.

Tap (in a transformer) 15.20.165

A tap in a transformer is a connection brought out of a winding at some point between its extremities, usually to permit changing the voltage ratio.

Rated Kva Tap (in a transformer) 15.20.170

A rated kva tap in a transformer is a tap through which the transformer can deliver its rated kva output without exceeding the specified temperature rise.

Reduced Kva Tap (in a transformer) 15.20.175

A reduced kva tap in a transformer is a tap through which the transformer can deliver only an output less than rated kva and keep within the specified temperature rise.

Conservator or Expansion Tank 15.20.180

A conservator or expansion tank is an auxiliary tank, normally only partly filled with oil or other cooling liquid and connected to the completely filled main tank.

Inert-Gas Equipment 15.20.182

Inert-gas equipment is equipment provided to maintain an inert gas, usually nitrogen, above the oil surface.

Rated Kva of a Transformer 15.20.185

The rated kva of a transformer is the output which can be delivered for the time specified at rated secondary voltage and rated frequency without exceeding the specified temperature limitations.

Rating of a Grounding Transformer 15.20.190

The rating of a grounding transformer is the rating determined by the current in the neutral for a specified time when one conductor is solidly grounded and the supply voltage is sustained.

* Deprecated.

Single-Voltage Rating of a Transformer   15.20.195

The single-voltage rating of a transformer is the rating applied to a transformer which has two separate windings (primary and secondary) with only one voltage rating assigned to each.

Double-Voltage Rating of a Transformer   15.20.200

The double-voltage rating of a transformer is the rating applied to a transformer which has two separate windings (primary and secondary) with two voltage ratings assigned to each, the turn ratio being the same for both ratings.

Normal-Voltage Rating of a Transformer Having a Double-Voltage Rating   15.20.205

The normal-voltage rating of a transformer having a double-voltage rating is the lower voltage rating.

Rated Secondary Voltage of a Constant-Potential Transformer   15.20.206

The rated secondary voltage of a constant-potential transformer is the secondary voltage at which the transformer is designed to deliver rated kva.

Rated Primary Voltage of a Constant-Potential Transformer   15.20.207

The rated primary voltage of a constant-potential transformer is the rated secondary voltage multiplied by the turn ratio in the case of a step-down transformer, or divided by the turn ratio in the case of a step-up transformer.

Rated Primary Voltage of a Constant-Current Transformer   15.20.209

The rated primary voltage of a constant-current transformer is the primary voltage for which the transformer is designed.

Rated Secondary Current of a Constant-Potential Transformer   15.20.210

The rated secondary current of a constant-potential transformer is the secondary current obtained by dividing the rated kva by the rated secondary voltage.

Rated Secondary Current of a Constant-Current Transformer   15.20.211

The rated secondary current of a constant-current transformer is the secondary current for which the transformer is designed.

Ratio of a Transformer   15.20.212

The ratio of a transformer is the turn ratio of the transformer, unless otherwise specified.

Turn Ratio of a Transformer   15.20.213

The turn ratio of a transformer is the ratio of the number of turns in the high-voltage winding to that in the low-voltage winding.

NOTE: In the case of a constant-potential transformer having taps for changing its voltage ratio, the turn ratio is based on the number of turns corresponding to the normal rated voltage of the respective windings, unless otherwise specified.

Voltage Ratio of a Transformer   15.20.215

The voltage ratio of a transformer is the ratio of the rms primary terminal voltage to the rms secondary terminal voltage, under specified conditions of load.

No-Load Losses of a Transformer   15.20.220

(Excitation Losses of a Transformer)

The no-load losses of a transformer are the losses in a transformer that is excited at rated voltage and frequency, but not supplying load.

NOTE: No-load losses include core loss, dielectric loss and copper loss in the windings due to exciting current.

Load Losses of a Transformer   15.20.225

(Impedance Losses of a Transformer)

The load losses of a transformer are those losses in a transformer which are incident to the carrying of load.

NOTE: Load losses include $I^2 R$ loss in the windings due to load current, stray loss due to stray fluxes in the windings, core clamps, etc., and to circulating currents, if any, in parallel windings.

Total Losses of a Transformer   15.20.230

The total losses of a transformer are the losses represented by the sum of the no-load losses and the load losses.

Regulation of a Constant-Potential Transformer 15.20.235

The regulation of a constant-potential transformer is the change in secondary voltage, expressed in percent of rated secondary voltage, which occurs when rated kva output at a specified power factor is reduced to zero, with the primary impressed terminal voltage maintained constant.

NOTE: In the case of multiwinding transformers, the loads on all windings, at specified power factors, are to be reduced from rated kva to zero simultaneously.

Regulation of a Constant-Current Transformer 15.20.236

The regulation of a constant-current transformer is the maximum departure of the secondary current from its rated value expressed in percent of the rated secondary current, with rated primary voltage and frequency applied and at rated secondary power factor and with the current variation taken between the limits of a short-circuit and rated load.

Impedance Voltage of a Transformer   15.20.240

The impedance voltage of a transformer is the voltage required to circulate rated current through a winding of the transformer when another winding is short-circuited, with the respective windings connected as for rated voltage operation, and is usually expressed in percent of the rated voltage of the winding in which the voltage is measured.

Exciting Current of a Transformer   15.20.245

(No-Load Current of a Transformer)

The exciting current of a transformer is the current which flows in any winding used to excite the transformer when all other windings are open-circuited, and is usually expressed in percent of the rated current of the winding in which it is measured.

Lead Polarity of a Transformer 15.20.250

The lead poiarity of a transformer is a designation of the relative instantaneous directions of currents in its leads. Primary and secondary leads are said to have the same polarity when at a given instant the current enters the primary lead in question and leaves the secondary lead in question in the same direction as though the two leads formed a continuous circuit.

The lead polarity of a single-phase distribution or power transformer may be either additive or subtractive. If one pair of adjacent leads from the two windings in question is connected together and voltage applied to one of the windings:

(a) The lead polarity io additivo if tho voltage acroos the other two leads of the windings in question is greater than that of the higher voltage winding alone.

(b) The lead polarity is subtractive if the voltage across the other two leads of the windings in question is less than that of the higher voltage winding alone.

The terms *additive* and *subtractive* are not always applicable to instrument transformers. The polarity of such transformers is indicated by markers on primary and secondary leads of like polarity.

The polarity of a three-phase transformer is fixed by the internal connections between phases as well as by the relative locations of leads; it is usually designated by means of a vector diagram showing the angular displacements of windings and a sketch showing the marking of leads. The vectors of the vector diagrams represent induced voltages and the recognized counterclockwise direction of rotation of the vectors is used. The vector representing any phase voltage of a given winding is drawn parallel to that representing the corresponding phase voltage of any other winding under consideration.

Angular Displacement of a Polyphase Transformer 15.20.260

The angular displacement of a polyphase transformer is the time angle between the line-to-neutral voltage of a specified high-voltage terminal (H_1) and the line-to-neutral voltage of a specified low-voltage terminal (X_1).

NOTE: These terminals are so designated that all possible connections of an n-phase transformer may be classified into a minimum number of groups. Thus, three-phase transformers are classified into two angular displacement groups, zero degrees and thirty degrees.

GROUP 15—TRANSFORMERS, REGULATORS, REACTORS AND RECTIFIERS

Section 30—Regulators

Induction Voltage Regulator 15.30.010

An induction voltage regulator is a device having a primary winding in shunt and a secondary winding in series with a circuit for gradually adjusting the voltage or the phase relation of the circuit by changing the relative position of the primary and secondary windings of the regulator.

Step Voltage Regulator 15.30.015

A step voltage regulator is a device consisting of a regulating transformer and means for adjusting the voltage or the phase relation of the system circuit in steps, usually without interrupting the load.

GROUP 15—TRANSFORMERS, REGULATORS, REACTORS AND RECTIFIERS

Section 40—Reactors

Reactor 15.40.005

A reactor is a device used for introducing reactance into a circuit for purposes such as motor starting, paralleling transformers and control of current.

See 05.45.085.

Current-Limiting Reactor 15.40.010

A current-limiting reactor is a form of reactor for limiting the current that can flow in a circuit under short-circuit conditions.

Bus Reactor 15.40.020

A bus reactor is a current-limiting reactor for connection between two different buses or two sections of the same bus for the purpose of limiting and localizing the disturbance due to a fault on either bus.

Feeder Reactor 15.40.030

A feeder reactor is a current-limiting reactor for connection in series with an alternating-current feeder circuit, for the purpose of limiting and localizing disturbances due to faults on the feeder.

Starting Reactor 15.40.040

A starting reactor is a reactor for decreasing the starting current of a machine or device.

Synchronizing Reactor 15.40.050

A synchronizing reactor is a current-limiting reactor for connecting momentarily across the open contacts of a circuit-interrupting device for synchronizing purposes.

Paralleling Reactor 15.40.060

A paralleling reactor is a reactor for correcting the division of load between parallel-connected transformers which have unequal impedance voltages.

GROUP 15—TRANSFORMERS, REGULATORS, REACTORS AND RECTIFIERS
Section 50—Rectifiers

Rectifier   15.50.010

A rectifier is a device which converts alternating current into unidirectional current by virtue of a characteristic permitting appreciable flow of current in only one direction.

Mercury-Arc Rectifier   15.50.020

A mercury-arc rectifier is a rectifier which makes use of the rectifying properties of an electron-emitting cathode and non-electron-emitting anodes enclosed in a chamber containing mercury vapor.

Metal-Tank Mercury-Arc Rectifier   15.50.030

A metal-tank mercury-arc rectifier is a mercury-arc rectifier with the anodes and mercury cathode enclosed in a metal container or chamber.

Controlled Mercury-Arc Rectifier   15.50.035

A controlled mercury-arc rectifier is a mercury-arc rectifier in which one or more electrodes are employed to control the starting of the discharge.

Rectifier Unit   15.50.040

A rectifier unit includes the rectifier with its essential auxiliaries and the rectifier transformer equipment.

Rectifier Anode   15.50.050

A rectifier anode is an electrode of the rectifier from which the current flows into the arc.

NOTE: The direction of current flow is considered in the conventional sense from positive to negative. The cathode is the positive direct-current terminal of the apparatus, and is usually a pool of mercury. The neutral of the transformer secondary system is the negative direct-current terminal of the rectifier unit.

Starting Anode   15.50.060

The starting anode is an electrode which is used in establishing the initial arc.

Excitation Anode   15.50.070

An excitation anode is an electrode which is used to maintain an auxiliary arc in the vacuum tank.

Anode Balancing Coil   15.50.075

An anode balancing coil is a set of mutually coupled windings used to maintain approximately equal currents in anodes operating in parallel from the same transformer terminal.

Rectifier Cathode   15.50.080

The rectifier cathode is the electrode of the rectifier into which the current flows from the arc.

NOTE: The direction of current flow is considered in the conventional sense from positive to negative. The cathode is the positive direct-current terminal of the rectifier unit, and is usually a pool of mercury. The neutral of the transformer secondary system is the negative direct-current terminal of the rectifier unit.

Grids   15.50.090

Grids are electrodes which are placed in the arc stream and to which a control voltage may be applied.

Vacuum Tank   15.50.100

The vacuum tank is the airtight metal chamber which contains the electrodes and in which the rectifying action takes place.

Vacuum Seal   15.50.110

The vacuum seal is the airtight junction between component parts of the evacuated system.

Vacuum Gauge   15.50.120

The vacuum gauge is a device which indicates the absolute gas pressure in the evacuated parts of the rectifier. The absolute gas pressure is expressed in microns, one micron being the pressure which will support a column of mercury 1/1000 of a millimeter high.

NOTE: There are two types of vacuum gauges in common use: the McLeod type, which measures only the sum of the partial pressure of the uncondensed (or non-condensing) gases; and the hot-wire type which measures the total pressure of all gases contained in the rectifier tank.

Degassing   15.50.130

Degassing of the rectifier is the process of driving out and exhausting occluded and remanent gases within the vacuum tank, anodes, cathode, etc., which are not removed by evacuation alone.

ELECTRICAL DEFINITIONS

GROUP 20—SWITCHING EQUIPMENT

SECTIONS

05 General
10 Switches
15 Interrupting Devices
20 Fuses
25 Relays

30 Lightning Arresters
35 Resistors
40 Regulators
45 Network Protectors
50 Switchgear Assemblies

Section 05—General

Switchgear   20.05.005

Switchgear is a general term covering switching and interrupting devices, also assemblies of those devices with control, metering, protective and regulatory equipment with the associated interconnections and supporting structures.

Properties and Characteristics of Switchgear

Distinctive Features
See 95.05.020.

Air (used as a prefix)
See 95.90.005.

Oil (used as a prefix)
See 95.90.010.

Indoor (used as a prefix)
See 95.90.190.

Outdoor (used as a prefix)
See 95.90.192.

Proof (used as a suffix)
See 95.90.015.

Resistant (used as a suffix)
See 95.90.020.

Tight (used as a suffix)
See 95.90.025.

Drip-Proof
See 95.90.150.

Dustproof
See 95.90.125.

Gasproof
See 95.90.105.

Sleetproof
See 95.90.170.

Splashproof
See 95.90.160.

Weatherproof
See 95.90.185.

Fume-Resistant
See 95.90.115.

Moisture-Resistant
See 95.90.140.

Driptight
See 95.90.155.

Dust-Tight
See 95.90.130.

Gastight
See 95.90.110.

Watertight
See 95.90.145.

Submersible
See 95.90.195.

Inverse Time
See 20.25.405.

Definite Time
See 20.25.380.

Instantaneous
See 20.25.400.

Service Classifications

Continuous Duty
See 05.50.015.

Short-Time Duty
See 05.50.020.

Intermittent Duty
See 05.50.025.

Periodic Duty
See 05.50.030.

Varying Duty
See 05.50.035.

Rating, Performance and Test

Ambient Temperature
See 25.95.005.

Rating
See 05.50.040.

Time Rating   20.05.165

Time rating is the period of a test run within which the

specified conditions of load and temperature rise shall not be exceeded.

Dielectric Tests

See 05.30.102.

Operating Voltage   20.05.171

The operating voltage of a circuit breaker is the rms voltage of the system on which it is to be operated.

Normal-Frequency Recovery Voltage   20.05.172

The normal-frequency recovery voltage is the normal frequency rms voltage impressed upon a circuit-interrupting device after the current has been interrupted and after high-frequency transients have subsided.

Transient Recovery Voltage   20.05.173

The transient recovery voltage is the transient voltage which occurs across the terminals of a circuit-interrupting device at the time of arc extinction. In a multipole interrupting device, it is usually applied to the voltage across the first pole to clear.

Transient Recovery Voltage Rate   20.05.174

The transient recovery voltage rate is the rate at which voltage rises across the contacts of a circuit-interrupting device at the time of arc extinction. It is usually measured as the slope of a line passing through zero voltage at the instant of arc current zero and thence through one of the peaks of the curve describing the transient recovery voltage. In case the transient recovery voltage curve does not have any definite or salient peaks, the line is drawn through some arbitrarily chosen point usually selected as a certain percentage of the crest value of the normal frequency recovery voltage at which the test is made.

Miscellaneous

Current-Carrying Parts

See 35.40.285.

Contacts

See 25.05.040.

Contact-Wear Allowance

See 25.30.010.

Voltage to Ground

See 35.15.025.

Grounded Parts

See 35.15.060.

Calibration Scale   20.05.200

A calibration scale is a set of graduations marked to indicate values, such as current, voltage or time, at which an automatic device can be set to operate.

Connection Diagram   20.05.205

A connection diagram is a diagram showing the relations and connections of devices and apparatus of a circuit or group of circuits.

Tank Fittings   20.05.210

Tank fittings are fittings which include the plug, valve and gauges used to handle or sample oils or to indicate the oil level.

GROUP 20—SWITCHING EQUIPMENT

Section 10—Switches

General

Switch

See 25.05.090.

Air Switch   20.10.010

An air switch is a switch in which the interruption of the circuit occurs in air.

Oil Switch   20.10.015

An oil switch is a switch in which the interruption of the circuit occurs in oil.

Low-Voltage Switches

NOTE: This classification applies to switches for voltages ordinarily below 750.

Knife Switch   20.10.050

A knife switch is a form of air switch in which the moving element, usually a hinged blade, enters or embraces the contact clips. In some cases, however, the blade is not hinged and is removable.

Field Discharge Switch   20.10.055

A field discharge switch is a switch, usually of the knife blade type, but also made in the form of an air circuit breaker, having auxiliary contacts for short-circuiting the field of a generator or motor through a resistor at the instant preceding the opening of the switch.

Field Break-Up Switch   20.10.060

A field break-up switch is a switch which, when open, separates a field winding into two or more sections, insulated from one another.

Instrument Switch   20.10.065

An instrument switch is a switch used to disconnect an instrument or to transfer it from one circuit or phase to another.

Examples: Ammeter switch; voltmeter switch.

Control Switch   20.10.070

A control switch is a switch for controlling electrically operated devices.

Indicating Control Switch   20.10.075

An indicating control switch is a control switch which indicates its last operation.

Auxiliary Switch   20.10.080

An auxiliary switch is a switch actuated by some main device such as a circuit breaker, for signaling, interlocking or other purpose.

Alarm Switch   20.10.085

An alarm switch is a form of auxiliary switch which closes the circuit to a bell or other audible signaling device upon the automatic opening of the circuit breaker or other apparatus with which it is associated.

High-Voltage Air Switches

NOTE: Switches in this classification are generally for voltages above 750.

Rating Terms

Rated Continuous Current (of a switch or circuit breaker)   20.10.100

The rated continuous current of a switch or circuit breaker is the designated limit in rms amperes or direct-current amperes which it will carry continuously without exceeding the limit of observable temperature rise.

Rated Voltage (of a switch or circuit breaker)   20.10.105

The rated voltage of a switch or circuit breaker is the highest rms voltage or the highest direct-current voltage at which it is designed to operate.

Rated Frequency (of a switch or circuit breaker)   20.10.110

The rated frequency of a switch or circuit breaker is the frequency of the circuit for which it is designed.

Rated Short-Time Current (of a switch or circuit breaker)   20.10.115

The rated short-time current of a switch or circuit breaker is the highest current, including the direct-current component, that it is required to carry without injury for specified short-time intervals. The ratings recognize the limitations imposed by both thermal and electromagnetic effects.

NOTE: Examples of short-time ratings now in current use are:

The rated momentary current is the maximum rms total current which it is required to carry for any time, however small, up to one second. The current is the rms value, including the direct-current component, during the maximum cycle as determined from the envelope of the current wave.

The rated five-second current is the rms total current, including the direct-current component, which it is required to carry for five seconds. For practical purposes, this current is measured at the end of the first second.

Classifications

Isolating Switch

See **25.05.110.**

Disconnecting Switch   20.10.130

A disconnecting switch is a form of air switch used for changing connections in a circuit or system, or for isolating purposes.

Selector Switch   20.10.135

A selector switch is a form of air switch arranged so that a conductor may be connected to any one of several other conductors.

Transfer Switch   20.10.140

A transfer switch is a form of air switch arranged so that a conductor connection can be transferred from one circuit to another without interrupting current.

Horn Gap Switch   20.10.145

A horn gap switch is a form of air switch provided with arcing horns.

Grounding Switch   20.10.150

(Ground Switch)

A grounding switch is a form of air switch by means of which a circuit or a piece of apparatus may be connected to ground.

See 35.15.185.

Construction Arrangements and Parts

Single-Break Switch   20.10.175

A single-break switch is a switch which opens the connected circuit at one point only.

Double-Break Switch   20.10.180

A double-break switch is a switch which opens the connected circuit at two points.

Single-Throw Switch   20.10.185

A single-throw switch is a switch by means of which the circuit can be closed or opened by moving the switch blade into or out of one set of contacts only.

Double-Throw Switch   20.10.190

A double-throw switch is a switch by means of which a change in circuit connections can be obtained by closing the switch blade into either of two sets of contacts.

Pole   20.10.195

A pole of a switch consists of the parts necessary to control one conductor of a circuit. A switch may be single pole or multipole, depending upon the number of single poles that are operated simultaneously.

Rotating-Insulator Switch   20.10.200

A rotating-insulator switch is a switch in which the opening and closing travel of the blade is accomplished by the rotation of one or more of the insulators supporting the conducting parts of the switch.

Tilting-Insulator Switch   20.10.205

A tilting-insulator switch is a switch in which the opening and closing travel of the blade is accomplished by a tilting movement of one or more of the insulators supporting the conducting parts of the switch.

Vertical Break Switch   20.10.210

A vertical break switch is a switch in which the travel of the blade is in a plane perpendicular to the plane of the base mounting.

Side Break Switch   20.10.215

(Horizontal Break Switch)

A side break switch is a switch in which the travel of the blade is in a plane parallel to the base of the switch.

Front Connected Switch   20.10.220

A front connected switch is a switch in which the current-carrying conductors are connected to the fixed terminal blocks in front of the mounting base.

Back Connected Switch   20.10.225

A back connected switch is a switch in which the current-carrying conductors are connected to the studs back of the mounting base.

Front and Back Connected Switch   20.10.230

A front and back connected switch is a switch in which one or more current-carrying conductors are connected directly to the fixed terminal blocks located at the front of the mounting base, the remaining conductors being connected to the studs back of the mounting base.

Quick-Make   20.10.235

A switch or circuit breaker is quick-make when it has a high contact-closing speed independent of the operator.

Quick-Break   20.10.240

A switch or circuit breaker is quick-break when it has a high contact-opening speed independent of the operator.

Live Parts   20.10.245

Live parts are those parts which are electrically connected to points of potential different from that of the earth.

Renewal Parts   20.10.250

Renewal parts are those parts necessary for the maintenance of switchgear apparatus.

Accessories   20.10.255

Accessories are devices which perform a secondary or minor duty as an adjunct or refinement to the primary or major duty of a unit of equipment.

Attachments   20.10.260

Attachments are accessories to be attached to switchgear apparatus, as distinguished from auxiliaries.

Auxiliaries   20.10.265

Auxiliaries are accessories to be used with switchgear apparatus but not attached to it, as distinguished from attachments.

Stationary Contact Member   20.10.270

A stationary contact member of a switch or circuit breaker is a conducting part which bears a contact surface which remains substantially stationary.

Moving Contact Member   20.10.275

A moving contact member of a switch or circuit breaker is a conducting part which bears a contact surface which moves to and from the stationary contact.

Main Contact   20.10.280

A main contact is a conducting part designed to be united by pressure to another conducting part for the purpose of carrying current. The contacts of a circuit breaker are composed of the surfaces brought together or separated by the operation of the breaker mechanism.

Arcing Contacts   20.10.285

Arcing contacts are the contacts on which the arc is drawn after the main contacts of a switch or circuit breaker have parted.

Arcing Horns   20.10.290

Arcing horns are forms of arcing contacts on which the arc is drawn after the main contacts of a horn gap switch have parted.

Contact Surfaces   20.10.295

Contact surfaces are the surfaces of contacts which meet and through which the current is transferred when the contacts are closed.

Contact Clip   20.10.300

A contact clip is the clip which the switch blade enters or embraces.

Blade   20.10.305

A blade of a switch is the moving contact member which enters or embraces the contact clips.

Trussed Blade   20.10.310

A trussed blade is a blade which is reinforced by truss construction to provide lateral stiffness.

Hinge Clip   20.10.315

A hinge clip is the clip to which the switch blade is movably attached.

Terminal Block   20.10.320

A terminal block of a switch is the extension provided on the switch to which the terminal connector is fastened.

Blade Latch   20.10.325

A blade latch is a latch used on a hook operated switch to hold the switch blade in the closed position.

Blade Guide   20.10.330

A blade guide of a switch is an attachment to secure proper alignment of blade and contact when closing the switch.

Wire Guide   20.10.335

A wire guide is an attachment to maintain a conductor in a definite position.

Outrigger 20.10.340

An outrigger is an attachment which is fastened to or adjacent to the terminal block of a switch and to which the conductor is clamped to relieve mechanical strain on the terminal and/or to maintain electrical clearance between the conductor and grounded parts.

Extended Outrigger Clamp 20.10.345

An extended outrigger clamp is an attachment fastened to the terminal block of a switch to which the conductor is clamped to relieve mechanical strain on the terminal.

Base 20.10.350

A base of a switch is the main member to which the conducting parts or the insulator units are attached.

Insulator Unit 20.10.355

An insulator unit of disconnecting switches, bus supports, or other switchgear equipment is the insulating part assembled with such metal parts as may be necessary for attaching the base and device parts.

Sleet Hood 20.10.360

A sleet hood of a switch is a cover for the contacts to prevent the accumulation of sleet from interfering with successful operation of the switch.

Break Distance 20.10.365

The break distance of a switch is the minimum open gap distance between the stationary and movable contacts, or live parts connected thereto, when the blade is in the open position.

Barrier

See 25.95.010.

Operating Mechanism 20.10.375

The operating mechanism of a switch or circuit breaker is a power operated or manual mechanism by which the contacts of all poles are actuated.

Operating Rods 20.10.380

(Operating Pipes)
Operating rods are the rods or pipes connecting the interphase connecting rods or pipes and the operating mechanism of a switch or circuit breaker.

Interphase Connecting Rods 20.10.385

(Interphase Connecting Pipes)
Interphase connecting rods are the rods connecting the several poles of a switch or circuit breaker together, and to the operating rods.

Bell Crank 20.10.390

A bell crank is a lever with two or more arms placed at an angle diverging from a given pivot point, by means of which the direction of motion of a mechanism is changed.

Bell-Crank Hanger 20.10.400

A bell-crank hanger is a support for a bell crank.

Interlock

See 25.95.060.

Switch Hook 20.10.410

A switch hook is a hook provided with an insulating handle for opening and closing hook operated switches.

Minimum Clearance to Ground 20.10.415

The minimum clearance to ground is the shortest distance between any live part and adjacent grounded parts.

Minimum Clearance Between Poles 20.10.420

The minimum clearance between poles is the shortest distance between any live parts of adjacent poles.

Mounting Position of a Switch or Fuse Support 20.10.425

The mounting position of a switch or fuse support is determined by and corresponds to the position of the base of the device. The usual positions are:

1. Horizontal upright
2. Horizontal underhung
3. Vertical
4. Angle underhung

Classes of Operation

Operation† 20.10.450

Operation, as applied to a switch or circuit breaker, is the method provided for its normal functioning.

Hook Operation† 20.10.455

Hook operation of a switch or circuit breaker is operation manually by means of a switch hook.

Mechanical Operation† 20.10.460

Mechanical operation of a switch or circuit breaker is operation by means of an operating mechanism connected to the switch by mechanical linkages.

NOTE: Mechanically operated switches may be actuated either manually, or electrically, or by other suitable means.

Electrical Operation† 20.10.461

Electrical operation of a switch or circuit breaker is power operation by electricity.

Manual Operation† 20.10.462

Manual operation of a switch or circuit breaker is operation by hand without using any other source of power.

Power Operation† 20.10.463

Power operation of a switch or circuit breaker is operation by power (electric, pneumatic, etc.) other than by hand.

Direct Operation† 20.10.465

Direct operation of a mechanically operated switch

† The above definitions relate to method of *operation* and should not be confused with method of *control*. For instance, electrical *operation* may involve automatic or non-automatic (hand or manual) *control*.

or circuit breaker is operation by means of a mechanism connected directly to the main operating shaft, or an extension of it.

Indirect Operation† 20.10.470

Indirect operation of a switch or circuit breaker is operation by means of an operating mechanism connected to the main operating shaft, or an extension of it, through offset linkages and bearings.

Group Operation† 20.10.475

Group operation of a multipole switch or circuit

breaker is the operation of all poles by means of one operating mechanism.

Remote Controlled Operation† 20.10.480

Remote controlled operation of a switch or circuit breaker is operation by means of an operating mechanism controlled from a distant point either manually and/or electrically or by other means.

___

† The above definitions relate to method of *operation* and should not be confused with method of *control*. For instance, electrical *operation* may involve automatic or non-automatic (hand or manual) *control*.

GROUP 20—SWITCHING EQUIPMENT

Section 15—Interrupting Devices

Circuit Breakers

Circuit Breaker 20.15.005

A circuit breaker is a device for interrupting a circuit between separable contacts under normal or abnormal conditions. Ordinarily circuit breakers are required to operate only infrequently, although some classes of breakers are suitable for frequent operation.

NOTE: *Normal* indicates the interruption of currents not in excess of the rated continuous current of the circuit breaker. *Abnormal* indicates the interruption of currents in excess of such rated continuous current such as short-circuits. In application, circuit breakers are selected whose rated interrupting current is as great or greater than the maximum current which they may be called upon to interrupt.

Oil Circuit Breaker 20.15.010

An oil circuit breaker is a circuit breaker in which the interruption occurs in oil.

Air Circuit Breaker 20.15.015

An air circuit breaker is a circuit breaker in which the interruption occurs in air.

Single-Throw Circuit Breaker 20.15.020

A single-throw circuit breaker is a circuit breaker by means of which the circuit can be closed or opened by moving one set of contacts only.

Double-Throw Circuit Breaker 20.15.025

A double-throw circuit breaker is a circuit breaker by means of which a change in the circuit connections can be obtained by closing either of two sets of contacts.

Multiple Multipole Circuit Breaker 20.15.030

A multiple multipole circuit breaker consists of two or more individual multipole circuit breakers electrically connected with two or more independent sets of contacts in multiple forming each pole of the breaker.

Rating and Duty Terms

Operating Duty 20.15.050

(Duty Cycle)

The operating duty of a circuit breaker consists of a specified number of unit operations at stated intervals.

Unit Operation of a Circuit Breaker 20.15.055

The unit operation of a circuit breaker consists of a closing followed immediately by its opening without purposely delayed action.

NOTE: The letters "CO" signify the operations of the breaker: CLOSING—OPENING.

Rated Interrupting Current 20.15.060

(Rated Interrupting Capacity)

The rated interrupting current of a circuit breaker is the highest rms current at a specified operating voltage which the breaker is required to interrupt under the operating duty specified and with a normal frequency recovery voltage equal to the specified operating voltage.

NOTE: The current is the rms value, including the direct-current component, at the instant of contact separation as determined from the envelope of the current wave. Where limited by testing equipment, the maximum tolerance for normal frequency recovery voltage is 15 percent of the specified operating voltage.

Characteristic Terms and Parts

Closing Time 20.15.075

The closing time of a circuit breaker is the interval between the making of contact at the closing switch and the contacting of the arcing contacts of the circuit breaker at rated control voltage.

NOTE: Where a closing relay is used with an electrically operated circuit breaker, the closing time includes the time consumed in the operation of the closing relay.

Reclosing Time 20.15.076

The reclosing time of a circuit breaker is the interval between the energizing of the trip coil (the breaker being in the closed position) and the contacting of the arcing contacts on the reclosing stroke, with rated control voltage applied.

Automatic Reclosing 20.15.077

A circuit breaker is automatic reclosing when means are provided for reclosing it automatically after it has tripped under abnormal conditions.

Opening Time 20.15.080

The opening time of a circuit breaker is the interval

existing between the energizing of the trip coil at rated voltage and the parting of the arcing contacts of the circuit breaker.

Interrupting Time 20.15.085

The interrupting time of a circuit breaker is the interval existing between the energizing of the trip coil at rated voltage and the interruption of the circuit.

NOTE: This is the summation of the opening time and the arcing time. If the tripping current of the circuit breaker is large enough to require the use of an individual auxiliary relay, the interrupting time includes the time consumed in the operation of such auxiliary relay.

Arcing Time 20.15.090

The arcing time of a switch or circuit breaker is the interval between the parting of the arcing contacts and the extinction of the arc.

Automatic Tripping 20.15.095

(Automatic Opening)

Automatic tripping is the opening of a circuit breaker under predetermined or other conditions without the intervention of an operator.

Series Overcurrent Tripping 20.15.100

Series overcurrent tripping signifies the tripping of a circuit breaker from a trip coil in series with the main circuit, responsive to an increase in the main-circuit current.

Transformer Overcurrent Tripping 20.15.105

Transformer overcurrent tripping signifies the tripping of a circuit breaker from a trip coil in series with the secondary winding of a current transformer whose primary winding is in series with the main circuit thus making the trip coil responsive to an increase in the main-circuit current.

Shunt Tripping 20.15.110

Shunt tripping signifies the tripping of a circuit breaker from a trip coil energized from the same or a separate shunt circuit or source of power, the trip-coil circuit being closed through a relay, switch or other means.

Reverse-Power Tripping 20.15.115

Reverse-power tripping signifies the tripping of a circuit breaker upon reversal of current in the main circuit.

Undervoltage Tripping 20.15.120

Undervoltage tripping signifies the tripping of a circuit breaker from a trip coil connected in shunt to the main circuit and responsive to a decrease in the main-circuit voltage.

Overvoltage Tripping 20.15.125

Overvoltage tripping signifies the tripping of a circuit breaker from a trip coil connected in shunt to the main circuit and responsive to an increase in the main-circuit voltage.

Series Undercurrent Tripping 20.15.130

Series undercurrent tripping signifies the tripping of a circuit breaker from a trip coil in series with the main circuit, responsive to a decrease in the main-circuit current.

Transformer Undercurrent Tripping 20.15.135

Transformer undercurrent tripping signifies the tripping of a circuit breaker from a trip coil in series with the secondary winding of a current transformer whose primary winding is in series with the main circuit thus making the trip coil responsive to a decrease in the main-circuit current.

Non-Automatic Tripping 20.15.140

(Non-Automatic Opening)

Non-automatic tripping is the opening of a circuit breaker only in response to an act of an operator.

Mechanically Trip Free 20.15.145

A circuit breaker is mechanically trip free when the tripping mechanism can trip it even though: (a) in a manually operated circuit breaker, the operating lever is held in the closed position; or, (b) in an electrically operated circuit breaker, the operating mechanism is held in the closing position either electrically or by means of an emergency closing lever.

Electrically Trip Free 20.15.150

An electrically operated circuit breaker is electrically trip free when the tripping mechanism can trip it even though the closing control circuit is energized, and the closing mechanism will not reclose it after tripping until the closing control circuit is opened and again closed. However, the breaker may be held closed by the emergency operating lever, unless it is also mechanically trip free.

Trip Free in Any Position 20.15.155

A circuit breaker is trip free in any position when it is trip free at any part of the closing operation. If the tripping circuit is completed through an auxiliary switch, electrical tripping will not take place until such auxiliary switch is closed.

Cell 20.15.160

A cell is a compartment for enclosing circuit breakers or other electric equipment.

Cell Door 20.15.165

A cell door is a door for closing the front or rear of a cell.

Cell Structure 20.15.170

A cell structure is a group of two or more cells.

Clevis 20.15.175

A clevis is a fitting having a U-shaped end and arranged for attaching to the end of a pipe or rod.

Dashpot 20.15.176

A dashpot is a device using a gas or liquid to absorb

energy, or retard the movement, of the moving parts of a circuit breaker or other electric device.

Indicating Lamp 20.15.177

An indicating lamp is a small lamp used in connection with the control system of a circuit breaker or other device to indicate the position of the device or condition of the circuit.

Circuit Breaker Mechanism 20.15.179

A circuit breaker mechanism is an assembly of levers and other parts which actuates the moving contacts of the circuit breaker.

Closing Coil of a Circuit Breaker 20.15.180

A closing coil of a circuit breaker is a coil used in the electromagnet which supplies power for closing a circuit breaker.

Tripping Mechanism 20.15.184

A tripping mechanism is an electrically or mechanically operated device which releases the holding means and permits the contacts of the circuit breaker to open.

Trip Coil of a Circuit Breaker 20.15.185

A trip coil of a circuit breaker is a coil used in the electromagnet which supplies power for tripping a circuit breaker.

Insulation 20.15.190

Insulation is material having the property of an insulator used to separate parts of the same or different potentials.

Bushing 20.15.195

(Insulating Bushing)

A bushing is a lining for a hole, intended to insulate and/or protect from abrasion one or more conductors which pass through it.

NOTE: The term bushing as related to circuit breakers is frequently employed to designate an assembly of the insulating member and the conductor passing through it.

Baffle 20.15.200

(Deflector)

A baffle is a device for deflecting oil or gas in a circuit breaker.

Oil Separator 20.15.205

(Separating Chamber)

An oil separator is that portion of a circuit breaker designed to facilitate the escape of gas and to prevent the escape of oil incident to circuit interruption.

Break (of a circuit-opening device) 20.15.210

The break of a circuit-opening device is the minimum distance between the stationary and movable contacts when these contacts are in the open position.

(a) The length of a single break is as defined above.

(b) The length of a multiple break (breaks in series) is the sum of the several breaks.

Laminated Brush 20.15.215

A laminated brush is a contact part consisting of thin sheets of conducting material fastened together so as to secure individual contact by the edges of the separate sheets.

Conduit Connections 20.15.220

Conduit connections are the means provided for bringing leads into or out of a circuit breaker through conduit.

Stud 20.15.225

A stud is a rigid current-carrying part which carries current from the terminals to the contacts of a circuit breaker.

Terminal Connector 20.15.230

A terminal connector is a connector for attaching a conductor to a lead, terminal block or stud of electric apparatus.

Cross Head 20.15.235

(Cross Bar)

A cross head is that part to which the moving contact rods of a circuit breaker are attached.

Moving Contact-Rods 20.15.240

Moving contact-rods are the rods to which the moving contacts of a circuit breaker are attached and through which they are operated.

Pipe End 20.15.245

(Rod End)

A pipe end is a fitting arranged to connect the end of a pipe or rod to a lever, bell crank or other part.

Coverplate and Handle 20.15.250

(Faceplate and Handle)

A coverplate and handle consists of the mounting bracket, handle lever and auxiliary parts for the manual operation of a circuit breaker from a panel or its equivalent.

Bearing Support 20.15.255

(Shaft Bearing Bracket)

A bearing support is a support provided for the bearing of a shaft.

Oil Tank of a Circuit Breaker 20.15.260

An oil tank of an oil circuit breaker is an oil container which surrounds the contacts and in which the circuit is interrupted.

Tank Lifter of a Circuit Breaker 20.15.265

A tank lifter is a device for raising or lowering the tank of a circuit breaker.

Tank Lining of a Circuit Breaker 20.15.270

Tank lining is material used for facing the interior of a tank of a circuit breaker to provide isolation and insulation.

Top Frame 20.15.275

(Base)

The top frame of a circuit breaker is the member which supports such parts as the bushings, mechanism and, in some cases, the tanks.

Pole Unit 20.15.280

A pole unit consists of the parts of a circuit breaker necessary to control one conductor of a circuit. A circuit breaker may be single pole or multipole.

Multipole Common-Frame Circuit Breaker 20.15.285

A multipole common-frame circuit breaker is a circuit breaker with two or more poles supported by one frame.

Circuit-Breaker Mounting 20.15.290

A circuit-breaker mounting is the means for supporting a circuit breaker.

Panel Mounting of a Circuit Breaker 20.15.295

Panel mounting is the mounting of a circuit breaker and its operating mechanism complete on a panel.

Panel-Frame Mounting of a Circuit Breaker 20.15.300

Panel-frame mounting is the mounting of a circuit breaker on a panel frame in the rear of a panel with the operating mechanism on the front of the panel.

Cell Mounting of a Circuit Breaker 20.15.305

Cell mounting is the mounting of a circuit breaker in a cell or with the poles in separate cells.

Wall Mounting of a Circuit Breaker 20.15.310

Wall mounting is the mounting of a circuit breaker and its operating mechanism on a wall.

Frame Mounting of a Circuit Breaker 20.15.315

Frame mounting is the mounting of a circuit breaker and its operating mechanism on a pipe or structural-iron framework.

Floor Mounting of a Circuit Breaker 20.15.320

Floor mounting is the mounting of a circuit breaker directly on the floor.

Remote Operation Frame Mounting of a Circuit Breaker 20.15.325

Remote operation frame mounting is the mounting of a circuit breaker on a pipe or structural-iron frame remote from the panel on which the operating mechanism is mounted.

Remote Operation Wall Mounting of a Circuit Breaker 20.15.330

Remote operation wall mounting is the mounting of a circuit breaker on a wall remote from the panel on which the operating mechanism is mounted.

Pole Mounting of a Circuit Breaker 20.15.335

Pole mounting is the mounting of a circuit breaker on a pole or tower.

GROUP 20—SWITCHING EQUIPMENT

Section 20—Fuses

Basic Term

Fuse 20.20.005

A fuse is an overcurrent protective device with a circuit opening fusible member directly heated and destroyed by the passage of overcurrent through it.

Ratings

High-Voltage Fuses

NOTE: Fuses in this classification are generally for voltages above 750.

Rating Terms

Voltage Rating of a Fuse 20.20.025

The voltage rating of a fuse is the rms alternating-current voltage or the direct-current voltage, at which it is designed to operate.

Current Rating of a Fuse 20.20.030

The current rating of a fuse is the designated rms alternating current or the direct current which the fuse will carry under the conditions specified.

Frequency Rating of a Fuse 20.20.035

The frequency rating of a fuse is the frequency at which it is designed to operate.

Interrupting Rating of a Fuse 20.20.040

The interrupting rating of a fuse is a rating based upon the highest rms alternating current or direct current which it will successfully interrupt under the conditions specified.

Time–Current Characteristic of a Fuse 20.20.045

The time–current characteristic of a fuse is the relation between the rms alternating current or direct current and the time for the fuse to perform the whole or some specified part of its interrupting function.

NOTE: The time–current characteristic is usually shown as a curve.

Melting Time of a Fuse 20.20.050

(Heating Time of a Fuse)

The melting time of a fuse is the time required for the current to melt the fuse link under the conditions specified, as indicated by the severance of the link.

Arcing Time of a Fuse 20.20.055

The arcing time of a fuse is the time elapsing from the severance of the fuse link to the final interruption of the circuit under the specified conditions.

Clearing Time   20.20.060

(Total Interrupting Time)

The clearing time of a fuse is the total time measured from the beginning of a specified overcurrent condition, for interruption of the circuit, at rated voltage. The clearing time is equal to the sum of the melting time plus the arcing time.

Parts

Fuse Link   20.20.075

(Fuse Element)

A fuse link is that part of a fuse which carries the current of the circuit, and all or part of which melts when the current exceeds a predetermined value.

Fuse Tube   20.20.080

A fuse tube is a tube of insulating material which encloses a fuse link.

Fuse Filler   20.20.085

A fuse filler is a material which is placed within the fuse tube to assist in the circuit interruption.

Fuse Holder   20.20.090

A fuse holder is an assembly of a fuse tube, or tubes, exclusive of fuse link, together with parts necessary to enclose, and provide means of making contact with, the fuse link and fuse clips.

Fuse Clips   20.20.100

(Fuse Contacts)

Fuse clips are the contacts on the fuse support for connecting the fuse holder into the circuit.

Fuse Unit   20.20.105

A fuse unit is an assembly comprising a fuse link mounted in a fuse holder with parts and materials in the fuse holder essential to the operation of the fuse link.

Fuse Support   20.20.110

A fuse support is an assembly of base, insulators and fuse clips for mounting a fuse holder and connecting it into the circuit.

Fuse Cutout   20.20.115

A fuse cutout is an assembly of a fuse support and a fuse holder which may or may not include the fuse link.

Enclosed Fuse Cutout   20.20.120

(Fuse Box)

An enclosed fuse cutout is a fuse cutout in which the fuse clips and fuse holder are mounted completely within an enclosure.

Open Fuse Cutout   20.20.125

An open fuse cutout is a fuse cutout in which the fuse support and fuse holder are exposed.

Oil Fuse Cutout   20.20.130

An oil fuse cutout is an enclosed fuse cutout in which all or a part of the fuse support is mounted in oil, with provision for partial or complete immersion of the fuse link.

Expulsion Fuse Unit   20.20.135

An expulsion fuse unit is a fuse unit which is characterized by expulsion of the arc gases when it operates.

Liquid Fuse Unit   20.20.140

A liquid fuse unit is a fuse unit in which the fuse link is immersed in a liquid, or provision is made for drawing the arc into the liquid when the fuse link melts.

Renewable Fuse Unit   20.20.145

A renewable fuse unit is a fuse unit which may be readily restored for service after operation by the replacement of the fused link.

Non-Renewable Fuse Unit   20.20.150

A non-renewable fuse unit is a fuse unit which cannot be readily restored for service after operation.

Fuse Disconnecting Switch   20.20.155

A fuse disconnecting switch is a disconnecting switch in which a fuse unit forms a part of the blade.

GROUP 20—SWITCHING EQUIPMENT

Section 25—Relays

Relay   20.25.005

A relay is a device that is operative by a variation in the conditions of one electric circuit to effect the operation of other devices in the same or another electric circuit.

NOTE: Where relays operate in response to changes in more than one condition, all functions should be mentioned.

Classes of Relays

Auxiliary Relay   20.25.050

An auxiliary relay is a relay which operates in response to the opening or closing of its operating circuit to assist another relay or device in the performance of a function.

Control Relay   20.25.055

A control relay is a relay which functions to initiate or to permit the next desired operation in a control circuit or scheme.

Protective Relay   20.25.060

A protective relay is a relay, the principal function of which is to protect service from interruption or to prevent or limit damage to apparatus.

Regulating Relay   20.25.065

A regulating relay is a relay which operates because of a departure from predetermined limits of a quantity and which functions through supplementary equipment to restore the quantity within these limits.

Specific Types of Relays

Alarm Relay (Alarm Signal)   20.25.075

An alarm relay is a relay which operates an audible or visible signal to attract attention to some action automatically performed or to some condition that requires attention.

Balanced Relay

See **20.25.110.**

Balanced Current Relay

See **20.25.110.**

Closing Relay   20.25.090

A closing relay is a form of auxiliary relay used with an electrically operated device to control the closing and opening of the operating circuit of the device so that the main operating current does not pass through the control switch or other initiating device.

Current Relay   20.25.095

A current relay is a relay which functions at a predetermined value of current. It may be an overcurrent relay, an undercurrent relay or a combination of both.

Current Balance Relay

See **20.25.110.**

Current Directional Relay   20.25.105

(Reverse-Current Relay)

A current directional relay is a relay which functions in conformance with the direction of current.

Differential Relay   20.25.110

A differential relay is a relay which functions by reason of the difference between two quantities of the same nature such as current or voltage, etc.

NOTE: This term includes relays heretofore known as "ratio balance relays", "biased relays" and "percentage differential relays".

Percentage Differential Relay   20.25.115

A percentage differential relay is a differential relay which functions when the difference between two quantities of the same nature exceeds a fixed percentage of the smaller quantity.

NOTE: This term includes relays heretofore known as "ratio balance relays", "biased relays" and "ratio differential relays".

Directional Relay   20.25.120

A directional relay is a relay which functions in conformance with the direction of power, or voltage, or current, or phase rotation, etc.

Directional Overcurrent Relay   20.25.125

A directional overcurrent relay is an overcurrent unit and a power directional unit combined to function on a predetermined fault location and value of current.

Power Directional Relay   20.25.135

A power directional relay is a relay which functions in conformance with the direction of power.

NOTE: This includes both unidirectional relays with single-throw contacts and duodirectional relays with double-throw contacts.

Voltage Directional Relay   20.25.140

(Polarity Directional Relay)

A voltage directional relay is a relay which functions in conformance with the direction of voltage.

Distance Relay   20.25.145

A distance relay is a protective relay, the operation of which is a function of the distance between the relay and the point of fault.

Impedance Relay   20.25.150

An impedance relay is a form of distance relay, the operation of which is a function of the impedance of the circuit between the relay and the fault.

Reactance Relay   20.25.155

A reactance relay is a form of distance relay, the operation of which is a function of the reactance of the circuit between the relay and the fault.

Resistance Relay   20.25.160

A resistance relay is a form of distance relay, the operation of which is a function of the resistance of the circuit between the relay and the fault.

Flow Relay   20.25.165

A flow relay is a relay which functions at a predetermined flow of gas or liquid.

Frequency Relay   20.25.170

A frequency relay is a relay which functions at a predetermined value of frequency. It may be an overfrequency relay, an underfrequency relay or a combination of both.

Ground Relay   20.25.175

A ground relay is a protective relay which functions in case of a fault to ground.

See **20.25.240.**

Locking Relay   20.25.180

A locking relay is a relay which renders some other relay or device inoperative under predetermined conditions.

Network Relay   20.25.185

A network relay is a form of voltage, power or other type of relay, for specific use in the protection and control of alternating-current low-voltage networks.

Network Master Relay   20.25.190

A network master relay is a relay which performs the chief functions of closing and tripping an alternating-current low-voltage network protector.

Network Phasing Relay   20.25.195

A network phasing relay is a relay which functions in conjunction with a master relay to limit closure of the network protector to a predetermined relationship between the voltage and the network voltage.

Open-Phase Relay 20.25.200

An open-phase relay is a relay which functions by reason of the opening of one or more phases of a polyphase circuit, when sufficient current is flowing in the remaining phase or phases.

Overcurrent Relay

See 20.25.095.

Overload Relay 20.25.210

An overload relay is an overcurrent relay.

See 20.25.095.

Phase Balance Relay 20.25.215

A phase-balance relay is a relay which functions by reason of a difference between two quantities associated with different phases of a polyphase circuit.

Phase-Reversal Relay

See 20.25.225.

Phase-Sequence Relay 20.25.225

(Phase-Rotation Relay)

A phase-sequence relay is a relay which functions in accordance with the order in which the phase voltages successively reach their maximum positive values.

Positive Phase-Sequence Relay 20.25.230

A positive phase-sequence relay is a relay which functions in conformance with the positive phase-sequence component of the current, voltage or power of the circuit.

Negative Phase-Sequence Relay 20.25.235

A negative phase-sequence relay is a relay which functions in comformance with the negative phase-sequence component of the current, voltage or power of the circuit.

Zero Phase-Sequence Relay 20.25.240

(Ground Relay) (Residual Relay)

A zero phase-sequence relay is a relay which functions in conformance with the zero phase-sequence component of the current, voltage or power of the circuit.

See 20.25.175.

Phase Undervoltage Relay 20.25.245

A phase undervoltage relay is a relay which functions by reason of the reduction of one phase voltage in a polyphase circuit.

Polarity Directional Relay

See 20.25.140.

Power Relay 20.25.255

A power relay is a relay which functions at a predetermined value of power. It may be an overpower relay, an underpower relay or a combination of both.

Pressure Relay 20.25.265

A pressure relay is a relay which functions at a predetermined pressure of gas or liquid.

Rate of Change Relay 20.25.275

A rate of change relay is a relay which functions in conformance with the rate of change of current, voltage, power, etc.

Reclosing Relay 20.25.285

A reclosing relay is a form of voltage, current, power or other type of relay which functions to reclose a circuit automatically.

Residual Relay

See 20.25.175 and 20.25.240.

Reverse-Current Relay

See 20.25.105.

Signal Alarm

See 20.25.075.

Step-Back Relay 20.25.320

A step-back relay is a relay which operates to limit the current peaks of a motor when the armature or line current increases. A step-back relay may, in addition, operate to remove such limitation when the cause of the high current has been removed.

Surge Relay

See 20.25.275.

Synchronizing Relay 20.25.330

A synchronizing relay is a relay which functions when two alternating-current sources are in agreement within predetermined limits of phase angle and frequency.

Temperature Relay 20.25.335

A temperature relay is a relay which functions at a predetermined temperature in the apparatus protected.

Temperature Overload Relay

See 20.25.095 and 20.25.335.

Thermostat Relay 20.25.345

A thermostat relay is a form of temperature relay which receives its operating energy by thermal conduction or convection from the device being protected.

Timing Relay 20.25.350

A timing relay is a form of auxiliary relay used to introduce a definite time delay in the performance of a function.

Trip-Free Relay 20.25.355

A trip-free relay is a relay which opens the closing circuit of an electrically operated circuit interrupting device such as a circuit breaker, so that the device is free to trip upon the action of its protective relay or other protective devices and which prevents more than one closing action of the circuit interrupting device for any one operation of the control switch or other initiating device.

Voltage Relay 20.25.360

A voltage relay is a relay which functions at a predetermined value of voltage. It may be an overvoltage relay, an undervoltage relay, or a combination of both.

General Qualifying Terms

Accelerating   20.25.375

Accelerating is a qualifying term applied to a relay indicating that it functions to control the acceleration of rotating electric apparatus.

Definite Time   20.25.380

Definite time is a qualifying term indicating that there is purposely introduced a delay in action, which delay remains substantially constant regardless of the magnitude of the quantity that causes the action.

Directional Control   20.25.385

Directional control is a qualifying term applied to a protective relay or relay scheme which indicates a means for preventing the protective relay or scheme from functioning until the power is in a predetermined direction.

Hand Reset   20.25.390

Hand reset is a qualifying term applied to a relay indicating that the contacts must be reset manually to their original positions when normal conditions are resumed.

Initiating   20.25.395

Initiating is a qualifying term applied to a relay indicating that its operation must precede that of other relays which depend upon its action in the performance of a function or operating sequence.

Instantaneous   20.25.400

Instantaneous is a qualifying term indicating that no delay is purposely introduced in the action of the device.

Inverse Time   20.25.405

Inverse time is a qualifying term indicating that there is purposely introduced a delayed action, which delay decreases as the operating force increases.

Notching   20.25.410

Notching is a qualifying term indicating that a predetermined number of separate impulses is required to complete operation.

Self Reset   20.25.415

Self reset is a qualifying term applied to a relay indicating that the contacts return to their original position when normal conditions are resumed.

Voltage Restraint   20.25.420

Voltage restraint is a qualifying term applied to a relay indicating that the operation of the relay is restrained by a force or torque dependent upon the magnitude of one or more voltages.

Parts of Relays

Target   20.25.430

A target is a supplementary device used in conjunction with a relay to indicate that it has functioned.

Performance Terms

Pick-Up†   20.25.435

The pick-up value of a relay is the minimum current, voltage, power, etc., at which its energized function will be completed.

Drop-Out†   20.25.440

The drop-out value of a relay is the maximum current, voltage, power, etc., at which it will recede from its energized position. For example, an overcurrent relay which closes its contacts on pick-up will just open the contacts on the drop-out.

Reset†   20.25.445

The reset value of a relay is the maximum current, voltage, power, etc., at which its deenergized function will be completed.

Differential Protection   20.25.450

Differential protection is the effect of a device operative on a difference between electrical quantities in excess of a predetermined amount or ratio to cause and maintain the interruption of power in the circuit. The electrical quantities may be current, voltage, power, frequency, etc.

Directional Overcurrent Protection   20.25.455

Directional overcurrent protection is the effect of a device operative on current in excess of a predetermined amount and in a predetermined direction to cause and maintain the interruption of power in the circuit.

Ground Protection   20.25.460

Ground protection is the effect of a device operative on faults to ground to cause and maintain the interruption of power in a circuit.

Overcurrent Protection   20.25.465

(Overload Protection)

Overcurrent protection is the effect of a device operative on excessive current to cause and maintain the interruption or reduction of current flow to the equipment governed.

Open-Phase Protection   20.25.475

Open-phase protection is the effect of a device operative on the loss of current in one phase of a polyphase circuit to cause and maintain the interruption of power in the circuit.

Phase-Failure Protection

See 20.25.475 and 20.25.485.

Phase Undervoltage Protection   20.25.485

Phase undervoltage protection is the effect of a device operative on the reduction of voltage in one phase of a polyphase circuit to cause and maintain the interruption of power in the circuit.

---

† Pick-up, drop-out and reset values for alternating-current relays are on the basis of rms values with a wave shape which conforms to good commercial practice.

Phase-Reversal Protection   20.25.490

Phase-reversal protection is the effect of a device operative on the reversal of the phase sequence in a polyphase circuit to cause and maintain the interruption of power in the circuit.

Rate-of-Change Protection   20.25.495

Rate-of-change protection is the effect of equipment operative in conformance with the rate of change of current, voltage, power, etc., to cause and maintain the interruption of power in the circuit. In alternating-current circuits the quantities are in rms values.

Surge Protection

See 20.25.495.

Undervoltage Protection   20.25.505

(Lowvoltage Protection)

Undervoltage or lowvoltage protection is the effect of a device operative on the reduction or failure of voltage to cause and maintain the interruption of power in the main circuit.

Undervoltage Release   20.25.510

(Lowvoltage Release)

Undervoltage or lowvoltage release is the effect of a device operative on the reduction or failure of voltage to cause the interruption of power in the main circuit, but not to prevent the reestablishment of the main circuit on return of voltage.

Time Undervoltage Protection   20.25.515

Time undervoltage protection is the effect of a device operative on the reduction or failure of voltage to cause and maintain the interruption of power in the main circuit if the voltage reduction continues for more than a predetermined time interval.

Current Phase-Balance Protection   20.25.520

Current phase-balance protection is the effect of a device operative on the current unbalance between the phases of a normally balanced polyphase system to cause and maintain the interruption of power in the circuit.

Voltage Phase-Balance Protection   20.25.525

Voltage phase-balance protection is the effect of a device operative on the voltage unbalance between the phases of a normally balanced polyphase system to cause and maintain the interruption of power in the circuit.

Overspeed Protection   20.25.530

Overspeed protection is the effect of a device operative on speed of rotating equipment in excess of a predetermined rate to cause and maintain the interruption of power to the protected equipment.

Overpower Protection   20.25.535

Overpower protection is the effect of a device operative on the power delivered to an electric circuit in excess of a predetermined amount, to cause and maintain the interruption of power in the circuit.

Distance Protection   20.25.540

Distance protection is the effect of a device operative on faults within a predetermined electrical distance on the protected circuit to cause and maintain the interruption of power in the circuit.

NOTE: Distance protection may be directional or non-directional and the distance may be determined by measurement of resistance, reactance or impedance. It may also be controlled in combination with other devices, for example by current.

Rating Terms

Rating of a Relay   20.25.545

The rating of a relay is the designated limit of its operating characteristics based on definite conditions. The rating is expressed in terms of voltage, current and frequency.

Continuous Rating of a Relay   20.25.550

The continuous rating of a relay is a rating which defines the current or voltage at specified frequency which may be sustained by the relay for an unlimited period without causing any of the prescribed limitations to be exceeded.

Periodic Rating of a Relay   20.25.555

The periodic rating of a relay is a rating which defines the current or voltage that may be sustained by the relay for the alternate periods of energization and de-energization specified in the rating with the apparatus starting cold and for the total time specified in the rating without causing any of the prescribed limitations to be exceeded.

Contact Interrupting Rating of a Relay   20.25.560

The contact interrupting rating of a relay is the maximum current which the device may be called upon to interrupt at a given alternating-current or direct-current voltage with a prescribed operating duty and circuit time constant.

Contact Current-Carrying Rating of a Relay   20.25.565

The contact current-carrying rating of a relay is the maximum current which may be carried continuously or at stated periodic intervals, without causing the prescribed temperature limitations to be exceeded.

Contact Current-Closing Rating of a Relay   20.25.570

The contact current-closing rating of a relay is the maximum current which the device may be called upon to close at a given alternating-current or direct-current voltage with a prescribed operating duty.

Duty Classification of a Relay   20.25.575

The duty classification of a relay is an expression of the frequency with which the relay may be required to operate without exceeding prescribed limitations.

GROUP 20—SWITCHING EQUIPMENT

Section 30—Lightning Arresters

Lightning 20.30.005

Lightning is an electric discharge occurring in the atmosphere, one terminal of which is a cloud.

Lightning Surge 20.30.010

A lightning surge is a transient electric disturbance in an electric circuit caused by lightning.

Lightning Arrester 20.30.015

A lightning arrester is a device which has the property of reducing the voltage of a surge applied to its terminals, is capable of interrupting follow current if present, and restores itself to its original operating conditions.

Discharge Current of a Lightning Arrester 20.30.020

Discharge current of a lightning arrester is the surge current which flows through the arrester upon application to its terminals of a lightning or test surge.

Follow Current 20.30.025

(Power Current)

Follow current is generated current which flows through the arrester following the passage of the surge current.

GROUP 20—SWITCHING EQUIPMENT

Section 35—Resistors

Resistor

See **05.45.015**.

Current-Limiting Resistor 20.35.010

A current-limiting resistor is a resistor inserted in an electric circuit to limit the flow of current to some predetermined value.

NOTE: A current-limiting resistor, usually in series with a fuse or circuit breaker, may be employed to limit the flow of circuit or system energy at the time of a fault or short-circuit.

Resistor Element 20.35.015

The resistor element of a current-limiting resistor is the material possessing the property of electric resistance.

Resistor Core 20.35.020

The resistor core of a current-limiting resistor is the insulating support on which the resistor element is wound.

Resistor Housing 20.35.025

The resistor housing of a current-limiting resistor is an enclosing member which surrounds the resistor element and the core.

Current-Limiting Resistor Unit 20.35.030

A current-limiting resistor unit is an assembly comprising a resistor element, resistor core and resistor housing and all parts for making necessary mechanical and electric connections.

Current-Limiting Resistor Support 20.35.035

A current-limiting resistor support is an assembly of base, insulators and necessary fittings for mounting the resistor unit.

GROUP 20—SWITCHING EQUIPMENT

Section 40—Regulators

Regulator 20.40.005

A regulator is a device which functions to maintain a designated characteristic at a predetermined value, or to vary it according to a predetermined plan.

Generator Voltage Regulator 20.40.010

A generator voltage regulator is a regulator which functions to maintain the voltage of a synchronous generator, condenser, motor, or of a direct-current generator, at a predetermined value, or vary it according to a predetermined plan.

Speed Regulator 20.40.015

A speed regulator is a regulator which functions to maintain the speed of a motor at a predetermined value or vary it according to a predetermined plan.

Power Factor Regulator 20.40.020

A power factor regulator is a regulator which functions to maintain the power factor of a line or an apparatus at a predetermined value or to vary it according to a predetermined plan.

Frequency Regulator 20.40.025

A frequency regulator is a regulator which functions to maintain the frequency of a generator at a predetermined value or to vary it according to a predetermined plan.

Load Regulator 20.40.030

A load regulator is a regulator which functions to maintain load as designated at a predetermined value or to vary it according to a predetermined plan.

GROUP 20—SWITCHING EQUIPMENT

Section 45—Network Protectors

Network Protector   **20.45.005**

A network protector is an assembly comprising a circuit breaker and its complete control equipment for automatically disconnecting a transformer from a secondary network in response to predetermined electrical conditions on the primary feeder or transformer, and for connecting a transformer to a secondary network either through manual control or automatic control responsive to predetermined electrical conditions on the feeder and the secondary network.

NOTE: The network protector is usually arranged to connect automatically its associated transformer to the network when conditions are such that the transformer will, when connected, supply power to the network and to automatically disconnect the transformer from the network when power flows from the network to the transformer.

GROUP 20—SWITCHING EQUIPMENT

Section 50—Switchgear Assemblies

Switchboard Classifications

Power Switchboard   **20.50.005**

A power switchboard is that part of switchgear which consists of one or more panels upon which are mounted the switching control, meters, protective and regulatory equipment. The panel or panel supports may also carry the main switching and interrupting devices together with their connections.

Live-Front Switchboard   **20.50.010**

A live-front switchboard is a switchboard having live parts on the front of the panels.

Dead-Front Switchboard   **20.50.015**

A dead-front switchboard is a switchboard having no live parts on the front of the panels.

Distribution Switchboard   **20.50.020**

A distribution switchboard is a power switchboard used for the distribution of electric energy at the voltages common for such distribution within a building.

NOTE: Knife switches, air circuit breakers, and fuses are generally used for circuit interruption on distribution switchboards, and voltages seldom exceed 600. However, such switchboards often include switchboard equipment for a high-tension incoming supply circuit and a stepdown transformer.

Construction Classification of Switchboards

Vertical Switchboard   **20.50.075**

A vertical switchboard is a switchboard composed of vertical panels.

Duplex Switchboard   **20.50.080**

A duplex switchboard is a structure with front and rear panels of metal or insulation material, separated a comparatively short distance, and enclosed at both ends.

NOTE: No primary switching devices are located between front and rear panels. The rear panels may be hinged for access to panel wiring.

Enclosed Switchboard   **20.50.085**

An enclosed switchboard is a dead front switchboard with an overall sheet-metal enclosure (not grille) covering back and ends of the entire structure. Access to the enclosure is usually provided by a door at one or both ends. Top may or may not be covered.

Benchboard   **20.50.090**
(Control Desk)

A benchboard is a switchboard having a horizontal or slightly inclined section for mounting control switches, indicating lamps and instrument switches; and constructed with or without vertical instrument sections.

Continuous Type of Benchboard   **20.50.095**

The continuous type of benchboard has no opening between the vertical instrument section and the bench.

Duplex Type of Benchboard   **20.50.100**

The duplex type of benchboard is a combination structure of a continuous type board and hinged rear panels of metal or insulation material, separated a comparatively short distance. Grille or solid end enclosures are provided, and the hinged panels give access to panel wiring and also serve to carry auxiliary equipment.

Open Type of Benchboard   **20.50.105**

The open type of benchboard has a space between the bench and the vertical instrument sections.

Separate Type of Benchboard   **20.50.110**

The separate type of benchboard consists of a bench or desk without vertical instrument sections.

Switchgear Pedestal   **20.50.115**

A switchgear pedestal is an individual enclosed indoor structure supported by a vertical hollow member of sufficient cross-section to accommodate its connection cables or wires; and which provides mounting for, and contains on its one or more sides, the switching, control, signal or meter equipment. The equipment panels may be either of metal or insulation material and access to interior is provided by hinged doors or removable plates.

General Terms
Parts Relating to Switchboards

Panel   **20.50.150**

A panel is a switchboard unit made up of one or more sections for mounting on common supports and drilled for or having mounted thereon switchgear apparatus.

Sectional Panel 20.50.155

A sectional panel is a panel of which the front is sectionalized.

Panel Framework 20.50.160

Panel framework is the framework which directly supports the panel and is constructed of either pipe or structural-steel shapes.

Panel Braces 20.50.165

Panel braces are braces from the panel framework to the floor, wall, column, ceiling or adjacent panel which support the panel in the desired position.

Sub-Base 20.50.170

(Sub-Section)

A sub-base is a bottom section of a panel composed of more than one section.

Sill 20.50.175

A sill is a base upon which the switchboard rests and is usually constructed of channel iron.

Bus 20.50.180

A bus conductor, or group of conductors, is a switchgear assembly which serves as a common connection for three or more circuits.

NOTE: The conductors of a bus are usually in the form of a bar.

Connection Bars 20.50.185

Connection bars are bar conductors used to interconnect machines, electric equipment and circuits, and/or buses, in a switchgear assembly.

Control Bus 20.50.190

Control buses are buses mounted in the rear of a switchboard or in the circuit breaker structure, to distribute power for operating electrically controlled devices.

Fault Bus 20.50.195

A fault bus is a bus which connects the grounded parts of electric equipment to ground through a fault-detecting device.

Enclosed Bus 20.50.200

An enclosed bus is a bus having its conductors confined within an insulating or metal enclosure.

Open Bus 20.50.205

An open bus is a bus without an enclosure.

Mimic Bus 20.50.210

A mimic bus is a single line diagram of the main connections of a system constructed on the face of a switchboard and so arranged that the circuit breakers are represented by their control switches. Disconnecting switches used for switching rather than for isolating are usually represented by mimic devices.

Main Switchgear Connections 20.50.215

(Primary Switchgear Connections)

Main switchgear connections are those which electrically connect together devices in the main circuit and/or connect them to the bus.

Small Wiring 20.50.220

(Secondary and Control Wiring)

Small wiring is the wiring used for control circuits and for interconnecting instruments, meters, relays, instrument-transformer secondaries, and other equipment mounted on the rear of panels, on the panel frame or on a structure integral with the panel supports.

Terminal Board 20.50.225

A terminal board is an insulating base or slab, usually mounted in the rear of a switchboard panel, equipped with terminals for connecting the small wiring to the outgoing instrument and control cables.

Calibrating or Testing Terminals 20.50.230

Calibrating or testing terminals are terminals arranged for the convenient testing and/or calibration of meters, instruments or relays.

Accessible

See 95.90.305 and 95.90.310.

Structural Classifications

Switching Structure 20.50.250

A switching structure is a framework supporting the main switching and associated equipment such as instrument transformers, buses, fuses and connections. It may be designed for indoor or outdoor use and the indoor type may be assembled with or without switchboard panels carrying the control equipment.

NOTE: A switching structure is frequently associated with a switchboard on which are mounted the control switches and the meter and protective devices.

Switchgear Cubicle 20.50.255

A switchgear cubicle is an indoor switching structure enclosed on all sides and top by metal or insulation material, having the control, meter and protective equipment mounted at the front, and the fixed primary switching devices with related equipment, including buses when required, located inside.

NOTE: The primary switching devices are generally located in a separate compartment from the secondary and control wiring and devices.

Removable Truck Type Switchgear 20.50.260

Removable truck type switchgear consists of an enclosed stationary housing for buses and cable connections, with a removable truck containing the switching, meter and protective equipment with other associated devices and connections. The truck may be completely isolated from the bus and line by removal from its stationary housing and is equipped with self-coupled primary and secondary disconnecting contacts. Interlocks are provided to prevent moving the truck from or into the connected position while the switching device is closed.

Parts and Terms Relating to Truck Type Switchgear

Housing   20.50.275

A housing is a stationary structure which contains the buses and connections and which receives the removable truck.

Removable Truck   20.50.280

A removable truck is a removable structure containing the main control equipment, circuit breaker, instruments and related apparatus.

Superstructure   20.50.285

A superstructure is a vertical extension, either integral or sectional, of the housing to accommodate equipment or connections, when space limitation does not permit their location in the truck or housing.

Primary Disconnecting Devices   20.50.290

Primary disconnecting devices of removable truck type or of metal-clad switchgear are separable contacts provided to connect or disconnect the main circuits between the removable truck and its housing or between the removable element and its stationary structure.

Secondary Disconnecting Devices   20.50.295

Secondary disconnecting devices of removable truck type or of metal-clad switchgear are separable contacts which connect or disconnect the auxiliary or control circuits between the removable truck and its housing or between the removable element and its stationary structure.

Disconnect Position   20.50.300

The disconnect position of removable truck type or of metal-clad switchgear is the position of the removable truck or of the removable element in which the primary disconnecting devices are separated by a safe distance, while the secondary disconnecting devices may still be in contact.

Metal-Clad Switchgear   20.50.305

Metal-clad switchgear consists of a metal structure containing a circuit breaker and other associated equipment such as instrument transformers, buses and connections. The transformers, buses and connections are placed in separate grounded metal compartments which may be either unfilled (dry type) or may contain fluid, semi-fluid or other insulating medium. The circuit breaker is equipped with self-coupling primary and secondary contacts and is arranged with a disconnecting mechanism for moving it physically (through either vertical or horizontal travel) from the connect to the disconnect position, after which it may be removed from the stationary structure. Interlocks are provided to insure proper sequence and safe operation.

In an alternative construction for circuit breakers of great weight or volume, disconnection is accomplished by switches which automatically ground the breaker when the switch is opened.

Parts and Terms Relating to Metal-Clad Switchgear

Stationary Structure   20.50.325

The stationary structure of metal-clad switchgear is that fixed portion which includes the compartment containing the buses, connections, and usually instrument transformers, and which also receives and supports the removable elements.

Removable Element   20.50.330

The removable element of metal-clad switchgear is that portion which carries the circuit breaker and/or other removable apparatus.

Compartments   20.50.335

The bus and connection compartments of metal-clad switchgear are those portions which contain the buses and connections and which are adaptable for filling with fluid, semi-fluid or other insulating mediums.

Connected Position   20.50.355

The connected position is that position of the removable element in which both primary and secondary disconnecting devices are in full contact.

Handling Device   20.50.360

The handling device of metal-clad switchgear is that accessory which is used for the removal and replacement of the removable element.

Outdoor Switchgear Assemblies

Switchhouse   20.50.375

A switchhouse is an outdoor switching structure enclosed on all sides and top to form a weatherproof construction. Control, protective, meter, fixed, primary switching and other related equipment are mounted inside. Access to interior is provided by doors, front and rear.

Outdoor Station   20.50.380

An outdoor station is a station in which the individual pieces of electric apparatus are designed to be self-protecting with respect to weather and therefore are not housed.

Automatic Switchgear

NOTE: Automatic switchgear assemblies employ the supporting frameworks and panels of switchboards, often in combination with a switching structure.

Automatic Station

See **35.10.070.**

Partial Automatic Station   20.50.405

A partial automatic station is a station which goes into operation by automatic sequence when given an indication by an attendant, and goes out of operation by automatic sequence when given the corresponding indication by an attendant or through protective equipment. Maintenance of the required character of service may be by automatic or manual control.

ELECTRICAL DEFINITIONS

Automatic Machine Equipment   20.50.410

An automatic machine equipment is an equipment which provides automatic control, as defined for Automatic Station, for any type of rotating machine or rectifier.

Automatic Feeder Equipment   20.50.415

An automatic feeder equipment is an equipment which provides automatic control, as defined for an Automatic Station.

Stub Feeder of an Automatic Station   20.50.420

(Radial Feeder of an Automatic Station)

A stub feeder is a feeder which connects a load with its only source of power.

Multiple Feeder of an Automatic Station   20.50.425

A multiple feeder is a feeder which is connected to a common load in multiple with one or more feeders from independent sources.

Stub Multiple Feeder of an Automatic Station   20.50.430

A stub multiple feeder is a feeder which may operate either to connect a load to a single source of power or to connect to a common load in multiple with one or more feeders from independent sources.

Tie Feeder of an Automatic Station   20.50.435

A tie feeder is a feeder which primarily connects two independent sources of power. A load may be connected between these two sources.

Parallel Feeder of an Automatic Station   20.50.440

A parallel feeder is a feeder which operates in parallel with one or more feeders of the same type from the same source. These feeders may be of the stub, multiple or tie feeder types.

Automatic Transfer Equipment   20.50.445

An automatic transfer equipment is an equipment which automatically transfers a load so that a source of power may be selected from one of several incoming lines.

Automatic Transformer Equipment   20.50.450

An automatic transformer equipment is an equipment which provides automatic control, as defined under Automatic Station, for connecting and disconnecting additional transformer capacity in response to overload and underload, respectively, of predetermined values for predetermined periods of time.

Load-Limiting Resistor

See 20.35.010.

Load-Shifting Resistor   20.50.460

A load-shifting resistor is a resistor used in an electric circuit to shift load from one circuit to another.

Load-Indicating Resistor   20.50.465

A load-indicating resistor is a resistor used, in conjunction with suitable relays and/or meters, in an electric circuit, for the purpose of determining the value of the connected load.

Classification of Switchgear Assemblies According to the Method of Control

Manual Control   20.50.475

Manual control is an arrangement of controls which provides for opening or closing the switching devices by hand.

Direct Manual Control   20.50.480

Direct manual control is an arrangement of controls in which the control handles are directly attached to their switching devices.

Remote Manual Control   20.50.485

Remote manual control is an arrangement of controls in which the auxiliary mechanism connects the control handles to their switching devices which are mounted apart from the point of control.

Electrical Control   20.50.490

Electrical control is an arrangement of controls in which the switching devices are operated by electric devices or other power means, energized by control devices located at the point of control.

Automatic Control   20.50.495

Automatic control is an arrangement of electrical controls which provides for opening and/or closing in an automatic sequence and under predetermined conditions, the switching devices which thereupon maintain the required character of service and provide adequate protection against all usual operating emergencies.

Supervisory Control   20.50.500

Supervisory control is a system for the selective control and automatic indication of remotely located units by electrical means, over a relatively small number of common transmission channels.

ELECTRICAL DEFINITIONS

GROUP 25—CONTROL EQUIPMENT

SECTIONS

05 General
10 Kinds of Protection
15 Relays
20 Qualifying Terms
25 Properties and Characteristics of Apparatus

30 Design Details
35 Duty and Service Classifications
40 Ratings
95 Not Otherwise Classified

Section 05—General

Electric Controller 25.05.005

An electric controller is a device, or group of devices, which serves to govern, in some predetermined manner, the electric power delivered to the apparatus to which it is connected.

Basic Functions 25.05.010

The basic functions of a controller are acceleration, retardation, line closing, reversing, etc.

Drum Controller 25.05.015

A drum controller is an electric controller which utilizes a drum switch as the main switching element.

NOTE: A drum controller usually consists of a drum switch and a resistor.

Electropneumatic Controller 25.05.020

An electropneumatic controller is an electric controller having its basic functions performed by air pressure.

Manual Controller 25.05.025

A manual controller is an electric controller having all of its basic functions performed by hand.

Full Magnetic Controller 25.05.030

A full magnetic controller is an electric controller having all of its basic functions performed by electromagnets.

Semi-Magnetic Controller 25.05.035

A semi-magnetic controller is an electric controller having only part of its basic functions performed by electromagnets.

Contacts 25.05.040

Contacts are conducting parts which coact to complete or to interrupt a circuit.

Auxiliary Contacts 25.05.045

Auxiliary contacts of a switching device are contacts in addition to the main circuit contacts and function with the movement of the latter.

Laminated Brush

See 20.15.215.

Contactor 25.05.050

A contactor is a device, operated other than by hand, for repeatedly establishing and interrupting an electric power circuit.

Magnetic Contactor 25.05.055

A magnetic contactor is a contactor actuated by electromagnetic means.

Resistance

See 05.20.150.

Resistor

See 05.45.015.

Constant-Torque Resistor 25.05.060

A constant-torque resistor is a resistor for use in the armature or rotor circuit of a motor in which the current remains practically constant throughout the entire speed range.

Current-Limiting Resistor

See 20.35.010.

Fan Duty Resistor 25.05.065

A fan duty resistor is a resistor for use in the armature or rotor circuit of a motor in which the current is approximately proportional to the speed of the motor.

Resistive Conductor

See 35.80.130.

Rheostat

See 05.45.025.

Starter 25.05.075

A starter is an electric controller for accelerating a motor from rest to normal speed.

Automatic Starter 25.05.080

An automatic starter is a starter which controls automatically the acceleration of a motor.

Autotransformer Starter 25.05.085

An autotransformer starter is a starter having an autotransformer to furnish a reduced voltage for starting. It includes the necessary switching mechanism and is frequently called a compensator or autostarter.

Switch 25.05.090

A switch is a device for making, breaking or changing the connections in an electric circuit.

NOTE: In controller practice a switch is considered to be a device operated by other than magnetic means.

Control Cutout Switch 25.05.095

A control cutout switch is a switch that isolates the control circuit of an electric controller.

Drum Switch   25.05.100

A drum switch is a switch in which the electric contacts are made on segments or surfaces on the periphery of a rotating cylinder or sector, or by the operation of a rotating cam.

General Use Switch   25.05.105

A general use switch is a switch intended for use in general distribution and branch circuits. It is rated in amperes and is capable of interrupting the rated current at the rated voltage.

Isolating Switch   25.05.110

An isolating switch is a switch intended for isolating an electric circuit from the source of power. It has no interrupting rating and is intended to be operated only after the circuit has been opened by some other means.

Master Switch   25.05.115

A master switch is a switch which dominates the operation of contactors, relays or other magnetically operated devices.

Motor-Circuit Switch   25.05.120

A motor-circuit switch is a switch intended for use in a motor branch circuit. It is rated in horsepower and is capable of interrupting the maximum operating overload current of a motor of the same rating at the rated voltage.

GROUP 25—CONTROL EQUIPMENT
Section 10—Kinds of Protection

Open-Phase Protection

See 20.25.475.

Overload Protection   25.10.005

(Overcurrent Protection)

Overload protection is the effect of a device operative on excessive current, but not necessarily on short-circuit, to cause and maintain the interruption of current flow to the device governed.

Phase-Failure Protection   25.10.010

Phase-failure protection is the effect of a device operative upon the failure of voltage in one leg of a polyphase circuit, to cause and maintain the interruption of power in all legs of the circuit.

Phase-Reversal Protection

See 20.25.490.

Undervoltage Protection

See 20.25.505.

Undervoltage Release

See 20.25.510.

GROUP 25—CONTROL EQUIPMENT
Section 15—Relays

Relay

See 20.25.005.

Current Relay

See 20.25.095.

Differential Relay

See 20.25.110.

Frequency Relay

See 20.25.170.

Open-Phase Relay

See 20.25.200.

Overload Relay   25.15.005

An overload relay is an overcurrent relay in the circuit to a motor and which functions at a predetermined value of overcurrent to cause the disconnection of the motor from the line.

NOTE: An overload relay is intended to protect the motor or controller and does not necessarily protect itself.

Phase-Sequence Relay

(Phase-Rotation Relay)

See 20.25.225.

Step-Back Relay

See 20.25.320.

Temperature Relay

See 20.25.335.

Voltage Relay

See 20.25.360.

GROUP 25—CONTROL EQUIPMENT

Section 20—Qualifying Terms

Automatic
See 95.90.420.

Definite Time
See 20.25.380.

Inverse Time
See 20.25.405.

Instantaneous
See 20.25.400.

Normally Open and Normally Closed   25.20.020
The terms "Normally Open" and "Normally Closed" when applied to a magnetically operated switching device, such as a contactor or relay, or to the contacts thereof, signify the position taken when the operating magnet is deenergized. These terms apply only to non-latching types of devices.

Notching
See 20.25.410.

GROUP 25—CONTROL EQUIPMENT

Section 25—Properties and Characteristics of Apparatus

Distinctive Features
See 95.05.020.

Air (used as a prefix)
See 95.90.005.

Oil (used as a prefix)
See 95.90.010.

Proof (used as a suffix)
See 95.90.015.

Resistant (used as a suffix)
See 95.90.020.

Tight (used as a suffix)
See 95.90.025.

Drip-Proof
See 95.90.150.

Dustproof
See 95.90.125.

Gasproof
See 95.90.105.

Sleetproof
See 95.90.170.

Splashproof
See 95.90.160.

Weatherproof
See 95.90.185.

Acid-Resistant
See 95.90.165.

Fume-Resistant
See 95.90.115.

Moisture-Resistant
See 95.90.140.

Driptight
See 95.90.155.

Dust-Tight
See 95.90.130.

Gastight
See 95.90.110.

Watertight
See 95.90.145.

Submersible
See 95.90.195.

GROUP 25—CONTROL EQUIPMENT

Section 30—Design Details

Break (of a circuit-opening device)
See 20.15.210.

Contact-Wear Allowance   25.30.010
Contact-wear allowance is the total thickness of material which may be worn away before the contact of two associated surfaces becomes inadequate to carry its rating.

Drop-Out Voltage (or Current)   25.30.015
The drop-out voltage (or current) of a magnetically operated device is the voltage (or current) at which the device will release to its deenergized position.

Pick-Up Voltage (or Current)   25.30.020
The pick-up voltage (or current) of a magnetically operated device is the voltage (or current) at which the device starts to operate.

Sealing Voltage (or Current)   25.30.025
The sealing voltage (or current) is the voltage (or current) necessary to seat the armature of a magnetic circuit closing device from the position at which the contacts first touch each other.

GROUP 25—CONTROL EQUIPMENT
Section 35—Duty and Service Classifications

Duty of a Controller   25.35.005

The duty of a controller means the specific function or functions which it is designed to accomplish with respect to the operation of the motor; such as starting, speed control, reversing and stopping; and, in addition, the frequency and length of time of operation.

Continuous Duty

See 05.50.015.

Intermittent Duty

See 05.50.025.

Periodic Duty

See 05.50.030.

Varying Duty

See 05.50.035.

Service of a Controller   25.35.010

The service of a controller is the specific application in which the controller is to be used, for example:

1. General purpose
2. Special purpose
   (a) Crane and hoist
   (b) Elevator
   (c) Machine tool
   etc.

GROUP 25—CONTROL EQUIPMENT
Section 40—Ratings

Rating   25.40.005

See 05.50.040.

NOTE: The rating of control apparatus in general is expressed in volts, amperes, horsepower or kilowatts as may be appropriate, except that resistors are rated in ohms, amperes and class of service.

Rating of a Controller   25.40.010

The rating of a controller is an arbitrary designation of an operating limit.† It is based on power governed, the duty and service required.

NOTE: Standard ratings do not provide for overload capacity unless specified.

Continuous Rating

See 05.50.045.

Periodic Rating   25.40.015

The periodic rating defines the load which can be carried for the alternate periods of load and rest specified in the rating, the apparatus starting cold, and for the total time specified in the rating without causing any of the specified limitations to be exceeded.

Short-Time Rating

See 05.50.050.

Eight-Hour Rating of a Magnetic Contactor   25.40.020

The eight-hour rating of a magnetic contactor is the rating based on its ampere carrying capacity for eight hours, starting with new clean contact surfaces, under conditions of free ventilation with full rated voltage on the operating coil and without causing any of the established limitations to be exceeded.

GROUP 25—CONTROL EQUIPMENT
Section 95—Not Otherwise Classified

Ambient Temperature   25.95.005

Ambient temperature is the temperature of the surrounding cooling medium, such as gas or liquid, which comes into contact with the heated parts of the apparatus.

Barrier   25.95.010

A barrier is a partition for the insulation or isolation of electric circuits or electric arcs.

Control Battery   25.95.015

A control battery is a battery used as a source of energy for the control of an electrically operated device.

† A rating is arbitrary in the sense that it must necessarily be established by definite fixed standards and cannot, therefore, indicate the safe operating limit under all conditions which may occur.

Control-Circuit Transformer   25.95.020

A control-circuit transformer is a voltage transformer utilized to supply a voltage suitable for the operation of shunt coil magnetic devices.

Elementary Controller Wiring Diagram   25.95.025

An elementary controller wiring diagram is a diagram using symbols and a plan of connections to illustrate, in simple form, the scheme of control.

Controller Wiring Diagram   25.95.030

A controller wiring diagram is a diagram showing the electric connections between the parts comprising the controller, and indicating the external connections.

External Controller Wiring Diagram   25.95.035

An external controller wiring diagram is a diagram showing the electric connections between the controller terminals and outside points; such as connections from the line, to the motor, and to auxiliary devices.

Controller Construction Diagram   25.95.040

A controller construction diagram is a diagram indicating the physical arrangement of parts such as wiring, buses, resistor units, etc.

Example: A diagram showing the arrangement of grids and terminals in a grid type resistor.

Control Sequence Table   25.95.045

A control sequence table is a tabulation of the connections which are made for each successive position of the controller.

Fuse

See **20.20.005.**

Grounded Parts   25.95.055

Grounded parts are those parts which are so connected that, when the installation is complete, they are substantially of the same potential as the earth.

Interlock   25.95.060

An interlock is a device actuated by the operation of some other device with which it is directly associated, to govern succeeding operations of the same or allied devices.

NOTE: Interlocks may be either electrical or mechanical.

Jogging   25.95.065

(Inching)

Jogging is the quickly repeated closure of the circuit to start a motor from rest for the purpose of accomplishing small movements of the driven machine.

Live Parts

See **20.10.245.**

Magnet Brake   25.95.070

A magnet brake is a friction brake controlled by electromagnetic means.

Operating Overload   25.95.075

Operating overload is the overcurrent to which electric apparatus is subjected in the course of the normal operating conditions that it may encounter.

NOTE: The maximum operating overload is considered to be six times normal full-load current for alternating-current industrial motors and control apparatus; four times normal full-load current for direct-current industrial motors and control apparatus used for reduced-voltage starting; and ten times normal full-load current for direct-current industrial motors and control used for full-voltage starting.

NOTE: It should be understood that these overloads are currents that may persist for a very short time only, usually a matter of seconds.

Percentage Speed Reduction   25.95.080

In speed reduction of motors as accomplished by control apparatus the various resulting speeds are customarily expressed as a percentage of full rated load speed.

Solenoid   25.95.085

A solenoid is an electromagnet having an energizing coil approximately cylindrical in form and operating on a movable core or plunger.

See **05.45.170.**

Thermal Cutout   25.95.090

A thermal cutout is an overcurrent protective device which contains a heater element in addition to and affecting a fusible member which opens the circuit.

GROUP 30—INSTRUMENTS, METERS AND METER TESTING

SECTIONS

20 Instruments
40 Specific Instruments
50 Meters
55 Demand Meters

60 Meter Testing
70 Accessory Apparatus
80 Instrument Transformers
95 Not Otherwise Classified

Section 20—Instruments

Instrument   30.20.005

An instrument is a device for measuring the present value of the quantity under observation. An instrument may be an indicating instrument or a recording instrument.

The term "instrument" is used in two different senses; (a) instrument proper and (b) to include not only the instrument proper but, in addition, any necessary auxiliary devices, such as shunts, shunt leads, resistors, reactors, capacitors or instrument transformers.

The term "meter" is also used in a general sense to designate any type of measuring device including all types of electric measuring instruments. Such use as a suffix or as part of a compound word (e. g., voltmeter, frequency meter) is universally accepted. "Meter" may be used alone with this wider meaning when the context is such as to prevent confusion with the narrower meaning of "electricity meter".

See 30.50.010.

Indicating Instrument   30.20.010

An indicating instrument is an instrument in which the present value of the quantity measured is indicated by the position of a pointer relative to a scale.

Recording Instrument   30.20.015

(Recorder) (Graphic Instrument)

A recording instrument is an instrument which makes a graphic record of the value of a quantity as a function of time.

Direct-Acting Recording Instrument   30.20.020

A direct-acting recording instrument is one in which the marking device is mechanically connected to, and directly operated by the moving element.

Relay Type Recording Instrument   30.20.025

A relay type recording instrument is one in which the marking device is moved by a secondary driving force which is controlled by the moving element.

Instrument Proper   30.20.030

The instrument proper consists of the actuating mechanism together with those auxiliary devices (scale, resistors, shunts, etc.) which are built into the case or made a corporate part thereof.

Self-Contained Instrument   30.20.035

A self-contained instrument is an instrument which has all the necessary equipment built into the case or made a corporate part thereof.

See 30.20.030.

Auxiliary Device to an Instrument   30.20.040

An auxiliary device to an instrument is a separate piece of equipment used with an instrument to extend its range, increase its accuracy or otherwise assist in making a measurement.

Mechanism of an Indicating Instrument   30.20.045

The mechanism of an indicating instrument is the arrangement of parts for producing and controlling the motion of the pointer.

It includes all the essential parts necessary to produce these results but does not include the base, cover, scale or any parts, such as series resistors or shunts, whose function is to adapt the range of the instrument to the quantity to be measured.

Zero Adjuster   30.20.046

A zero adjuster is a device for bringing the pointer of an electric instrument to zero when the electrical quantity is zero.

Mechanism of a Recording Instrument   30.20.050

The mechanism of a recording instrument includes (a) the arrangement for producing and controlling the motion of the marking device; (b) the marking device; (c) the device (clockwork, constant-speed motor, or equivalent) for driving the chart at a controlled speed; (d) the parts necessary to carry the chart.

It includes all the essential parts necessary to produce these results but does not include the base, cover, fixed scale, chart or any parts, such as series resistors or shunts, whose function is to adapt the range of the instrument to the quantity to be measured.

Moving Element of an Instrument   30.20.055

The moving element of an instrument comprises those parts which move as a direct result of a variation in the electrical quantity which the instrument is measuring.

The weight of a moving element includes one-half the weight of the springs, if there are any. The weight is expressed in grams.

Current Circuit of an Instrument   30.20.060

The current circuit of an instrument is that conductor or winding of the instrument proper which carries the current of the circuit in which a given electrical quantity is to be measured, or a definite fraction of that current, or a current dependent upon it.

Voltage Circuit of an Instrument   30.20.065

The voltage circuit of an instrument is that conductor or winding of the instrument proper to which is applied the voltage of the circuit in which a given electrical quantity is to be measured, or a definite fraction of that voltage, or a voltage dependent upon it.

Fixed Scale of a Recording Instrument   30.20.070

A fixed scale is one rigidly attached to the recording instrument, and upon which the value of the recorded quantity at the time of observation may be read from the position of a pointer or its equivalent attached to or operated by the marking device.

Chart of a Recording Instrument   30.20.075

The chart of a recording instrument is the paper or other material upon which the graphic record is made.

Chart Scale of a Recording Instrument   30.20.080

The chart scale of a recording instrument is the scale marked on the chart. This may include a time scale or the scale of the electrical quantity being recorded, or both.

Scale Length of an Indicating Instrument   30.20.085

The scale length of an indicating instrument is the length of the path described by the end of the pointer in moving from one end of the scale to the other.

In the case of knife-edge pointers and others extending beyond the scale divisions, the pointers shall be considered as ending at the outer edge of the shortest scale divisions.

Scale Length of a Recording Instrument   30.20.090

The scale length of a recording instrument is the length of the path described by the marking device in moving from one end of the scale to the other.

Measurement Range of an Instrument   30.20.095

The measurement range of an instrument is that part of the total range throughout which the requirements for accuracy are to be met.

Torque of an Instrument   30.20.100

The torque of an instrument is the turning moment produced by the electrical quantity to be measured acting through the mechanism.

This is also termed the "deflecting torque", and in instruments having control systems is opposed by the controlling torque, which is the turning moment produced by the mechanism of the instrument tending to return it to a fixed position. Torque is expressed in millimeter-grams. The particular value of the torque for the condition of full-scale deflection should be designated "full-scale torque" and should be accompanied by a statement of the angle corresponding to this deflection.

Restoring Torque Gradient of an Instrument   30.20.105

The restoring torque gradient of an instrument is the rate of change, with respect to the deflection, of the resultant of the electric or electric and mechanical torques tending to restore the moving element to any position of equilibrium when displaced from that position.

It should be expressed as the rate of change in resultant turning moment in millimeter-grams per degree at that position.

Deflecting Force of a Recording Instrument   30.20.110

The deflecting force of a recording instrument is the force at the recording point, in the direction of its motion, produced by the electrical quantity to be measured acting through the mechanism.

With the marking device free of contact with the chart, the deflecting force is balanced by the controlling force. Deflecting force is expressed in grams. The particular value of the deflecting force for the condition of full-scale deflection should be designated "full-scale deflecting force" and should be accompanied by a statement of the travel of the marking device, in millimeters, corresponding to this deflection.

Restoring Force Gradient of a Direct-Acting Recording Instrument   30.20.115

The restoring force gradient of a direct-acting recording instrument is the rate of change, with respect to the displacement, of the resultant of the electric or electric and mechanical forces tending to restore the marking device to any position of equilibrium when displaced from that position.

It should be expressed in grams per centimeter and should be accompanied by statements of the length of the marking device in millimeters and the position of equilibrium to which it refers. The force gradient may be constant throughout the entire travel of the recording point, or it may vary greatly over this travel, depending upon the operating principles and the details of construction.

Period of an Instrument   30.20.120

The period of an instrument, sometimes called the "periodic time", is the time between two consecutive transits of the pointer (or marking device) in the same direction through the rest position.

Damping of an Instrument   30.20.125

The damping of an instrument is the dissipation of the kinetic energy of its moving element.

Two general classes of damping are distinguished: namely, (a) periodic, in which the pointer oscillates about the final position before coming to rest; (b) aperiodic, in which the pointer comes to rest without overshooting the rest position. The point of change between periodic and aperiodic damping is called critical damping.

Damping Factor of an Instrument   30.20.130

The damping factor of an instrument is the ratio of the deviations of the pointer (or marking device) in two consecutive swings from the position of equilibrium, the greater deviation being divided by the lesser.

For practical purposes it is sometimes convenient to express the performance of an instrument in terms of the reciprocal of the damping factor. This reciprocal is the ratio of the excess of the maximum momentary deflection (over the steady deflection) to the steady deflection, both expressed in angular degrees, and when expressed as a percentage is denoted by the term "percentage overshoot".

Responsiveness of an Instrument   30.20.135

The response time of an instrument is the time required for the pointer of the instrument to come to apparent rest after a specified change in the value of the measured quantity.

For portable instruments the pointer is to be considered as having come to apparent rest when it has reached the actual rest point within ± 0.2 percent of the scale length. For switchboard instruments the corresponding tolerance is ± 1 percent of the scale length.

Rating of an Instrument   30.20.140

The rating of an instrument is a designation assigned by the manufacturer to indicate its operating limitations.

The full-scale marking of an instrument does not necessarily correspond to its rating.

Accuracy of an Instrument   30.20.145

The accuracy of an instrument is a number or a quantity which defines its limit of error.

Error and Correction   30.20.150

The error of indication is the difference between the indication and the true value of the quantity being measured. It is the quantity which algebraically subtracted from the indication gives the true value. A positive error denotes that the indication of the instrument is greater than the true value.

The correction has the same numerical value as the error of indication, but the opposite sign. It is the quantity which algebraically added to the indication gives the true value. If T, I, E and C represent, respectively, the true value, the indicated value, the error, and the correction, the following equations hold:

$$E = I - T$$
$$C = T - I$$

Example: A voltmeter reads 112 volts when the voltage applied to its terminals is actually 110 volts.
Then

$$\text{Error} = 112 - 110 = +2 \text{ volts}$$
$$\text{Correction} = 110 - 112 = -2 \text{ volts}$$

Influence Upon an Instrument   30.20.155

The influence upon an instrument is measured by the effect upon the indication caused by a change in a specified single quantity or condition.

Among these are frequency influence, external-field influence, power-factor influence, temperature influence, voltage influence, position influence, friction influence (pen to paper in a recording instrument), inkwell influence (in a recording instrument), etc.

Electrodynamic Instrument   30.20.200

An electrodynamic instrument is an instrument which depends for its operation on the reaction between the current in one or more moving coils and the current in one or more fixed coils. (Also known as an electrodynamometer instrument.)

Electrostatic Instrument   30.20.205

An electrostatic instrument is an instrument which depends for its operation on the forces of attraction and/or repulsion between bodies charged with electricity.

Electrothermic Instrument   30.20.210

An electrothermic instrument is an instrument which depends for its operation on the heating effect of a current.

Two distinct types are (a) the expansion type, including the "hot-wire" and "hot-strip" instruments; (b) the thermocouple type.

Hot-Wire Instrument   30.20.215

A hot-wire instrument is an instrument which depends for its operation on the expansion by heat of a wire carrying a current.

The hot-strip instrument differs from the hot-wire instrument only in having a metallic strip in place of a wire.

See 30.20.210.

Thermocouple Instrument   30.20.220

A thermocouple instrument is an instrument in which one or more thermojunctions are heated directly or indirectly by an electric current, and supply a direct current which flows through the coil of a suitable direct-current mechanism, such as one of the permanent-magnet moving-coil type.

Induction Instrument   30.20.225

An induction instrument is an instrument which depends for its operation on the reaction between a magnetic flux (or fluxes) set up by one or more currents in fixed windings, and electric currents set up by electromagnetic induction in conducting parts of the moving system.

Moving-Iron Instrument   30.20.230

A moving-iron instrument is an instrument which depends for its operation on the reactions resulting from the current in one or more fixed coils acting upon one or more pieces of soft iron or magnetically similar materials in the moving system.

Various forms of this instrument (plunger, vane, repulsion, attraction, repulsion-attraction) are distinguished chiefly by mechanical features of construction.

The above definition is not intended to include the polarized-vane type of instrument which is applicable to direct-current measurements only.

Permanent-Magnet Moving-Coil Instrument   30.20.235
(D'Arsonval Instrument)*

A permanent-magnet moving-coil instrument is an instrument which depends for its operation on the reaction between the current in a movable coil and the field of a fixed permanent magnet.

Permanent-Magnet Moving-Iron Instrument   30.20.240

A permanent-magnet moving-iron instrument is an instrument which depends for its operation on the action of an iron vane in aligning itself in the resultant field of a permanent magnet and an adjacent coil carrying current.

Electronic (Thermionic) Instrument   30.20.245

An electronic (thermionic) instrument is an instrument which utilizes for its operation the action of an electronic (thermionic) tube.

Rectifier Instrument   30.20.250

A rectifier instrument is the combination of an instrument sensitive to direct current and a rectifying device whereby alternating currents (or voltages) may be measured.

The instrument proper is usually one of the unidirectional current types of mechanism; the instrument is specially suitable for the measurement of alternating currents of small magnitude.

* Deprecated.

Suppressed-Zero Instrument   30.20.255

A suppressed-zero instrument is an indicating or recording instrument in which the zero position is beyond the end of the scale.

Flush Type Instrument   30.20.260

A flush type instrument is an instrument which is designed to be mounted with its face projecting only slightly beyond the front of the panel.

Dustproof

See **95.90.125.**

Dust-Tight

See **95.90.130.**

Moistureproof

See **95.90.015.**

Moisturetight

See **95.90.025.**

Corrosion-Resistant

See **95.90.020.**

Submersible (Watertight)

See **95.90.145** and **95.90.195.**

GROUP 30—INSTRUMENTS, METERS AND METER TESTING
Section 40—Specific Instruments

Ammeter   30.40.005

An ammeter is an instrument for measuring electric current.

Ammeters are provided with a scale, usually graduated in amperes, milliamperes or microamperes.

Bridge   30.40.010

A bridge is an instrument which embodies part or all of a bridge circuit,† and by means of which one or more of the electrical constants of a bridge circuit may be determined.

The operation of a bridge consists of the insertion of a suitable electromotive force and a suitable detecting device in branches which can be made conjugate and which do not include the branch whose constants are to be determined, followed by the adjustment of one or more of the remaining branches until the response of the detecting device becomes zero or an amount measurable by the detector for the purpose of interpolation.

Corona Voltmeter   30.40.015

A corona voltmeter is a voltmeter in which voltage is determined by the inception of corona.

Crest Voltmeter   30.40.020

A crest voltmeter is a voltmeter depending for its indications upon the crest, or maximum value of the voltage applied to its terminals.

Crest voltmeters should have clearly marked on the instrument proper whether readings are in equivalent root-mean-square values or in true crest volts. It is preferred that the marking should be root-mean-square values of the sinusoidal wave having the same crest value as that of the wave measured.

Electrometer   30.40.025

An electrometer is an instrument for indicating or measuring potential difference by electrostatic means.

See **05.45.110** and **30.20.205.**

Electrostatic Voltmeter   30.40.030

An electrostatic voltmeter is a voltmeter depending for its action upon electrostatic forces.

† See **05.45.090.**

Faradmeter   30.40.035

A faradmeter is an instrument for measuring electric capacitance.

Faradmeters are provided with a scale usually graduated in microfarads.

Fluxmeter   30.40.040

A fluxmeter is an instrument for measuring magnetic flux.

Frequency Meter   30.40.045

A frequency meter is an instrument for measuring the frequency of an alternating current.

Galvanometer   30.40.050

A galvanometer is an instrument for indicating or measuring a small electric current, or a function of the current, by means of a mechanical motion derived from electromagnetic or electrodynamic forces which are set up as a result of the current.

Magnetometer   30.40.055

A magnetometer is an instrument for measuring the magnitude and sometimes also the direction of a magnetic force.

Ohmmeter   30.40.060

An ohmmeter is an instrument for measuring electric resistance.

Ohmmeters are provided with a scale, usually graduated in ohms or megohms.

Oscillograph   30.40.065

An oscillograph is an apparatus for producing a continuous curve representing the instantaneous values of a rapidly varying electrical quantity as a function of the time or of another electrical quantity.

Permeameter   30.40.070

A permeameter is an instrument for measuring the magnetic flux or flux density produced in a test specimen by a given magnetic intensity so that the magnetic permeability of the material may be computed.

Phase Meter   30.40.075

A phase meter is an instrument for measuring the difference in phase between two alternating quantities of the same frequency.

Potentiometer   30.40.080

A potentiometer is an instrument which embodies part or all of a potentiometer circuit,† and by means of which the value of an electromotive force or potential difference, in one of the arms of this circuit, may be measured in terms of one or more other electromotive forces or potential differences and the constants of the potentiometer circuit when the response of a suitable detecting device has been reduced to zero or to an amount which is measurable by the detecting device.

Power Factor Meter   30.40.085

A power factor meter is an instrument for measuring power factor.

Power factor meters are provided with a scale, usually graduated in power factor.

Reactive Factor Meter   30.40.090

A reactive factor meter is an instrument for measuring reactive factor.

Reactive Volt-Ampere Meter   30.40.095

(Var Meter)

A reactive volt-ampere meter is an instrument for measuring reactive volt-amperes.

Electric Telemetering   30.40.150

Electric telemetering is the indicating, recording or integrating of a quantity at a distance by electrical translating means.

Electric Telemeter   30.40.155

An electric telemeter is the complete measuring, transmitting and receiving apparatus for indicating, recording or integrating at a distance, by electrical translating means, the value of a quantity. (A telemeter which measures current is called a teleammeter; voltage, a televoltmeter; power, a telewattmeter. The names of the various component parts making up the telemeter are, in general, self-defining; e. g., the transmitter, pilot wires, receiver, indicator, etc.)

Direct-Relation Telemeter   30.40.160

A direct-relation telemeter is a telemeter in which the translating means (voltage, current, frequency, etc.) increases in value with increase in the measured quantity.

Inverse-Relation Telemeter   30.40.165

An inverse-relation telemeter is a telemeter in which the translating means (voltage, current, frequency, etc.) decreases in value with increase in the measured quantity.

Position Type Telemeter   30.40.170

A position type telemeter is a telemeter which employs the relative phase position between, or the magnitude relation of, two (or more) electrical quantities as the translating means.

Voltage Type Telemeter   30.40.175

A voltage type telemeter is a telemeter which employs voltage as the translating means.

Current Type Telemeter   30.40.180

A current type telemeter is a telemeter which employs current as the translating means.

Frequency Type Telemeter   30.40.185

A frequency type telemeter is a telemeter which employs frequency as the translating means.

Impulse Type Telemeter   30.40.190

An impulse type telemeter is a telemeter which employs electric impulses as the translating means.

Voltmeter   30.40.205

A voltmeter is an instrument for measuring voltage.

Voltmeters are provided with a scale, usually graduated in volts, millivolts or kilovolts.

Line-Drop Voltmeter Compensator   30.40.210

A line-drop voltmeter compensator is a device used in connection with a voltmeter which causes the latter to indicate the voltage at some distant point of the circuit.

Wattmeter   30.40.215

A wattmeter is an instrument for measuring electric power.

Wattmeters are provided with a scale, usually graduated in watts or kilowatts.

GROUP 30—INSTRUMENTS, METERS AND METER TESTING

Section 50—Meters

Electricity Meter   30.50.010

(Meter)

An electricity meter is a device that measures and registers the integral of an electrical quantity with respect to time.

The term "meter" is also used in a general sense to designate any type of measuring device including all types of electric measur-

ing instruments. Such use as a suffix or as part of a compound word (e. g., voltmeter, frequency meter) is universally accepted. "Meter" may be used alone with this wider meaning when the context is such as to prevent confusion with the narrower meaning here defined.

Watthour Meter   30.50.015

A watthour meter is an electricity meter that measures and registers electric energy in watthours (or kilowatthours).

† See 05.45.095.

Ampere-Hour Meter   30.50.020

An ampere-hour meter is an electricity meter that registers the quantity of electricity in ampere-hours.

Ampere-hour meters are sometimes adapted to register in kilowatthours at the rated voltage of the circuit.

Reactive Volt-Ampere-Hour Meter   30.50.025

(Var-Hour Meter)

A reactive volt-ampere-hour meter is a meter for measuring and registering reactive volt-ampere-hours (or reactive kilovolt-ampere-hours).

Coulometer   30.50.030

(Voltameter)

A coulometer is an electrolytic cell arranged for the measurement of a quantity of electricity by the chemical action produced.

Portable Standard Watthour Meter   30.50.035

(Rotating Standard)*

A portable standard watthour meter is a portable form of watthour meter usually provided with several current and voltage ranges and with dials indicating revolutions and fractions of a revolution of the rotating element, thus enabling an accurate comparison to be made between the standard and the meter under test.

Motor Type Watthour Meter   30.50.040

A motor type watthour meter consists essentially of a motor element in conjunction with a braking element in which the resultant speed is proportional to the power (i. e., rate at which energy is being delivered) and a register connected thereto by suitable gearing so as to count in terms of equivalent kilowatthours the revolutions of the rotating element.

Mercury Motor Meter   30.50.045

A mercury motor meter is a motor type meter in which a portion of the rotating element is immersed in mercury, which serves to direct the current through the driving element.

Induction Motor Meter   30.50.050

An induction motor meter is a motor type meter in which the rotating element moves under the reaction between the currents induced in it and a magnetic field.

Dial of a Meter   30.50.055

A dial of a meter is a graduated circle over which a dial pointer moves.

First Dial of a Meter   30.50.060

The first dial of a meter is the graduated circle over which the most rapidly moving dial pointer moves.

The test dial or dials, if any, are not considered.

Dial Train of a Meter   30.50.065

A dial train of a meter comprises all the gear wheels and pinions used to interconnect the dial pointers.

* Deprecated.

Dial Pointer of a Meter   30.50.070

A dial pointer of a meter is that part of the register which moves over the dial and points to the numbers on the divisions of the dial.

Gear Ratio   30.50.075

The gear ratio is the number of revolutions of the rotating element for one revolution of the first dial pointer.

Register of a Meter   30.50.080

The register is that part of the meter which registers the revolutions of the rotating element in terms of units of electric energy (or of quantity).

Standard Register   30.50.085

A standard register is a register in which each of the four dials is divided into ten equal parts, the division marks being numbered from zero to nine, and the gearing between the dial pointers is such that the relative movements of adjacent dial pointers are in opposite directions and in a 10 to 1 ratio.

Register Ratio   30.50.090

The register ratio is the number of revolutions of the wheel meshing with the worm or pinion on the rotating element, for one revolution of the first dial pointer.

Register Face   30.50.095

The register face is that part of the register on which the dials are printed.

Register Reading   30.50.100

A register reading is the numerical value indicated on the dials by the dial pointers. Neither the register constant nor the test dial or dials, if any exist, is considered.

Register Constant   30.50.105

The register constant is a factor used in conjunction with the register reading in order to ascertain, in the desired unit, the total amount of electric energy (or the total quantity of electricity) that has passed through the meter.

Registration of a Meter   30.50.110

The registration of a meter is the apparent amount of electric energy (or quantity of electricity) that has passed through the meter, as shown by the register reading. It is equal to the product of the register reading and the register constant. The registration during a given interval of time is equal to the product of the register constant and the difference between the register readings at the beginning and the end of the interval.

Rotating Element of a Meter   30.50.115

The rotating element of a meter is that part of the motor element which rotates.

In a watthour meter the element rotates at a speed substantially proportional to the power being integrated by the meter. In an ampere-hour meter the element rotates at a speed substantially proportional to the current being integrated by the meter.

Current Circuit of a Meter   30.50.120

The current circuit of a meter is that winding of the meter which carries the current of the circuit in which a given electrical quantity is to be registered, or a definite fraction of that current, or a current dependent upon it.

Voltage Circuit of a Meter   30.50.125

The voltage circuit of a meter is that winding of the meter to which is applied the voltage of the circuit in which a given electrical quantity is to be registered, or a definite fraction of that voltage, or a voltage dependent upon it.

GROUP 30—INSTRUMENTS, METERS AND METER TESTING
Section 55—Demand Meters

Demand Meter   30.55.005

A demand meter is a device which indicates or records the demand or maximum demand.

A demand meter records or indicates the maximum average load over any specified time interval, or the average load over a number of equal time intervals.

Electric Element of a Demand Meter   30.55.010

The electric element of a demand meter is that portion, the action or effect of which in response to the electrical quantity to be measured gives a measurement of that electrical quantity.

For example, the electric element of certain demand meters is similar to an ordinary ammeter or wattmeter of the deflection type, and in others it is a watthour meter or other integrating meter, and in still others it is a resistance unit which introduces a heating effect, which is interpreted in terms of amperes or watts.

Recording Element of a Demand Meter   30.55.015

The recording element of a demand meter is that mechanism or that feature of the device which records the measurement of the electrical quantity as related to the time interval of the device.

In many classes of demand meters this is distinct from the electric and timing elements, but in certain other classes the electric, timing and recording elements are interdependent through the principles employed, or through the design.

Timing Element of a Demand Meter   30.55.020

The timing element of a demand meter is that mechanism or that feature of the device through which the demand interval is introduced into the result.

While the principal function of the timing element of a demand meter is to measure the demand interval, its subsidiary function in the case of certain types of demand meters is to provide a record of the time of day at which any demand has occured. The timing element consists either of a clock or its equivalent (for example, an electric motor) or of a lagging device which delays the indications of the electric element.

Integrated-Demand Meter   30.55.025

An integrated-demand meter is one which indicates or records the demand obtained through integration.

Lagged-Demand Meter   30.55.030

A lagged-demand meter is one in which the indication of the maximum demand is subject to a characteristic time lag.

Excess Meter   30.55.035

An excess meter is a meter that records either exclusively or separately that portion of the energy consumption taken in addition to a predetermined load.

Multirate Meter   30.55.040

A multirate meter is a meter which registers at different rates or on different dials at different hours of the day.

GROUP 30—INSTRUMENTS, METERS AND METER TESTING
Section 60—Meter Testing

NOTE: Definitions **30.60.005** to **30.60.090**, inclusive, apply to tests of electricity meters (watthour meters) that are to be or are installed on the premises of customers of public service companies or corporations.

Installation Test of a Meter   30.60.005

An installation test of a meter is a test made within a limited period of time after installation of the meter on a consumer's premises.

Inspection of a Meter   30.60.010

An inspection of a meter is an examination of the meter and the conditions surrounding it for the purpose of discovering mechanical defects or conditions which are likely to be detrimental to its accuracy.

Such an examination may or may not include an approximate determination of the percentage accuracy of the meter.

Laboratory Test of a Meter   30.60.015

A laboratory test of a meter is a test made in the laboratory of the meter department of a public service corporation prior to the installation of the meter.

Office Test of a Meter   30.60.020

An office test of a meter is a test originating with the company and made to determine the cause of apparently abnormal registration of a meter.

Periodic Test of a Meter   30.60.025

A periodic test of a meter is a test made at regular intervals.

Referee Test of a Meter 30.60.030

A referee test of a meter is a test made in the presence of one or more representatives of regulatory bodies or a disinterested authority.

Repair Test of a Meter 30.60.035

A repair test of a meter is a test made after a meter has been repaired in service.

Request Test of a Meter 30.60.040

A request test of a meter is a test made upon request of a customer.

Service Test of a Meter 30.60.045

A service test of a meter is a test made at the place where the meter is installed.

Meter Watts 30.60.050

Meter watts is the term used to designate the ratio of registration in wattseconds to the number of seconds during which the registration took place.

Meter Watthours 30.60.055

Meter watthours is the actual registration in watt-hours for the meter test interval of the meter being tested.

Percentage of Accuracy of a Meter 30.60.060

The percentage of accuracy of a meter is the ratio, expressed as a percentage, of the registration in a given time to the true kilowatthours.

It is commonly referred to as the "accuracy", "percentage accuracy" or "percentage registration" of the meter.

Percentage Error of a Meter 30.60.065

The percentage error of a meter is the difference between its percentage of accuracy and one hundred percent (100%).

A meter whose percentage of accuracy is ninety-five percent (95%) is said to be five percent (5%) slow, or its error is minus five percent (−5%). A meter whose percentage of accuracy is one hundred and five percent (105%) is five percent (5%) fast, or its error is plus five percent (+5%).

Reference Performance of a Meter 30.60.070

The reference performance of a meter as established for each test furnishes a means of comparing the performance of the meter under normal (reference) and test conditions.

The variations from reference-performance accuracy are known as deviations from reference performance.

True Watts 30.60.075

True watts is a term used to designate the average rate at which electric energy is delivered through the meter during a meter test, as indicated by standard instruments.

Watthour Constant of a Meter 30.60.080

The watthour constant of a watthour meter is the registration of one revolution of the rotating element expressed in watthours.

Wattsecond Constant of a Meter 30.60.085

The wattsecond constant of a watthour meter is the registration of one revolution of the rotating element expressed in wattseconds.

Calibration Voltage 30.60.090

The calibration voltage is the voltage applied to a watthour meter during calibration or checking.

GROUP 30—INSTRUMENTS, METERS AND METER TESTING

Section 70—Accessory Apparatus

Series Resistor of an Instrument 30.70.005

A series resistor of an instrument is a resistor which forms an essential part of the voltage circuit of an instrument and is used to adapt the instrument to operate on some designated voltage or voltages. It may be included in the instrument's structure or it may be separate therefrom.

Instrument Multiplier 30.70.006

An instrument multiplier is a particular type of series resistor which is used to extend the voltage range of an instrument beyond some particular value for which the instrument is already complete.

Instrument Shunt 30.70.010

An instrument shunt is a particular type of resistor designed to be connected in parallel with the measuring device to extend the current range beyond some particular value for which the instrument is already complete.

Shunt Leads 30.70.015

Shunt leads are leads which connect the current circuit of an instrument to the shunt and are essentially a part of the instrument.

Compensatory Leads 30.70.020

Compensatory leads are connections between an instrument and the point of observation so contrived that variations in the properties of leads, such as variations of resistance with temperature, are so compensated that they do not affect the accuracy of the instrument readings.

Standard Cell

See **60.11.065.**

Resistance Standard 30.70.030

A resistance standard is a resistor which is adjusted with high accuracy to a specified value, is but slightly affected by variations in temperature and is substantially constant over long periods of time.

Volt Box 30.70.035

A volt box is a series of resistors so arranged that a definite fraction of a given voltage may be measured and the given voltage computed therefrom.

GROUP 30—INSTRUMENTS, METERS AND METER TESTING
Section 80—Instrument Transformers

Instrument Transformer   30.80.005

An instrument transformer is a transformer in which the conditions of current or voltage and of phase position in the primary circuit are represented with acceptable accuracy in the secondary circuit. Instrument transformers are classified according to their accuracy under specified conditions. An instrument transformer may be either an instrument current transformer or an instrument potential (voltage) transformer.

Current Transformer   30.80.010

A current transformer is a transformer, intended for measurement or control purposes, designed to have its primary winding connected in series with a circuit carrying the current to be measured or controlled.

Potential (Voltage) Transformer   30.80.015

A potential (voltage) transformer is a transformer, intended for measurement or control purposes, which is designed to have its primary winding connected in parallel with a circuit, the voltage of which is to be measured or controlled.

Primary and Secondary Windings   30.80.020

The terms "primary" and "secondary" serve to distinguish the windings in regard to energy flow, the primary being that which receives the energy from the supply circuit, and the secondary that which receives the energy by electromagnetic induction from the primary.

The term "primary winding" is intended to include the cable or bus bar which links with the iron circuit of certain types of current transformers to form a single effective primary turn.

Burden of an Instrument Transformer   30.80.025

The burden of an instrument transformer is that property of the circuit connected to its secondary which determines the flow of true and reactive power from the transformer. It is expressed either as total ohms impedance, together with the effective resistance and reactance components of the impedance, or as the total volt-amperes and power factor of the secondary devices and leads. The values expressing the burden apply to the condition of rated secondary current or voltage of the instrument transformer and a stated frequency, both of which must also be included with the burden expression.

The impedance expression is more applicable to current transformers, the volt-ampere power factor expression to potential (voltage) transformers.

True Ratio of an Instrument Transformer   30.80.030

The true ratio of a current or a potential instrument transformer is the ratio of rms primary current or voltage, as the case may be, to the rms secondary current or voltage under specified conditions.

Marked Ratio of an Instrument Transformer 30.80.035

The marked ratio of a current or a potential instrument transformer is the ratio of the primary current or voltage, as the case may be, to the secondary current or voltage, as given on the rating plate.

Ratio Correction Factor   30.80.040

The ratio correction factor is that factor by which the marked ratio of a current or a potential transformer must be multiplied to obtain the true ratio.

This factor is expressed as the ratio of true ratio to marked ratio. If both a current transformer and a potential transformer are used in conjunction with a wattmeter or watthour meter, the combined ratio correction factor is the product of the individual ratio correction factors.

Phase Angle of a Current Transformer   30.80.045

The phase angle of a current transformer is the angle between the primary current vector and the secondary current vector reversed. This angle is conveniently considered as positive when the reversed secondary current vector leads the primary current vector.

It is preferably designated by the symbol β.

Phase Angle of a Potential Transformer   30.80.050

The phase angle of a potential transformer is the angle between the primary voltage vector and the secondary voltage vector reversed. This angle is conveniently considered as positive when the reversed secondary voltage vector leads the primary voltage vector.

It is preferably designated by the symbol γ.

Phase Angle Correction Factor   30.80.055

The phase angle correction factor is that factor by which the reading of a wattmeter or watthour meter, operated from the secondary of a current or a potential transformer or both, must be multiplied to correct for the effect of phase displacement of current and voltage due to the measuring apparatus.

This factor equals the ratio of the true power factor to the apparent power factor.

Rated Primary Current of a Current Transformer 30.80.060

The rated primary current of a current transformer defines a current which can be carried for an unlimited period, without causing the established limitations to be exceeded.

Rated Primary Voltage   30.80.065

The rated primary voltage of a current transformer or of a potential (voltage) transformer defines a voltage which can be applied to the transformer for an unlimited period without causing the established limitations to be exceeded.

Rated Burden   30.80.070

The rated burden of an instrument transformer defines a burden which can be carried at a specified accuracy for an unlimited period without causing the established limitations to be exceeded.

ELECTRICAL DEFINITIONS

GROUP 30—INSTRUMENTS, METERS AND METER TESTING

Section 95—Not Otherwise Classified

To Test   30.95.005

To test an instrument or meter is to determine its performance characteristics while functioning under controlled conditions.

To Check   30.95.010

To check an instrument or meter is to determine the error of its indication or registration.

To Calibrate a Deflection Instrument   30.95.015

To calibrate a deflection instrument or meter is to adjust its mechanism or auxiliary devices until it indicates or registers correctly within limits.

This definition of "to calibrate" is to be considered as reflecting usage only in the electric meter and instrument industry and in electric metering practice.

Proof Test   30.95.020

A proof test of an instrument or meter is a test made to demonstrate that the device is in satisfactory condition in one or more respects.

Acceptance Test   30.95.025

An acceptance test is a test made to demonstrate the degree of compliance of an instrument or meter with purchaser's requirements.

GROUP 35—GENERATION, TRANSMISSION AND DISTRIBUTION

SECTIONS

10 Generation
15 Grounds and Grounding
20 Systems
40 Components of Systems

60 Details of Construction (Overhead)
70 Details of Construction (Underground)
80 Wires and Cables
90 Surges and Impulse Testing

Section 10—Generation

Combustion Control   35.10.005

Combustion control is the regulation of the rate of combination of fuel with air in a furnace.

Automatic Combustion Control   35.10.010

Automatic combustion control is a method of combustion control which is effected automatically by mechanical or electric devices.

Efficiency, Station or System   35.10.015

Efficiency, station or system, is the ratio of the energy delivered from the station or system to the energy received by it under specified conditions.

Excitation Voltage   35.10.030

Excitation voltage is the nominal voltage of the excitation circuit.

High-Speed Excitation System   35.10.035

A high-speed excitation system is an excitation system capable of changing its voltage rapidly in response to a change in the excited generator field circuit.

Frequency Control   35.10.040

Frequency control is the regulation of the frequency of a generating station or system within a narrow range.

Holding Frequency   35.10.045

(Take the Swings)

Holding frequency is a condition of operating a generator or station at substantially constant frequency irrespective of variations in load. A plant so operated is said to be regulating frequency.

Regulated Frequency   35.10.050

Regulated frequency is frequency so adjusted that the average value does not differ from a predetermined value by an appreciable amount.

Fuel Economy   35.10.060

Fuel economy is the ratio of the chemical energy input to a generating station to its net electric output.

NOTE: Fuel economy is usually expressed in Btu per kwhr.

Generating Station   35.10.065

A generating station is a plant wherein electric energy is produced from some other form of energy (e. g., chemical, mechanical or hydraulic) by means of suitable apparatus.

Automatic Station   35.10.070

An automatic station is a station (usually unattended) which, under predetermined conditions, goes into operation by an automatic sequence; which thereupon by automatic means maintains the required character of service; which goes out of operation by automatic sequence under other predetermined conditions and which provides protection against usual operating emergencies.

NOTE: This definition applies equally to Automatic Generating Station and to Automatic Substation.

Generating Station Auxiliaries   35.10.075

Generating station auxiliaries are accessory units of equipment necessary for the operation of the plant.

Example: Pumps, stokers, fans, etc.

NOTE: Auxiliaries may be classified as "essential auxiliaries" or those which must not sustain service interruptions of more than 15 seconds to 1 minute, such as boiler feed pumps, forced draft fans, pulverized fuel feeders, etc.; and "non-essential auxiliaries" which may, without serious effect, sustain service interruptions of 1 to 3 minutes or more, such as air pumps, clinker grinders, coal crushers, etc.

Generating Station Auxiliary Power   35.10.080

Generating station auxiliary power is the power required for operation of the generating station auxiliaries.

Generating Station Capacity   35.10.085

Generating station capacity is the maximum net power output that a generating station can produce without exceeding the operating limits of its component parts.

Generating Station Efficiency

See **35.10.015.**

Generating Station Reserve

See **35.10.190.**

House Turbine   35.10.096

A house turbine is a turbine installed to provide a source of auxiliary power.

Balanced Polyphase Load   35.10.100

A balanced polyphase load is a load to which symmetrical currents are supplied when it is connected to a system having symmetrical voltages.

NOTE: The term "balanced polyphase load" is applied also to a load to which are supplied two currents having the same wave form and rms value and differing in phase by 90 electrical degrees when it is connected to a quarter-phase (or two-phase) system having voltages of the same wave form and rms value.

Base Load   35.10.105

Base load is the minimum load over a given period of time.

Holding Load   35.10.110

Holding load is a condition of operating a generator or station at substantially constant load irrespective of variations in frequency. A plant so operated is said to be operating on base load.

See **35.10.105.**

Load Curve 35.10.115

Load curve is a curve of power *vs.* time showing the value of a specific load for each unit of the period covered.

Load Duration Curve 35.10.116

The load duration curve is a curve showing the total time, within a specified period, during which the load equalled or exceeded the power values shown.

Connected Load 35.10.120

The connected load on a system, or part of a system, is the sum of the continuous ratings of the load consuming apparatus connected to the system, or part of the system, under consideration.

Load Diversity 35.10.121

Load diversity is the difference between the sum of the peaks of two or more individual loads and the peak of the combined load.

Load Diversity Power 35.10.122

Load diversity power is the rate of transfer of energy necessary for the realization of a saving of system capacity brought about by load diversity.

Load Factor 35.10.125

Load factor is the ratio of the average load over a designated period of time to the peak load occurring in that period.

Plant Factor 35.10.126

(Plant Capacity Factor)

The plant factor is the ratio of the average load on the plant for the period of time considered, to the aggregate rating of all the generating equipment installed in the plant.

Capacity Factor 35.10.127

The capacity factor is the ratio of the average load on a machine or equipment for the period of time considered, to the rating of the machine or equipment.

Operation Factor 35.10.128

The operation factor is the ratio of the duration of actual service, of a machine or equipment, to the total duration of the period of time considered.

Output Factor 35.10.129

The output factor is the ratio of the actual energy output, in the period of time considered, to the energy output which would have occurred if the machine or equipment had been operating at its full rating throughout its actual hours of service during the period.

Loss Factor 35.10.130

The loss factor is the ratio of the average power loss to the peak load power loss, during a specified period of time.

Peak Load 35.10.135

Peak load is the maximum load consumed or produced by a unit or group of units in a stated period of time. It may be the maximum instantaneous load or the maximum average load over a designated interval of time.

NOTE: Maximum average load is ordinarily used. In commercial transactions involving peak load (peak power) it is taken as the average load (power) during a time interval of specified duration occurring within a given period of time, that time interval being selected during which the average power is greatest.

Dump Power 35.10.160

Dump power is hydro power in excess of load requirements that is made available by surplus water.

Peak Power

See **35.10.135.**

Firm Power 35.10.170

Firm power is the power intended to be always available even under emergency conditions.

Prime Power 35.10.175

Prime power is the maximum potential power (chemical, mechanical or hydraulic) constantly available for transformation into electric power.

Cold Reserve 35.10.184

Cold reserve is that reserve generating capacity available for service but not in operation.

Hot Reserve 35.10.185

Hot reserve is that reserve generating capacity in operation but not in service.

Reserve Equipment 35.10.190

Reserve equipment is the installed equipment in excess of that required to carry peak load.

NOTE: Reserve equipment not in operation is sometimes referred to as "Standby Equipment".

Spinning Reserve 35.10.195

Spinning reserve is that reserve generating capacity connected to the bus and ready to take load.

System Reserve 35.10.200

System reserve is the capacity, in equipment and conductors, installed on the system in excess of that required to carry the peak load.

Run-of-River Station 35.10.205

Run-of-river station is a hydroelectric generating station which utilizes the stream flow without storage.

Spare Equipment 35.10.225

Spare equipment is equipment complete or in parts, on hand for repair or replacement.

See **35.10.190.**

Standby

See **35.10.190.**

Stream Flow 35.10.245

Stream flow is the quantity rate of water passing a given point.

GROUP 35—GENERATION, TRANSMISSION AND DISTRIBUTION
Section 15—Grounds and Grounding

Ground 35.15.005

(Earth)†

A ground is a conducting connection, whether intentional or accidental, between an electric circuit or equipment and earth, or to some conducting body which serves in place of the earth.

Grounded 35.15.010

(Earthed)†

Grounded means connected to earth or to some conducting body which serves in place of the earth.

Ground-Return Circuit 35.15.015

(Earth-Return Circuit)

A ground-return circuit is a circuit in which the earth is utilized to complete the circuit.

Ground Current 35.15.020

A ground current is any current flowing in the earth.

NOTE: Specifically, currents flowing to earth through ground conductors or currents flowing in conductors embedded in the earth are commonly referred to as ground currents.

Voltage to Ground 35.15.025

The voltage to ground is the voltage between any live conductor of a circuit and earth.

NOTE: Where safety considerations are involved, the voltage to ground for ungrounded circuits shall be taken as the highest voltage between the conductors of the circuit.

Rating of a Ground (Grounding) Transformer

See 15.20.190.

Ground Indication 35.15.040

A ground indication is an indication of the presence of a ground on one or more of the normally ungrounded conductors of a system.

Things Grounded

Grounded Parts 35.15.060

Grounded parts are those parts which are so connected that they are intentionally grounded.

Grounded Capacitance

See 05.15.075.

Grounded Conductor 35.15.065

A grounded conductor is a conductor which is intentionally grounded, either solidly or through a current-limiting device.

Grounded Circuit 35.15.070

A grounded circuit is a circuit in which one conductor or point (usually the middle wire or neutral point of transformer or generator windings) is intentionally grounded, either solidly or through a current-limiting device.

† British.

Grounded System 35.15.075

A grounded system is a system of conductors in which at least one conductor or point (usually the middle wire or neutral point of transformer or generator windings) is intentionally grounded, either solidly or through a current-limiting device.

Grounded Concentric Wiring System 35.15.080

A grounded concentric wiring system is a grounded system in which the external (outer) conductor is solidly grounded and completely surrounds the internal (inner) conductor throughout its length. The external conductor is usually uninsulated.

Parts Used in Grounding

Grounding Electrode 35.15.100

(Ground Electrode)

A grounding electrode is a conductor imbedded in the earth, used for maintaining ground potential on conductors connected to it, and for dissipating into the earth current conducted to it.

Grounding Connection 35.15.105

(Ground Connection)

A grounding connection is a connection used in establishing a ground and consists of a grounding conductor, a grounding electrode and the earth (soil) which surrounds the electrode.

Grounding Conductor 35.15.110

(Ground Conductor)

A grounding conductor is a conductor used to connect an equipment, device or wiring system with a grounding electrode or electrodes.

Ground Wire of an Overhead Line 35.15.115

A ground wire of an overhead line is a conductor having grounding connections at intervals, which is suspended usually above, but not necessarily over the line conductor to provide a degree of protection against lightning discharges.

Guard Wire 35.15.120

A guard wire is a grounded wire erected near a low-voltage circuit or public crossing in such a position that a high-voltage overhead conductor cannot come into accidental contact with the low-voltage circuit, or with persons or objects on the crossing, without first becoming grounded by contact with the guard wire.

System Grounding Conductor 35.15.125

A system grounding conductor is an auxiliary solidly grounded conductor which connects together the individual grounding conductors in a given area.

NOTE: This conductor is not normally a part of any current-carrying circuit including the system neutral.

See 35.40.080.

Ground Plate 35.15.130

(Grounding Plate)

A ground plate is a plate of conducting material buried in the earth to serve as a grounding electrode.

Ground Clamp 35.15.140

(Grounding Clamp)

A ground clamp is a clamp used in connecting a grounding conductor to a grounding electrode or to a thing grounded.

Ground Lug 35.15.145

A ground lug is a lug used in connecting a grounding conductor to a grounding electrode or to a thing grounded.

Ground Cable Bond 35.15.150

A ground cable bond is a cable bond used for grounding the armor and/or sheaths of cables.

Ground Conduit 35.15.155

A ground conduit is a conduit used solely to contain one or more grounding conductors.

Ground Outlet 35.15.160

(Safety Outlet)*

A ground outlet is an outlet equipped with a receptacle of the polarity type, having, in addition to the current carrying contacts, one grounded contact which can be used for the connection of an equipment grounding conductor.

NOTE: This type of outlet is used for connection of portable appliances.

Ground Relay

See 20.25.175.

Ground Transformer

(Grounding Transformer)

See 15.20.045.

Ground Detector 35.15.175

A ground detector is an instrument or an equipment used for indicating the presence of a ground on an ungrounded system.

Ground Bus 35.15.180

A ground bus is a bus used to connect a number of grounding conductors to one or more grounding electrodes.

Ground Switch 35.15.185

(Grounding Switch)

A ground switch is a switch used to connect or disconnect a grounding conductor.

See 20.10.150.

_____

* Deprecated.

Degree or Manner of Grounding

Solidly Grounded 35.15.200

(Directly Grounded)

Solidly grounded means grounded through an adequate ground connection in which no impedance has been inserted intentionally.

NOTE: "Adequate" as used herein means "suitable for the purpose intended".

Effectively Grounded 35.15.205

Effectively grounded means grounded through a ground connection of sufficiently low impedance (inherent and/or intentionally added) that fault grounds which may occur cannot build up voltages dangerous to connected equipment.

Resistance Grounded 35.15.210

Resistance grounded means grounded through a resistance.

Reactance Grounded 35.15.215

Reactance grounded means grounded through a reactance.

NOTE: The reactance may be in the form of a reactor, a ground transformer, or one or more power transformers or generators, the remaining power transformers or generators operating with isolated neutral.

Kinds of Grounds

Interior Wiring System Ground 35.15.225

An interior wiring system ground is a ground connection to one of the current carrying conductors of an interior wiring system.

Equipment Ground 35.15.230

An equipment ground is a ground connection to non-current-carrying metal parts of a wiring installation or of electric equipment, or both.

Ground System of an Antenna

See 65.30.105.

Service Ground 35.15.240

A service ground is a ground connection to a service equipment and/or a service conductor.

Neutral Ground 35.15.245

A neutral ground is a ground connection to the neutral point or points of a circuit, transformer, rotating machine or system.

GROUP 35—GENERATION, TRANSMISSION AND DISTRIBUTION
Section 20—Systems

Alternating-Current Distribution   35.20.005

Alternating-current distribution is the supply to points of utilization of electric energy by alternating current from its source or one or more main receiving stations.

NOTE: Generally a voltage is employed which is not higher than that which could be delivered or utilized by rotating electric machinery. Step-down transformers of a capacity much smaller than that of the line are usually employed as links between the moderate voltage of distribution and the lower voltage of the consumer's apparatus.

Direct-Current Distribution   35.20.010

Direct-current distribution is the supply to points of utilization of electric energy by direct current from its point of generation or conversion.

Edison Distribution System   35.20.015

An Edison distribution system is a three-wire direct-current system, usually about 120–240 volts, for combined light and power service from a single set of mains.

Network Primary Distribution System   35.20.021

A network primary distribution system is a system of alternating-current distribution in which the primaries of the distribution transformers are connected to a common network supplied from the generating station or substation distribution buses.

Network Secondary Distribution System   35.20.022

A network secondary distribution system is a system of alternating-current distribution in which the secondaries of the distribution transformers are connected to a common network for supplying light and power directly to consumers' services.

Primary Distribution System   35.20.025

A primary distribution system is a system of alternating-current distribution for supplying the primaries of distribution transformers from the generating station or substation distribution buses.

Secondary Distribution System   35.20.030

A secondary distribution system is a low-voltage alternating-current system which connects the secondaries of distribution transformers to the consumers' services.

See 35.20.005.

Series Distribution System   35.20.035

A series distribution system is a distribution system for supplying energy to units of equipment connected in series.

Closed Loop Series Street Lighting System   35.20.040

A closed (or parallel) loop series street lighting system is one which employs two-wire series circuits in which the return wire is always adjacent.

Constant-Current Street Lighting System   35.20.045

(Series Street Lighting System)

A constant-current street lighting system is a street lighting system employing a series circuit in which the current is maintained substantially constant.

NOTE: Special generators or rectifiers are used for direct current while suitable regulators or transformers are used for alternating current.

Mixed Loop Series Street Lighting System   35.20.050

A mixed loop series street lighting system is one which comprises both open loops and closed loops.

Multiple Street Lighting System   35.20.055

A multiple street lighting system is a system in which street lights, connected in multiple, are supplied from a low-voltage distribution system.

Open Loop Series Street Lighting System   35.20.060

An open loop series street lighting system is one in which the circuits each consist of a single line wire which is connected from lamp to lamp and returned by a separate route to the source of supply.

Cascade Control of a Street Lighting System   35.20.061

Cascade control of a street lighting system is a method of turning street lights on and off in sections, each section being controlled by the energizing and deenergizing of the preceding section.

Balanced Polyphase System   35.20.065

A balanced polyphase system is a polyphase system in which both the currents and voltages are symmetrical.

NOTE: The term "balanced polyphase system" is applied also to a quarter-phase (or two-phase) system in which the voltages have the same wave form and rms value and in which the currents have the same wave form and rms value and differ in phase by 90 electrical degrees.

Balanced Three-Wire System   35.20.070

A balanced three-wire system is a three-wire system in which no current flows in the conductor connected to the neutral point of the supply.

See 35.20.140.

Demand of an Installation or System   35.20.075

The demand of an installation or system is the load at the receiving terminals averaged over a specified interval of time.

NOTE: Demand is expressed in kilowatts, amperes or other suitable units.

Maximum Demand   35.20.076

The maximum demand of an installation or system is the greatest of all the demands which have occurred during a given period of time.

NOTE: The maximum demand is determined by measurement, according to specification, over a definitely prescribed time interval.

See 30.55.005.

Demand Factor   35.20.077

The demand factor is the ratio of the maximum demand of a system, or part of a system, to the total connected load of the system, or part of system, under consideration.

Diversity Factor   35.20.078

The diversity factor is the ratio of the sum of the individual maximum demands of the various subdivisions of a system, or part of a system, to the maximum demand of the whole system, or part under consideration.

Utilization Factor   35.20.079

The utilization factor is the ratio of the maximum demand of a system, or part of a system, to the rated capacity of the system, or part of the system, under consideration.

Low-Voltage System   35.20.095

A low-voltage system is an electric system having an operating voltage less than 750 volts.

Radial System   35.20.100

A radial system is a system in which independent feeders branch out radially from a common source of supply.

Voltage Drop (in a supply system)   35.20.110

Voltage drop (in a supply system) is the difference between the voltages at the transmitting and receiving ends of a feeder, main or service.

With alternating current the voltages are not necessarily in phase, and hence the voltage drop is not necessarily equal to the algebraic sum of the voltage drops along the several conductors.

System Interconnection   35.20.120

System interconnection is the connecting together of two or more power systems.

Three-Phase Three-Wire System   35.20.125

A three-phase three-wire system is a system of alternating-current supply comprising three conductors between successive pairs of which are maintained alternating differences of potential successively displaced in phase by one-third of a period.

Three-Phase Four-Wire System   35.20.130

A three-phase four-wire system is a system of alternating-current supply comprising four conductors, three of which are connected as in a three-phase three-wire system, the fourth being connected to the neutral point of the supply, which may be grounded.

Three-Phase Seven-Wire System   35.20.135

A three-phase seven-wire system is a system of alternating-current supply from groups of three single-phase transformers connected in Y so as to obtain a three-phase four-wire grounded neutral system for lighting and a three-phase three-wire grounded neutral system of a higher voltage for power, the neutral wire being common to both systems.

Three-Wire System   35.20.140

A three-wire system (d-c or single-phase a-c) is a system of electric supply comprising three conductors, one of which (known as the "neutral wire") is maintained at a potential midway between the potential of the other two (referred to as the outer conductors).

NOTE: Part of the load may be connected directly between the outer conductors, the remainder being divided as evenly as possible into two parts each of which is connected between the neutral and one outer conductor.

There are thus two distinct voltages of supply, the one being twice the other.

Two-Phase Three-Wire System   35.20.145

A two-phase three-wire system is a system of alternating-current supply comprising three conductors between one of which (known as the common return) and each of the other two are maintained alternating differences of potential displaced in phase by one-quarter of a period with relation to each other.

Two-Phase Four-Wire System   35.20.150

A two-phase four-wire system is a system of alternating-current supply comprising two pairs of conductors between one pair of which is maintained an alternating difference of potential displaced in phase by one-quarter of a period from an alternating difference of potential of the same frequency maintained between the other pair.

Two-Phase Five-Wire System   35.20.155

A two-phase five-wire system is a system of alternating-current supply comprising five conductors, four of which are connected as in a four-wire two-phase system, the fifth being connected to the neutral points of each phase.

NOTE: The neutral is usually grounded. Although this type of system is usually known as the two-phase five-wire system, it is strictly a four-phase five-wire system.

Two-Wire System   35.20.160

A two-wire system (d-c or single-phase a-c) is a system of electric supply comprising two conductors between which the load is connected.

Ungrounded System   35.20.165

(Insulated Supply System)

An ungrounded system is one in which no point is deliberately connected to earth except through potential or ground detecting transformers or other very high impedance devices.

Alternating-Current Transmission   35.20.170

Alternating-current transmission is the transfer of electric energy by alternating current from its source to one or more main receiving stations for subsequent distribution.

NOTE: Generally a voltage is employed which is higher than that which would be delivered or utilized by electric machinery. Transformers of a capacity comparable to that of the line are usually employed as links between the high voltage of transmission and the lower voltage used for distribution or utilization.

Direct-Current Transmission   35.20.175

Direct-current transmission is the transfer of electric energy by direct current from its source to one or more main receiving stations.

NOTE: For transmitting large blocks of power high voltage may be used such as obtained with generators in series, rectifiers, etc.

Thury Transmission System 35.20.190

The Thury transmission system is a system of direct-current transmission with constant current and a variable high voltage.

NOTE: High voltage used on this system is obtained by connecting series direct-current generators in series at the generating station; and is utilized by connecting series direct-current motors in series at the substations.

Stability 35.20.200

Stability, when used with reference to a power system, is that attribute of the system, or part of the system, which enables it to develop restoring forces between the elements thereof, equal to or greater than the disturbing forces so as to restore a state of equilibrium between the elements.

NOTE: If automatic devices are used to aid stability their use will modify the steady-state and transient stability terms to:

Steady-state stability with automatic devices
Transient stability with automatic devices

Automatic devices as defined for this purpose are those devices which are operating to increase stability during the period preceding and following a disturbance as well as during the disturbance. Thus relays and circuit breakers are excluded from this classification and all forms of voltage regulators included. Devices for inserting and removing shunt or series impedance may or may not come within this classification depending upon whether or not they are operating during the periods preceding and following the disturbance.

Steady-State Stability 35.20.201

Steady-state stability is a condition which exists in a power system if it operates with stability when there is no aperiodic disturbance on the system.

See 35.20.200.

Transient Stability 35.20.202

Transient stability is a condition which exists in a power system if, after an aperiodic disturbance has taken place, the system regains steady-state stability.

See 35.20.200.

Stability Limit 35.20.203

(Power Limit)

A stability limit is the maximum power flow possible through some particular point in the system when the entire system or the part of the system to which the stability limit refers is operating with stability.

Steady-State Stability Limit 35.20.204

(Steady-State Power Limit)

The steady-state stability limit is the maximum power flow possible through some particular point in the system when the entire system or the part of the system to which the stability limit refers is operating with steady-state stability.

Transient Stability Limit 35.20.205

(Transient Power Limit)

The transient stability limit is the maximum power flow possible through some particular point in the system when the entire system or the part of the system to which the stability limit refers is operating with transient stability.

Stability Factor 35.20.206

Stability factor is the ratio of a stability limit (power limit) to the nominal power flow at the point of the system to which the stability limit is referred.

NOTE: In determining stability factors it is essential that the nominal power flow be specified in accordance with the one of several bases of computation such as rating or capacity of, or average or maximum load carried by the equipment or the circuits.

Steady-State Stability Factor 35.20.207

The steady-state stability factor of a system or part of a system is the ratio of the steady-state stability limit to the nominal power flow at the point of the system to which the stability limit is referred.

See 35.20.206.

Transient Stability Factor 35.20.208

The transient stability factor of a system or part of a system is the ratio of the transient stability limit to the nominal power flow at the point of the system to which the stability limit is referred.

See 35.20.206.

GROUP 35—GENERATION, TRANSMISSION AND DISTRIBUTION

Section 40—Components of Systems

Center of Distribution 35.40.005

The center of distribution is the point from which the electric energy must be supplied if the minimum weight of conducting material is to be used.

NOTE: The center of distribution is commonly considered to be that fixed point which, in practice, most nearly meets the ideal conditions stated above.

Circuit 35.40.010

A circuit is a conducting part or a system of conducting parts through which an electric current is intended to flow.

Balanced Circuit 35.40.015

A balanced circuit is a circuit in which there are substantially equal currents, either alternating or direct, in all main wires and substantially equal voltages between main wires and between each main wire and neutral (if one exists).

Leg of a Circuit 35.40.025

A leg of a circuit is any one of the conductors of an electric supply circuit between which is maintained the maximum supply voltage.

Multiple Circuit 35.40.030

A multiple circuit consists of two or more circuits connected in parallel.

Polyphase Circuit 35.40.035

A polyphase circuit is a circuit of more than a single phase. This term is ordinarily applied to symmetrical systems.

See 05.21.090.

Quarter-Phase or Two-Phase Circuit 35.40.040

A quarter-phase or two-phase circuit is a combination of circuits energized by alternating electromotive forces which differ in phase by a quarter of a cycle, *i. e.*, 90 degrees.

NOTE: In practice the phases may vary several degrees from the specified angle.

Series Circuit 35.40.045

A series circuit is a circuit supplying energy to a number of devices connected in series, *i. e.*, the same current passes through each device in completing its path to the source of supply.

Single-Phase Circuit 35.40.050

A single-phase circuit is a circuit energized by a single alternating electromotive force.

NOTE: A single-phase circuit is usually supplied through two wires. The currents in these two wires, counted outward from the source, differ in phase by 180 degrees or a half cycle.

See 05.21.035.

Six-Phase Circuit 35.40.055

A six-phase circuit is a combination of circuits energized by alternating electromotive forces which differ in phase by one-sixth of a cycle, *i. e.*, 60 degrees.

NOTE: In practice the phases may vary several degrees from the specified angle.

Three-Phase Circuit 35.40.060

A three-phase circuit is a combination of circuits energized by alternating electromotive forces which differ in phase by one-third of a cycle, *i. e.*, 120 degrees.

NOTE: In practice the phases may vary several degrees from the specified angle.

Two-Wire Circuit 35.40.065

A two-wire circuit is a metallic circuit formed by two adjacent conductors insulated from each other.

Common Return 35.40.070

A common return is a return conductor common to several circuits.

Negative Conductor 35.40.075

A negative conductor is a conductor connected to the negative terminal of a source of supply.

NOTE: A negative conductor is frequently used as an auxiliary return circuit in a system of electric traction.

Neutral Conductor 35.40.080

A neutral conductor is that conductor of an electric supply system that is connected to a neutral point of the system.

Positive Conductor 35.40.085

A positive conductor is a conductor connected to the positive terminal of a source of supply.

Feeder 35.40.095

A feeder is a conductor or group of conductors connecting (a) two generating stations, (b) two substations, (c) a generating station and a substation or feeding point, or (d) a substation and a feeding point.

See "Direct Feeder"—35.40.100, "Distribution Feeder"—35.40.106, "Interconnection Tie"—35.40.190, "Loop Feeder"—35.40.110, "Multiple Feeder"—35.40.115, "Network Feeder"—35.40.120, "Radial Feeder"—35.40.135, "Teed Feeder"—35.40.155, "Tie Feeder"—35.40.160, "Transmission Feeder"—35.40.165, "Trunk Feeder"—35.40.170.

Direct Feeder 35.40.100

A direct feeder is a feeder which connects a generating station, substation or other supply point to one point of utilization.

See 35.40.135.

Distribution Feeder

See 35.40.106 and 35.40.107.

Primary Distribution Feeder 35.40.106

A primary distribution feeder is a feeder operating at primary voltage supplying a distribution circuit.

NOTE: A primary feeder is usually considered as that portion of the primary conductors between the substation or point of supply and the center of distribution.

Secondary Distribution Feeder 35.40.107

A secondary distribution feeder is a feeder operating at secondary voltage supplying a distribution circuit.

Loop Feeder 35.40.110

A loop feeder consists of a number of tie feeders in series, forming a closed loop.

NOTE: There are two routes by which any point on a loop feeder can receive electric energy, so that the flow can be in either direction.

Multiple Feeder 35.40.115

A multiple feeder consists of two or more feeders connected in parallel.

Network Feeder 35.40.120

A network feeder is a feeder that supplies energy to a network.

Parallel Feeder

See 35.40.115.

Primary Transmission Feeder 35.40.130

A primary transmission feeder is a feeder connected to a primary transmission circuit.

Radial Feeder 35.40.135

A radial feeder is a feeder supplying electric energy to a substation or a feeding point which receives energy by no other means.

NOTE: The normal flow of energy in such a feeder is in one direction only.

Radial Distribution Feeder

See **35.40.135.**

Radial Transmission Feeder

See **35.40.135.**

Single Feeder   35.40.150

A single feeder is a feeder which forms the only connection between two points, along the route considered.

Teed Feeder   35.40.155

A teed feeder is a feeder which supplies two or more feeding points.

Tie Feeder   35.40.160

A tie feeder is a feeder which is connected at each end to a source of electric energy.

NOTE: The source of energy may be a generating system, substation or feeding point. The normal flow of energy in such a feeder may be in either direction.

Transmission Feeder   35.40.165

A transmission feeder is a feeder forming part of a transmission circuit.

Trunk Feeder   35.40.170

A trunk feeder is a feeder connecting two generating stations or a generating station and an important substation.

Floating Neutral   35.40.175

A floating neutral is one whose voltage to ground is free to vary when circuit conditions change.

Direct-Current Neutral Grid   35.40.180

A direct-current neutral grid is a network of neutral conductors, usually grounded, formed by connecting together within a given area all of the neutral conductors of a low-voltage direct-current supply system.

Secondary Neutral Grid   35.40.185

A secondary neutral grid is a network of neutral conductors, usually grounded, formed by connecting together within a given area all the neutral conductors of individual transformer secondaries of the supply system.

Interconnection Tie   35.40.190

An interconnection tie is a feeder interconnecting two electric supply systems.

NOTE: The normal flow of energy in such a feeder may be in either direction.

Distribution Trunk Line

See **35.40.196** and **35.40.197.**

Primary Distribution Trunk Line   35.40.196

A primary distribution trunk line is a line acting as a main source of supply to a distribution system.

Secondary Distribution Trunk Line   35.40.197

A secondary distribution trunk line is a line acting as a main source of supply to a secondary distribution system.

Duplicate Lines   35.40.200

Duplicate lines are lines of substantially the same capacity and characteristics, normally operated in parallel, connecting the same supply point with the same distribution point.

Electric Supply Lines   35.40.205

Electric supply lines are those conductors and their necessary supporting or containing structures which are located entirely outside of buildings and are used for conveying electric energy.

NOTE: This does not include open wiring on buildings, in yards or similar locations where spans are less than 20 feet, and all the precautions required for stations or utilization equipment, as the case may be, are observed.

Short-Circuit   35.40.208

A short-circuit is an abnormal connection of relatively low resistance, whether made accidentally or intentionally, between two points of different potential in a circuit.

Leakage Current   35.40.209

Leakage current is a stray current of relatively small value which flows through or across the surface of solid or liquid insulation when a voltage is impressed across the insulation.

Fault Current   35.40.210

A fault current is a current that flows from one conductor to ground or to another conductor owing to an abnormal connection (including an arc) between the two.

NOTE: A fault current flowing to ground may be called a ground fault current.

Primary Fault   35.40.211

A primary fault is the initial breakdown of the insulation of a conductor, usually followed by a flow of power current.

Secondary Fault   35.40.212

A secondary fault is an insulation breakdown occurring as a result of a primary fault.

Fault (wire or cable)   35.40.213

A wire or cable fault is a partial or total local failure in the insulation or continuity of a conductor.

Transmission Line   35.40.215

A transmission line is a line used for electric power transmission.

Charging Current of a Transmission Line   35.40.216

Charging current of a transmission line is the current that flows into the capacitance of a transmission line when voltage is applied at its terminals.

Trunk Transmission Line   35.40.220

A trunk transmission line is a transmission line acting as a source of main supply to a number of other transmission circuits.

Mains

See **35.40.231** and **35.40.235.**

Distribution Main

See **35.40.231** and **35.40.235.**

Primary Distribution Mains   35.40.231

Primary distribution mains are the conductors which feed from the center of distribution to direct primary loads or to transformers which feed secondary circuits.

Secondary Distribution Mains   35.40.235

Secondary distribution mains are the conductors connected to the secondaries of distribution transformers from which consumers' services are supplied.

Electric Power Substation   35.40.240

An electric power substation is an assemblage of equipment for purposes other than generation or utilization, through which electric energy in bulk is passed for the purpose of switching or modifying its characteristics. Service equipment, distribution transformer installations or other minor distribution or transmission equipment are not classified as substations.

NOTE: A substation is of such size or complexity that it incorporates one or more buses, a multiplicity of circuit breakers, and usually is either the sole receiving point of commonly more than one supply circuit, or it sectionalizes the transmission circuits passing through it by means of circuit breakers.

Network   35.40.245

A network is an aggregation of interconnected conductors, consisting of feeders, mains and services for the distribution of electric energy.

Distribution Network

See **35.40.251** and **35.40.252.**

Primary Distribution Network   35.40.251

A primary distribution network is a network consisting of primary distribution mains.

Secondary Distribution Network   35.40.252

A secondary distribution network is a network consisting of secondary distribution mains.

Pilot Wire Controlled Network   35.40.255

A pilot wire controlled network is a network whose switching devices are controlled by means of pilot wires.

Primary Network   35.40.260

A primary network is a network supplying the primaries of transformers whose secondaries may be independent or connected to a secondary network.

See **35.40.251.**

Transmission Network   35.40.265

A transmission network is a group of interconnected transmission lines or feeders.

Pilot Wire   35.40.270

A pilot wire is an auxiliary conductor used in connection with remote measuring devices or for operating apparatus at a distant point.

Feeding Point   35.40.275

A feeding point is the point of junction of a distribution feeder with a distribution main or service connection.

Neutral Point   35.40.280

The neutral point of a system is that point which has the same potential as the point of junction of a group of equal non-reactive resistances if connected at their free ends to the appropriate main terminals or lines of the system.

NOTE: The number of such resistances is 2 for direct-current or single-phase alternating-current, 4 for two-phase (applicable to 4-wire systems only) and 3 for three-, six- or twelve-phase systems.

Current-Carrying Part   35.40.285

Current-carrying part is a conducting part intended to be connected in an electric circuit to a source of voltage.

NOTE: Non-current-carrying parts are those not intended to be so connected.

Service   35.40.290

A service is the conductors and equipment for delivering energy from the main or feeder or from the transformer to the wiring system of the premises served.

Service Equipment   35.40.291

Service equipment usually consists of a circuit breaker or switch and fuses and their accessories, located near the point of entrance of the service conductors to a building and intended to constitute the main control and means of cutoff for the supply to that building.

Service Conductors   35.40.292

The service conductors is that portion of the supply conductors which extends from the street mains or feeder or transformer to the service equipment of the premises served. For an overhead system it includes the conductors from the last line pole to the service equipment.

See **35.40.291.**

Service Entrance Conductors   35.40.293

The service entrance conductors is that portion of the service conductors between the terminals of the service equipment and a point outside the premises served, clear of the building walls, where it is joined by tap or splice to the service drop or to service conductors or other source of supply.

See **35.40.292** and **35.40.294.**

Service Drop   35.40.294

(Service Loop)*

The service drop is that portion of overhead service conductors between the last pole and the premises served extending from the pole to the junction with the service entrance conductors.

See **35.40.292** and **35.40.293.**

_____

* Deprecated.

Service Cable 35.40.295

The service cable is the service conductors made up in the form of a cable.

See 35.40.292.

Dual Service 35.40.296

(Plural Service)

A dual service consists of two separate services usually of different characteristics, supplying one consumer.

See 35.40.290, 35.40.300, 35.40.305 and 35.40.310.

NOTE: A dual service might consist of an alternating-current and direct-current service, or of 120-208-volt 3-phase, 4-wire service for light and some power and a 13.2-kv service for power, etc.

Service Pipe 35.40.297

A service pipe is the pipe or conduit that contains underground service conductors and extends from the junction with outside supply wires into the customer's premises.

See 35.70.135.

Duplicate Service 35.40.300

A duplicate service consists of two services, usually supplied from separate sources, of substantially the same capacity and characteristics.

See 35.40.290, 35.40.296, 35.40.305 and 35.40.310.

NOTE: The two services may be operated in parallel on the consumer's premises, but either one alone is of sufficient capacity to carry the entire load.

Emergency Service 35.40.305

An emergency service is an additional service intended only for use under emergency conditions.

See 35.40.290, 35.40.296, 35.40.300 and 35.40.310.

Loop Service 35.40.310

A loop service is two services, of substantially the same capacity and characteristics supplied from adjacent sections of a loop feeder. The two sections of the loop feeder are normally tied together on the consumer's bus through switching devices.

Single Service 35.40.315

A single service consists of one service only supplying a consumer.

NOTE: Either or both lighting and power load may be connected to the service.

Transmission Route 35.40.325

A transmission route is the route followed by a transmission circuit.

GROUP 35—GENERATION, TRANSMISSION AND DISTRIBUTION

Section 60—Details of Construction (Overhead)

Guy Anchor 35.60.005

A guy anchor is a device so installed (usually buried in the earth or in rock) as to provide a firm point of attachment for a guy.

NOTE: In addition to anchor logs (see 35.60.010) there are many forms of metal devices.

Anchor Log 35.60.010

(Dead Man)

An anchor log is a length of rigid material (e. g., wood, concrete or metal) buried in the earth to provide anchorage for guys.

Insulator Arcing Horn 35.60.020

An insulator arcing horn is a metal part placed at one or both ends of an insulator or of a string of insulators for the purpose of reducing or eliminating damage by arcover to the insulator and/or conductor.

Insulator Arcing Ring 35.60.025

An insulator arcing ring is a metal part, usually circular or oval in shape, placed at one or both ends of an insulator or of a string of insulators for the purpose of reducing or eliminating damage by arcover to the insulator and/or conductor.

Insulator Arcing Shield

See 35.60.140.

Bull Ring 35.60.035

A bull ring is a metal ring used in overhead construction at the junction point of three or more strain wires.

Buzz Stick 35.60.040

A buzz stick is a device for testing suspension insulator units for fault when the units are in position on an energized line. It consists of an insulating stick, on one end of which are metal prongs of the proper dimensions for spanning and short-circuiting the porcelain of one insulator unit at a time.

Clearance (transmission and distribution) 35.60.070

Clearance is the minimum distance between two conductors, between conductors and supports or other objects, or between conductors and ground.

Combined Mechanical and Electrical Strength of an Insulator 35.60.080

The combined mechanical and electrical strength of an insulator is the loading in pounds at which the insulator fails to perform its function either electrically or mechanically, voltage and mechanical stress being applied simultaneously.

NOTE: The value will depend upon the conditions under which the test is made. (For AIEE standard conditions see AIEE Standard No. 41.)

Lateral Conductor 35.60.090

A lateral conductor, in pole wiring work, is a wire or cable extending in a general horizontal direction approximately at right angles to the general direction of the line conductors.

Line Conductor 35.60.095

A line conductor is one of the wires or cables carrying electric current, supported by poles, towers or other structures, but not including vertical or lateral connecting wires.

Vertical Conductor 35.60.100

A vertical conductor, in pole wiring work, is a wire or cable extending in an approximately vertical direction.

Structure Conflict 35.60.120

Structure conflict (as applied to a pole line) means that the line is so situated with respect to a second line that the overturning (at the ground line) of the first line will result in contact between its poles or conductors and the conductors of the second line, assuming that no conductors are broken in either line.

Exceptions: Lines are not considered as conflicting under the following conditions:

(1) Where one line crosses another.
(2) Where two lines are on opposite sides of a highway, street, or alley and are separated by a distance not less than 60 percent of the height of the taller pole line and not less than 20 feet.

Corona 35.60.125

Corona is a luminous discharge due to ionization of the air surrounding a conductor around which exists a voltage gradient exceeding a certain critical value.

Cross Arm 35.60.130

A cross arm is a horizontal member (usually wood or steel) attached to a pole, post or tower generally perpendicularly to the direction of the line, and normally used for the support of line insulators.

Footings 35.60.135

(Foundations)

Footings are structures set in the ground to support the bases of towers, poles or other overhead structures.

NOTE: Footings are usually skeleton steel pyramids, grilles or piers of concrete.

Insulator Grading Shield 35.60.140

An insulator grading shield is an arcing ring so shaped and located as to improve the voltage distribution across or along the insulator or insulator string.

Guy 35.60.145

A guy is a tension member having one end securely held and the other attached to a pole, cross arm or other structural part which it supports.

Pole Guy 35.60.150

A pole guy is a tension member having one end securely anchored and the other end attached to a pole or other structure, which it supports against overturning.

Pin Insulator 35.60.160

A pin insulator is a complete insulator, consisting of one insulating member or an assembly of such members without tie wires, clamps, thimbles or other accessories, the whole being of such construction that when mounted on an insulator pin it will afford insulation and mechanical support to a conductor which has been properly attached with suitable accessories.

Semi-Strain Insulator 35.60.170

(Semi-Tension Assembly)

A semi-strain insulator consists of two insulator strings at right angles, each making an angle of about 45 degrees with the line conductor.

NOTE: These assemblies are used at intermediate points where it may be desirable to partially anchor the conductor to prevent too great movement in case of a broken wire.

Strain Insulator 35.60.175

A strain insulator is a single insulator, an insulator string, or two or more strings in parallel, designed to transmit to the tower or other support the entire pull of the conductor and to insulate it therefrom.

Suspension Insulator 35.60.180

A suspension insulator is a shell assembled with its necessary attaching members.

Insulator Arcover 35.60.185

Insulator arcover is a discharge of power current in the form of an arc, following a surface discharge over an insulator.

Conductor Loading (mechanical) 35.60.195

Conductor loading is the combined load per unit length of a conductor due to the weight of the wire plus the wind and ice loads.

Tower Loading 35.60.200

Tower loading is the load placed on a tower by its own weight, the weight of the wires with or without ice covering, the insulators, the wind pressure normal to the line acting both on the tower and the wires and the pull from the wires in the direction of the line.

Mast

See 35.60.215.

Open Wire

See 65.25.435.

Pole 35.60.215

A pole is a column of wood or steel, or a similar structure of some other material, supporting overhead conductors, usually by means of arms or brackets, span wires or bridges.

NOTE: Broad base lattice steel supports are often known as "towers"; narrow base steel supports are often known as "masts".

Pole Steps 35.60.220

Pole steps are devices attached to the side of a pole, conveniently spaced to provide a means for climbing the pole.

Apparent Sag of Wire in a Span 35.60.230

Apparent sag of wire in a span is the maximum departure of the wire in a given span from the straight line between the two points of support of the span.

NOTE: Where the two supports are at the same level this will be the normal sag.

Apparent Sag at Any Point   35.60.235

Apparent sag at any point is the departure of the wire at the particular point in the span from the straight line between the two points of support.

Normal Sag   35.60.240

Normal sag is the difference in elevation between the highest point of support of the conductor in a span and the lowest point of the conductor in the span (or in the curve of the conductor in the span produced).

See 35.60.230.

Shell   35.60.245

A shell is a single insulating member without cement or other connecting devices intended to form a part of an insulator assembly.

Climbing Space   35.60.250

Climbing space is the vertical space reserved along the side of a pole or tower to permit ready access for linemen to equipment and conductors located thereon.

Lateral Working Space   35.60.255

Lateral working space is the space reserved for working between conductor levels outside the climbing space, and to its right and left.

Span   35.60.265

Span is the horizontal distance between two adjacent supporting points of a conductor.

Insulator String   35.60.270

An insulator string is two or more suspension insulators connected in series.

Tower

See 35.60.215.

Angle Tower   35.60.280

An angle tower is a tower located where the line changes horizontal direction sufficiently to require special design of the tower to withstand the resultant pull of the wires and to provide adequate clearance.

Dead-End Tower   35.60.285

A dead-end tower is a tower designed to withstand unbalanced pull from all of the conductors in one direction together with wind and vertical loads.

Flexible Tower   35.60.290

(Frame)

A flexible tower is a tower which is dependent on the line conductors for longitudinal stability but is designed to resist transverse and vertical loads.

Rigid Tower   35.60.295

A rigid tower is a tower which depends only upon its own structural members to withstand the load that may be placed upon it.

See 35.60.280, 35.60.285 and 35.60.290.

Insulated Turnbuckle   35.60.305

An insulated turnbuckle is one so constructed as to constitute an insulator as well as a turnbuckle.

Dry Flashover Voltage   35.60.310

Dry flashover voltage is the voltage at which the air surrounding a clean dry insulator or shell completely breaks down between electrodes.

NOTE: The value will depend upon the conditions under which the test is made. (For AIEE standard conditions see AIEE Standard No. 41.)

Puncture Voltage   35.60.315

Puncture voltage is the voltage at which an insulator or shell is electrically punctured when subjected to a gradually increasing voltage.

NOTE: The value will depend upon the conditions under which the test is made. (For AIEE standard conditions see AIEE Standard No. 41.)

Wet Flashover Voltage   35.60.320

Wet flashover voltage is the voltage at which the air surrounding a clean wet insulator or shell completely breaks down between electrodes.

NOTE: The value will depend on the conditions under which the test is made. (For AIEE standard conditions see AIEE Standard No. 41.)

Suspension Insulator Weights   35.60.325

Suspension insulator weights are devices, usually cast iron, hung below the conductor on a special spindle supported by the conductor clamp.

NOTE: Suspension insulator weights will limit the swing of the insulator string, thus maintaining adequate clearances. In practice, weights of several hundreds of pounds are sometimes used.

Transposition   35.60.330

Transposition is the interchange of the position of the several conductors of a circuit.

Tie Wire   35.60.336

A tie wire is an auxiliary wire used to attach a conductor to an insulator.

Aerial Cable

See 65.25.330

GROUP 35—GENERATION, TRANSMISSION AND DISTRIBUTION
Section 70—Details of Construction (Underground)

Cable Bond   35.70.005

A cable bond is an electric connection across a joint in the armor or lead sheath of a cable, or between the armor or lead sheath and the earth, or between the armor or sheath of adjacent cables.

See 35.70.010 and 35.70.015.

Continuity Cable Bond   35.70.010

A continuity cable bond is a cable bond used for bonding cable sheaths and armor across joints between contiguous lengths of cable.

See 35.70.005 and 35.70.015.

Cross Cable Bond   35.70.015

A cross cable bond is a cable bond used for bonding between the armor or lead sheath of adjacent cables.

See 35.70.005 and 35.70.010.

Bonding   35.70.025

Bonding is the electrical interconnecting of cable sheaths or armor to sheaths or armor of adjacent conductors.

See 35.70.005, 35.70.010 and 35.70.015.

Cable Rack   35.70.030

(Shelf)* (Hanger)

A cable rack is a device usually secured to the wall of a manhole, cable raceway or building to provide support for the cables.

Distributor Box   35.70.040

A distributor box is a box or pit through which cables are inserted or removed in a draw-in system of mains. It contains no links, fuses or switches and its usual function is to facilitate tapping into a consumer's premises.

Junction Box   35.70.050

A junction box is an enclosed distribution panel for connecting or branching one or more corresponding electric circuits without the use of permanent splices.

Pull or Transfer Box   35.70.060

A pull or transfer box is a box without a distribution panel, within which one or more corresponding electric circuits are connected or branched.

Connector (Splicing Sleeve)   35.70.070

A connector is a metal sleeve, usually copper, that is slipped over and secured to the butted ends of the conductors in making up a joint.

See 35.80.165.

Sealed End of a Cable   35.70.080

(Shipping Seal)

The sealed end of a cable is the end of a cable fitted with a cap for protection against the loss of compound or the entrance of moisture.

Live Cable Test Cap   35.70.090

A live cable test cap is a protective structure at the end of a cable which insulates the conductors and seals the cable sheath.

Test Cap   35.70.091

A test cap is a protective structure which is placed over the exposed end of the cable to seal the sheath or other covering completely against the entrance of dirt, moisture, air or other foreign substances.

NOTE: Test caps are often provided with facilities for vacuum treatment, oil filling or other special field operations.

See 35.70.090.

---

* Deprecated.

Submarine Cable   35.70.095

A submarine cable is a cable designed for service under water.

NOTE: Submarine cable is usually a lead-covered cable with a steel armor applied between layers of jute.

Underground Cable   35.70.100

An underground cable is a cable designed for operation buried in the ground or installed in an underground duct or conduit.

Splicing Chamber

See 35.70.220.

Armor Clamp   35.70.115

An armor clamp is a fitting for gripping the armor of a cable at the point where the armor terminates or where the cable enters a junction box or other piece of apparatus.

Fireproofing of Cables   35.70.120

Fireproofing of cables is the application of a fire-resisting covering to protect them from arcs in an adjacent cable or from fires from any cause.

Conduit   35.70.124

A conduit is a structure containing one or more ducts.

NOTE: Conduit may be designated as iron pipe conduit, tile conduit, etc. If it contains one duct only it is called "single-duct conduit", if it contains more than one duct it is called "multiple-duct conduit", usually with the number of ducts as a prefix, viz., two-duct multiple conduit.

Trunk Line Conduit   35.70.125

A trunk line conduit is a duct bank provided for main or trunk line cables.

Duct   35.70.130

A duct is a single enclosed runway for conductors or cables.

Distributor Duct   35.70.135

A distributor duct is a duct installed for occupancy of distribution mains.

See 35.40.297.

Duct Bank   35.70.140

(Conduit Run)

A duct bank is an arrangement of conduit providing one or more continuous ducts between two points.

NOTE: An underground runway for conductors or cables, large enough for workmen to pass through, is termed a gallery or tunnel.

Duct Edge Shield   35.70.145

(Cable Shield)

A duct edge shield is a collar or thimble, usually flared, inserted at the duct entrance in a manhole for the purpose of protecting the cable sheath or insulation from being worn away by the duct edge.

Duct Entrance   35.70.150

Duct entrance is the opening of a duct at a manhole, distributor box or other accessible space.

Monolithic Conduit   35.70.160

Monolithic conduit is a monolithic concrete structure built to the desired duct formation by an automatic conduit forming machine or flexible tubular rubber forms.

Duct Rodding   35.70.165

(Rodding a Duct)

Duct rodding is the threading of a duct by means of a jointed rod of suitable design for the purpose of pulling in the cable-pulling rope, mandrel or the cable itself.

Duct Sealing   35.70.170

Duct sealing is the closing of the duct entrance for the purpose of excluding water, gas or other undesirable substances.

Stuffing Box   35.70.185

(Watertight Gland)

A stuffing box is a device for use where a cable passes into a junction box or other piece of apparatus and is so designed as to render the joint watertight.

Wiping Gland   35.70.190

(Wiping Sleeve)

A wiping gland is a projecting sleeve on a junction box or other piece of apparatus serving to make a connection to the lead sheath of a cable by means of a plumber's wiped joint.

Handhole   35.70.195

A handhole is a subsurface chamber, not large enough for a man to enter, in the route of one or more conduit runs, and affording facilities for placing and maintaining in the runs, conductors, cables and any associated apparatus.

Branch Joint   35.70.200

(T Joint) (Tee Joint) (Y Joint) (Multiple Joint)

A branch joint is a joint used for connecting a branch conductor or cable to a main conductor or cable, where the latter continues beyond the branch.

See 35.70.206, 35.70.215 and 35.70.216.

NOTE: A branch joint may be further designated by naming the cables between which it is made, e. g., single-conductor cables; three-conductor main cable to single-conductor branch cable, etc. With the term "multiple joint" it is customary to designate the various kinds as 1-way, 2-way, 3-way, 4-way, etc., multiple joint.

Cable Joint   35.70.206

(Splice)

A cable joint is a connection between two or more separate lengths of cable with the conductors in one length, connected individually to conductors in other lengths, and with the protecting sheaths so connected as to extend protection over the joint.

See 35.70.200, 35.70.215 and 35.70.216.

NOTE: Cable joints are designated by naming the conductors between which the joint is made, e. g., 1 single-conductor to 2 single-conductor cables; 1 single-conductor to 3 single-conductor cables; 1 concentric to 2 concentric cables; 1 concentric to 1 single-conductor cable; 1 concentric to 2 single-conductor cables; 1 concentric to 4 single-conductor cables; 1 three-conductor to 3 single-conductor cables.

Shielded Joint   35.70.208

A shielded joint is a cable joint having its insulation so enveloped by a conducting shield that substantially every point on the surface of the insulation is at ground potential or at some predetermined potential with respect to ground.

Insulating Joint   35.70.210

An insulating joint is a device which mechanically couples and electrically insulates the sheath and armor of contiguous lengths of cable.

Straight Joint   35.70.215

A straight joint is a joint used for connecting two lengths of cable in approximately the same straight line in series.

See 35.70.200, 35.70.206 and 35.70.216.

NOTE: A straight joint is made between two like cables, e. g., between two single-conductor cables, between two concentric cables or between two triplex cables.

Reducing Joint   35.70.216

A reducing joint is a joint between two lengths of cable the conductors of which are not the same size.

See 35.70.200, 35.70.206 and 35.70.215.

Looping-In   35.70.217

Looping-in is a method in wiring of avoiding tee joints by carrying the conductor or cable to and from the point to be supplied.

Manhole   35.70.220

A manhole is a subsurface chamber, large enough for a man to enter, in the route of one or more conduit runs, and affording facilities for placing and maintaining in the runs, conductors, cables and any associated apparatus.

Manhole Chimney   35.70.225

A manhole chimney is a vertical passageway for workmen and equipment between the roof of the manhole and the street level.

Manhole Cover Frame   35.70.230

The manhole cover frame is the structure which caps the manhole chimney at ground level and supports the cover.

Oil Feeding Reservoirs   35.70.235

Oil feeding reservoirs are oil storage tanks situated at intervals along the route of an oil filled cable or at oil filled joints of solid cable for the purpose of keeping the cable constantly filled with oil under pressure.

Cable Terminal (power work)   35.70.240

(Pothead) (End Bell)

A cable terminal (power work) is a device which seals the end of a cable, and provides insulated egress for the conductors.

Pulling Eye   35.70.245

A pulling eye is a device which may be fastened to the conductor or conductors of a cable or formed by or fastened to the wire armor and to which a hook or rope may be directly attached in order to pull the cable into or from a duct.

NOTE: Pulling eyes are sometimes equipped, like test caps, with facilities for oil feed or vacuum treatment.

Transformer Vault   35.70.250

A transformer vault is an isolated enclosure either above or below ground, with fire-resistant walls, ceiling and floor, for unattended transformers and their auxiliaries.

Troughing   35.70.255

Troughing is an open channel of earthenware, wood or other material in which a cable or cables may be laid and protected by a cover.

Electrolysis of Underground Structures   35.70.260

Electrolysis of underground structures is the destructive chemical action caused by stray or local electric currents to pipes, cables and other metal work.

Subsidiary Conduit (lateral)

See **65.25.425**

Buried Cable

See **65.25.325**.

GROUP 35—GENERATION, TRANSMISSION AND DISTRIBUTION

Section 80—Wires and Cables

Cable   35.80.005

A cable is either a stranded conductor (single-conductor cable), or a combination of conductors insulated from one another (multiple-conductor cable).

Armored Cable   35.80.010

An armored cable is a cable provided with a wrapping of metal, usually steel wires, primarily for the purpose of mechanical protection.

See **35.80.045**.

Cable Filler   35.80.020

Cable filler is the material used in multiple-conductor cables to occupy the spaces formed by the assembly of the insulated conductors, thus forming a core of the desired shape.

Cable Sheath   35.80.025

Cable sheath is the protective covering usually lead, applied to cables.

See **35.80.045**.

Concentric-Lay Cable   35.80.030

A concentric-lay cable is either:

(a) A concentric-lay conductor as defined in **35.80.105** or

(b) A multiple-conductor cable composed of a central core surrounded by one or more layers of helically laid insulated conductors.

"D" Cable   35.80.035

A "D" cable is a two-conductor cable each conductor having the shape of the capital letter "D" with insulation between the conductors themselves and between conductors and sheath.

Duplex Cable   35.80.040

A duplex cable is a cable composed of two insulated stranded conductors twisted together.

NOTE: They may or may not have a common insulating covering.

Lead Covered Cable   35.80.045

(Lead Sheathed Cable)

A lead covered cable is a cable provided with a sheath of lead for the purpose of excluding moisture and affording mechanical protection.

See **35.80.010**.

N-Conductor Cable   35.80.050

An n-conductor cable is a combination of n conductors insulated from one another and from sheath and armor where used.

NOTE: It is not intended that the name as here given be actually used. One would, instead, speak of a 3-conductor cable, a 12-conductor cable, etc. In referring to the general case, one may speak of a multiple-conductor cable. See **35.80.005**.

N-Conductor Concentric Cable   35.80.055

An n-conductor concentric cable is a cable composed of an insulated central conductor with $(n-1)$ tubular stranded conductors laid over it concentrically and separated by layers of insulation.

NOTE: This kind of cable usually has only two or three conductors. The remark on the expression n-conductor as given in **35.80.050** also applies here.

Oil Filled Cable   35.80.057

An oil filled cable is a cable having insulation impregnated with an oil which is fluid at all operating temperatures and provided with facilities such as longitudinal ducts or channels and with reservoirs, or their equivalent, by means of which positive oil pressure can be maintained within the cable at all times, incipient voids promptly filled during period of contraction and all surplus oil adequately taken care of during periods of expansion.

Serving of a Cable   35.80.060

Serving of a cable is a wrapping applied over the core of a cable before the cable is leaded, or over the lead if the cable is armored.

NOTE: Materials commonly used for serving are jute, cotton, duck tape.

The serving is for mechanical protection and not for insulating purposes.

Shielded-Conductor Cable   35.80.065

A shielded-conductor cable is a cable in which the insulated conductor or conductors is/are enclosed in a conducting envelope or envelopes, so constructed that substantially every point on the surface of the insulation is at ground potential or at some predetermined potential with respect to ground.

Split-Conductor Cable   35.80.070

A split-conductor cable is one in which each conductor is composed of two or more insulated conductors normally connected in parallel.

Triplex Cable   35.80.075

A triplex cable is a cable composed of three insulated single-conductor cables twisted together.

NOTE: They may or may not have a common insulating covering.

Twin Cable   35.80.080

A twin cable is a cable composed of two insulated stranded conductors laid parallel, having a common covering.

Conductor   35.80.085

A conductor is a wire or combination of wires not insulated from one another, suitable for carrying electric current.

Service Entrance Conductors

See 35.40.293.

Service Drop

See 35.40.294.

Service Cable

See 35.40.295.

Aluminum Conductor   35.80.090

An aluminum conductor is a conductor made wholly of aluminum.

Aluminum-Steel Conductor   35.80.095

An aluminum-steel conductor is a composite conductor made up of a combination of aluminum and steel wires. In the usual construction the aluminum wires surround the steel.

Bare Conductor   35.80.100

A bare conductor is a conductor not covered with insulating material.

Concentric-Lay Conductor   35.80.105

A concentric-lay conductor is a conductor composed of a central core surrounded by one or more layers of helically laid wires.

NOTE: In the most common type of concentric-lay conductor, all wires are of the same size and the central core is a single wire.

Copper Conductor   35.80.110

A copper conductor is a conductor made wholly of copper.

Copper-Covered Steel Wire   35.80.115

A copper-covered steel wire is a wire having a steel core to which is fused an outer shell of copper.

Cross-Sectional Area of a Conductor   35.80.120

(Cross-Section of a Conductor)

The cross-sectional area of a conductor is the sum of the cross-sectional areas of its component wires, that of each wire being measured perpendicular to its individual axis.

Plain Conductor   35.80.125

A plain conductor is a conductor consisting of one metal only.

Resistive Conductor   35.80.130

A resistive conductor is a conductor used primarily because it possesses the property of high electric resistance.

Rope-Lay Conductor or Cable   35.80.135

A rope-lay cable is a cable composed of a central core surrounded by one or more layers of helically laid groups of wires.

NOTE: This kind of cable differs from a concentric-lay conductor in that the main strands are themselves stranded. In the most common type of rope-lay conductor or cable, all wires are of the same size and the central core is a concentric-lay conductor.

Round Conductor   35.80.140

A round conductor is either a solid or stranded conductor of which the cross-section is substantially circular.

Sector Cable   35.80.145

A sector cable is a multiple-conductor cable in which the cross-section of each conductor is substantially a sector, an ellipse or a figure intermediate between them.

NOTE: Sector cables are used in order to obtain decreased overall diameter and thus permit the use of larger conductors in a cable of given diameter.

Solid Conductor   35.80.150

A solid conductor is a conductor consisting of a single wire.

Stranded Conductor   35.80.155

A stranded conductor is a conductor composed of a group of wires, or of any combination of groups of wires.

NOTE: The wires in a stranded conductor are usually twisted or braided together.

Connection Strap   35.80.160

A connection strap is a short separate connecting conductor used to join two or more conducting parts.

Connector (temporary or test)   35.80.165

A connector is a device attached to two or more wires or cables for the purpose of connecting electric circuits without the use of splices.

NOTE: This type of connector is commonly used for making temporary repairs or for making test connections.

See 35.70.070.

Cord 35.80.170

A cord is a small, very flexible insulated cable.

NOTE: There is no sharp dividing line in respect to size between a cord and a cable.

Factor of Assurance of Wire or Cable Insulation 35.80.180

The factor of assurance of wire or cable insulation is the ratio of the voltage at which completed lengths are tested to that at which it is used.

Insulation of a Cable 35.80.185

The insulation of a cable is that part which is relied upon to insulate the conductor from other conductors or conducting parts or from ground.

Insulation Resistance of an Insulated Conductor 35.80.190

The insulation resistance of an insulated conductor is the resistance offered by its insulation, to an impressed direct voltage tending to produce a leakage of current through the same.

Thermal Resistance of a Cable 35.80.191

The thermal resistance of a cable is the resistance offered by the insulation to the flow of heat from the conductor or conductors to the sheath.

NOTE: The thermal resistance of a cable is equal to the difference of temperature between the conductor and outside of the cable, divided by the rate of flow of heat produced thereby. It is preferably expressed by the number of degrees centigrade per watt.

Lay 35.80.195

The lay of any helical element of a cable is the axial length of a turn of the helix of that element.

NOTE: Among the helical elements of a cable may be each strand in a concentric-lay cable, or each multiple conductor in a multiple-conductor cable.

Direction of Lay 35.80.200

The direction of lay is the lateral direction in which the strands of a cable run over the top of the cable as they recede from an observer looking along the axis of the cable.

Jumper 35.80.205

A jumper is a short length of conductor used to make a connection between terminals or around a break in a circuit, or around an instrument. It is usually a temporary connection.

Strand 35.80.215

A strand is one of the wires, or groups of wires, of any stranded conductor.

Twisted Pair 35.80.220

A twisted pair is a cable composed of two small insulated conductors, twisted together without a common covering.

NOTE: The two conductors of a twisted pair are usually substantially insulated, so that the combination is a special case of a cord.

Wire 35.80.225

A wire is a slender rod or filament of drawn metal.

NOTE: The definition restricts the term to what would be ordinarily understood by the term solid wire. In the definition, the word slender is used in the sense that the length is great in comparison with the diameter. If a wire is covered with insulation, it is properly called an insulated wire; while primarily the term wire refers to the metal, nevertheless when the context shows that the wire is insulated, the term wire will be understood to include the insulation.

Composite Conductor 35.80.230

A composite conductor consists of two or more strands of different metals, such as aluminum and steel or copper and steel, assembled and operated in parallel.

Bronze Conductor 35.80.231

A bronze conductor is a conductor made wholly of an alloy of copper with other than pure zinc.

NOTE: The copper may be alloyed with tin, silicon, cadmium, manganese or phosphorus, for instance, or several of these in combination.

Stranded Wire

See 35.80.155.

Twin Wire 35.80.250

A twin wire is a cable composed of two small insulated conductors laid parallel, having a common covering.

GROUP 35—GENERATION, TRANSMISSION AND DISTRIBUTION

Section 90—Surges and Impulse Testing

Disruptive Discharge 35.90.005

Disruptive discharge is the sudden and large increase in current through an insulating medium due to the complete failure of the medium under the electrostatic stress.

Flashover 35.90.010

A flashover is a disruptive discharge around or over the surface of a solid or liquid insulator.

Sparkover 35.90.015

A sparkover is a disruptive discharge between electrodes of a measuring gap, such as a sphere gap or oil testing gap.

See 05.45.115, 05.45.120 and 05.45.125.

Breakdown 35.90.020

(Puncture)

A breakdown is a disruptive discharge through insulation.

Wave (in an electric circuit) 35.90.050

A wave (in an electric circuit) is the variation of current and/or potential at any point in the electric circuit.

See 05.05.405.

Traveling Wave 35.90.055

A traveling wave is the resulting wave when the electric variation in a circuit takes the form of translation of energy along a conductor, such energy being always equally divided between current and potential forms.

Standing Wave 35.90.060

A standing wave is the resulting wave when the electric variation in a circuit takes the form of periodic exchange of energy between current and potential forms without translation of energy.

See 05.05.420.

Surge (in an electric circuit) 35.90.075

A surge in an electric circuit is a transient variation in the current and/or potential at a point in the circuit.

Oscillatory Surge 35.90.080

An oscillatory surge is a surge which includes both positive and negative polarity values.

Impulse 35.90.100

An impulse is a surge of unidirectional polarity.

Wave Front (of an impulse in a conductor) 35.90.105

The wave front of an impulse in a conductor is that part (in time or distance) between the initial point of the impulse and the point at which the impulse reaches its crest value.

NOTE: For an interpretation of the nominal value of the wave front of an impulse in a conductor, reference should be made to the test code relating to the particular apparatus concerned.

See 05.05.425.

Wave Tail (of an impulse in a conductor) 35.90.110

The wave tail of an impulse in a conductor is that part (in time or distance) between the point of crest value and the end of the impulse.

NOTE: For an interpretation of the nominal value of the wave tail of an impulse in a conductor, reference should be made to the test code relating to the particular apparatus concerned.

Wave Shape (of an impulse test wave) 35.90.115

The wave shape of an impulse test wave is the graph of the wave as a function of time or distance.

NOTE: It is customary in practice to express the wave shape by a combination of two numbers, the first part of which represents the wave front and the second the time between the beginning of the impulse and the instant at which one-half crest value is reached on the wave tail, both values being expressed in microseconds such as a 1×5 wave or a 1.5×40 wave.

Flashover Voltage (for an impulse) 35.90.120

The flashover voltage for an impulse is the highest value attained by any voltage impulse which causes flashover.

Minimum Flashover Voltage (for an impulse) 35.90.125

The minimum flashover voltage for an impulse is the crest value of the lowest voltage impulse of a given wave shape and polarity which causes flashover.

Impulse Ratio 35.90.130

The impulse ratio is the ratio of the flashover, sparkover or breakdown voltage of an impulse to the crest value of the power-frequency flashover, sparkover or breakdown voltage.

Impulse Inertia 35.90.150

Impulse inertia is that property of insulation whereby more voltage must be applied to produce disruptive discharge, the shorter the time of voltage application.

Time to Impulse Flashover 35.90.155

The time to impulse flashover is the time between the initial point of the voltage impulse causing flashover and the point at which the abrupt drop in the voltage impulse takes place.

Time Lag of Impulse Flashover 35.90.160

The time lag of impulse flashover is the time between the instant when the voltage of the impulse wave first exceeds the power-frequency flashover crest voltage and the instant when the impulse flashover causes the abrupt drop in the testing wave.

Impulse Flashover Volt—Time Characteristic 35.90.165

An impulse flashover volt—time characteristic is a curve plotted between flashover voltage for an impulse and time to impulse flashover, or time lag of impulse flashover.

Surge Generator 35.90.200

(Impulse Generator) (Lightning Generator)*

A surge generator is an electric apparatus suitable for the production of surges.

NOTE: Surge generator types common in the art are:

Transformer-capacitor
Transformer-rectifier
Transformer-rectifier capacitor, parallel charging, series discharging

Charging Circuit of a Surge Generator 35.90.205

The charging circuit of a surge generator is that portion of the surge generator connections through which electric energy is stored up prior to the production of a surge.

Discharge Circuit of a Surge Generator 35.90.210

The discharge circuit of a surge generator is that portion of the surge generator connections in which exist the current and voltage variations constituting the surge generated.

Voltage Divider (for surge measurement) 35.90.215

The voltage divider for surge measurement is that portion of the measuring circuit which provides for the reduction of the surge generator voltage for application to the surge-measuring or surge-recording instrument.

NOTE: Voltage divider types common in the art are:

Capacitance
Resistance
Resistance-capacitance
Resistance cable

_____
* Deprecated.

ELECTRICAL DEFINITIONS

GROUP 40—TRANSPORTATION
Section 05—General

Diesel-Electric Drive   40.05.005

(Oil-Electric Drive)

A diesel-electric drive is a self-contained system of power conversion in which a diesel engine supplies power to the driving motors through an electric generator which it operates.

NOTE: The prefix "diesel-electric" is applied to ships, locomotives, cars, buses, etc., which are equipped with this drive.

Gas-Electric Drive   40.05.010

A gas-electric drive is a self-contained system of power conversion in which a gas engine supplies power to the driving motors through an electric generator which it operates.

NOTE: The prefix "gas-electric" is applied to ships, locomotives, cars, buses, etc., which are equipped with this drive.

Coasting Recorder   40.05.015

A coasting recorder is a device which registers the amount of coasting time in the operation of a vehicle.

Motive Power Unit   40.05.020

(Tractive Power Unit)*

A motive power unit is the least number of wheel bases together with superstructure capable of independent propulsion, but not necessarily equipped with an independent control.

Electrified Track   40.05.025

An electrified track is a suitably equipped track in association with a contact conductor or conductors for the operation of electrically propelled vehicles.

Maximum Equipment Line   40.05.030

The maximum equipment line is the contour which embraces cross-sections of all rolling stock under all normal operating conditions.

Third-Rail Clearance Line   40.05.035

The third-rail clearance line of a railroad is the contour which embraces all cross-sections of third-rail and its insulators, supports and guards located at an elevation higher than the top of the track rail.

Tractive Effort   40.05.040

Tractive effort is the total propelling force measured at the rims of the driving wheels.

NOTE: When the term "tractive effort" is used, it is commonly preceded by one of the following limiting words: "maximum start", "one-hour" or "continuous."

Draw Bar Pull   40.05.045

Draw bar pull is the force exerted at the coupler of the propelling vehicle.

NOTE: When the term "draw bar pull" is used it is commonly preceded by one of the following limiting words: "maximum start", "one-hour" or "continuous."

* Deprecated.

Free Running Speed   40.05.050

(Balancing Speed)

The free running speed of a vehicle or train is the speed at which the total tractive effort is exactly balanced by those forces which resist vehicle or train movements.

NOTE: This is usually assumed to be on level tangent track, in still air, with full power applied.

Train Resistance   40.05.055

Train resistance is the sum of frictional and atmospheric forces which resist vehicle or train movement, with the exception of the resistance due to grades and curves.

Stray Current   40.05.060

Stray current is that portion of the total current which flows through paths other than the intended circuit.

Single-End Control   40.05.065

Single-end control is a control in which provision is made for operating a vehicle from one end only.

Double-End Control   40.05.070

Double-end control is a control in which provision is made for operating a vehicle from either end.

Multiple-Unit Control   40.05.075

Multiple-unit control is a control in which each motive power unit is provided with its own controlling apparatus, all such units throughout a train being controlled from any one of a number of points on the train by means of a master controller.

Automatic Acceleration   40.05.080

Automatic acceleration of a vehicle is its acceleration under the control of devices which function automatically to maintain a predetermined value or values of accelerating current.

Ignition System   40.05.085

An ignition system for internal combustion engines is a method of electrically igniting the compressed combustible mixture in the engine cylinders.

NOTE: This may be accomplished electrically by the use of spark plugs and high-tension magneto, together with necessary wiring; or by electric energy from a storage battery together with suitable interrupting mechanism, induction coil, etc. For internal combustion engines of the diesel type using oil as fuel, the heat of compression ignites the combustible mixture.

Projector

See 55.30.025.

Series-Parallel Control   40.05.105

Series-parallel control is a method of controlling motors whereby the motors, or groups of them, may be connected in series first and then in parallel.

Bridge Transition 40.05.110

Bridge transition is a method of changing the connection of motors from series to parallel in which all of the motors carry the same amount of current throughout the transfer due to the Wheatstone bridge connection of motors and resistors.

Shunt Transition 40.05.115

Shunt transition is a method of changing the connection of motors from series to parallel in which one motor, or group of motors, is first shunted, then open-circuited and finally connected in parallel with the other motor or motors.

Open-Circuit Transition 40.05.120

Open-circuit transition is a method of changing the connection of motors from series to parallel in which the circuits of all motors are open during the transfer.

Reverser 40.05.125

A reverser is a switching device for interchanging electric circuits to reverse the direction of motor rotation.

Sequence Switch 40.05.130

A sequence switch is a remotely controlled power operated switching device used as a secondary master controller.

Changeover Switch 40.05.135

A changeover switch is a switching device for changing electric circuits from one combination to another.

NOTE: It is usual to qualify the term "changeover switch" by stating the purpose for which it is used, such as a series-parallel changeover switch, trolley shoe changeover switch, etc.

Line Breaker 40.05.140

A line breaker is a device which combines the function of a contactor and circuit breaker.

Equipment Clearance Line 40.05.145

The equipment clearance line is that line which shows the existing or proposed (as specified) maximum equipment outline.

Double Reduction Drive 40.05.150

A double reduction drive is a method of transmitting power from the motor shaft to the driven axle by means of two sets of gear reductions.

Electric Depth Finder 40.05.155

An electric depth finder is any electrically operated device which determines exactly the lapse of time between the emission of oscillator signals or other mechanically or electrically propagated sound waves downward from ships at sea or from aircraft over land, and the return of the echo to an electric receiver from the ocean bottom or from the surface of the land, as the case may be.

NOTE: Knowing the speed at which sound travels through the water or air, the depth of water beneath the ship or the depth of air beneath the airplane (the actual height above land—not the altitude above sea level) may be calculated once the time lapse is determined. Calculations are not always necessary, since most depth finders are calibrated to read directly in feet.

GROUP 41—TRANSPORTATION—AIR

Section 10—Aircraft Equipment

Shielded Ignition Wiring   41.10.005

Shielded ignition wiring on an aircraft is the high- and low-tension ignition system wiring which is completely covered usually with a flexible braided steel mesh, the mesh being grounded to the engine and metal frame of the aircraft at frequent intervals.

NOTE: The purpose of shielding the wiring of the ignition system is to eliminate electric interference with aircraft radio communication.

Radio Shielding   41.10.010

Radio shielding on an aircraft is the metallic covering over all electric wiring and ignition apparatus, which covering is grounded at frequent intervals to the frame of the aircraft for the purpose of eliminating electric interference with aircraft radio communication.

Aircraft Bonding   41.10.015

Aircraft bonding is electrically connecting together all of the metal structure of the aircraft, including the engine and metal covering on the wiring.

NOTE: Bonding of aircraft is to prevent electric interference with aircraft radio communication and to prevent fires arising from arcing between adjacent metallic parts from static or radio frequency electric voltages.

Electric Parachute Flare Launching Tubes   41.10.030

Electric parachute flare launching tubes are tubes mounted on an aircraft through which a metal container carrying a parachute flare is launched, the tubes being so designed that as the container passes through the tube an electric circuit is completed which ignites a slow burning fuse in the parachute flare container, the fuse being so designed as to permit the parachute flare container to clear the aircraft before it ignites the parachute flare.

Induction Compass   41.10.035

An induction compass is a compass, the indications of which depend on the current generated in a coil revolving in the earth's magnetic field.

Electric-Capacity Altimeter   41.10.040

An electric-capacity altimeter is an altimeter, the indications of which depend on the variation of an electric capacity with distance from the earth's surface.

Shielding Harness   41.10.045

A shielding harness is a composite shielding system furnishing a metallic covering for all the low- and high-tension cables up to magneto and plugs.

Wind-Driven Generator for Aircraft   41.10.050

A wind-driven generator for aircraft is a generator used on aircraft which derives its power from the air stream applied on its own air screw or propeller, during flight.

Engine-Driven Generator for Aircraft   41.10.055

An engine-driven generator for aircraft is a radio or charging generator deriving its power from a geared connection to the main aircraft engine.

GROUP 42—TRANSPORTATION—LAND

SECTIONS

Section 10—Distribution and Contact Conductors

Catenary System   42.10.005

A catenary system is that form of overhead contact system in which the contact wire is supported from one or more longitudinal messengers, either directly by hangers or by hangers in combination with auxiliary conductors and clamps.

NOTE: Attachment of the contact wire to the messenger is made at frequent and uniform intervals so as to produce a contact surface nearly parallel to the top of the track rails.

Direct Suspension

See 42.10.011.

Direct Suspension System   42.10.011

A direct suspension system is that form of overhead contact system in which contact wire or wires are suspended by suitable attachments directly from the supporting structures.

Simple Catenary Suspension   42.10.015

(Single Catenary Suspension)

Simple catenary suspension is that construction in which the contact wire or wires are suspended from a single messenger.

Compound Catenary Suspension   42.10.020

Compound catenary suspension is that construction in which the contact wire or wires are suspended from a secondary messenger, which in turn is suspended from a primary messenger.

Double Catenary Suspension   42.10.025

Double catenary suspension is that construction in which the contact wire or wires together with the auxiliary wires, if any, are suspended from two messengers having substantially the same vertical sag and supported at substantially the same level at point of attachment to structure.

Tangent Chord Catenary Suspension   42.10.030

Tangent chord catenary suspension is that construction in which, on curves, the messenger and contact wires are maintained in the same vertical relation as on tangents, by means of pull-offs.

Inclined Catenary Suspension   42.10.035

Inclined catenary suspension is that construction in which, on curves, the messenger not only supports the vertical load but also carries the horizontal load component of the entire system, the hangers assuming the direction of the resultant force on the contact wire or wires.

Inclined Chord Catenary Suspension   42.10.040

Inclined chord catenary suspension is that construction in which, on curves, the catenary suspension is the same as that used for inclined catenary construction but suitably deflected horizontally at proper intervals by pull-offs.

Messenger   42.10.045

A messenger is the longitudinal wire or cable of a catenary system from which the contact wire is suspended, either directly or indirectly.

NOTE: In compound catenary construction the top messenger carrying all of the load is termed the primary (or main) messenger and the one suspended from it to which the contact wire is attached is termed the secondary messenger.

Lacing Messenger   42.10.050

A lacing messenger is a flexible continuous wire or cable which is attached alternately to the messenger and the contact wire or wires at more or less regular intervals as a substitute for hangers.

Catenary Hanger   42.10.055

A catenary hanger is a device for suspending a contact wire from a messenger, or a secondary messenger from a primary messenger.

NOTE: (a) When a hanger supports a messenger it is termed a messenger hanger, and when it supports a contact wire it is termed a contact wire hanger.

(b) When the hanger is relatively short it is commonly termed a clamp or clip.

Direct Suspension Hanger   42.10.060

A direct suspension hanger is a device, commonly insulated, used in connection with an ear for suspending contact wires from an overhead structure or a mine roof.

Contact Conductor   42.10.065

A contact conductor is that part of the distribution system other than the traffic rails, which is in immediate electric contact with the current collectors of the vehicle.

Double or Twin Contact Wires   42.10.070

Double or twin contact wires consist of two adjacent contact wires of the same potential and polarity held in approximately the same horizontal plane, usually by alternate hangers.

Contact Wire   42.10.075

(Trolley Wire)

A contact wire is a contact conductor in the form of a wire, with which a trolley, customarily mounted on the top of a vehicle, makes electric contact.

Supporting Structure   42.10.080

A supporting structure is a pole, tower, bridge or other stationary structure used for supporting a catenary system, or a direct suspension system, and includes foundations, anchors, guys, braces and similar reinforcing attachments.

Bracket Type Supporting Structure   42.10.085

A bracket type supporting structure is an arm, or arms, with supporting pole, tower or other stationary structure, located at one side of the track or between tracks.

Bridge Type Supporting Structure   42.10.090

A bridge type supporting structure is a transverse beam, truss or similar rigid member, extending over the track or tracks, together with its supports.

Cross Span Type Supporting Structure   42.10.095

A cross span type supporting structure is a transverse cable or cables, or similar flexible member, together with the necessary supporting structures located at both sides of the track or tracks.

Simple Cross Span Type Supporting Structure   42.10.100

A simple cross span type supporting structure is a single cable attached to and together with the supporting structures located at both sides of the track or tracks.

Compound Cross Span Type Supporting Structure   42.10.105

A compound cross span type supporting structure is two or more cables attached to and together with the supporting structures located at both sides of the tracks, the upper cables carrying all or part of the suspended load.

Trolley System   42.10.110

(Overhead Contact System)

A trolley system is a system for supplying electric power to a vehicle by means of one or more contact wires.

Trackless Trolley System   42.10.115

(Railless System)

A trackless trolley system is a trolley system in which electrically propelled vehicles run on the ordinary roadway, the power supply being obtained from two contact wires, of opposite potential.

Steady Brace   42.10.120

A steady brace is a rigid member, normally unstressed, which restrains lateral displacement of the contact wire

and connects it or the messenger to the supporting structure from which it is insulated.

Steady Span   42.10.125

A steady span is the transverse cable, or flexible member, used with bridge or cross span construction, which restrains lateral displacement of the contact wire and connects it or the messenger to the supporting structure from which it is insulated.

Pull-Off   42.10.130

A pull-off is a tension member between the contact wire or messenger and the supporting structure from which it is usually insulated.

Push-Off   42.10.135

A push-off is a compression member between the contact wire or messenger and the supporting structure from which it is usually insulated.

Bridle   42.10.140

A bridle is a tension member extending longitudinally between supporting structures and attached to the catenary system, or direct suspension system, at points between supports.

Wind Bracing   42.10.145

Wind bracing is a system of steady braces, steady spans or bridles, used for the purpose of reducing contact wire deflection due to winds.

Deflector   42.10.150

A deflector is a device or construction used in a catenary system at track switches or turnouts to hold the contact wires over each track in the same horizontal plane to prevent the current-collecting device on the vehicle from fouling when passing from one contact wire to another.

Bull Ring

See 35.60.035.

Ear   42.10.160

An ear is a metal fitting attached to a contact wire, commonly for the purpose of suspending it.

NOTE: Ears which are bent or formed around a contact wire are commonly termed "clinch ears"; and those which are fastened mechanically are termed "clamp ears". In the railway and railroad field these ears are frequently referred to as "trolley anchor clamps", "trolley clamps", etc.

Feeder Ear   42.10.165

A feeder ear is an ear for making connection between a contact wire and a feeder tap.

Strain Ear   42.10.170

A strain ear is an ear for making connection between a contact wire and a strain wire.

Splicing Ear   42.10.175

A splicing ear is an ear used for joining two sections of a contact wire.

ELECTRICAL DEFINITIONS

Overhead Crossing   42.10.180

An overhead crossing is a device used at the crossing of two contact wires to permit the passage of current collectors along either wire.

Trolley Frog   42.10.185

A trolley frog is a device used at the junction of a branch contact wire with the main contact wire to permit the passage of current collectors along either wire.

Contact Rail   42.10.190

A contact rail is a metal rail used as a contact conductor.

Overhead Contact Rail   42.10.195

An overhead contact rail is a contact rail which is above the elevation of the maximum equipment line.

Center Contact Rail   42.10.200

A center contact rail is a contact rail placed between the track rails, customarily having its contact surface above the level of the top of the track rails.

Underground Contact Rail   42.10.205

An underground contact rail is a contact rail placed in an open conduit below the level of the track rails.

Third-Rail   42.10.210

A third-rail is a contact rail placed at either side of the track, the contact surface of which is customarily a few inches above the level of the top of the track rails.

Third-Rail System   42.10.215

A third-rail system is a system for supplying electric power to a vehicle by means of a third-rail.

Slot System   42.10.220

(Conduit System)

A slot system is a system for supplying electric power to a vehicle by means of one or more underground contact rails.

Overrunning Third-Rail   42.10.225

An overrunning third-rail is a third-rail so supported that the current collector makes contact with the top surface of the rail.

Underrunning Third-Rail   42.10.230

An underrunning third-rail is a third-rail so supported that the current collector makes contact with the under surface of the rail.

Rail Bond   42.10.235

(Bond)

A rail bond is an electric connection across a joint between abutting lengths of rail.

NOTE: Bonds may be applied to the rails by arc welding, gas welding, brazing or by mechanical means.

Section Insulator   42.10.240

A section insulator is an insulator used for dividing a contact conductor into electrical sections while maintaining mechanical continuity.

Contact Rail Anchor   42.10.245

A contact rail anchor is a device for anchoring a contact rail to prevent longitudinal movement.

End or Side Approach   42.10.250

An end or side approach of a contact rail is a device which is so shaped as to guide the current collector on or off the contact rail.

Sectionalizing Switch   42.10.255

A sectionalizing switch is a switch used for connecting or disconnecting adjacent sections of contact conductors or feeders.

Metallic Return Circuit   42.10.260

A metallic return circuit is a type of electric power distribution circuit for vehicles wherein grounded parts are not used as a portion of the circuit.

Track Return Circuit   42.10.265

A track return circuit is a type of electric power distribution circuit for rail vehicles wherein the track is included as a portion of the circuit.

Return Feeder   42.10.270

A return feeder is a conductor used to supplement the current-carrying capacity of the return portion of the circuit.

Return   42.10.275

A return in the electric power distribution for rail vehicles is that portion of the circuit normally at or near earth potential, from the utilization equipment to the source of supply.

Phase Section Break   42.10.280

(Phase Break)

A phase section break in an alternating-current contact system is a section insulator between sections having different phase relations.

Air Section Break   42.10.285

(Air Break)

An air section break is a section insulator wherein the sections are insulated from each other by air.

NOTE: The sections usually overlap each other in the horizontal plane to provide smooth transition of the current collector from one section to the other without interruption of the power supply.

Wood Stick Section Break   42.10.290

(Wood Stick Break)

A wood stick section break is a section insulator wherein the sections are insulated from each other by a wooden section over which the current collector passes smoothly from one section to the other.

Three-Wire System (single-phase a-c)   42.10.295

In a single-phase alternating-current railway electrification, a three-wire system is a system for supplying power to vehicles in which a transmission circuit and the trolley circuit utilize the trolley wires as a common conductor, energy being transferred from the former circuit to the latter by means of autotransformers.

NOTE: The voltage of the transmission circuit is usually two or three times the voltage of the trolley circuit.

ELECTRICAL DEFINITIONS

GROUP 42—TRANSPORTATION—LAND

Section 11—Distribution Systems

Distribution Feeder (three-wire system)   42.11.005

In a three-wire system of distribution for single-phase railway electrification, a distribution feeder is a conductor which, alone or in parallel with other similar conductors, forms one side of the transmission circuit of which the other side consists of a trolley wire or trolley wires in parallel.

GROUP 42—TRANSPORTATION—LAND

Section 20—Vehicles

Electric Locomotive   42.20.005

An electric locomotive is a vehicle on wheels, designed to operate on a railway for haulage purposes only, the propulsion of which is effected by electrical means.

NOTE: The prefix "electric" is applied to cars, buses, etc., of this type.

Combination Electric Locomotive   42.20.010

A combination electric locomotive is an electric locomotive, the power for which may be drawn from two or more sources, either located on the locomotive or elsewhere.

NOTE: The prefix "combination" is applied to cars, buses, etc., of this type.

Self-Propelled Electric Locomotive   42.20.015

A self-propelled electric locomotive is an electric locomotive requiring no external source of electric energy during its operation.

NOTE: (a) Storage battery, diesel-electric and gas-electric locomotives are examples of self-propelled locomotives.
(b) The prefix "self-propelled" is also applied to cars, buses, etc., of this type.

Trolley Car   42.20.020

A trolley car is a car operated on rails and propelled by one or more electric motors, the power for which is collected from a trolley system.

Trolley Bus   42.20.025

(Trackless Trolley Bus)

A trolley bus is a passenger vehicle operating without track rails and propelled by one or more electric motors, the power for which is collected from an overhead trackless trolley system.

GROUP 42—TRANSPORTATION—LAND

Section 21—Railway Vehicles

Electric Freight Locomotive   42.21.005

An electric freight locomotive is an electric locomotive, commonly used for hauling freight trains and generally designed to operate at higher tractive effort values and lower speeds than a passenger locomotive of equal horsepower capacity.

Electric Passenger Locomotive   42.21.010

An electric passenger locomotive is an electric locomotive, commonly used for hauling passenger trains and generally designed to operate at higher speeds and lower tractive effort values than a freight locomotive of equal horsepower capacity.

Electric Switching Locomotive   42.21.015

An electric switching locomotive is an electric locomotive designed for yard movements of freight or passenger cars, its speed and continuous capacity usually being low.

Electric Industrial Locomotive   42.21.020

An electric industrial locomotive is an electric locomotive, used for industrial purposes, which does not necessarily conform to government safety regulations as applied to railroads.

NOTE: Electric industrial locomotives of this character are used principally above ground in such places as factories and industrial plants, steel works, open strip mines, highway construction and contracting work.

Electric Motor-Generator Locomotive   42.21.025

An electric motor-generator locomotive is an electric locomotive in which the main power supply for the traction motors is changed from one electrical characteristic to another by means of a motor-generator set carried on the locomotive.

Electric Single-Phase Locomotive   42.21.030

An electric single-phase locomotive is an electric locomotive which collects its power supply from a single phase of an alternating-current distribution system.

Electric Three-Phase Locomotive   42.21.035

An electric three-phase locomotive is an electric locomotive which collects its power supply from three phases of an alternating-current distribution system.

Electric Split-Phase Locomotive   42.21.040

An electric split-phase locomotive is a single-phase electric locomotive equipped with electric devices to change the single-phase energy to polyphase energy without complete conversion of the power supply.

Electric Motor Car   42.21.045

An electric motor car is an electrically propelled rail vehicle which is provided with space for revenue loads.

Electric Tower Car   42.21.050

An electric tower car is a rail vehicle which is provided with an elevated platform, generally arranged for raising and lowering, for the installation, inspection and repair of a contact wire system.

Electric Trail Car   42.21.055

(Electric Trailer)

An electric trail car is a car not provided with motive power, which is used in a train with one or more motor cars.

Electric Control Trail Car   42.21.060

An electric control trail car is a trail car in a multiple-unit train, provided at one or both ends with a master controller and other apparatus necessary for controlling the train.

Electric Direct-Current Locomotive   42.21.065

A electric direct-current locomotive is an electric locomotive which collects its power supply from a direct-current distribution system.

GROUP 42—TRANSPORTATION—LAND

Section 22—Mine Vehicles

Electric Crab Reel Mine Locomotive   42.22.005

An electric crab reel mine locomotive is an electric mine locomotive equipped with an electrically driven winch, or crab reel, for the purpose of hauling cars by means of a wire rope from the unelectrified working faces to the electrified track.

Electric Cable Reel Locomotive   42.22.010

An electric cable reel locomotive is an electric locomotive equipped with a reel for carrying a cable which may be used to conduct power to the locomotive when operating on unelectrified tracks.

Electric Explosion Tested Mine Locomotive   42.22.015

An electric explosion tested mine locomotive is an electric mine locomotive in which the electric equipment is so housed or shielded that ignition of ambient inflammable or explosive gases does not occur due to the electric apparatus.

Electric Gathering Mine Locomotive   42.22.020

An electric gathering mine locomotive is an electric mine locomotive the chief function of which is to gather cars from the working faces and make up trains for the haulage locomotives.

Electric Haulage Mine Locomotive   42.22.025

An electric haulage mine locomotive is an electric mine locomotive used for hauling trains of cars, which have been gathered from the working faces of the mine, to the point of delivery of the cars.

Electric Mine Locomotive   42.22.030

An electric mine locomotive is an electric locomotive used in underground mines, tunnels or similar sub-surface operations, and is commonly built to restricted dimensions on account of space limitations, especially in height.

Electric Permissible Mine Locomotive   42.22.035

An electric permissible mine locomotive is an electric mine locomotive in which the electric equipment has passed the United States Bureau of Mines explosion tests and conforms to the requirements of the United States Bureau of Mines.

GROUP 42—TRANSPORTATION—LAND

Section 25—Current Collection

Current Collector   42.25.005

A current collector is a device for maintaining electric contact between a contact conductor and the electric circuit of the vehicle on which the collector is mounted.

Overhead Rail Collector   42.25.010

An overhead rail collector is a current collector the function of which is to make contact with an overhead contact rail.

Third-Rail Collector   42.25.015

A third-rail collector is a current collector the function of which is to make contact with a third-rail.

Underground Collector or Plow   42.25.020

An underground collector or plow is a current collector, the function of which is to make contact with underground contact rails.

Trolley   42.25.025

A trolley is a current collector, commonly mounted on the top of the vehicle, the function of which is to make contact with a contact wire.

Bow Trolley   42.25.030

A bow trolley is a trolley, the collecting member of which is bow shaped, mounted on a frame or pole.

Pantograph Trolley   42.25.035

A pantograph trolley is a trolley, the collecting member of which is carried by a collapsible pantograph frame.

Pole Trolley   42.25.040

A pole trolley is a trolley consisting of a rotatable base, a pole and a collecting member which is carried at the end of the pole.

Shoe or Pan   42.25.045

A shoe or pan is the collecting member of a current collector of the sliding contact type.

NOTE: This term is usually preceded by a designating name, thus: third-rail shoe, trolley shoe, pantograph pan, etc.

Trolley Base   42.25.050

A trolley base is that part of a pole trolley on which the trolley pole is mounted, so pivoted as to permit of free horizontal movement, and which is provided with means whereby the current collecting member is pressed against the contact wire.

Trolley Wheel   42.25.055

A trolley wheel is the collecting member of a pole trolley which maintains a rolling contact with a contact wire.

Trolley Pole   42.25.060

A trolley pole is the member of a pole trolley, one end of which carries the collecting member, the other end being attached to the trolley base.

Trolley Harp   42.25.065

A trolley harp is the member of a pole trolley which carries the trolley wheel or shoe.

Trolley Head   42.25.070

A trolley head is a fitting, commonly used with a swivel harp, attached to the end of a trolley pole for carrying a trolley harp.

GROUP 42—TRANSPORTATION—LAND
Section 30—Lighting

Headlamp or Headlight
See 55.30.030.

Backing Lamp (Backing Light)   42.30.010
(Back-Up Lamp) (Back-Up Light)

A backing lamp or backing light is a lighting unit mounted on the rear of a vehicle and intended to illuminate the road to the rear of the vehicle.

Classification Lamp (Classification Light)   42.30.015

A classification lamp or classification light is a signal lamp placed at the side of the front end of a vehicle, displaying lights of a particular color to note the class of service of the train or vehicle.

Marker Lamp (Marker Light)   42.30.020

A marker lamp or marker light is a signal lamp placed at the side of the rear end of a vehicle, displaying lights of a particular color to indicate the rear end and to serve for identification purposes.

Dimming Resistor   42.30.025

A dimming resistor is a resistor connected in a headlamp circuit for reducing the voltage applied to the lamp.

Head-End System   42.30.030

A head-end system of electric power supply is a system in which electric current for the requirements of the train is supplied from a generator, or generators, located on the locomotive or in one of the cars, customarily at the forward part of the train.

NOTE: The generators may be driven by steam turbine, internal combustion engine or, if located in one of the cars, by a mechanical drive from the car axle.

Straight Storage System   42.30.035

A straight storage system of electric power supply is a system in which electric current for the requirements of the car is supplied solely from a storage battery carried on the car.

Axle Generator System   42.30.040

An axle generator system of electric power supply is a system in which electric current for the requirements of the car is supplied from an axle driven generator carried on the car, supplemented by a storage battery.

Variable-Speed Axle Generator   42.30.045

A variable-speed axle generator is an axle driven generator in which the speed of the generator varies directly with the speed of the car.

Controlled-Speed Axle Generator   42.30.050

A controlled-speed axle generator is an axle driven generator in which the speed of the generator is maintained approximately constant for a given load after the car attains a certain speed.

NOTE: This is usually accomplished by so designing the generator suspension that the belt will slip on the generator pulley when the load exceeds a predetermined value.

Axle Generator Regulator   42.30.055

An axle generator regulator is a control device for controlling the voltage and current of a variable speed axle generator.

Lamp Regulator   42.30.060

A lamp regulator is a device for automatically maintaining constant voltage on the lamp circuit with a varying higher voltage on the generator to permit charging of batteries.

Axle Generator Pole Changer   42.30.065

An axle generator pole changer is a mechanical or electric device for maintaining constant polarity at the terminals of an axle generator when the direction of the rotation of the armature is reversed due to a change in direction of movement of the car.

Truck Generator Suspension   42.30.070

A truck generator suspension is a design of support for

an axle generator in which the generator is attached to the car truck.

Body Generator Suspension   42.30.075

A body generator suspension is a design of support for an axle generator in which the generator is attached to the car body.

Total-Current Regulation   42.30.080

Total-current regulation for an axle generator is that type of regulation in which the generator regulator controls the total current output of the generator.

Battery-Current Regulation   42.30.085

Battery-current regulation for an axle generator is that type of regulation in which the generator regulator controls only the current used for battery charging purposes.

Constant-Voltage Regulation   42.30.090

Constant-voltage regulation for an axle generator is that in which the generator regulator maintains the voltage of the generator constant.

Constant-Current Regulation   42.30.095

Constant-current regulation for an axle generator is that in which the generator regulator maintains a constant-current output from the generator.

Combination Current and Voltage Regulation   42.30.100

Combination current and voltage regulation is that in which the generator regulator controls both the voltage and current output of the generator.

NOTE: This type of control is designed primarily for the purpose of insuring proper charging of the storage batteries on cars.

GROUP 42—TRANSPORTATION—LAND
Section 35—Braking

Magnetic Braking   42.35.005

Magnetic braking is a system of electric braking in which brakes are applied by magnetic force, the current for exciting the electromagnets being derived either from the traction motors, acting as generators, or from an independent source.

Dynamic Braking   42.35.010

Dynamic braking is a system of electric braking in which the traction motors are used as generators, and the kinetic energy of the vehicle is employed as the actuating means of exerting a retarding force.

Regenerative Braking   42.35.015

Regenerative braking is a system of dynamic braking in which the traction motors are used as generators, returning energy to the supply system, and thus exerting a retarding force.

Rheostatic Braking   42.35.020

(Resistance Braking)

Rheostatic braking is a system of dynamic braking in which the traction motors are used as generators, dissipating energy in resistors, and thus exerting a retarding force.

Track Braking   42.35.025

Track braking is a system of braking in which a shoe or slipper is applied to the track rails by mechanical, pneumatic or magnetic means.

Magnetic Track Braking

See 42.35.005 and 42.35.025.

Electropneumatic Brake   42.35.030

An electropneumatic brake is an air brake which is provided with electrically controlled valves for the application and release of the brakes.

NOTE: The electric control is usually in addition to a complete air brake equipment to provide a more prompt and synchronized operation of the brakes.

GROUP 42—TRANSPORTATION—LAND
Section 40—Traction Equipment

Traction Motor   42.40.005

A traction motor is an electric propulsion motor used for driving the wheels of a vehicle.

Gearless Motor   42.40.010

A gearless motor is a traction motor in which the armature is commonly mounted directly on the driving axle, or is carried by a sleeve or quill which surrounds the axle.

Axle Hung Motor   42.40.015

An axle hung motor is a traction motor, a portion of

the weight of which is supported directly on the axle of a vehicle by means of the motor axle bearings.

Axle Suspension

See 42.40.015.

Nose Suspension Motor

See 42.40.025.

Nose Suspension   42.40.025

Nose suspension is a method of mounting an electric traction motor to give three points of support, consisting of the two axle bearings (or equivalent) and a lug or nose projecting from the opposite side of the motor frame and supported by the truck frame.

Quill Drive 42.40.030

Quill drive is a form of drive in which the motor is geared to a hollow cylindrical sleeve or quill, or the armature is directly mounted on a quill, in either case the quill being mounted substantially concentrically with the driving axle and flexibly connected to the driving wheels.

Axle Bearing 42.40.035

An axle bearing of a traction motor is the bearing which supports a portion of the motor weight on the driving axle.

GROUP 42—TRANSPORTATION—LAND

Section 50—Signals and Interlocking

Alternating-Current Floating Storage Battery System 42.50.005

An alternating-current floating storage battery system is a combination of alternating-current power supply, storage battery and rectifying devices so constructed as to charge continuously the storage battery and at the same time furnish power for the operation of signal devices.

Highway Crossing Bell 42.50.010

A highway crossing bell is an audible signal at a highway grade crossing to give warning of the approach of trains.

Block 42.50.015

A block is a length of track of defined limits, the use of which by trains is governed by block signals.

Absolute Block 42.50.020

An absolute block is a block based on the fundamental principle that no train shall be permitted to enter the block while it is occupied by another train.

Absolute Permissive Block 42.50.025

An absolute permissive block is a term used for an automatic block signal system on single track in which "Stop" signals are used for opposing movements between fixed points, and "Stop then Proceed" signals are used for following movements.

Permissive Block 42.50.030

A permissive block is a block in manual or controlled manual territory, based on the principle that a train other than a passenger train may be permitted to follow a train other than a passenger train in the block.

Track Indicator Chart 42.50.035

A track indicator chart is a maplike reproduction of railway tracks controlled by track circuits so arranged as to indicate automatically, for defined sections of track, whether or not such sections are occupied.

Battery Chute 42.50.040

A battery chute is a small cylindrical receptacle for housing track batteries and set in the ground below the frost line.

Approach Circuit 42.50.045

Approach circuit is a term applied to a circuit generally used in connection with announcing the approach of trains at block or interlocking stations.

Clearing Circuit 42.50.050

Clearing circuit is a term applied to a circuit used in connection with the operation of a signal in advance of an approaching train.

Line Circuit 42.50.055

Line circuit is a term applied to a signal circuit on an overhead or underground line.

Stick Circuit 42.50.060

Stick circuit is a term applied to a circuit used to maintain a relay or similar unit energized through its own contact.

Track Circuit 42.50.065

A track circuit is an electric circuit of which the rails of the track form a part.

Trap Circuit 42.50.070

A trap circuit is a term applied to a stick circuit used at locations where it is impracticable to have a complete track circuit.

Normal Clear 42.50.075

Normal clear is a term used to express the normal indication of the signals in an automatic block system in which an indication to proceed is always displayed except when the block is occupied.

Standard Code 42.50.080

The standard code is the train, block signal and interlocking rules of the Association of American Railroads.

Back Contact 42.50.085

A back contact is a part of a relay against which, when the relay is deenergized, the current-carrying portion of the movable neutral member rests so as to form a continuous path for current.

Closed Contact 42.50.090

A closed contact is a current-carrying member which is closed when the operating unit is in the normal position.

Dependent Contact 42.50.095

A dependent contact is a contacting member designed to complete any one of two or three circuits, depending on whether a two- or three-way device is considered.

Front Contact 42.50.100

A front contact is a part of a relay against which,

when relay is energized, the current-carrying portion of the movable neutral member is held so as to form a continuous path for current.

Independent Contact 42.50.105

An independent contact is a contacting member designed to complete one circuit only.

Normal Contact 42.50.110

Normal contact is a term used to designate a current-carrying member, when the operated unit is in the normal position.

Open Contact 42.50.115

An open contact is a current-carrying member which is open when the operating unit is in the normal position.

Polar Contact 42.50.120

A polar contact is a part of a relay against which the current-carrying portion of the movable polar member is held so as to form a continuous path for current.

Reverse Contact 42.50.125

Reverse contact is a term used to designate a current-carrying member when the operated unit is in the reverse position.

Sliding Contact 42.50.130

A sliding contact is an electric contact obtained by a sliding motion of one conductor over another.

Spring Contact 42.50.135

A spring contact is an electric contact that is actuated by a spring.

Drawbridge Coupler 42.50.140

A drawbridge coupler is a device for engaging and disengaging signal or interlocking connections between the shore and movable bridge span.

Drop-Away 42.50.145

Drop-away is the electrical value which in the gradual reduction of the current energizing an electromagnetic instrument will cause the moving member to move to the position which will open the front and make the back contacts and/or visually indicate its deenergized position.

Track Instrument 42.50.150

A track instrument is a device in which the vertical movement of the rail or the blow of the wheel operates a contact to open or close an electric circuit.

Interlocking 42.50.155

Interlocking is an arrangement of switch, lock and/or signal appliances so interconnected that their movements must succeed each other in a predetermined order.

Automatic Interlocking 42.50.160

Automatic interlocking is an arrangement of signals at railroad grade crossings which function through the exercise of inherent power as distinguished from those whose functions are controlled manually.

Insulated Rail Joint 42.50.165

An insulated rail joint is a joint used to insulate electrically abutting rail ends.

Strap Key 42.50.170

A strap key is a push button circuit controller which has a spring metal strip for opening and/or closing a circuit momentarily.

Ballast Leakage 42.50.175

Ballast leakage is the leakage of current from one rail of a track circuit to the other through the ballast, ties, etc.

Electric Lock 42.50.180

An electric lock is a device to prevent or restrict the movement of a lever, a switch or a drawbridge unless the locking member is withdrawn by an electric device, such as an electromagnet, solenoid or motor.

Electric Drawbridge Lock 42.50.185

An electric drawbridge lock is an electric lock used in connection with a drawbridge to prevent its operation until released.

Electric Indication Lock 42.50.190

An electric indication lock is an electric lock connected to a lever of an interlocking machine to prevent the release of the lever or latch until the signals, switches or other units operated, or directly affected by such lever, are in the proper position.

Electric Switch Lock 42.50.195

An electric switch lock is an electric lock connected with a switch or switch movement to prevent its operation until released.

Electric Switch-Lever Lock 42.50.200

An electric switch-lever lock is an electric lock connected to a lever of an interlocking machine to prevent the movement of lever or latch until released.

Electric Locking 42.50.205

Electric locking is the term applied to the combination of one or more electric locks and controlling circuits by means of which levers of an interlocking machine, or switches or other units operated in connection with signaling and interlocking, are secured against operation under certain conditions as follows:

1. Approach locking   2. Indication locking
3. Switch-lever locking 4. Time locking
5. Traffic locking

Electric Approach Locking 42.50.210

Electric approach locking is electric locking effective while a train is approaching a signal that has been displayed for it to proceed, and adapted to prevent manipulation of levers or units that would endanger that train.

Electric Indication Locking 42.50.215

Electric indication locking is electric locking adapted to prevent manipulation of levers that would bring about an unsafe condition in case a signal, switch or other operated unit fails to make a movement corresponding with that of the operating lever; or adapted directly to prevent the operation of one unit in case another unit to be operated first, fails to make the required movement.

Electric Route Locking 42.50.220

Electric route locking is electric locking effective when a train passes a signal and adapted to prevent manipulation of levers that would endanger the train while it is within the limits of the route entered. It may be so arranged that a train in clearing each section of the route releases the locking affecting that section.

Electric Section Locking 42.50.225

Electric section locking is electric locking effective while a train occupies a given section of a route and adapted to prevent manipulation of levers that would endanger the train while it is within that section.

Electric Switch-Lever Locking 42.50.230

Electric switch-lever locking is a general term for route or section locking.

Electric Time Locking 42.50.235

Electric time locking is electric locking effective upon the displaying of a signal for a train to proceed until released by the train passing or by a time release, and adapted to prevent the manipulation of levers that would endanger an approaching train.

Electric Traffic Locking 42.50.240

Electric traffic locking is electric locking adapted to prevent the manipulation of levers or units for changing the direction of traffic on a section of track while that section is occupied or while a signal is displayed for a train to proceed into that section.

Electric Interlocking Machine 42.50.245

An electric interlocking machine is an interlocking machine designed for operating and controlling the units electrically.

Electromechanical Interlocking Machine 42.50.250

An electromechanical interlocking machine is an interlocking machine which is a combination of mechanical and electrical levers.

Electropneumatic Interlocking Machine 42.50.255

An electropneumatic interlocking machine is an interlocking machine designed to control the units electrically and operate them pneumatically or electrically.

Mechanical Interlocking Machine 42.50.260

A mechanical interlocking machine is an interlocking machine designed to operate the units mechanically although some of the units may be controlled and operated electrically.

Overlap 42.50.265

Overlap is the distance the control of one signal ex-

tends into the territory which another signal, or signals, governs.

Interlocking Plant 42.50.270

An interlocking plant is an assemblage of switch, lock and/or signal appliances interlocked.

Cross Protection 42.50.275

Cross protection is an arrangement of electric circuits and apparatus to prevent the improper operation of switches and/or signals from the effect of a cross.

Approach Lighting Relay 42.50.280

An approach lighting relay is a relay used to close the lighting circuit for signals upon the approach of a train.

Centrifugal Relay 42.50.285

A centrifugal relay is an alternating-current frequency selective relay in which the contacts are operated by a flyball governor or centrifuge driven by an induction motor.

Interlocking Relay 42.50.290

An interlocking relay is a relay having two sets of coils with their armatures so arranged that with either set of coils deenergized it prevents the other armature from closing or opening a circuit through its contacts.

Line Relay 42.50.295

A line relay is a relay receiving its operating energy through conductors of which the track rails form no part.

Neutral Relay 42.50.300

A neutral relay is a relay which operates in response to a predetermined change of the current in the controlling circuit, irrespective of the direction of the current.

Power Transfer Relay 42.50.305

A power transfer relay is a relay so connected to the normal source of power supply that the failure of such source of power supply causes the load to be transferred to another source of power supply.

Single Element Relay 42.50.310

A single element relay is an alternating-current relay having a set of coils energized by a single circuit.

Three Position Relay 42.50.315

A three position relay is a relay which operates in three positions.

Track Relay 42.50.320

A track relay is a relay receiving all or part of its operating energy through conductors of which the track rails are an essential part.

Transformer Relay 42.50.325

A transformer relay is a relay in which the coils act as a transformer.

Two Element Relay 42.50.330

A two element relay is an alternating-current relay having two sets of coils energized by two circuits.

ELECTRICAL DEFINITIONS

Vane Type Relay 42.50.335

A vane type relay is a type of alternating-current relay in which a light metal disk or vane moves in response to a change of the current in the controlling circuit.

Time Release 42.50.340

A time release is a device used to prevent the operation of an operative unit until after the lapse of a specified time.

Block Signal 42.50.345

A block signal is a fixed signal at the entrance of a block to govern trains entering and using that block.

Color Light Signal 42.50.350

A color light signal is a fixed signal in which the indications are given by the color of a light only.

Flashing Light Signal 42.50.355

A flashing light signal is a highway crossing signal, the indication of which is given by two horizontal red lights flashing alternately at predetermined intervals.

Highway Crossing Signal 42.50.360

A highway crossing signal is an electrically or mechanically operated signal used for the protection of highway traffic at railroad grade crossings.

Position Light Signal 42.50.365

A position light signal is a fixed signal in which the indications are given by the position of two or more lights.

Color Position Light Signal 42.50.370

A color position light signal is a fixed signal in which the indications are given by color and the position of two or more lights.

Smashboard Signal 42.50.375

A smashboard signal is a signal so designed that the arm will be broken when passed in the "Stop" position.

Wig-Wag Signal 42.50.380

A wig-wag signal is a highway crossing signal, the indication of which is given by a horizontally swinging disk with or without a red light attached.

Interlocking Signals 42.50.385

Interlocking signals are the fixed signals of an interlocking plant.

Automatic Block System 42.50.390

An automatic block system is a series of consecutive blocks governed by block signals operated by electric, pneumatic or other agency actuated by a train, or by certain conditions affecting the use of a block.

Block System 42.50.395

A block system is a series of consecutive blocks.

Working Value 42.50.400

Working value is the electrical value which, when applied to an electromagnetic instrument, will cause the moving member to move to its full energized position to provide maximum front contact pressure.

First Voltage Range 42.50.405

The first voltage range is 30 volts or less.

Second Voltage Range 42.50.410

The second voltage range is over 30 volts to and including 175 volts.

Third Voltage Range 42.50.415

The third voltage range is over 175 volts to and including 250 volts.

Fourth Voltage Range 42.50.420

The fourth voltage range is over 250 volts to and including 660 volts.

Fifth Voltage Range 42.50.425

The fifth voltage range is over 660 volts.

Signal Aspect 42.50.430

Signal aspect is the appearance of a signal conveying an indication as received from the direction of an approaching train.

Back Light 42.50.435

A back light is a light showing through a small glass-covered opening in the back of a signal lamp.

Impedance Bond 42.50.440

(Reactance Bond)

An impedance bond is an iron core coil of low resistance and relatively high reactance, providing a continuous path for the return propulsion current around insulated joints, while impeding from one track circuit to another the flow of the alternating current used in signaling and confining the flow of that current to one track circuit.

Remote Control 42.50.445

Remote control is a term applied to power operated switches and/or signals controlled from a distant point.

Circuit Controller 42.50.450

A circuit controller is a device for closing and/or opening electric circuits.

Cutout 42.50.455

A cutout is an electric device to interrupt the flow of current through any particular apparatus or instrument, either automatically or by hand.

Cut-Section 42.50.460

A cut-section is a location other than a signal location where two adjacent track circuits end within a block.

Train Describer 42.50.465

A train describer is an instrument used to give information regarding the origin, destination, class or character of trains, engines or cars moving or to be moved between given points.

Detector Point   42.50.470

A detector point is a device used with certain types of power switch machines to insure that the switch point is within a specified distance to the stock rail.

Focusing Device   42.50.475

A focusing device is an instrument used to sight the light emanating from a signal lamp.

Lever Indication   42.50.480

Lever indication is the information conveyed by means of an indication lock that the movement of an operated unit has been completed.

Signal Indication   42.50.485

Signal indication is the information conveyed by the aspect of a visual signal.

Interlocking Limits   42.50.490

Interlocking limits is that portion of the track of an interlocking plant between opposing home signals over which movements are controlled by interlocking signals.

Operated Unit   42.50.495

An operated unit is a switch, signal, lock or other device, which it is the function of a lever or other operating means to operate.

Pick-Up   42.50.500

Pick-up is the electrical value which, when applied to an electromagnetic instrument, will cause the moving member to move to the position which will just close the front contacts and/or visually indicate its energized position.

Fouling Point   42.50.505

Fouling point is the location in a turnout back of the frog at which insulated joints are placed.

Polarized Relay   42.50.510

A polarized relay is a neutral relay equipped with polar armatures and contacts.

Semaphore Signal   42.50.515

A semaphore signal is a signal in which the day indications are given by the position of a semaphore arm.

Switch-and-Lock Movement   42.50.520

A switch-and-lock movement is a device for the operation of a switch, movable point frog, or derail, the complete movement of which performs the three operations of unlocking, operating and locking.

GROUP 42—TRANSPORTATION—LAND

Section 55—Automatic Train Control

Application Magnet   42.55.005

An application magnet is a magnet located on the track to impart a restrictive impulse to the vehicle apparatus.

Automatic Train Control   42.55.010

Automatic train control is a system or an installation so arranged that its operation will automatically result in either one or the other or both of the following conditions:

(a) Automatic Train Stop

The application of the brakes until the train has been brought to a stop.

(b) Automatic Speed Control

The application of the brakes when the speed of the train exceeds a prescribed rate and continued until the speed has been reduced to a predetermined and prescribed rate.

1. One-Speed Control

A device which, under prescribed conditions, restricts the speed of trains to a prescribed rate.

2. Two-Speed Control

A device which, under prescribed conditions, restricts the speed of trains to each one of two predetermined rates.

3. Three-Speed Control

A device which, under prescribed conditions, restricts the speed of trains to each one of three predetermined rates.

Acknowledge   42.55.015

(Acknowledging) (Acknowledgment)

Acknowledge is the operation by the engineman of a specific part of the automatic train control apparatus, in order to prevent an application of the brakes by the device.

Automatic Train Control Application   42.55.020

Automatic train control application is an application of the brakes through the medium of the automatic train control device.

Axle Circuit   42.55.025

An axle circuit is the circuit through which signal current flows along one of the track rails to the train, through the first wheels and axles of the train and returns to the source along the other track rail.

Axle Current

See 42.55.025.

Actuator Valve   42.55.035

An actuator valve is an electropneumatic valve used to control the operation of a brake valve actuator.

Acknowledging Circuit   42.55.040

An acknowledging circuit is the circuit which is established by the act of acknowledgment for the purpose of preventing an automatic train control application of the brakes.

Acknowledging Contactor   42.55.045

(Forestaller)

An acknowledging contactor is a manually operated electric contactor, used to prevent an automatic train control application of the brakes when passing a restrictive signal or when entering and operating through restrictive territory.

Acknowledging Switch or Forestalling Switch

See 42.55.045.

Acknowledging Whistle or Forestalling Whistle   42.55.055

An acknowledging whistle or forestalling whistle is an air operated whistle which is sounded when a restrictive signal is acknowledged.

Brake Valve Actuator   42.55.060

A brake valve actuator is a device for operating the engineer's brake valve automatically.

Brake Application Valve   42.55.065

A brake application valve is an air valve through the medium of which brakes are automatically applied.

Cab Indicator   42.55.070

A cab indicator is a device located in the cab which indicates a condition of one or more elements of the automatic train control apparatus.

Cab Signal   42.55.075

A cab signal is a device located in the cab which displays an indication of the condition of the controlling section or of fixed signals in advance.

Continuous Train Control   42.55.080

(Continuous Inductive Train Control)

Continuous train control is a form of automatic train control in which information as to the roadway condition in advance is transmitted continuously to the locomotive.

Controlling Section   42.55.085

A controlling section is a length of track consisting of one or more track circuit sections, by means of which the track elements or the device which governs approach to or movement within a block are controlled.

Cut-In   42.55.090

Cut-in is the condition of an automatic train control system under which the coordination of the roadway and the vehicle apparatus will, under prescribed conditions, effect an application of the brakes.

Cut-Out   42.55.095

Cut-out is the condition of an automatic train control system under which the vehicle apparatus will not be affected by the roadway apparatus.

Cut-In Loop   42.55.100

A cut-in loop is a circuit on the roadway to produce a cut-in.

Cut-Out Loop   42.55.105

A cut-out loop is a circuit on the roadway to produce a cut-out.

Code System   42.55.110

A code system is a system of automatic train control in which an electric current of suitable character is fed into the track rails for transmitting "Proceed" indications to a moving train by periodically interrupting or modulating the current in different manners; each indication being controlled by its own distinctive code.

Code Transmitter   42.55.115

A code transmitter is a device the function of which is to open and close automatic train control circuits periodically.

Coder   42.55.120

A coder is a device to interrupt or modulate the track current in various manners in order to establish corresponding controls on the vehicle.

Delayed Application   42.55.125

Delayed application is the withholding for a predetermined time after its initiation by the roadway apparatus, of an application of the brakes by means of the automatic train control system.

Delay Time   42.55.130

Delay time is the period or interval after the initiation of an automatic train control application by the roadway apparatus, and before the application of the brakes becomes effective.

Decoder   42.55.135

A decoder is a device adapted to control vehicle carried apparatus in a manner corresponding to the code to which the track circuit is subjected.

Engine Relay

See 42.55.285.

Forestall   42.55.145

(Forestalling)

Forestall is the operation of a specific part of the automatic train control device in response to an acknowledgment by the engineman, which prevents an application of the brakes.

Forestalling Circuit Controller   42.55.150

A forestalling circuit controller is an air operated circuit controller of the diaphragm operated plunger type used to close electric contacts which cause a sounding of the forestalling whistle.

Indication Point   42.55.155

An indication point is the point at which the impulse is transmitted to the locomotive or vehicle.

Intermittent Train Control   42.55.160

(Intermittent Inductive Train Control)

Intermittent train control is a system of automatic

train control in which impulses are communicated to the locomotive or vehicle at fixed points only.

Inductor (in train control) 42.55.165

An inductor is æ mass of iron, with or without a winding, used to effect inductively a roadway indication to a locomotive or vehicle.

Inductor Circuit 42.55.170

(Inductor Control Circuit)

An inductor circuit is a circuit including the inductor coil and the two lead wires leading therefrom taken through relay and signal mechanism contacts as required.

Loop Circuit 42.55.175

A loop circuit is a circuit which includes a source of electric energy, a line the length of a block and connections to the track rails at both ends of the block.

Loop Current

See 42.55.175.

Operation 42.55.185

Operation is the functioning of the automatic train control device which results from the movement of an equipped vehicle over the track element, or elements, for each block with the automatic train control device in service, or which results from the failure of some part of the device.

Proper Operation 42.55.190

Proper operation is the functioning of the device to create or continue a condition of the vehicle apparatus which corresponds with the condition of the track of the controlling section when the vehicle apparatus is in operative relation with the track elements of the device.

False-Restrictive Operation 42.55.195

False-restrictive operation is the creation or continuance of a condition of the vehicle apparatus which is more restrictive than is required by the condition of the track of the controlling section when the vehicle apparatus is in operative relation with the controlling track elements or which is caused by failure or derangement of some part of the device.

False-Proceed Operation 42.55.200

False-proceed operation is the creation or continuance of a condition of the vehicle apparatus which is less restrictive than is required by the condition of the track of the controlling section when the vehicle is at a point where its apparatus is or should be in operative relation with the controlling track elements.

Potential False-Proceed Operation 42.55.205

Potential false-proceed operation is the existence of a condition of vehicle or roadway apparatus under which a false-proceed operation would have occurred had a vehicle approached or entered a section where normally a restrictive operation would occur.

Ramp 42.55.210

A ramp is a metal bar of limited length, with inclined ends, fixed on the roadway, designed to make contact with and raise vertically a member supported on the vehicle.

Receiver 42.55.215

A receiver is a device on the vehicle so placed that it is in position to be influenced inductively by the train control roadway apparatus.

Reset 42.55.220

(Reset Contactor) (Reset Switch)

A reset is a device to be operated manually in order to permit the release of the brakes after an automatic train control application.

Reset Magnet 42.55.225

A reset magnet is a track magnet to restore the vehicle apparatus to condition for unrestricted operation.

Rail Effect 42.55.230

Rail effect is the term generally applied to the electrical inductive effect on the receiver resulting from passing over the rails in turn-outs or crossings.

NOTE: The changes in the current normally existent in the primary relay caused by such rails can be detected by a meter in the circuit, but are not of sufficient magnitude to cause any interference with the proper operation of the relay.

Shoe 42.55.235

(Ramp Shoe)

A shoe is the part of the vehicle apparatus making contact with the ramp.

Maximum Speed 42.55.240

Maximum speed is that speed beyond which an automatic train control brake application will take place when running under clear signals.

Medium Speed 42.55.245

Medium speed is that speed beyond which an automatic train control brake application will take place when running under medium speed signals.

Low Speed 42.55.250

Low speed is that speed beyond which an automatic train control brake application will take place when running under stop or low-speed signals.

Speed Controller 42.55.255

A speed controller is a device to regulate the speed of a train in accordance with predetermined requirements.

Speed Limit Indicator 42.55.260

A speed limit indicator is a series of lights, controlled by a relay, to indicate the speeds permitted corresponding to the track conditions.

Train Control Territory 42.55.265

Train control territory is that portion of a division or district equipped with an automatic train control system.

Track Element   42.55.270

(Trackway Element) (Wayside Element)

A track element is that portion of the roadway apparatus of an automatic train control system to which the vehicle apparatus is directly responsive.

Trip   42.55.275

Trip is a movement of a vehicle over all or any portion of train control territory between the terminals for that vehicle or the train to which it is assigned; a movement in one direction.

Mechanical Trip   42.55.280

A mechanical trip is a roadway device which, when in operative position, engages apparatus on the locomotive to effect an application of the brakes by the train control system.

Train Control Relay   42.55.285

(Engine Relay)

A train control relay is a relay used to control speed restriction indicating lights; also to control a local circuit energizing an electropneumatic valve which in turn is so arranged that when deenergized a brake application results.

Transmitted Code   42.55.290

A transmitted code is a train control code transmitted to the track circuit.

Train Control

See 42.55.010.

Electropneumatic Valve   42.55.300

An electropneumatic valve is a valve electrically operated which, when operated, will permit or prevent passage of air.

Whistle Valve   42.55.305

A whistle valve is an electropneumatic valve used to control the sounding of a whistle.

Acknowledger or Forestaller   42.55.310

An acknowledger or forestaller is the specific part of the automatic train control apparatus which must be operated in order to prevent an automatic train control application.

See 42.55.045.

GROUP 42—TRANSPORTATION—LAND

Section 60—Car Retarders

Car Retarder   42.60.005

A car retarder is a stationary track brake device, electrically controlled, for reducing the speed of cars, such as in hump yards, through the medium of friction between brake shoes and the sides of the wheels.

Car Retarder Mechanism   42.60.010

A car retarder mechanism is an electrically controlled power operated mechanism used for moving retarder shoes to and from the sides of the car wheels.

Car Retarder Motor   42.60.015

A car retarder motor is a motor for operating a car retarder mechanism, commonly provided with a magnetic brake whose coil is in series with the motor armature circuit, the brake being released by the presence of current and applied by spring pressure.

Car Retarder Lever   42.60.020

A car retarder lever is a lever mechanically operating contacts which control the operation of the contactors in the controller panel which in turn control the movement of the car retarder mechanism.

Dimmer Lever   42.60.025

A dimmer lever is a lever mechanically operating contacts which connect the switch signals to a reduced voltage.

Hump Signal   42.60.030

A hump signal is a signal located at the hump to designate to the engineman information in connection with the direction and speed of movements toward the hump.

Hump Repeater Signal   42.60.035

A hump repeater signal is a signal which repeats the hump signal indication.

Hump Signal Controller   42.60.040

A hump signal controller is a unit located at the hump which includes the hump signal lever, the trimmer signal lever and the signal repeater lights.

Hump Signal Lever or Hump Signal Emergency Lever   42.60.045

A hump signal lever or hump signal emergency lever is a lever usually located in one of the control towers and mechanically operates electric contacts which control the hump signal circuit to change it to a stop indication when in an emergency the operator desires to stop operation.

Hump Engine Cab Signal System   42.60.050

A hump engine cab signal system is a system of signals displayed in the engine cab giving information concerning direction and speed of movements toward the hump.

Lever Machine   42.60.055

A lever machine is a group of levers mechanically operating the electric contacts which control the circuits of the various electric devices in the system with the light indicators which give information concerning the operation of the devices.

Master Controller   42.60.060

A master controller of a car retarder is a cam operated group of electric contacts designed to coordinate the movement of the retarder with the movement of the retarder lever.

Magnetic Time Relay   42.60.065

A magnetic time relay of a car retarder is a relay magnetically operated to limit the permissible time of one retarder movement.

Power Off Indicators   42.60.070

Power off indicators are two light indicators which may be either normally lighted or made dark, one of the lights indicating when alternating-current power is off, and the other when direct-current power is off.

Skate Machine   42.60.075

A skate machine is a mechanism, electrically controlled, for placing on, or removing from, the rails a "skate" which, if allowed to engage with the wheels of a car, provides a continuous braking until the car is stopped.

NOTE: A skate machine may be electrically or pneumatically operated.

Skate Machine Controller   42.60.080

A skate machine controller is a group of electric contacts designed to limit the movement of the machine in either direction.

Skate Machine Brake   42.60.085

A skate machine brake is an electrically operated brake, the coils of which are connected in series with the skate machine motor, designed to hold the mechanism in a fixed position when not being operated.

Skate Machine Lever   42.60.090

A skate machine lever is a lever mechanically operating electric contacts which control the direction of the movement of the skate machine.

Switch Machine   42.60.095

A switch machine for car retarder yards is a quick-acting mechanism, electrically controlled, for positioning track switch points, and so arranged that the accidental "trailing" of the switch points does not cause damage.

NOTE: A switch machine may be operated by a pneumatic or electric motor.

Switch Machine Pole Changer   42.60.100

A switch machine pole changer is a group of electric contacts mechanically operated to limit the move-

ment of the switch machine and change connections for reversing movement.

Switch Machine Point Detector   42.60.105

A switch machine point detector is a group of contacts designed to open an electric circuit if switch points are not properly set for the movement of trains.

Switch Machine Lever   42.60.110

A switch machine lever is a lever mechanically operating electric contacts which control the direction of movement of the switch machine.

Switch Machine Lever Lock   42.60.115

A switch machine lever lock is a lock electrically controlled by the switch machine current, which prevents the movement of the switch machine lever while the switch machine is taking current.

Switch Machine Lever Lights   42.60.120

Switch machine lever lights are a group of lights indicating the position of the switch machine.

Signal Repeater Lights   42.60.125

Signal repeater lights are a group of lights indicating the signal displayed for humping and trimming.

Switch Signal Lever   42.60.130

A switch signal lever is a lever mechanically operating electric contacts which cut off current to the switch signals.

Switch Signal   42.60.135

A switch signal is a color light or rotary signal located at each switch to indicate the position of the switch.

Thermal Relay   42.60.140

A thermal relay is a relay controlled by the heating effect of motor current for the purpose of cutting off current if the motor approaches an unsafe degree of heating.

Trimmer Signal   42.60.145

A trimmer signal is a signal which gives information to the engineman concerning movements to be made from the classification tracks into the switch and retarder area.

Trimmer Signal Lever   42.60.150

A trimmer signal lever is a lever operating contacts which control the trimmer signal indications.

GROUP 42—TRANSPORTATION—LAND

Section 95—Not Otherwise Classified

Bus Line   42.95.005

A bus line is a continuous electric circuit other than the electric train line, extending through two or more vehicles of a train, for the distribution of electric energy.

Electric Coupler   42.95.010

An electric coupler is a group of devices which pro-

vides for readily connecting or disconnecting electric circuits between vehicles.

Electric Coupler Socket or Receptacle   42.95.015

An electric coupler socket or receptacle is the fixed portion of an electric coupler.

ELECTRICAL DEFINITIONS

Electric Coupler Plug 42.95.020

An electric coupler plug is the removable portion of an electric coupler.

Electric Train Line 42.95.025

An electric train line in a multiple unit control system is a continuous multiple electric circuit extending between vehicles provided with control stations to permit the control of the traction motors and other equipment from any one of several points on the train.

An electric train line as applied to electric car lighting and power supply is a continuous electric circuit extending the length of the car with electric train line coupler, for transmitting current from one car to another.

Grounded Parts

See **35.15.060.**

Jumper 42.95.035

A jumper is a conductor used to make electric connection between terminals, or around a break in a circuit.

NOTE: As applied to vehicles it usually consists of two electric coupler plugs with connecting cable although sometimes one end of the connecting cable is permanently attached to the vehicle.

Electric Train Line Coupler 42.95.040

An electric train line coupler is a group of devices which connects electric train line circuits between vehicles.

Deadman's Handle 42.95.045

A deadman's handle is a safety attachment to the handle of a controller, or to a brake valve, causing the current to the traction motors to be cut off, and/or the brakes to be applied, if the pressure of the operator's hand on the handle is released.

Electric Air Compressor Governor 42.95.050

An electric air compressor governor is a device responsive to variations in air pressure, which automatically starts or stops the operation of a compressor for the purpose of maintaining air pressure in a reservoir between predetermined limits.

Deadman's Feature 42.95.055

A deadman's feature is that feature of a control system which acts to cause the current to the traction motors to be cut off, and/or the brakes to be applied if the operator becomes incapacitated.

GROUP 45—ELECTROMECHANICAL APPLICATIONS

SECTIONS

02   Methods of Speed Control of D-C Motors
10   Elevators
11   Cranes, Derricks and Hoists

Section 02—Methods of Speed Control of Direct-Current Motors

Motor-Field Control   45.02.005

Motor-field control is a method of controlling the speed of a motor by means of a change in the magnitude of the field current.

Armature-Voltage Control   45.02.010

Armature-voltage control is a method of controlling the speed of a motor by means of a change in the magnitude of the voltage impressed on its armature winding.

Multivoltage Control   45.02.015

Multivoltage control is a form of armature-voltage control obtained by impressing successively on the armature of the motor a number of substantially fixed voltages such as may be obtained from multicommutator generators common to a group of motors.

Adjustable-Voltage Control   45.02.020

Adjustable-voltage control is a form of armature-voltage control obtained by impressing on the armature of the motor a voltage which may be changed in small increments, but when once adjusted, it and consequently the speed of the motor are practically unaffected by a change in load. Such a voltage may be obtained from an individual shunt-wound generator with adjustable field current, for each motor.

Varying-Voltage Control   45.02.025

Varying-voltage control is a form of armature-voltage control obtained by impressing on the armature of the motor a voltage which varies considerably with change in load, with a consequent change in speed, such as may be obtained from a differentially compound-wound generator or by means of resistance in the armature circuit.

Adjustable Varying-Voltage Control   45.02.030

Adjustable varying-voltage control is a form of armature-voltage control obtained by impressing on the armature of the motor a voltage which may be changed by small increments, but when once adjusted for a given load will vary considerably with change in load with a consequent change in speed, such as may be obtained from a differentially compound-wound generator with adjustable field current or by means of an adjustable resistance in the armature circuit.

GROUP 45—ELECTROMECHANICAL APPLICATIONS

Section 10—Elevators

Elevator   45.10.005

An elevator is a hoisting and lowering mechanism equipped with a car or platform which moves in guides in a substantially vertical direction.

> NOTE: Dumbwaiters, endless belts, conveyors, chains, buckets, etc., used for the purpose of elevating materials and tiering, piling or feeding machines giving service within one story, are not included in the term "elevator".

Electric Elevator   45.10.010

An electric elevator is one in which the motion of the car is obtained through an electric motor directly applied to the elevator machinery.

Electrohydraulic Elevator   45.10.015

An electrohydraulic elevator is one in which the lifting of the car is obtained by means of an electric motor driving a pump, which pumps liquid directly into the cylinder.

Signal-Control Electric Elevator

See 45.10.140.

Electric Automatic Push-Button (Self-Service) Elevator   45.10.025

An electric automatic push-button (self-service) elevator is one that is operated by means of momentary pressure of push buttons at the landings with or without push buttons in the car.

Continuous-Pressure Electric Elevator   45.10.030

A continuous-pressure electric elevator is one operated by means of push buttons or switches in the car and at the landings, which requires a button or switch to be held manually in contact to keep the car in motion.

Elevator Machine   45.10.035

An elevator machine is the machinery and its equipment used in raising and lowering the elevator car or platform.

Traction Machine   45.10.040

A traction machine is an elevator machine in which the motion of the car is obtained through friction between the hoisting ropes and the traction sheave.

Geared Traction Machine   45.10.045

A geared traction machine is a traction machine which employs gearing between the electric motor and the traction sheave.

Gearless Traction Machine 45.10.050

A gearless traction machine is a traction machine which has the traction sheave and the brake drum mounted directly on the electric motor shaft.

Winding-Drum Machine 45.10.055

A winding-drum machine is an elevator machine in which the cables are fastened to and wind on a drum.

Electric-Elevator Controller 45.10.059

An electric-elevator controller is a device, or a group of devices, which serves to govern, in some predetermined manner, the electric energy delivered to the apparatus to which it is connected.

Control of an Elevator 45.10.060

The control of an elevator is a system of regulation by which the starting, stopping, direction of motion, acceleration, speed and retardation of an elevator are governed.

Rheostatic Control 45.10.065

Rheostatic control is a system in which control is accomplished primarily by varying resistance and/or reactance in the armature and/or field circuit of the hoisting motor.

Multivoltage Control

See 45.02.015

Generator-Field Control 45.10.075

Generator-field control is a system in which control is primarily accomplished by the use of an individual generator for each elevator in which the voltage applied to the hoisting motor is adjusted by varying the strength and direction of the generator field.

Two-Speed, Alternating-Current Elevator Control 45.10.080

A two speed, alternating-current elevator control is a control for a two-speed induction elevator motor which is arranged to run at two different, practically constant speeds, by connecting the motor windings so as to obtain different numbers of poles.

Operation 45.10.085

Operation is the method of actuating the controller.

See 25.05.005.

Operating Device 45.10.090

The operating device is the car switch, push button, rope, wheel, lever, treadles or other means employed to enable the operator to actuate the controller.

Car-Switch Operation 45.10.095

Car-switch operation is operation wherein the movement of the car is directly and solely under the control of the operator by means of a switch in the car.

Automatic Operation 45.10.100

Automatic operation is operation by means of buttons or switches at the landings, with or without buttons or switches in the car, the momentary pressing of which will cause the car to start and automatically stop at the landing corresponding to the button pressed.

Single-Automatic Operation 45.10.105

Single-automatic operation is automatic operation by means of one button in the car for each landing level served and one button at each landing, so arranged that if any car or landing button has been pressed the pressure of any other car or landing operating button will have no effect on the operation of the car until the response to the first button has been completed.

Non-Selective Collective Automatic Operation 45.10.110

Non-selective collective automatic operation is automatic operation by means of one button in the car for each landing level served and one button at each landing, wherein all stops registered by the momentary pressure of landing or car buttons are made irrespective of the number of buttons pressed or of the sequence in which the buttons are pressed. With this type of operation the car stops at all landings for which buttons have been pressed, making the stops in the order in which the landings are reached after the buttons have been pressed but irrespective of its direction of travel.

Selective Collective Automatic Operation 45.10.115

Selective collective automatic operation is automatic operation by means of one button in the car for each landing level served and by "Up" and "Down" buttons at the landings, wherein all stops registered by the momentary pressure of the car buttons are made as defined under non-selective collective automatic operation but wherein the stops registered by the momentary pressure of the landing buttons are made in the order in which the landings are reached in each direction of travel after the buttons have been pressed. With this type of operation, all "Up" landing calls are answered when the car is traveling in the "Up" direction and all "Down" landing calls are answered when the car is traveling in the "Down" direction, except in the case of the uppermost or lowermost calls which are answered as soon as they are reached, irrespective of the direction of travel of the car.

Dual Operation 45.10.120

Dual operation is a system of operation whereby the elevator controller is arranged for automatic operation by means of landing and car buttons or switches, or for manual operation by an operator in the car who may either use a car switch or the car push buttons. When operated by an operator, upon the throwing of a suitable switch or switches, the car can no longer be started by the landing push buttons; which buttons may, however, be used to signal the operator that the car is desired at certain landings.

Continuous-Pressure Operation 45.10.125

Continuous-pressure operation is operation by means of push buttons or switches in the car and at landings, any one of which may be used to control the movement of the car so long as the button or switch is manually held in the operating position.

ELECTRICAL DEFINITIONS

Car Switch Automatic Floor-Stop Operation 45.10.130

Car switch automatic floor-stop operation is operation in which the stop is initiated by the operator from within the car with a definite reference to the landing at which it is desired to stop, after which the slowing down and stopping of the elevator is automatically effected.

Preregister Operation 45.10.135

Preregister operation is operation in which signals to stop are registered in advance by buttons in the car and at the landings. At the proper point in the car travel the operator in the car is notified by a signal, visual, audible or otherwise, to initiate the stop, after which the landing stop is automatic.

Signal Operation 45.10.140

Signal operation is operation by means of signal buttons or switches (or both) in the car, and "Up" or "Down" direction buttons (or both) at the landings, by which predetermined landing stops may be set up or registered for an elevator or for a group of elevators. The stops set up by the momentary pressure of the car buttons are made automatically in succession as the car reaches those landings, irrespective of its direction of travel or the sequence in which the buttons are pressed. The stops set up by the momentary pressure of the "Up" and "Down" buttons at the landing are made automatically by the first available car in the group approaching the landing in the corresponding direction, irrespective of the sequence in which the buttons are pressed. With this type of operation the car can be started only by means of a starting switch or button in the car.

Emergency-Stop Switch 45.10.145

An emergency-stop switch (safety switch) is a device in the car used to cut off the power from the elevator machine independently of the operating devices.

Non-Stop Switch 45.10.155

A non-stop switch is a switch which, when thrown, will prevent the elevator from making hall stops and will automatically transfer these hall-stop signals to the next car following.

Signal Transfer Switch 45.10.160

A signal transfer switch is a switch in the car which may be thrown by the operator when the car is filled or when, for some other reason, it is desirable to pass a signal, and which thereby transfers the signal to the next car approaching in the same direction.

Elevator Potential Switch 45.10.165

An elevator potential switch is a switch which disconnects the power from the elevator apparatus when the supply voltage fails or decreases below a definite value and which is usually opened by various electric safety devices. These switches are of the magnetic type.

Elevator Slack-Cable Switch 45.10.170

An elevator slack-cable switch is a device for automatically cutting off the power in case the hoisting cables become slack.

Hoistway-Door Interlock 45.10.175

A hoistway-door interlock is a device, the purpose of which is:

First—To prevent the operation of the elevator machine in a direction to move the car away from a landing unless the hoistway door at that landing at which the car is stopping or is at rest is locked in the closed position.

Second—To prevent the opening of the hoistway door from the landing side except by special key; unless the car is at rest within the landing zone, or is coasting through the landing zone with its operating device in the stop position.

A hoistway-door interlock may be used in a *door unit system*, which meets the above requirements, but does not require all the hoistway doors to be locked in the closed position; or in a *hoistway unit system* which, in addition to fulfilling the above first and second requirements, will also prevent the operation of the car unless all hoistway doors are locked in the closed position.

Hoistway-Door or Hoistway-Gate Electric Contact 45.10.180

A hoistway-door or hoistway-gate electric contact is a device the purpose of which is to open the operating circuit, or an auxiliary circuit, unless the hoistway door or gate at which the car is standing is in the closed position and thus prevents operation of the elevator in a direction to move the car away from the landing by the normal operating device.

Elevator Emergency Terminal Slowdown Device 45.10.185

An elevator emergency terminal slowdown device is one so arranged that when the elevator does not slow down properly when approaching the terminal landings, an emergency retarding force is applied.

Elevator Automatic Shutdown Device 45.10.190

An elevator automatic shutdown device is one that automatically disconnects the elevator apparatus, usually the motor-generator set, after the elevator has remained stopped for a definite time interval, which time interval may be adjustable.

Emergency Release 45.10.195

An emergency release is a device the purpose of which is to make inoperative door or gate electric contacts or door interlocks in case of emergency.

Normal Terminal-Stopping Device 45.10.200

A normal terminal-stopping device is an automatic device for stopping the elevator car within the overtravel independently of the operating device.

Final Terminal-Stopping Device 45.10.205

A final terminal-stopping device is an automatic device for stopping the car and counterweight from contract speed, within the top clearance and bottom overtravel, independently of the operation of the normal terminal-stopping device, and the operating device.

Car-Door or Car-Gate Electric Contact　　45.10.210

A car-door or car-gate electric contact is a device the purpose of which is to open the operating circuit, or an auxiliary circuit, unless the car door or car gate is in the closed position, and thus prevent operation of the elevator in a direction to move the car away from the landing by the normal operating device.

Car-Leveling Device　　45.10.215

A car-leveling device is any mechanism or control that will move the car within a limited zone toward, and stop the car at, the landing.

Position Indicator　　45.10.220

A position indicator is a device that indicates the position of the elevator car in the hoistway. It is called a hall position indicator when placed in the hall or a car position indicator when placed in the car.

Elevator Starter's Panel　　45.10.225

An elevator starter's panel is an assembly of devices by means of which the starter is kept informed of the condition of the elevator service. This panel is generally located in the elevator hallway on the main entrance level.

Automatic Dispatching Device　　45.10.230

An automatic dispatching device is a device whose principal function is to operate automatically a signal in the car to indicate when that car should leave the terminal.

Elevator Separate Signal System　　45.10.235

An elevator separate signal system is one providing push buttons in the hallways, which, when momentarily pressed by a person desiring elevator service, indicate in the car where the operator is to stop, by illuminating a flash signal or operating an annunciator.

Elevator Automatic Signal Transfer Device　　45.10.240

An elevator automatic signal transfer device is one used with manually operated elevators, by means of which the signal is automatically transferred to the next car following, in case a car passes a set signal without making a stop.

Waiting-Passenger Indicator　　45.10.245

A waiting-passenger indicator is an indicator which shows for a single elevator or a group of elevators where and for which direction hall buttons have been pressed, and also indicates when these calls have been answered. This indicator is usually located at the lower terminal.

Elevator Car Annunciator　　45.10.250

An elevator car annunciator is an electric device in the car, which indicates the landings at which hall buttons have been pressed.

Elevator Car Flash-Signal Device　　45.10.255

An elevator car flash-signal device is one providing a signal light in the car, which is illuminated when approaching the landings at which hall buttons have been pressed.

Elevator Electric Door Operator　　45.10.260

An elevator electric door operator is an electric device for operating the hoistway or car door or both.

Elevator Hall Signal Button　　45.10.265

An elevator hall signal button is a push button placed in the elevator hallways, by momentary pressure of which a stop signal is registered in the car.

Elevator Hall Stop Button　　45.10.270

An elevator hall stop button is a push button placed in the elevator hallway, which, when momentarily pressed, automatically causes the elevator car to stop at that floor.

Elevator Electric Traveling Cable　　45.10.275

An elevator electric traveling cable is a cable made up of electric conductors, which provides electric connection between the car and stationary apparatus.

Dumbwaiter　　45.10.280

A dumbwaiter is a hoisting and lowering mechanism equipped with a car, which moves in guides in a substantially vertical direction, the floor area of which does not exceed nine (9) square feet, whose compartment height does not exceed four (4) feet, the capacity of which does not exceed 500 pounds, and which is used exclusively for carrying freight.

Electric Dumbwaiter　　45.10.285

An electric dumbwaiter is one in which the motion of the car is obtained through an electric motor directly applied to the dumbwaiter machinery.

Escalator　　45.10.290

An escalator is a moving inclined continuous stairway or runway used for raising or lowering passengers.

Electric Escalator　　45.10.295

An electric escalator is one in which the motion is obtained through an electric motor directly applied to the escalator machinery.

Electric Stage Lift　　45.10.300

An electric stage lift is an electrically driven mechanism for raising and lowering various sections of a stage.

Electric Console Lift　　45.10.305

An electric console lift is an electrically driven mechanism for raising and lowering an organ console and the organist.

Electric Orchestra Lift　　45.10.310

An electric orchestra lift is an electrically driven mechanism for raising and lowering the musicians' platform and the musicians.

Electric Incline Railway　　45.10.315

An electric incline railway consists of an electric hoist operating a single car with or without counterweights, or two cars in balance, which car or cars travel on inclined tracks.

GROUP 45—ELECTROMECHANICAL APPLICATIONS

Section 11—Cranes, Derricks and Hoists

Crane   45.11.005

A crane is a machine for lifting or lowering a load and moving it horizontally, in which the hoisting mechanism is an integral part of the machine. It may be driven manually or by power and may be a fixed or a mobile machine.

Derrick   45.11.010

A derrick is an apparatus consisting of a mast or equivalent members held at the top by guys or braces, with or without a boom, for use with a hoisting mechanism and operating ropes.

Hoist   45.11.015

A hoist is an apparatus for moving a load by the application of a pulling force, and not including a car or platform running in guides.

Overhead Electric Hoist   45.11.020

An overhead electric hoist is a motor driven hoist having one or more drums or sheaves for rope or chain, and supported overhead. It may be fixed or traveling.

Base-Mounted Electric Hoist   45.11.025

A base-mounted electric hoist is a hoist similar to an overhead electric hoist, except that it has a base or feet and may be mounted overhead, on a vertical plane or in any position for which it is designed.

Electrically Operated Brake   45.11.030

An electrically operated brake is a friction brake actuated or controlled by electric means.

Collectors   45.11.035

Collectors are contacting devices for collecting current from the contact conductors.

Contact Conductors   45.11.040

Contact conductors are the fixed electric conductors from which current is collected by moving contacts or shoes for operating the motors of an electric traveling crane.

Emergency-Stop Switch   45.11.045

An emergency-stop switch is a manually operated electric switch to cut off electric power independently of the regular operating devices.

Limit Switch   45.11.050

A limit switch is a device designed to cut off the power automatically at or near the limit of travel of a crane, trolley, hoist or similar mechanism, independently of the operating devices.

GROUP 50—ELECTRIC WELDING AND CUTTING

SECTIONS

05 General
10 Arc Welding and Cutting

15 Resistance Welding
95 Not Otherwise Classified

Section 05—General

Weld   50.05.005

A weld is a localized consolidation of metals by a welding process.

Fusion Welding   50.05.010

Fusion welding is a group of processes in which metals are welded together by bringing them to the molten state at the surfaces to be joined, with or without the addition of filler metal, without the application of mechanical pressure or blows.

Manual Weld   50.05.015

A manual weld is a weld wherein the arc is controlled or the torch is manipulated by hand.

Automatic Welding   50.05.020

Automatic welding is welding with equipment which automatically controls the entire welding operation. (Including feed, speed, oscillation, interruption, etc.)

Welded Joint   50.05.030

A welded joint is a localized union of two or more parts by welding.

Base Metal   50.05.035

(Parent Metal)
Base metal is the metal to be welded or cut.

Weld Metal   50.05.040

Weld metal is the metal resulting from the fusion of the filler or base metals or both.

Filler Metal   50.05.045

Filler metal is material to be added in making a weld.

Deposited Metal   50.05.050

Deposited metal is metal that has been added by a welding process.

Bond   50.05.065

A bond is the junction of the weld metal and the base metal.

Electric Brazing   50.05.070

Electric brazing is a group of brazing processes wherein the heat is obtained from electric current.

Electrode   50.05.075

A. *In Metal Arc Welding:* The filler metal in the form of a wire or rod, either bare or covered, through which current is conducted between the electrode holder and the arc.

B. *In Carbon Arc Welding:* A carbon or graphite rod through which current is conducted between the electrode holder and the arc.

C. *In Atomic Hydrogen Welding:* One or two tungsten rods between the points of which the arc is maintained.

D. *In Resistance Welding:* A bar, wheel, clamp or die through which the current is conducted and the pressure applied to the work.

Ground Connections

See **50.05.090.**

Induction Brazing   50.05.080

Induction brazing is an electric brazing process wherein the heat is obtained from induced current.

Non-Pressure Welding   50.05.085

Non-pressure welding is a group of welding processes wherein the weld is made without pressure.

Welding Ground   50.05.090

A welding ground (in arc welding) is the side of the circuit opposite the welding electrode.

Welding Leads   50.05.095

Welding leads are conductors furnishing an electric path between source of welding power and electrodes.

Crater   50.05.100

A crater is a depression at the termination of an arc weld.

GROUP 50—ELECTRIC WELDING AND CUTTING

Section 10—Arc Welding and Cutting

Arc Welding   50.10.005

Arc welding is a non-pressure (fusion) welding process wherein the welding heat is obtained from an arc either between the base metal and an electrode, or between two electrodes.

Carbon Arc Welding   50.10.010

Carbon arc welding is an arc welding process wherein

a carbon or graphite electrode or electrodes is used with or without the use of filler metal.

Shielded Carbon Arc Welding   50.10.015

Shielded carbon arc welding is a carbon arc welding process wherein the arc and molten weld metal are protected from the atmosphere by a shielding medium.

Unshielded Carbon Arc Welding   50.10.016

Unshielded carbon arc welding is a carbon arc welding process wherein no shielding medium is used.
See **50.10.015.**

Metal Arc Welding   50.10.020

Metal arc welding is an arc welding process wherein the electrode supplies the filler metal in the weld.

Semi-Automatic Metal Arc Weld   50.10.021

A semi-automatic metal arc weld is a weld made with equipment which automatically controls the feed of the electrode—the manipulation of the electrode being controlled by hand.

Shielded Metal Arc Welding   50.10.025

Shielded metal arc welding is a metal arc welding process wherein the arc and weld metal are protected from the atmosphere by a shielding medium.
See **50.10.026.**

Unshielded Metal Arc Welding   50.10.026

Unshielded metal arc welding is a metal arc welding process wherein no shielding medium is used.
See **50.10.025.**

Atomic Hydrogen Welding   50.10.030

Atomic hydrogen welding is an alternating-current arc welding process wherein the welding heat is obtained from an arc between two suitable electrodes in an atmosphere of hydrogen.

Carbon Arc Cutting   50.10.035

Carbon arc cutting is the process of severing metals by melting with the heat of the carbon arc.

Metal Arc Cutting   50.10.040

Metal arc cutting is the process of severing metals by melting with the heat of the metal arc.

Arc Welding Electrode

See **50.05.075.**

Carbon Electrode

See **50.05.075.**

Metal Electrode

See **50.05.075.**

Welding Rod   50.10.060

A welding rod is filler metal, in wire or rod form, used in the gas welding process and those arc welding processes wherein the electrode does not furnish the metal.

Bare (Lightly Coated) Electrode   50.10.065

A bare electrode is a solid metal electrode with no coating other than that incidental to the manufacture of the electrode or with a light coating.

Alternating-Current Arc Welding   50.10.070

Alternating-current arc welding is an arc welding process wherein the power supply at the arc is alternating current.

Arc Brazing   50.10.075

Arc brazing is an electric brazing process wherein the heat is obtained from an arc formed between the base metal and an electrode or between two electrodes.

Arc Voltage   50.10.080

Arc voltage is the voltage across the arc.

Coated Electrode

See **50.10.090.**

Covered (Shielded Arc) Electrode   50.10.090

A covered electrode is a metal electrode which has a relatively thick covering material serving the dual purpose of stabilizing the arc and improving the properties of the weld metal.

Composite Electrode   50.10.095

A composite electrode is an electrode with or without a flux having more than one filler material combined mechanically.

Electrode Holder   50.10.100

An electrode holder is a device used for holding the electrode mechanically.

Direct-Current Arc Welding   50.10.105

Direct-current arc welding is an arc welding process wherein the power supply at the arc is direct current.

Welding Arc Voltage   50.10.110

Welding arc voltage is the total voltage between the electrode holder and the base metal immediately adjacent to the arc terminal. It is the summation of the arc stream voltage, the cathode drop, the anode drop, the drop in the electrode and the contact drop between the electrode holder and the electrode.†

† In the case of the Zerener process employing two electrodes, the welding arc voltage is the total voltage between the two electrode holders.

True Arc Voltage   50.10.115

True arc voltage is the summation of the arc stream voltage, the cathode drop and the anode drop. It is determined by deducting from the welding arc voltage, the drop in the electrode and the contact drop between the electrode holder and the electrode.

Open-Circuit Voltage   50.10.120

Open-circuit voltage is the voltage between the terminals of the welding source when no current is flowing in the welding circuit.

Arc Stream Voltage   50.10.125

Arc stream voltage is the voltage across the gaseous zone which varies with the length of the arc.

Cathode Drop   50.10.130

Cathode drop is the voltage drop between the arc stream and the negative electrode.

Anode Drop   50.10.135

Anode drop is the voltage drop between the arc stream and the positive electrode.

Electrode Drop   50.10.140

Electrode drop is the voltage drop in the electrode due to its resistance (or impedance).

Single Operator Motor-Generator Set   50.10.145

A single operator motor-generator set is a motor-generator set designed to supply current to only one welding arc from one generator.

Multiple Operator Motor-Generator Set   50.10.150

A multiple operator motor-generator set is a motor-generator set designed to supply current to two or more welding arcs at the same time from one generator or from two or more single operator generators mechanically connected.

Constant-Voltage Welding Source   50.10.155

A constant-voltage welding source is one which automatically maintains its voltage within 5 percent of the rated full-load setting over the range from full-load to no-load and has a time of recovery of not more than 0.3 second.

Variable-Voltage Welding Source   50.10.160

A variable-voltage welding source is one in which the voltage automatically reduces as the current increases but not in such a way as to qualify the source as a constant-energy source.

Constant-Current Welding Source   50.10.165

A constant-current welding source is one which, when adjusted to give rated current output with normal arc voltage, will automatically maintain this current output within 5 percent of the rated value with a variation in arc voltage of 10 percent above or below the normal arc voltage and has a time of recovery of not more than 0.3 second.

Constant-Power Welding Source   50.10.170

A constant-power welding source is one which, when adjusted to give rated power output with normal arc voltage, will automatically maintain this power output within 5 percent of the rated value with a variation in arc voltage of 10 percent above or below the normal arc voltage and has a time of recovery of not more than 0.3 second.

Time of Recovery   50.10.175

Time of recovery is the time required to assume conditions which are within a specified amount of their final value in an automatically regulated welding circuit after a definitely specified disturbance has taken place.

NOTE: The standard procedure for determining the time of recovery of a welding machine is as follows: With the machine operating on open-circuit, short-circuit the welding circuit and then abruptly remove the short-circuit. The time which has elapsed between the removal of the short-circuit and the attainment of 50 percent of the open-circuit voltage for the particular current setting is taken as the time of recovery.

Reversed Polarity (Electrode Positive)   50.10.180

Reversed polarity is the arrangement of direct-current arc welding leads wherein the work is the negative pole and the electrode is the positive pole of the arc circuit.

Straight Polarity (Electrode Negative)   50.10.185

Straight polarity is the arrangement of direct-current arc welding leads wherein the work is the positive pole and the electrode is the negative pole of the arc circuit.

GROUP 50—ELECTRIC WELDING AND CUTTING

Section 15—Resistance Welding

Resistance Welding   50.15.005

Resistance welding is a pressure welding process wherein the welding heat is obtained by passing an electric current between the contact areas to be welded.

Pressure Welding   50.15.010

Pressure welding is a group of welding processes wherein the weld is consummated by pressure.

Spot Welding   50.15.015

Spot welding is a resistance welding process wherein the fusion is confined to a relatively small portion of the area of the lapped parts to be joined.

Resistance Butt Welding   50.15.020

Resistance butt welding is a group of resistance welding processes wherein the fusion occurs simultaneously over the entire contact area of the parts being joined.

Upset Butt Welding   50.15.025

Upset butt welding is a resistance butt welding process wherein the potential is applied after the parts to be welded are brought in contact.

Flash Butt Welding   50.15.030

Flash butt welding is a resistance butt welding process wherein the potential is applied before the parts are brought in contact and where the heat is derived principally from a series of arcs between the parts being welded.

Electrode Tip   50.15.035

(Point)

An electrode tip is a replaceable tip of metal on an electrode having the electrical and physical characteristics required for spot and projection welding.

Seam Welding   50.15.040

Seam welding is a resistance welding process wherein overlapping or tangent spot welds are made progressively.

Flash   50.15.045

(Fin)

Flash is metal expelled from a joint made by the resistance welding process.

Interrupted Spot Welding   50.15.050

Interrupted spot welding is a spot welding process wherein fusion is accomplished by means of successive applications of electric energy between contact electrodes during a single application of pressure to the electrodes.

Contact Jaw   50.15.055

A contact jaw is an electric terminal used in a resistance butt welding machine to securely clamp the parts to be welded and conduct the electric current to those parts.

Multiple Resistance Welding   50.15.060

Multiple resistance welding is a resistance welding process wherein two or more separate welds are made simultaneously.

Poke Welding   50.15.065

Poke welding is a spot welding process wherein pressure is applied manually to one electrode only.

Progressive Spot Welding   50.15.070

Progressive spot welding is a resistance spot welding process wherein two or more spot welds are made automatically one after the other by the actuation of a single control device.

Resistance Brazing   50.15.075

Resistance brazing is an electric brazing process wherein the heat is obtained from the resistance to the flow of an electric current.

Resistance Flash Butt Welding

See **50.15.030.**

Resistance Welding Time   50.15.085

Resistance welding time is the time of duration of the welding current.

Projection Welding   50.15.090

Projection welding is a pressure resistance welding process wherein localization of heat between two surfaces or between the end of one member and the surface of another is effected by projections.

Series Welding   50.15.095

Series welding is a resistance welding process wherein two or more welds are made simultaneously in a single welding circuit with the total current passing through every weld.

Butt Resistance Welding

See **50.15.020.**

Percussive Welding   50.15.155

Percussive welding is a resistance welding process utilizing electric energy suddenly discharged.

Electrostatic Percussive Welding   50.15.160

Electrostatic percussive welding is a percussive welding process wherein a condenser is used to supply the energy.

Electromagnetic Percussive Welding   50.15.165

Electromagnetic percussive welding is a percussive welding process wherein the stored energy in a magnetic field is transformed by the collapse of the field to supply the energy.

Induction Resistance Welding   50.15.170

Induction resistance welding is a resistance welding process wherein the heating current is caused to flow in the parts to be welded by electromagnetic induction without any electric contact between the source and the work.

Progressive Induction Seam Welding   50.15.175

Progressive induction seam welding is an induction resistance welding process wherein the heating current is caused to flow in the parts to be welded and to cross the seam of the weld in a localized zone while there is relative progressive traversing movement of the parts to be welded and the welding zone along the seam.

GROUP 50—ELECTRIC WELDING AND CUTTING
Section 95—Not Otherwise Classified

Qualified Welder   50.95.005

A qualified welder is a welder who, under specified conditions, can consistently make welds having specified properties.

GROUP 55—ILLUMINATING ENGINEERING

SECTIONS

Section 05—Photometric Quantities

Light   55.05.005

For the purposes of illuminating engineering, *light* is radiant energy (see **55.10.005**) evaluated according to its capacity to produce visual sensation.

NOTE: The standard basis for the evaluation of radiant energy as light (or of radiant flux as luminous flux) when different spectral distributions are involved, is the set of relative luminosity (visibility) factors adopted by the Illuminating Engineering Society and the International Commission on Illumination in 1924 and by the International Committee on Weights and Measures in 1933.
See **55.05.095** to **55.05.100**.

Luminous Flux,[†] F   55.05.010

Luminous flux is the time rate of flow of light.

Lumen,[†] lm   55.05.015

The lumen is the unit of luminous flux. It is equal to the flux through a unit solid angle (steradian) from a uniform point source of one candle, or to the flux on a unit surface all points of which are at unit distance from a uniform point source of one candle.

NOTE: For some purposes the kilolumen, equal to 1,000 lumens, is a convenient unit.

Luminous Intensity,[†] $I = dF/d\omega$ 55.05.020

Luminous intensity, of a source of light, in a given direction, is the solid-angular flux density in the direction in question. Hence, it is the luminous flux on a small surface normal to that direction, divided by the solid angle (in steradians) which the surface subtends at the source of light.

NOTE: Mathematically a solid angle must have a point as its apex; the definition of luminous intensity therefore applies strictly only to a point source. In practice, however, light emanating from a source whose dimensions are negligible in comparison with the distance from which it is observed may be considered as coming from a point. For extended sources, see **55.25.065**.

Candle,[†] c   55.05.025

The candle is the unit of luminous intensity. The unit used in the United States is a specified fraction of the average horizontal candlepower of a group of 45 carbon-filament lamps preserved at the National Bureau of Standards, when the lamps are operated at specified voltages. This unit is identical, within the limits of uncertainty of measurement, with the International Candle established in 1909 by agreement between the national standardizing laboratories of France, Great Britain and the United States, and adopted in 1921 by the International Commission on Illumination.

NOTE: The international agreement of 1909 fixed only the unit at low color temperatures as represented by carbon-filament lamps. In rating lamps at higher temperatures, differences developed between the units used in different countries. The International Committee on Weights and Measures adopted in 1937 a new system of units based upon (1) assigning 60 candles per square centimeter as the brightness of a blackbody at the temperature of freezing platinum, and (2) deriving values for standards having other spectral distributions by use of the accepted luminosity factors. (See **55.05.095** to **55.05.100**.) It was planned to introduce the new units into use January 1, 1940, but this step has been deferred until further international comparisons of standards can be made.

Candlepower, $I = dF/d\omega$; abbreviation, cp   55.05.030

Candlepower is luminous intensity expressed in candles.

See **55.25.040** to **55.25.065**.

Illumination,[†] $E = dF/dA$ 55.05.035

Illumination is the density of the luminous flux on a surface; it is the quotient of the flux by the area of the surface when the latter is uniformly illuminated.

NOTE: The term "illumination" is also commonly used in a qualitative or general sense to designate the act of illuminating or the state of being illuminated. Usually the context will indicate which meaning is intended, but occasionally it is desirable to use the expression *amount of illumination* to indicate that the quantitative meaning is intended. (See Transactions IES, Vol. 33, No. 2 p. 173, 1938.)

Foot-Candle,[†] ft-c   55.05.040

The foot-candle is the unit of illumination when the foot is taken as the unit of length. It is the illumination on a surface one square foot in area on which there is a uniformly distributed flux of one lumen, or the illumination produced at a surface all points of which are at a distance of one foot from a uniform point source of one candle.

Lux,[†] lx   55.05.045

The lux is the practical unit of illumination in the metric system, and is equivalent to the "meter-candle". It is the illumination on a surface one square meter in area on which there is a uniformly distributed flux of one lumen, or the illumination produced at a surface all points of which are at a distance of one meter from a uniform point source of one candle.

Phot,[†] ph   55.05.050

The phot is the unit of illumination when the centime-

---

† For terms bearing this reference, the definitions given are substantially equivalent to definitions adopted by the International Commission on Illumination.

ter is taken as the unit of length; it is equal to one lumen per square centimeter.

NOTE: 1 foot-candle = 10.764 lux = 1.0764 milliphot.

Quantity of Light,[†] $Q = \int F\, dt$ 55.05.055

Quantity of light is the product of the luminous flux by the time it is maintained. It is the time integral of luminous flux.

Compare **55.05.005** and **55.05.010**.

Lumen-Hour, lm-hr   55.05.060

The lumen-hour is the unit of quantity of light. It is the quantity of light delivered in one hour by a flux of one lumen.

Brightness,[†] $B = dI/(dA \cos \theta)$ 55.05.065

Brightness is the luminous intensity of any surface in a given direction per unit of projected area of the surface as viewed from that direction.

NOTE: In the defining equation, θ is the angle between the direction of observation and the normal to the surface.

In practice no surface follows exactly the cosine formula of emission or reflection; hence the brightness of a surface generally is not uniform but varies with the angle at which it is viewed. Brightness can be measured not only for sources and illuminated surfaces, but also for virtual surfaces such as the sky.

In common usage the term brightness usually refers to the intensity of *sensation* which results from viewing surfaces or spaces from which light comes to the eye. This sensation is determined in part by the definitely measurable "brightness" defined above and in part by conditions of observation such as the state of adaptation of the eye.

Units of Brightness   55.05.070

The practice recognized internationally is to express brightness in candles per unit area of surface. The brightness of *any* surface, in a specified direction, can also be expressed in terms of the lumens per unit area from a perfectly diffusing surface of equal brightness.

Stilb,[†] sb   55.05.075

The stilb is a unit of brightness equal to one candle per square centimeter.

NOTE: The name "stilb" has been adopted by the International Commission on Illumination, and is commonly used in European publications. In America the preferred practice is to use self-explanatory terms such as candle per square inch and candle per square centimeter.

The *apostilb*, asb, is a unit of brightness defined by the German Illuminating Engineering Society (DLTG) as $1/(\pi \times 10^4)$ stilb. It is therefore equal to the brightness of a perfectly diffusing surface emitting or reflecting one lumen per square meter.

Lambert, L   55.05.080

The lambert is a unit of brightness equal to $1/\pi$ candle per square centimeter, and therefore is equal to the uniform brightness of a perfectly diffusing surface emitting or reflecting light at the rate of one lumen per square centimeter.

[†] See footnote on page 169.

NOTE: The lambert is also the average brightness of *any* surface emitting or reflecting light at the rate of one lumen per square centimeter. For the general case the average must take account of variation of brightness with angle of observation and also of its variation from point to point on the surface considered.

The lambert has a magnitude suitable for expressing the brightness of bright sources of light but for most other purposes the *millilambert*, mL, 0.001 lambert, is a preferable unit.

Foot-Lambert, ft-L   55.05.085

The foot-lambert is a unit of brightness equal to $1/\pi$ candle per square foot, or to the uniform brightness of a perfectly diffusing surface emitting or reflecting light at the rate of one lumen per square foot, or to the average brightness of any surface emitting or reflecting light at that rate.

NOTE: The average brightness of any reflecting surface in foot-lamberts is therefore the product of the illumination in foot-candles by the reflection factor of the surface.

The foot-lambert is the same as the "apparent foot-candle".

Brightness Ratio   55.05.090

Brightness ratio is the ratio of the brightnesses of any two surfaces. When the two surfaces are adjacent, the brightness ratio is commonly called the "brightness contrast".

Luminosity Factor,[†, ††] $K = F_\lambda/\Phi_\lambda$ 55.05.095

The luminosity factor for radiation of a particular wavelength is the ratio of the luminous flux at that wavelength to the corresponding radiant flux. (See **55.10.015**.) It is expressed in lumens per watt.

Relative Luminosity Factor[†, ††]   55.05.100

The relative luminosity factor for a particular wavelength is the ratio of the luminosity factor for that wavelength to the value at the wavelength of maximum luminosity.

Luminous Efficiency   55.05.105

The luminous efficiency of radiant energy is the ratio of the luminous flux to the radiant flux.

NOTE: Luminous efficiency is usually expressed in lumens per watt of radiant flux. It should not be confused with the term efficiency as applied to a practical source of light (see **55.25.020**), since the latter is based upon the power supplied to the source instead of the radiant flux from the source.

For energy radiated at a single wavelength, luminous efficiency is synonymous with luminosity factor (**55.05.095**).

The reciprocal of the luminous efficiency of radiant energy is sometimes called the "mechanical equivalent of light". The value most commonly cited is the *minimum* "mechanical equivalent", that is, the watts per lumen at the wavelength of maximum luminosity. The best experimental value is 0.00154 watt per lumen, corresponding to 650 lumens per watt as the maximum possible efficiency of a source of light. When expressed in terms of the new value of the lumen (see note under **55.05.025**) these numerical values become, respectively, 0.00151 watt per (new) lumen and 660 (new) lumens per watt.

[††] In these terms *luminosity* replaces the word *visibility* formerly used.

GROUP 55—ILLUMINATING ENGINEERING
Section 10—Radiation

Radiant Energy, U   55.10.005

Radiant energy is energy traveling in the form of electromagnetic waves. It is measured in units of energy such as ergs, joules, calories or kilowatthours.

Spectral Radiant Energy, $U_\lambda = dU/d\lambda$ 55.10.010

Spectral radiant energy is radiant energy per unit wavelength interval at wavelength λ, e. g., ergs / micron.

Radiant Flux, $\Phi = dU/dt$; (alternate symbol, P) 55.10.015

Radiant flux is the time rate of flow of radiant energy. It is expressed preferably in watts, or in ergs per second.

Radiant Energy Density, $u = dU/dV$ 55.10.020

Radiant energy density is radiant energy per unit volume, e. g., ergs/cm³.

Radiant Flux Density, $W = d\Phi/dA$ 55.10.025

Radiant flux density at an element of surface is the ratio of radiant flux at that element of surface to the area of that element; e.g., watts/cm². When referring to a source of radiant flux this is also called *radiancy*.

Radiant Intensity, $J = d\Phi/d\omega$ 55.10.030

The radiant intensity of a source is the energy emitted per unit time, per unit solid angle about the direction considered; e. g., watts/steradian.

Spectral Radiant Intensity, $J_\lambda = dJ/d\lambda$ 55.10.035

Spectral radiant intensity is radiant intensity per unit wavelength interval; e. g., watts/(steradian, micron).

Steradiancy, $N = d^2\Phi/d\omega\ (dA \cos \Theta) = dJ/(dA \cos \Theta)$, (alternate symbol, $\mathcal{B}$)   55.10.040

Steradiancy of an element of a source in any direction is the radiant flux per unit solid angle per unit of projected area of the element of source as observed from that direction. It is equivalent to the radiant intensity per unit of projected area of the source.

NOTE: In the defining equation, Θ is the angle between the normal to the element of source and the direction of observation. For this quantity the term *radiance* is proposed by the Committee on Colorimetry of the Optical Society of America.

Irradiancy, $H = d\Phi/dA$ (alternate symbol, $\mathcal{E}$) 55.10.045

Irradiancy of an element of surface is the incident radiant flux per unit area; e. g., watt / cm².

Temperature Radiator   55.10.050

A temperature radiator is one whose radiant flux density (radiancy) is determined by its temperature and the material and character of its surface, and is independent of its previous history.

Blackbody   55.10.055

A blackbody is a temperature radiator of uniform temperature whose radiant flux in all parts of the spectrum is the maximum obtainable from any temperature radiator at the same temperature.

Such a radiator is called a blackbody because it will absorb all the radiant energy that falls upon it. All other temperature radiators may be classed as nonblackbodies. They radiate less in some or all wavelength intervals than a blackbody of the same size and the same temperature.

NOTE: The blackbody is practically realized in the form of a cavity with opaque walls at uniform temperature and with a small opening for observation purposes. It is variously called standard radiator, complete radiator or ideal radiator.

Total Emissivity, e_t   55.10.060

The total emissivity of an element of surface of a temperature radiator is the ratio of its radiant flux density (radiancy) to that of a blackbody at the same temperature.

Spectral Emissivity, e_λ   55.10.065

The spectral emissivity of an element of surface of a temperature radiator at any wavelength is the ratio of its radiant flux density per unit wavelength interval (spectral radiancy), at that wavelength, to that of a blackbody at the same temperature.

Graybody   55.10.070

A graybody is a temperature radiator whose spectral emissivity is less than unity and the same at all wavelengths.

Stefan-Boltzmann Law   55.10.075

The Stefan-Boltzmann law is the statement that the emitted radiant flux density (or radiancy) of a blackbody is proportional to the fourth power of its absolute temperature; that is

$$W = \sigma T^4$$

NOTE: Experimental values of the constant σ, called the Stefan-Boltzmann constant, average about 5.70×10^{-12} watts cm⁻² deg K⁻⁴, but recent determinations have generally given results somewhat larger.

Wien Displacement Law   55.10.080

The Wien displacement law is an expression representing, in a functional form, the spectral radiant intensity of a blackbody as a function of the wavelength (or frequency) and the temperature.

$$J_\lambda / A' = N_\lambda = c_1 \lambda^{-5} f (\lambda T)$$

The two principal corollaries of this law are

$$\lambda_m T = \text{constant}$$
$$J_m / (A' T^5) = \text{constant}$$

which show how the maximum spectral radiant intensity J_m, and the wavelength λ_m at which it occurs, are related to the absolute temperature T.

NOTE: A' is the projected area of the radiating aperture.

The numerical values of the two constants are now somewhat uncertain. The present International Temperature Scale makes $\lambda_m T$ equal 0.2884 cm deg K (or 2884 micron deg K), but 0.2892 is more nearly correct. (See note under **55.10.085**.) $J_m / A' T^5$ = 4.13×10^{-12} watt cm⁻³ steradian⁻¹ deg K⁻⁵.

Planck Radiation Law   55.10.085

The Planck radiation law is an expression representing the spectral radiant intensity of a blackbody as a function of the wavelength (or the frequency) and temperature. This law is commonly expressed by the formula

$$J_\lambda / A' = N_\lambda = c_{1N}\lambda^{-5}(e^{c_2/\lambda T} - 1)^{-1}$$

in which J_λ represents the spectral radiant intensity, A' is the projected area ($A \cos \theta$) of the aperture of the blackbody, e is the base of natural logarithms $2.718 +$; T is absolute temperature, c_{1N} and c_2 are constants designated as the first and second radiation constants.

NOTE: The designation c_{1N} is used to indicate that the equation in the form here given refers to the intensity J, or to the steradiancy, N, of the source. Numerical values commonly given for c_1 apply to energy radiated in a hemisphere, so that $c_1 = \pi c_{1N}$

The value of c_2 adopted as a basis for the International Temperature Scale is 1.432 centimeter degrees Kelvin (14,320 micron degK). It is now known that 1.436 is more nearly correct, but the temperature scale has not been revised accordingly. With the quantities defined as above, power being expressed in watts and all lengths in centimeters,

$$c_{1N} = 15 \pi^{-5} c_2^4 \sigma$$

Then if $c_2 = 1.436$ and $\sigma = 5.70$, $c_{1N} = 1.188 \times 10^{-12}$ watt cm². If wavelengths are expressed in microns, and area in square centimeters, $c_{1N} = 1.188 \times 10^4$, J_λ being given in watts per steradian per micron.

The Planck law in the following form, in which c_1 is π times c_{1N} as given above, shows the energy radiated from the blackbody in a given wavelength interval:

$$U = U_\lambda d\lambda = A \cdot t \cdot c_1 \lambda^{-5} (e^{c_2/\lambda T} - 1)^{-1} d\lambda$$

If A is area of the radiation aperture or surface in square centimeters, t is time in seconds, λ is wavelength in microns, and $c_1 = 3.732 \times 10^4$ watt micron⁴ cm⁻², then $U_\lambda d\lambda$ is energy in wattseconds, emitted from this area, in time t, in the solid angle 2π, within the wavelength interval $d\lambda$ at wavelength λ.

NOTE: It is often convenient, as is done here, to use different units of length in specifying wavelengths and areas, respectively. If both quantities are expressed in centimeters, and the corresponding value for c_1 (3.732×10^{-5} erg cm² sec⁻¹) is used, this equation gives the emission of energy in ergs from area A in the solid angle 2π, at wavelength λ, for time t, and for the interval $d\lambda$ in centimeters.

The values of the constants here used are consistent among themselves, but not consistent with the present International Temperature Scale. (See H. T. Wensel, Journal of Research, National Bureau of Standards, Vol. 22, p. 375, 1939; Research Paper 1189. For earlier discussion of experimental values, see R. T. Birge, Physical Review Supplement, Vol. 1, p. 64, 1929.)

Wien Radiation Law   55.10.090

The Wien radiation law is an expression representing approximately the spectral radiant intensity of a blackbody as a function of its wavelength (or frequency) and temperature. It is commonly expressed by the formula:

$$J_\lambda / A' = N_\lambda = c_{1N} \lambda^{-5} e^{-(c_2/\lambda T)}$$

This law is accurate to 1 percent or better for values of λT less than 3,000 micron degrees Kelvin.

Units of Wavelength   55.10.095

Spectral radiant-energy measurements necessitate some statement as to the unit of wavelength used, since four different units are in use, as shown in the table.

WAVELENGTH UNITS

Name	Abbreviation		Value
Micron	μ	1μ	$= 10^{-3}$ mm
Millimicron	$m\mu$	$1 m\mu$	$= 10^{-6}$ mm
Angstrom	A	$1 A$	$= 10^{-7}$ mm
X-unit	X U	$1 X U$	$= 10^{-10}$ mm

NOTE: It was formerly thought satisfactory to express wavelength in microns, but if this unit is used, the wavelengths of the entire visible and ultraviolet spectrum are expressed by fractions. To avoid the use of fractions, many authors express wavelengths in millimicrons. Using this unit, the wavelengths of the visible spectrum are expressed by three figures before the decimal point. For most work in radiation measurements, wavelengths expressed by three figures seem to be accurate enough, but some workers express wavelengths in angstrom units in all cases; hence it seems impossible to get unity of action even among workers in radiation measurements. The spectroscopist uses angstrom units for all of his work except in the x-ray region, where the unit XU (XU = 0.001 A) is often used.

GROUP 55—ILLUMINATING ENGINEERING

Section 15—Evaluation of Ultraviolet Radiation

Erythemal Flux   55.15.005

Erythemal flux is radiant flux evaluated according to its capacity to produce erythema (temporary reddening) of the untanned human skin.

Relative Erythemal Factor   55.15.010

The relative erythemal factor for radiation of a particular wavelength is a factor which gives the relative erythemal effectiveness of radiation of that wavelength as compared with that of wavelength 296.7 millimicrons (2,967 angstroms) taken as unity.

Unit of Erythemal Flux   55.15.015

The recommended practical unit of erythemal flux is such an amount of radiant flux as will give the same erythemal effect as 10 microwatts of radiant power at 296.7 millimicrons (2,967 angstroms).

NOTE: This unit has been called the *E-viton*; the name *erytheme* has also been proposed.

Finsen   55.15.020

The finsen is the recommended practical unit of erythemal flux density or intensity of irradiation. It is equal to one unit of erythemal flux per square centimeter.

Erythemal Exposure   55.15.025

Erythemal exposure is the product of erythemal flux density on a surface and the duration of the exposure. It is therefore the amount of effective radiant energy received per unit of area exposed.

GROUP 55—ILLUMINATING ENGINEERING

Section 25—Illuminants

Lamp   55.25.005

Lamp is a generic term for an artificial source of light.

Electric Filament Lamp   55.25.010

An electric filament lamp is a light source consisting of a glass bulb containing a filament electrically maintained at incandescence.

NOTE: A lighting unit consisting of an electric filament lamp with shade, reflector, enclosing globe, housing or other accessories, is also commonly called a "lamp". In such cases in order to distinguish between the assembled lighting unit and the light source within it, the latter is often called a "bulb".

See 55.30.035.

Electric Discharge Lamp   55.25.015

An electric discharge lamp is a lamp in which light is produced by the passage of electricity through a metallic vapor or a gas enclosed in a tube or bulb.

Fluorescent Lamp   55.25.016

A fluorescent lamp is an electric discharge lamp in which the radiant energy from the electric discharge is transferred by suitable materials (phosphors) into wavelengths giving higher luminosity.

Efficiency (of a source of light)[†]   55.25.020

The efficiency of a source is the ratio of the total luminous flux to the total power input. In the case of an electric lamp it is expressed in lumens per watt. In the case of a source depending upon combustion it may be expressed in lumens per thermal unit consumed per unit of time.

Specific Consumption   55.25.025

The specific consumption of an electric lamp is its watt consumption per lumen. "Watts per candle" is a term formerly used in connection with electric incandescent lamps to denote watts per mean horizontal candle.

Color Temperature   55.25.030

The color temperature of a source of light is the temperature at which a blackbody (see **55.10.055**) must be operated to give a color matching that of the source in question.

NOTE: Color temperatures are usually assignable only for sources which have a spectral distribution of energy not greatly different from that of a blackbody.

Hemispherical Ratio   55.25.035

Hemispherical ratio for a given lighting unit is the ratio of the luminous flux in the upper hemisphere to that in the lower hemisphere.

† See footnote on page 169.

Mean Horizontal Candlepower,[†] mhcp   55.25.040

The mean horizontal candlepower of a lamp is the average candlepower in the horizontal plane passing through the luminous center of the lamp.

NOTE: It is assumed that the lamp (or other light source) is mounted in the usual manner, or, as in the case of an incandescent lamp, with its axis of symmetry vertical.

Spherical Candlepower,[†] scp   55.25.045

The (mean) spherical candlepower of a lamp is the average candlepower of the lamp in all directions in space. It is equal to the total luminous flux of the lamp in lumens divided by 4π.

Hemispherical Candlepower[†]   55.25.050

The (mean) upper, or lower, hemispherical candlepower of a lamp is the average candlepower of the lamp in the hemisphere considered. It is equal to the luminous flux in that hemisphere divided by 2π.

Zonal Candlepower   55.25.055

The (mean) zonal candlepower of a lamp is the average candlepower of the lamp over the given zone. It is equal to the luminous flux in that zone divided by the solid angle of the zone.

Spherical Reduction Factor[†]   55.25.060

The spherical reduction factor of a lamp is the ratio of the mean spherical to the mean horizontal candlepower of the lamp.

NOTE: In the case of a uniform point source, this factor would be unity, and for a straight cylindrical filament obeying the cosine law it would be $\pi/4$.

Apparent Candlepower   55.25.065

The apparent candlepower of an extended source of light measured at a specified distance is the candlepower of a point source of light which would produce the same illumination at that distance.

Total Flux[†]   55.25.070

The total flux of a source is the flux from that source in all directions.

Upward Flux   55.25.075

The upward flux is the flux from the source above the horizontal plane passing through its center.

Downward Flux   55.25.080

The downward flux is the flux from the source below the horizontal plane passing through its center.

GROUP 55—ILLUMINATING ENGINEERING

Section 30—Materials and Accessories Modifying Distribution of Light

Reflector 55.30.005

A reflector is a device, the chief use of which is to redirect the light of a lamp by reflection in a desired direction or directions.

Refractor 55.30.010

A refractor is a device, usually of prismatic glass (see 55.30.245), which redirects the light of a lamp in desired directions principally by refraction.

Shade 55.30.015

A shade is a device, the chief use of which is to diminish or to intercept the light from a lamp in certain directions where such light is not desirable. Frequently the functions of a shade and a reflector are combined in the same unit.

Globe 55.30.020

A globe is an enclosing device of clear or diffusing material; the chief uses of a globe are to protect the lamp, to diffuse or redirect its light, and/or to modify its color.

Projector 55.30.025

A projector is a device which concentrates luminous flux within a small angle from a single axis.

Headlamp or Headlight 55.30.030

A headlamp or headlight is a lighting unit on the front of a vehicle intended primarily to illuminate the road ahead of the vehicle.

Luminaire 55.30.035

A luminaire is a complete lighting unit consisting of a light source, together with its direct appurtenances, such as globe, reflector, refractor, housing and such support as is integral with the housing.

NOTE: The term "luminaire" is used to designate separable devices, such as completely equipped lighting fixtures, wall brackets, portable lamps, so-called removable units or street-lighting units. It does not include permanent parts of a building, such as a ceiling or other structural element; and in street-lighting units the pole, post or bracket is not considered a part of the luminaire.

Diffusing Surfaces and Media 55.30.040

Diffusing surfaces and media are those which break up the incident light and distribute it more or less in accordance with the cosine law, as, for example, rough plaster and opal glass.

See 55.35.015.

Perfect Diffusion 55.30.045

Perfect diffusion is that in which light is scattered uniformly in all directions by the diffusing medium.

NOTE: This is a hypothetical case, since no medium is perfectly diffusing. A flat plate of such a diffusing medium would appear equally bright irrespective of the direction of the incident light or the direction from which it is observed, but on account of the foreshortening effect when the plate is observed obliquely the light flux would be distributed in accordance with Lambert's cosine formula.

Wide-Angle Diffusion 55.30.050

Wide-angle diffusion is that in which light is scattered over a wide angle so that the diffusing medium appears of approximately the same brightness when observed from any angle.

NOTE: The particular degree of diffusion exhibited by a sample can be represented by plotting on a polar diagram the values of brightness obtained by measurements at different angles.

Narrow-Angle Diffusion 55.30.055

Narrow-angle diffusion is that in which light is scattered in all directions from the diffusing medium but in which the intensity is notably greater over a narrow angle in the general direction which the light would take by regular reflection or transmission.

NOTE: A polar diagram of brightness as measured at different angles is required to represent the particular type of diffusion exhibited by a sample showing diffusion of this general type.

Complete Diffusion 55.30.060

Complete diffusion is that in which the diffusing medium scatters the light incident upon it so that none is regularly reflected or transmitted and objects from which the light originally comes cannot be seen sharply defined by the reflected or transmitted light.

Partial or Incomplete Diffusion 55.30.065

Partial or incomplete diffusion is that in which the diffusing medium scatters part of the light incident upon it but allows part to be regularly reflected or transmitted so that objects from which the light originally comes (such as the filament of a lamp) can be seen sharply defined by the reflected or transmitted light.

Redirecting Surfaces and Media 55.30.070

Redirecting surfaces and media are those which change the direction of the light in a definite manner; as, for example, a mirror or a prism.

Scattering Surfaces and Media 55.30.075

Scattering surfaces and media are those which redirect the light into a multiplicity of separate pencils by reflection or transmission, as, for example, rippled glass.

Regular or Specular Reflection 55.30.080

Regular or specular reflection is that in which the angle of reflection is equal to the angle of incidence.

Diffuse Reflection 55.30.085

Diffuse reflection is that in which the light is reflected in all directions.

NOTE: The reflection from a body may be regular, diffuse or mixed. In most practical cases there is a superposition of regular and diffuse reflection.

Regular Reflection Factor 55.30.090

The regular reflection factor of a surface or a body is the ratio of the regularly reflected light to the incident light.

Diffuse Reflection Factor   55.30.095

The diffuse reflection factor of a surface or a body is the ratio of the diffusely reflected light to the incident light.

Reflection Factor[†], $\rho = F_r/F_i$ 55.30.100

(Reflectance)

The reflection factor of a body is the ratio of the light reflected by the body to the incident light.

Diffuse Transmission   55.30.105

Diffuse transmission is that in which the transmitted light is emitted in all directions from the transmitting body.

Regular Transmission   55.30.110

Regular transmission is that in which the transmitted light is not diffused. In such transmission the direction of a transmitted pencil of light has a definite geometrical relation to the corresponding incident pencil. When the direction of the light is not changed, the transmission is called direct.

NOTE: The transmission of light by a body may be regular, diffuse or mixed. In many practical cases there is a superposition of regular and diffuse transmission.

It should be noted also that transmission factors as defined below refer to the ratio of light emerging from the body concerned to the light incident upon it. Reflections at the surfaces, as well as absorption within the body, therefore operate to reduce the transmission.

Since transmission and reflection factors depend in general on the angle of incidence, this angle should be stated. If the angle is not given, incidence is assumed to be practically normal. Transmission and reflection factors frequently vary also with the quality of light used, and consequently the quality of the light or the characteristics of the illuminant used should be specified.

Regular Transmission Factor   55.30.115

The regular transmission factor of a body is the ratio of the regularly transmitted light to the incident light.

Diffuse Transmission Factor   55.30.120

The diffuse transmission factor of a body is the ratio of the diffusely transmitted light to the incident light.

Transmission Factor[†], $\tau = F_t/F_i$ 55.30.125

The transmission factor of a body is the ratio of the light transmitted by the body to the incident light.

Transmittance   55.30.126

The transmittance of a body is the ratio of the light reaching the second surface of the body to the light which enters the surface where it is incident.

NOTE: This definition of "transmittance" as distinguished from "transmission factor" is adopted tentatively. The distinctive use of the two terms is not generally accepted. This note applies also to 55.30.130 and 55.30.131.

Absorption Factor[†], $\alpha = F_a/F_i$ 55.30.130

The absorption factor of a body is the ratio of the light absorbed by the body to the incident light.

NOTE: The absorbed light is the difference between the incident light and the sum of the transmitted and the reflected light.

See 55.30.126 Note.

---

† See footnote on page 169.

Absorptance   55.30.131

The absorptance of a body is the ratio of the light absorbed by the body to the light which enters it.

See 55.30.126 Note.

The remaining definitions in this section have been adopted by a joint committee representing the Illuminating Engineering Society, the Glass Division of the American Ceramic Society and the Illuminating Glassware Guild (see Transactions IES, Vol. **29**, p. 677, September, 1934).

Illuminating Glasses

Opal Glass   55.30.205

Opal glass is highly diffusing glass having a nearly white, milky or gray appearance. The diffusing properties are an inherent, internal characteristic of the glass.

Opalescent Glass   55.30.206

Opalescent glass is opal glass having the properties of selectively transmitting and diffusing light, with a resultant fire appearance when used with concentrated incandescent sources of light. It is sometimes referred to as fire opal.

Alabaster Glass   55.30.210

Alabaster glass is glass simulating natural alabaster and having a gray or paraffin-like appearance. For a given thickness, it usually has less diffusion than opal glass.

The true alabaster appearance results from the internal structure of glass of proper composition, rather than from surface treatment or casing. An alabaster appearance can also be obtained by casing an opal glass with clear glass, and while this should be classed as a cased glass, it is sometimes referred to as alabaster.

Cased Glass   55.30.215

Cased glass is glass composed of two or more layers of different glasses, usually a clear, transparent layer to which is added a layer of opal, opalescent or colored glass. This glass is sometimes referred to as flashed, multilayer, polycased, etc.

Homogeneous Glass   55.30.220

Homogeneous glass is glass of essentially uniform composition throughout its structure. (This term is used to distinguish the type from cased glass which is composed of two or more layers of different compositions, rather than to appraise the glass on the basis of freedom from streaks, striae, etc.)

Enameled Glass   55.30.225

Enameled glass is glass which has had applied to its surface a coating of enamel. The enamel may be white or colored and may have varying degrees of diffusion.

Decorated Glass   55.30.230

Decorated glass is glass to which etchings, stains, enamels, etc., have been applied, primarily for decorative purposes.

Mat-Surface Glass   55.30.235

Mat-surface glass is glass whose surface has been altered by etching, sand blasting, grinding, etc., to increase the diffusion. Either one or both surfaces may be so treated.

Configurated Glass   55.30.240

Configurated glass is glass having a patterned or irregular surface. The surface configuration is usually applied during fabrication. Such glasses are not transparent and are somewhat diffusing.

Glasses falling under this classification are often referred to as pebbled, stippled, rippled, hammered, patterned, chipped, crackled, cathedral, etc., depending upon the particular type of surface.

Prismatic Glass   55.30.245

Prismatic glass is clear glass into whose surface is fabricated a series of prisms, the function of which is to direct the incident light in desired directions.

Antique Glass   55.30.250

Antique glass is glass of relatively smooth surface having a slight degree of non-uniform diffusion due to the intentional presence of bubbles, striae, fissures, etc.

Transparent Glass   55.30.255

Transparent glass is glass having no apparent diffusing properties. Varieties of such glass are sometimes referred to as flint, crystal, clear.

Polished Plate Glass   55.30.260

Polished plate glass is glass whose surface irregularities have been removed by grinding and polishing, so that the surfaces are approximately plane and parallel.

Window Glass   55.30.265

Window glass is transparent, relatively thin, flat glass having glossy, fire-finished, apparently plane and smooth surfaces, but having a characteristic waviness of surface which is visible when viewed at an acute angle or in reflected light.

GROUP 55—ILLUMINATING ENGINEERING

Section 35—Classes and Characteristics of Illumination

Unidirectional Illumination   55.35.005

Unidirectional illumination on a surface is that produced by a single light source of relatively small dimensions. It is characterized by the fact that a small opaque object placed near the illuminated surface casts a sharp shadow.

Multidirectional Illumination   55.35.010

Multidirectional illumination on a surface is that produced by several separated light sources of relatively small area. It is characterized by the fact that a small opaque object placed near the illuminated surface casts several shadows.

Diffused Illumination   55.35.015

Diffused illumination is that produced by either primary or secondary light sources having dimensions relatively large with respect to the distance from the point illuminated, and emitting or scattering light in all directions. It is characterized by relative lack of shadow. Diffused illumination may be derived principally from a single direction as in the light from a skylit window, or from all directions as in the open air.

NOTE: In any practical case of illumination on a surface there is usually a mixture of the above types.

See 55.30.040 to 55.30.065.

Coefficient of Utilization   55.35.020

Coefficient of utilization of an illumination installation on a given plane is the total flux received by that plane divided by the total flux from the lamps illuminating it. When not otherwise specified, the plane of reference is assumed to be a horizontal plane 30 inches (76 cm) above the floor.

Variation Factor   55.35.025

Variation factor of an illumination installation is the ratio of either the maximum or minimum illumination on a given plane to the average illumination on that plane.

Variation Range   55.35.030

Variation range of illumination on a given plane is the ratio of the maximum illumination to the minimum illumination on that plane.

Outline Lighting   55.35.035

Outline lighting is an arrangement of incandescent lamps or gaseous tubes to outline and call attention to certain features such as the shape of a building or the decoration of a window.

GROUP 55—ILLUMINATING ENGINEERING

Section 40—Photometric Standards and Tests

Primary Luminous Standard   55.40.005

A primary luminous standard is one by which the unit of light is established and from which the values of other standards are derived. A satisfactory primary standard must be reproducible from specifications.

See 55.05.025.

Secondary Luminous Standard   55.40.010

A secondary luminous standard is one calibrated by comparison with a primary standard. The use of the term may also be extended to include standards which have not been directly measured against the primary standards, but derive their assigned values indirectly from the primary standards.

NOTE: The photometric units are actually maintained in most laboratories by electric filament lamps serving as reference standards.

Working Standard 55.40.015

A working standard is any standardized luminous source for daily use in photometry.

Comparison Lamp 55.40.020

A comparison lamp is a lamp of constant but not necessarily known candlepower against which standard and test lamps are successively compared in a photometer.

Test Lamp 55.40.025

A test lamp, in a photometer, is a lamp to be tested.

Performance Curve 55.40.030

A performance curve is a curve representing the behavior of a lamp in any particular (candlepower, consumption, etc.) at different periods during its life.

Characteristic Curve 55.40.035

A characteristic curve is a curve expressing a relation between two variable properties of a luminous source, as candlepower and volts, candlepower and rate of fuel consumption, etc.

Curve of Light Distribution 55.40.040

A curve of light distribution is a curve showing the variation of luminous intensity of a lamp, or luminaire, with angle of emission.

Curve of Horizontal Distribution 55.40.045

A curve of horizontal distribution is a curve, usually polar, representing the luminous intensity of a lamp, or luminaire, at various angles of azimuth in the horizontal plane through its light center.

NOTE: It is recommended that in horizontal distribution curves there be indicated the relative positions of parts of the equipment affecting the symmetry of distribution.

Curve of Vertical Distribution 55.40.050

A curve of vertical distribution is a curve, usually polar, representing the luminous intensity of a lamp, or luminaire, at various angles of elevation, in a vertical plane passing through its light center.

NOTE: Unless otherwise specified, a vertical distribution curve is assumed to be an average vertical distribution curve, such as may in many cases be obtained by rotating the unit about its axis, and measuring the average intensities at different angles of elevation. It is recommended that in vertical distribution curves, angles of elevation shall be counted positively from the nadir as zero, to the zenith as 180 degrees. In the case of filament lamps, it is assumed that the vertical distribution curve is taken with the base of the lamp upward.

Solid of Light Distribution 55.40.055

A solid of light distribution is a solid whose surface is such that the radius vector from the origin to the surface in any direction is proportional to the luminous intensity of the light source in the corresponding direction.

Symmetrical Light Distribution 55.40.060

A symmetrical light distribution is one in which the curves of vertical distribution are substantially the same for all planes.

Asymmetrical Light Distribution 55.40.065

An asymmetrical light distribution is one in which the curves of vertical distribution are not the same for all planes.

Isocandle Line 55.40.070

An isocandle line is a line plotted on any appropriate coordinates to show directions in space, about a source of light, in which the candlepower is the same. The line, for a complete exploration, is always a closed curve.

Isocandle Diagram 55.40.071

An isocandle diagram is a collection of isocandle lines showing the distribution of candlepowers about a source of light. The isocandle lines are usually drawn for equal increments of candlepower.

NOTE: For a detailed description of the isocandle diagram and its uses see article by Benford in General Electric Review, Vol. 28, p. 271, April, 1925, and Transactions IES, Vol. 21, p. 129, February, 1926. A clear and simple exposition of the isocandle system is given by Walsh in Illuminating Engineer (London), Vol. 26, p. 169, July, 1933.

Equal-Area Web 55.40.075

An equal-area web is a set of coordinates formed by the development of the lines of latitude and longitude of a sphere so that they may be drawn on a plane and still preserve the true area of all parts of the sphere. In the usual form, the lines of latitude become straight lines, equally spaced; the lines of longitude become sine curves convergent at the poles and equally spaced at the equator.

Isolux Line 55.40.080

An isolux line is a line, plotted on any appropriate coordinates, showing points of equal illumination. The line, for a complete exploration, is always a closed curve.

Isolux Diagram 55.40.081

An isolux diagram is a collection of isolux lines showing the distribution of illumination on a surface.

GROUP 55—ILLUMINATING ENGINEERING

Section 50—Aeronautic Lighting

Light‡   55.50.005

A light, for the purpose of the definitions in this section, is a luminous signal.

NOTE: The term "light" in combination with other terms is sometimes used to denote a device used as a source of luminous energy.

Fixed Light   55.50.010

A fixed light is a light which is constant in intensity when viewed from a fixed point.

Intermittent Light‡   55.50.015

An intermittent light is a light which has alternate dark and light intervals, when viewed from a fixed point.

Flashing Light‡   55.50.020

A flashing light is an intermittent light in which the light interval is shorter than the dark interval.

Occulting Light‡   55.50.025

An occulting light is an intermittent light in which the light interval is equal to or longer than the dark interval.

Blinker Light   55.50.030

A blinker light is an intermittent light having more than 60 flashes per minute.

Code Light‡   55.50.035

A code light is an intermittent light having characteristic groups of flashes by which it can be identified.

Undulating Light   55.50.040

An undulating light is a light which when viewed from a fixed location varies rhythmically in intensity without being completely occulted.

Illuminated   55.50.045

A surface is illuminated when luminous flux is distributed over it.

Lighted   55.50.050

A body is lighted when it is either illuminated or marked by means of lights.

Beacon‡   55.50.055

A beacon is a light used to indicate a geographical location.

NOTE: This term is also applied to a device to be used for this purpose.

‡ Identical with or practically equivalent to definitions adopted by the Committee on Aviation Ground Lighting and the Committee on Aircraft Lighting of the International Commission on Illumination.

Flashing Beacon   55.50.060

A flashing beacon is a beacon having the characteristics of a flashing light.

See 55.50.020.

Occulting Beacon   55.50.065

An occulting beacon is a beacon having the characteristics of an occulting light.

See 55.50.025.

Code Beacon   55.50.070

A code beacon is a beacon having the characteristics of a code light.

See 55.50.035.

Rotating Beacon   55.50.075

A rotating beacon is a beacon having variations in light intensity, when viewed from a fixed point, which are produced by rotating a projector about a vertical axis.

Airway Beacon‡   55.50.205

An airway beacon is a beacon, other than an airport beacon, located on or near an airway and used for the purpose of indicating the location of the airway.

Airport Beacon‡   55.50.210

An airport beacon is a beacon located at or near an airport for the purpose of indicating the location of the airport.

Landmark Beacon‡   55.50.215

A landmark beacon is a beacon other than an airport beacon or an airway beacon.

Course Light‡   55.50.220

A course light is a light directed along the course of an airway so as to be chiefly visible from points on or near that airway.

NOTE: In American practice a course light is generally used as part of a beacon.

Approach Light   55.50.225

An approach light is one of a group of lights located outside of a landing area to indicate the projection of a runway or landing stretch.

Marker Light   55.50.230

Marker light is a general term which includes boundary lights, contact lights, obstruction lights, range lights and circle lights.

Obstruction Light‡   55.50.235

(Obstacle Light)*

An obstruction light is a light which indicates the presence of a fixed object which is dangerous to aircraft in motion.

Boundary Light‡   55.50.240

A boundary light is one of a series of lights used to indicate the limits of the landing area of a landing field.

Contact Light   55.50.245

(Runway Light)*

A contact light is one of a series of marker lights, set substantially flush in the ground along a runway, for the purposes of indicating the location of the runway and assisting aircraft to land or take off.

Landing-Direction Light‡   55.50.250

A landing-direction light is a light designed to indicate, either by itself or in conjunction with other lights, the favored direction for landings.

Traffic-Control Projector‡   55.50.255

A traffic-control projector is a device designed to produce from the ground a controllable distinctive signal, directed at an individual aircraft for the purpose of directing its operation.

Pistol Light   55.50.256

A pistol light is a traffic-control projector designed to be operated in the hands.

Lighted Wind Indicator‡   55.50.260

A lighted wind indicator is a lighted device designed to indicate the direction and, in some cases, the velocity of the surface wind.

Lighted Wind Tee‡   55.50.261

A lighted wind tee is a lighted wind indicator having the form of a tee in a horizontal or slightly tilted plane.

Lighted Tetrahedron   55.50.262

A lighted tetrahedron is a lighted wind indicator having the form of a horizontally elongated tetrahedron and designed to indicate by its orientation the direction of the surface wind.

Illuminated Wind Cone‡   55.50.263

An illuminated wind cone is a flexible illuminated wind indicator having the form of a truncated cone and so supported as to be affected by the action of the wind so as to indicate by its position the direction and the approximate velocity of the wind.

Ceiling Projector‡   55.50.265

A ceiling projector is a device designed to produce a well-defined illuminated spot on the lower portion of a cloud for the purpose of providing a reference mark for the determination of the height of that part of the cloud.

Landing-Area Floodlight‡   55.50.270

A landing-area floodlight is a device designed for location at a landing field to illuminate all or part of the surface of the landing area.

Landing-Area Floodlight System‡   55.50.275

A landing-area floodlight system is an assembly of landing-area floodlights together with the necessary conductors and controls, designed to illuminate a single landing area.

General Field Floodlight System   55.50.276

A general field floodlight system is a landing-area floodlight system so operated that the entire area of landing is illuminated from one floodlight or bank of floodlights.

Distributed Floodlight System   55.50.277

A distributed floodlight system is a landing-area floodlight system so operated that the flux from floodlights located a material distance apart is combined to illuminate the area.

Directional Floodlight System   55.50.278

A directional floodlight system is a landing-area floodlight system so operated that aircraft land essentially parallel with the direction of the rays.

Runway Floodlight System   55.50.279

A runway floodlight system is a landing-area floodlight system so operated that the runway to be used lies within a narrow floodlighted area.

Shadow Bar   55.50.285

A shadow bar is a device designed to be used with a single floodlight operated as a general field floodlight, to insert a shaded region which can be so directed as to envelope a moving aircraft.

Apron Floodlight   55.50.290

An apron floodlight is a floodlight designed to illuminate an apron or loading area.

Flare   55.50.295

A flare is a pyrotechnic device designed to produce either a luminous signal or illumination.

Position Light‡   55.50.405

(Navigation Light)* (Running Light)*

A position light is a light used aboard an aircraft to indicate its position and direction of motion.

Auxiliary Position Light   55.50.410

(Passing Light)* (Courtesy Light)* (Warning Light)*

An auxiliary position light is a light used to supplement normal position lights in the forward direction.

Formation Light   55.50.415

A formation light is a position light of modified characteristics, used to facilitate formation flying.

---

* Deprecated.

‡ See footnote on page 178.

Toplight 55.50.420

A toplight is a supplementary position light designed to be used on marine aircraft while on the water.

Riding Light[‡] 55.50.425

(Anchor Light)*

A riding light is a light designed for use on floating aircraft to indicate its position when anchored.

Landing Light[‡] 55.50.430

A landing light is a device designed for use aboard an aircraft to illuminate a ground area from the aircraft.

* Deprecated.
[‡] See footnote on page 178.

Instrument Lamp[‡] 55.50.435

An instrument lamp is a device designed to be used on board an aircraft to illuminate or irradiate an instrument or instruments.

Indicator Light[‡] 55.50.440

(Control Light) (Pilot Light)*

An indicator light is a light, used in association with a control, which by means of position or color indicates the functioning of the control.

Parachute Flare[‡] 55.50.445

A parachute flare is a flare attached to a parachute and designed to illuminate an area from an altitude.

See **55.50.290**.

GROUP 60—ELECTROCHEMISTRY AND ELECTROMETALLURGY

SECTIONS

Section 05—General

Electrochemistry 60.05.005

Electrochemistry is that branch of science and technology which deals with reciprocal transformations of chemical and electric energy.

Electrothermics 60.05.010

Electrothermics is that branch of science and technology which deals with the direct transformations of electric energy and heat.

Electrometallurgy 60.05.015

Electrometallurgy is that branch of science and technology which deals with the application of electrochemistry or electrothermics to the extraction or treatment of metals.

Electrolyte 60.05.020

(Electrolytic Conductor) (Conductor of the Second Class)

An electrolyte is a conducting medium in which the flow of electric current is accompanied by the movement of matter.

Electrolyte 60.05.021

An electrolyte is a substance which when dissolved in a specified solvent (usually water) produces a conducting medium.

Ionogen 60.05.025

An ionogen is a substance which when dissolved in a specified medium (usually water) produces an electrolyte.

Electrode 60.05.030

An electrode is a conductor belonging to the class of metallic conductors, but not necessarily a metal, through which a current enters or leaves an electrolytic cell, arc, furnace, vacuum tube, gaseous discharge tube, or any conductor of the non-metallic class.

Specifically, in an electrolytic cell, an electrode is a conductor of the metallic-conductor class, at which there is a change from conduction by electrons to conduction by ions or colloidal particles.

Electrolysis 60.05.035

Electrolysis is the production of chemical changes by the passage of current through an electrolyte.

Anode 60.05.040

An anode is an electrode through which current enters any conductor of the non-metallic class. Specifically, an electrolytic anode is an electrode at which negative ions are discharged, or positive ions are formed, or at which other oxidizing reactions occur.

Cathode 60.05.045

A cathode is an electrode through which current leaves any conductor of the non-metallic class. Specifically, an electrolytic cathode is an electrode at which positive ions are discharged, or negative ions are formed, or at which other reducing reactions occur.

Electrolytic Cell 60.05.050

An electrolytic cell is a unit apparatus designed for carrying out an electrochemical reaction and includes a vessel, two or more electrodes, and one or more electrolytes.

Ion

See 05.10.050

Anion 60.05.060

An anion is an ion that is negatively charged.

Cation 60.05.065

A cation is an ion that is positively charged.

Anolyte 60.05.070

An anolyte is the portion of an electrolyte in an electrolytic cell adjacent to an anode. If a diaphragm is present, it is the portion of electrolyte on the anode side of the diaphragm.

Catholyte 60.05.075

A catholyte is the portion of an electrolyte in an electrolytic cell adjacent to a cathode. If a diaphragm is present, it is the portion of electrolyte on the cathode side of the diaphragm.

Diaphragm 60.05.080

A diaphragm, as used in electrolytic cells, is a porous or permeable membrane, usually flexible, separating anode and cathode compartments of an electrolytic cell from each other or from an intermediate compartment for the purpose of preventing admixture of anolyte and catholyte.

Colloidal Particles 60.05.085

Colloidal particles are electrically charged particles, suspended in a medium, that are larger than atomic or molecular dimensions, but sufficiently small to exhibit the Brownian movement.

Electrode (Electrolytic) Potential 60.05.090

An electrode potential is the difference in potential between an electrode and the immediately adjacent electrolyte, expressed in terms of some standard electrode potential difference.

Static Electrode Potential 60.05.095

A static electrode potential is an electrode potential measured when no current is flowing between the electrode and the electrolyte.

Equilibrium Electrode Potential 60.05.100

An equilibrium electrode potential is a static electrode potential that is measured when the electrode and electrolyte are in equilibrium with respect to a specified electrochemical reaction.

Single Electrode Potential 60.05.105

A single electrode potential is an equilibrium electrode potential of an electrode in an electrolyte of specified composition.

Standard Electrode Potential 60.05.110

A standard electrode potential is an equilibrium electrode potential, measured or computed, for an electrode in contact with an electrolyte in which one or more specified ions have a specified ion activity; and is the equilibrium potential involved in a specified electrochemical reaction under specified standard conditions.

Dynamic Electrode Potential 60.05.115

A dynamic electrode potential is an electrode potential measured when current is passing between the electrode and the electrolyte.

Half Cell 60.05.120

A half cell consists of an electrode immersed in a suitable electrolyte, and designed for measurements of single potentials.

Calomel Half Cell 60.05.125

(Calomel Electrode)

A calomel half cell is a half cell containing a mercury electrode in contact with a solution of potassium chloride of specified concentration that is saturated with mercurous chloride of which an excess is present.

Quinhydrone Half Cell 60.05.130

(Quinhydrone Electrode)

A quinhydrone half cell is a half cell with a platinum or gold electrode in contact with a solution saturated with quinhydrone.

Glass Half Cell 60.05.135

(Glass Electrode)

A glass half cell is a half cell in which the potential measurements are made through a glass membrane.

Polarization (electrolytic) 60.05.140

Polarization (electrolytic) is a change in the potential of an electrode produced during electrolysis, such that the potential of an anode always becomes more positive (more noble), or that of a cathode becomes more negative (less noble), than their respective equilibrium potentials. The polarization is equal to the difference between the equilibrium potential for the specified electrode reaction and the dynamic potential (that is, the potential when current is flowing).

Anodic Polarization 60.05.145

Anodic polarization is polarization of an anode.

Cathodic Polarization 60.05.150

Cathodic polarization is polarization of a cathode.

Overvoltage 60.05.155

Overvoltage is the minimum polarization at which a particular reaction occurs at an appreciable rate on a specified electrode, or at which, with a small increase in voltage, there is a marked increase in current density.

Polarizer 60.05.160

A polarizer is a substance which when added to an electrolyte increases the polarization.

Depolarization 60.05.165

Depolarization is a decrease in the polarization of an electrode at a specified current density.

Depolarizer 60.05.170

A depolarizer is a substance which produces depolarization.

Electrolytic Oxidation 60.05.175

Electrolytic oxidation is an electrolytic process whereby electrons are removed from, or positive charges are added to, an atom or ion. It occurs only at an anode.

Electrolytic Reduction 60.05.180

Electrolytic reduction is an electrolytic process whereby electrons are added to, or positive charges are removed from, an atom or ion. It occurs only at a cathode.

Electrolytic Dissociation 60.05.185

Electrolytic dissociation in a solution is a process whereby some fraction of the molecules of a solute are decomposed to form ions.

Ion Concentration 60.05.190

The ion concentration of any species of ion is equal to the number of those ions, or of mols or equivalents of those ions contained in a unit volume of an electrolyte.

Ion Activity 60.05.195

The ion activity of any species of ion is equal to the "thermodynamic ion concentration", i. e., the ion concentration corrected for the deviations from the laws of ideal solutions.

pH 60.05.200

The pH of an electrolyte is the cologarithm of the hydrogen ion activity of that medium, *i. e.,*

$$pH = \log \frac{1}{(H^+)}$$

Buffers 60.05.205

(Buffer Salts)

Buffers are salts or other compounds which prevent large changes in the pH of a solution upon the addition of an acid or alkali.

pM 60.05.210

The pM of a metal M in any electrolyte is the cologarithm of the metal ion activity in that medium, *i. e.,*

$$pM = \log \frac{1}{(M^{+\cdots})}$$

Electromotive Series 60.05.215

(Electrochemical Series)

The electromotive series is a table which lists in order the standard potentials of specified electrochemical reactions.

Reversible Process 60.05.220

A reversible electrolytic process is an electrochemical reaction which takes place reversibly at the equilibrium electrode potential.

Irreversible Process 60.05.225

An irreversible electrolytic process is an electrochemical reaction in which polarization occurs.

Bath Voltage 60.05.230

The bath voltage is the total voltage between the anode and cathode of an electrolytic cell during electrolysis. It is equal to the sum of (a) equilibrium reaction potential, (b) IR drop, (c) anode polarization and (d) cathode polarization.

See **60.21.325.**

Equilibrium Reaction Potential 60.05.235

The equilibrium reaction potential is the minimum voltage at which an electrochemical reaction can take place. It is equal to the algebraic difference of the equilibrium potentials of the anode and cathode with respect to the specified reaction. It can be computed from the free energy of the reaction.

Thus $\quad \Delta F = - \, N \, F \, E$

where ΔF = the free energy of the reaction, N is the number of chemical equivalents involved in the reaction, F is the value of the Faraday expressed in calories per volt (23,074) and E is the equilibrium reaction potential (in volts).

Decomposition Potential 60.05.236

The decomposition potential (or decomposition voltage) is the minimum potential (excluding IR drop), at

which an electrochemical process can take place continuously at an appreciable rate.

IR Drop 60.05.240

The IR drop in an electrolytic cell is equal to the product of the current passing through the cell and the resistance of the cell.

Electrophoresis 60.05.245

Electrophoresis is a movement of colloidal particles produced by the application of an electric potential.

Electrosmosis 60.05.250

(Electroendosmose)

Electrosmosis is the movement of fluids through porous diaphragms produced by the application of an electric potential.

Electrostenolysis 60.05.255

Electrostenolysis is the discharge of ions or colloidal particles in capillaries through the application of an electric potential.

Ion Migration 60.05.260

Ion migration is a movement of ions produced in an electrolyte by the application of an electric potential between electrodes.

Contact Potential 60.05.265

Contact potential is the difference in potential existing at the contact of two media or phases.

Liquid-Junction Potential 60.05.270

Liquid-junction potential is the contact potential between two electrolytes.

Current Density 60.05.275

The current density on a specified electrode in an electrolytic cell is the current per unit area of that electrode.

Current Efficiency 60.05.280

The current efficiency for a specified process is the proportion of the current that is effective in carrying out that process in accordance with Faraday's Law.

Cathode Efficiency 60.05.285

The cathode efficiency is the current efficiency of a specified cathodic process.

Anode Efficiency 60.05.290

The anode efficiency is the current efficiency of a specified anodic process.

Gassing 60.05.295

Gassing is the evolution of gases from one or more of the electrodes during electrolysis.

Voltage Efficiency 60.05.300

Voltage efficiency of a specified electrochemical process is the ratio of the equilibrium reaction potential to the bath voltage.

Energy Efficiency   60.05.305

Energy efficiency of a specified electrochemical process is the product of the current efficiency and the voltage efficiency.

Passivity (electrolytic)   60.05.310

Passivity (electrolytic) is the polarization of an anode, resulting in retardation of a reaction involving anodic solution of the material of the anode.

Passivity (chemical)   60.05.315

Passivity (chemical) is the condition of a surface which retards a specified chemical reaction at that surface.

Isoelectric Point   60.05.320

The isoelectric point of a colloid is that condition in which the colloid is electrically neutral with respect to the surrounding medium.

Coulometer

(Voltameter)
See **30.50.030.**

Faraday   60.05.330

A faraday is the number of coulombs (96,500) required for an electrochemical reaction involving one chemical equivalent.

Electrochemical Equivalent   60.05.335

An electrochemical equivalent of an element, compound, radical or ion is the weight of that substance involved in a specified electrochemical reaction during the passage of a specified quantity of electricity, such as a faraday, ampere-hour or coulomb.

Equivalent Conductivity   60.05.340

The equivalent conductivity of an ionogen at a specified concentration is the conductance of that volume of solution which contains one gram equivalent of the ionogen when placed between parallel electrodes one centimeter apart. The equivalent conductivity is numerically equal to the conductivity of the solution multiplied by the volume in cubic centimeters containing one gram equivalent of the ionogen.

Equivalent Resistivity   60.05.345

The equivalent resistivity of an ionogen is the reciprocal of the equivalent conductivity.

Molar Conductivity   60.05.350

The molar conductivity of an ionogen at a specified concentration is the conductance of that volume of solution which contains one gram mol of the ionogen when placed between parallel electrodes one centimeter apart.

Molar Resistivity   60.05.355

The molar resistivity of an ionogen is the reciprocal of the molar conductivity.

Cell Constant   60.05.360

The cell constant of an electrolytic cell is the resistance in ohms of that cell when filled with a liquid of unit resistivity.

Counter Electromotive Force   60.05.365

The counter electromotive force of any system is the effective emf within the system which opposes the passage of current in a specified direction.

GROUP 60—ELECTROCHEMISTRY AND ELECTROMETALLURGY
Section 10—Electric Batteries (General)

Galvanic Cell   60.10.005

A galvanic cell is an electrolytic cell that is capable of producing electric energy by electrochemical action.

Battery   60.10.010

A battery is a combination of two or more galvanic cells electrically connected to work together to produce electric energy. (Common usage permits this designation to be applied also to a single cell used independently. In the following definitions, unless otherwise specified, the term battery will be used in this dual sense.)

Terminals   60.10.015

The terminals of a battery are the parts to which the external electric circuit is connected.

Positive Terminal   60.10.020

The positive terminal of a battery is the terminal from which current flows† (as ordinarily conceived) through the external circuit to the negative terminal when the cell discharges.

Negative Terminal   60.10.025

The negative terminal of a battery is the terminal toward which current flows† (as ordinarily conceived) in the external circuit from the positive terminal.

Open-Circuit Voltage   60.10.030

The open-circuit voltage of a battery is the voltage at its terminals when no appreciable current is flowing.

Closed-Circuit Voltage   60.10.035

(Working Voltage)
The closed-circuit voltage of a battery is the voltage at the terminals when a specified current is flowing

---

† The flow of electrons in the external circuit is to the positive terminal and from the negative terminal.

through an external circuit. For storage batteries, this applies to either charge or discharge.

Initial Voltage 60.10.040

The initial voltage of a battery is the closed-circuit voltage at the beginning of a discharge. It is usually measured after the current has flowed for a sufficient period for the rate of change of voltage to become practically constant.

Cut-Off Voltage 60.10.045

(Final Voltage)

The cut-off voltage of a battery is the prescribed voltage upon reaching which the discharge is considered complete. The cut-off or final voltage is usually chosen so that the useful capacity of the battery is realized. The cut-off voltage varies with the type of battery, the rate of discharge, the temperature and the kind of service in which the battery is used. The term "cut-off voltage" is applied more particularly to primary batteries, and "final voltage" to storage batteries.

Polarity 60.10.050

The polarity of a battery is an electrical condition determining the direction in which current tends to flow. By common usage the discharge current is said to flow from the positive electrode through the external circuit.

Polarization (in a battery) 60.10.055

Polarization in a battery is the change in voltage at the terminals of the cell or battery when a specified current is flowing, and is equal to the difference between the actual and the equilibrium (constant open-circuit condition) potentials of the plates, exclusive of the IR drop.

See 60.05.140.

Local Action 60.10.060

(Self Discharge)

Local action in a battery is the loss of otherwise usable chemical energy by currents which flow within the cell or battery regardless of its connections to an external circuit.

Internal Resistance 60.10.065

The internal resistance of a cell or battery is the resistance within the cell or battery to the flow of an electric current and is measured by the ratio of the change in voltage at the terminals of the cell or battery corresponding to a specified change in current for short time intervals.

$$R_b = \frac{E_1 - E_2}{I_2 - I_1}$$

External Resistance 60.10.070

The external resistance is the resistance of the complete electric circuit outside the cell or battery between its positive and negative terminals.

GROUP 60—ELECTROCHEMISTRY AND ELECTROMETALLURGY

Section 11—Primary Batteries

Primary Cell 60.11.005

A primary cell is a cell designed to produce electric current through an electrochemical reaction which is not efficiently reversible and hence the cell, when discharged, cannot be efficiently recharged by an electric current.

Primary Battery 60.11.010

A primary battery is a battery consisting of primary cells.

Wet Cell 60.11.015

A wet cell is a cell whose electrolyte is in liquid form and free to flow and move.

Dry Cell 60.11.020

A dry cell is a cell in which the electrolyte exists in the form of a jelly or is absorbed in a porous medium, or is otherwise restrained from flowing from its intended position, such a cell being completely portable and the electrolyte non-spillable.

Sal Ammoniac Cell 60.11.025

A sal ammoniac cell is a cell in which the electrolyte consists primarily of a solution of ammonium chloride.

Caustic Soda Cell 60.11.030

A caustic soda cell is a cell in which the electrolyte consists primarily of a solution of sodium hydroxide.

Gas Cell 60.11.035

A gas cell is a cell in which the action of the cell depends on the absorption of gases by the electrodes.

Air Cell 60.11.040

An air cell is a gas cell in which depolarization at the positive electrode is accomplished through the reduction of oxygen of the air.

Carbon-Consuming Cell 60.11.045

(Carbon-Combustion Cell)

A carbon-consuming cell is a cell intended for the production of electric energy by voltaic oxidation of carbon.

Bichromate Cell 60.11.050

A bichromate cell is a cell having an electrolyte consisting of a solution of sulphuric acid and a bichromate.

One-Fluid Cell 60.11.055

A one-fluid cell is a cell having the same electrolyte in contact with both electrodes.

Two-Fluid Cell 60.11.060

A two-fluid cell is a cell having different electrolytes at the electrodes.

Standard Cell 60.11.065

A standard cell is a cell which serves as a standard of electromotive force.

Weston Normal Cell 60.11.070

A Weston normal cell is a standard cell of the saturated cadmium type.

Unsaturated Standard Cell 60.11.075

An unsaturated standard cell is a cell usually of the cadmium type, in which the electrolyte is not saturated at ordinary temperatures. (This is the commercial type of cadmium standard cell commonly used in the United States.)

Concentration Cell 60.11.080

A concentration cell is a cell of the two-fluid type in which the same ionogen is employed in the two solutions, but differs in concentration at the electrodes.

"B" Battery 60.11.085

A "B" battery is a battery designed or employed to furnish the plate current in a vacuum tube circuit.

See 65.20.125.

"C" Battery 60.11.090

A "C" battery is a battery designed or employed to furnish voltage used as a grid bias in a vacuum tube circuit.

See 65.20.130.

"A" Battery 60.11.095

An "A" battery is a battery designed or employed to furnish current to heat the filaments of the tubes in a vacuum tube circuit.

See 65.20.120.

Flashlight Battery 60.11.100

A flashlight battery is a battery designed or employed to furnish power to light a lamp in an electric lantern or flashlight.

Drain 60.11.105

Drain (current drain) is the current passing through the cell or battery when in service.

Series Connection 60.11.110

Series connection is the arrangement of cells in a battery by connecting the positive terminal of each cell to the negative terminal of the next adjacent cell, all cells being electrically in line so that their voltages are additive.

Multiple Connection 60.11.115

Multiple connection is the arrangement of cells in a battery by connecting all positive terminals together and all negative terminals together, the voltage of the group being only that of one cell and the current drain through the battery being divided among the several cells.

Multiple Series Connection 60.11.120

Multiple series connection is the arrangement of cells in a battery by connecting two or more series-connected groups, each having the same number of cells, so that the positive terminals of each group are connected together and the negative terminals are connected together in a corresponding manner.

Positive Electrode 60.11.125

The positive electrode in a primary cell is the body of conducting material which serves as the cathode when the cell is discharging and to which the positive terminal is connected.

Negative Electrode 60.11.130

The negative electrode in a primary cell is the body of conducting material which serves as the anode when the cell is discharging and to which the negative terminal is connected.

Depolarizer 60.11.135

The depolarizer of a primary cell is a cathodic depolarizer which is adjacent to or a part of the positive electrode.

See 60.05.170.

Depolarizing Mix 60.11.140

The depolarizing mix of a primary cell is a mixture containing a depolarizer and an electrically conducting material which together constitute the positive electrode.

Bobbin 60.11.145

A bobbin is a body in a dry cell consisting of depolarizing mix molded around a central rod of carbon or other conducting material and constituting the positive electrode used in the assembly of the cell.

Liner 60.11.150

A liner in a dry cell is the paper or cloth sheet placed between the depolarizing mix and the negative electrode to separate them physically or to protect the surface of the mix.

Paste 60.11.155

Paste in a dry cell is a medium in the form of a paste or jelly containing electrolyte which lies adjacent to the negative electrode.

Paper-Lined Construction 60.11.160

Paper-lined construction of a dry cell is a type of construction in which a paper liner, wet with electrolyte, forms the principal medium between the negative electrode, usually zinc, and the depolarizing mix.

(A layer of paste may lie between the paper liner and the negative electrode.)

Bag Type Construction   60.11.165

Bag type construction of a dry cell is a type of construction in which a layer of paste forms the principal medium between the depolarizing mix, contained within a cloth wrapper, and the negative electrode.

Non-Lined Construction   60.11.170

Non-lined construction of a dry cell is a type of construction in which a layer of paste forms the only medium between the depolarizing mix and the negative electrode.

Cup   60.11.175

(Can)

The cup of a dry cell is a metal container, usually zinc, in which the cell is assembled and which constitutes also its negative element.

Jacket   60.11.180

The jacket of a dry cell is a cylindrical covering of insulating material, closed at the bottom.

Tube   60.11.185

A tube for a dry cell or battery is a cylindrical covering of insulating material, without closure at the bottom.

Amperage   60.11.190

Amperage of a primary cell is the maximum electric current indicated by an ammeter of the dead-beat type when connected directly to the terminals of the cell or battery by wires which together with the meter have a resistance of 0.01 ohm.

Working Voltage

See 60.10.035.

Cut-Off Voltage

See 60.10.045.

Service Test   60.11.195

A service test of a primary battery is a test designed to measure the capacity of a cell or battery under specified conditions comparable with some particular service for which such cells are used.

Service Life   60.11.200

The service life of a primary cell or battery is the length of time required for a cell or battery on a service test to reach a specified final electrical condition.

Service Capacity   60.11.205

The service capacity of a primary cell or battery is the electric output of the cell or battery on a service test delivered before the cell reaches a specified final electrical condition and may be expressed in ampere-hours, watt-hours or similar units.

Initial Test   60.11.210

An initial test is a service test begun shortly after the manufacture of the battery. (Uusally less than one month.)

Shelf Test   60.11.215

A shelf test is a test designed to measure the ability of a primary cell to maintain its initial electrical condition for a specified period of time while unused.

Shelf Depreciation   60.11.220

Shelf depreciation is the depreciation in service capacity of a primary cell as measured by a shelf test on similar cells of the same lot.

Continuous Test   60.11.225

A continuous test is a service test in which the battery is subjected to an uninterrupted drain until the cut-off voltage is reached.

Intermittent Test   60.11.230

An intermittent test is a service test in which the battery is subjected to alternate discharges and periods of recuperation according to a specified program until the cut-off voltage is reached.

Delayed Test   60.11.235

A delayed test is a service test of a battery made after a specified period of time and is usually made for comparison with an initial test to determine shelf depreciation.

Shelf Corrosion   60.11.240

The shelf corrosion of a dry cell is the consumption of the negative electrode as a result of local action.

Service Corrosion   60.11.245

Service corrosion of a dry cell is the consumption of the negative electrode as a result of useful current delivered by the cell.

Creepage   60.11.250

Creepage is the travel of electrolyte up the surface of electrodes or other parts of the cell above the level of the main body of electrolyte.

GROUP 60—ELECTROCHEMISTRY AND ELECTROMETALLURGY

Section 12—Secondary Batteries

Storage Cell   60.12.005

A storage cell is an electrolytic cell for the generation of electric energy in which the cell after being discharged may be restored to a charged condition by an electric current flowing in a direction opposite to the flow of current when the cell discharges.

Storage Battery 60.12.010

(Secondary Battery or Accumulator)

A storage battery is a connected group of two or more storage cells. (Common usage permits this term to be applied to a single cell used independently.)

Stationary Battery 60.12.015

A stationary battery is a storage battery designed for service in a permanent location.

Portable Battery 60.12.020

A portable battery is a storage battery designed for convenient transportation.

Active Materials 60.12.025

The active materials of a storage battery are the materials of the plates which react chemically to produce electric energy when the cell discharges and which are restored to their original composition, in the charged condition, by oxidation or reduction processes produced by the charging current.

Grid 60.12.030

A grid is a metallic framework employed in a storage cell or battery for conducting the electric current and supporting the active material.

Positive Plate 60.12.035

The positive plate of a storage battery consists of the grid and active material from which current flows to the external circuit when the battery is discharging.

Negative Plate 60.12.040

The negative plate of a storage battery consists of the grid and active material to which current flows from the external circuit when the battery is discharging.

Separator 60.12.045

A separator is a device employed in a storage battery for preventing metallic contact between the plates of opposite polarity within the cell.

Group 60.12.050

A group for a storage cell is an assembly of a set of plates of the same polarity for one cell.

Element 60.12.055

The element of a storage cell consists of the positive and negative groups with separators, assembled for one cell.

Couple 60.12.060

A couple is an element of a storage cell consisting of two plates, one positive and one negative. The term couple is also applied to a positive and a negative plate connected together as one unit for installation in adjacent cells.

Jar 60.12.065

A jar is a glass or composition container for the element and electrolyte of a lead-acid storage cell.

Tank 60.12.070

A tank is a lead container usually supported by wood, for the element and electrolyte of a storage cell. (This is restricted to some relatively large types of lead-acid cells.)

Can 60.12.075

A can is a steel container for the element and electrolyte of a nickel-iron storage cell.

Case 60.12.080

A case is a container for several storage cells. Specifically wood cases are containers for cells in individual jars; rubber or composition cases are provided with compartments for the cells.

See **60.12.085**.

Tray 60.12.085

A tray is a support or container for one or more storage cells.

See **60.12.080**.

Terminal Posts 60.12.090

The terminal posts are the points of the storage battery to which the external circuit is connected.

Cell Connector 60.12.095

A cell connector is an electric conductor used for carrying current between adjacent storage cells.

Counter Electromotive Force Cells 60.12.100

Counter electromotive force cells, frequently called "counter cells", are cells of practically no ampere-hour capacity used to oppose the line voltage.

End Cells 60.12.105

End cells are cells of a storage battery which may be cut in or cut out of the circuit for the purpose of adjusting the battery voltage.

Emergency Cells 60.12.110

Emergency cells are end cells which are held available for use exclusively during emergency discharges.

Pilot Cell 60.12.115

A pilot cell is a selected cell of a storage battery whose temperature, voltage and specific gravity are assumed to indicate the condition of the entire battery.

Ampere-Hour Capacity 60.12.120

The ampere-hour capacity of a storage battery is the number of ampere-hours which can be delivered under specified conditions as to temperature, rate of discharge and final voltage.

Watthour Capacity 60.12.125

The watthour capacity of a storage battery is the number of watthours which can be delivered under specified conditions as to temperature, rate of discharge and final voltage.

Time Rate   **60.12.130**

The time rate is the current in amperes at which a storage battery will be fully discharged in a specified time, under specified conditions of temperature and final voltage.

Average Voltage   **60.12.135**

The average voltage of a storage battery is the average value of the voltage during the period of charge or discharge. (It is conveniently obtained from the time-integral of the voltage curve.)

Final Voltage

See **60.10.045**.

Charge   **60.12.140**

Charge, applied to a storage battery, is the conversion of electric energy into chemical energy within the cell or battery. Specifically, charge consists in the restoration of the active materials by passing a unidirectional current through the cell or battery in the opposite direction to that of the discharge; a cell or battery which is said to be "charged" is understood to be fully charged.

Charging Rate   **60.12.145**

The charging rate of a storage battery is the current expressed in amperes at which a battery is charged.

Constant-Current Charge   **60.12.150**

A constant-current charge of a storage battery is a charge in which the current is maintained at a constant value. (For some types of lead-acid batteries this may involve two rates called the starting and finishing rates.)

Constant-Voltage Charge   **60.12.155**

A constant-voltage charge of a storage battery is a charge in which the voltage at the terminals of the battery is held at a constant value.

Modified Constant-Voltage Charge   **60.12.160**

A modified constant-voltage charge of a storage battery is a charge in which the voltage of the charging circuit is held substantially constant, but a fixed resistance is inserted in the battery circuit, producing a rising voltage characteristic at the battery terminals as the charge progresses.

Boost Charge   **60.12.165**

A boost charge of a storage battery is a partial charge, usually at a high rate for a short period.

Equalizing Charge   **60.12.170**

An equalizing charge of a storage battery is an extended charge which is given to a storage battery to insure the complete restoration of the active materials in all the plates of all the cells.

Trickle Charge   **60.12.175**

A trickle charge of a storage battery is a continuous charge at a low rate approximately equal to the internal losses and suitable to maintain the battery in a fully charged condition. (This term is also applied to very low rates of charge suitable not only for compensating for internal losses, but to restore intermittent discharges of small amount delivered from time to time to the load circuit.)

See **60.12.195**.

Finishing Rate   **60.12.180**

The finishing rate for a storage battery is the rate of charge expressed in amperes to which the charging current for some types of lead batteries is reduced near the end of charge to prevent excessive gassing and temperature rise.

Discharge   **60.12.185**

Discharge of a storage battery is the conversion of the chemical energy of the battery into electric energy.

Reversal   **60.12.190**

Reversal of a storage battery is a change in normal polarity of the cell or battery.

Floating   **60.12.195**

Floating is a method of operation for storage batteries in which a constant voltage is applied to the battery terminals sufficient to maintain an approximately constant state of charge.

See **60.12.175**.

Gassing

See **60.05.295**.

Efficiency (of a storage battery)   **60.12.200**

The efficiency of a storage battery is the ratio of the output of the cell or battery to the input required to restore the initial state of charge under specified conditions of temperature, current rate and final voltage.

Ampere-Hour Efficiency   **60.12.205**

The ampere-hour efficiency of a storage battery is the electrochemical efficiency expressed as the ratio of the ampere-hours output to the ampere-hours input required for the recharge.

Volt Efficiency   **60.12.210**

The volt efficiency of a storage battery is the ratio of the average voltage during the discharge to the average voltage during the recharge.

Watthour Efficiency   **60.12.215**

The watthour efficiency of a storage battery is the energy efficiency expressed as the ratio of the watthours output to the watthours of the recharge.

Reference Temperature   **60.12.220**

The reference temperature for a storage battery is the average temperature of the electrolyte in all cells at the beginning of discharge.

Note: The standard reference temperature is 25C (77F) initially, without limit on the final temperature, but the ambient temperature on discharge shall be 5 degrees to 8 degrees centigrade lower than the temperature of the electrolyte at the beginning of the discharge and shall be kept constant during discharge.

Temperature Coefficient of Electromotive Force 60.12.225

The temperature coefficient of electromotive force of a storage cell or battery is the change in open-circuit voltage per degree centigrade relative to the electromotive force of the cell or battery at a specified temperature.

Temperature Coefficient of Capacity 60.12.230

The temperature coefficient of capacity of a storage cell or battery is the change in delivered capacity (ampere-hour or watthour capacity) per degree centigrade relative to the capacity of the cell or battery at a specified temperature.

Critical Temperature 60.12.235

The critical temperature of a storage cell or battery is the temperature of the electrolyte at which an abrupt change in capacity occurs.

Cycle of Operation 60.12.240

The cycle of operation of a storage cell or battery is the discharge and subsequent recharge of the cell or battery to restore the initial conditions.

Rating of Storage Batteries 60.12.245

The rating of storage batteries is expressed as the number of ampere-hours which they are capable of delivering when fully charged and under specified conditions as to temperature, rate of discharge and final voltage, but for particular classes of service different time rates (see **60.12.130**) are frequently used.

Service Life 60.12.250

The service life of a storage battery is the period of useful service under specified conditions, and is usually expressed as the period elapsed when the ampere-hour capacity has fallen to a specified percentage of the rated capacity.

GROUP 60—ELECTROCHEMISTRY AND ELECTROMETALLURGY

Section 20—Electrodeposition (General)

Electrodeposition 60.20.005

Electrodeposition is the process of depositing a substance upon an electrode by electrolysis. Electrodeposition includes electroplating, electroforming, electrorefining and electrowinning.

Electrodissolution 60.20.010

Electrodissolution is the process of dissolving a substance from an electrode by electrolysis.

Electroanalysis 60.20.015

Electroanalysis is the electrodeposition of an element or compound for the purpose of determining its quantity in the solution electrolyzed.

Reguline 60.20.020

Reguline is a descriptive word for electrodeposited metal which is firm and metallic in physical characteristics as contrasted with loose, spongy, dull or nonmetallic appearing surfaces.

Sponge 60.20.025

Sponge is a loose cathode deposit which is fluffy and of the nature of a sponge, contrasted with a firm reguline metal.

Slime 60.20.030

Slime is finely divided insoluble metal or compound forming on the surface of an anode or in the solution during electrolysis.

Re-Solution 60.20.035

Re-solution is the passing back into solution of metal already deposited on the cathode.

Agitator 60.20.040

An agitator is any device introduced into an electrolytic cell for the purpose of moving the electrolyte relative to the electrodes or of keeping solid or liquid particles in suspension.

Trees 60.20.045

Trees are macroscopic projections upon electrodeposited metal surfaces.

Pits 60.20.050

Pits are depressions produced in metal surfaces by non-uniform electrodeposition or from electrodissolution; e. g., corrosion.

GROUP 60—ELECTROCHEMISTRY AND ELECTROMETALLURGY

Section 21—Electroplating

Electroplating 60.21.005

Electroplating is the electrodeposition of an adherent coating upon an electrode for the purpose of securing a surface with properties or dimensions different from those of the base metal.

Coating 60.21.010

The coating is the layer deposited by electroplating.

Base 60.21.015

(Base Metal)

The base is the material upon which the metal is plated.

Throwing Power 60.21.020

The throwing power of a solution is a measure of its

adaptability to deposit metal uniformly upon a cathode of irregular shape. In a given solution under specified conditions it is equal to the improvement (in percent) of the metal distribution ratio above the primary current distribution ratio.

Metal Distribution Ratio   60.21.025

The metal distribution ratio is the ratio of the thicknesses (weights per unit areas) of metal upon two specified parts of a cathode.

Primary Current Ratio   60.21.030

The primary current ratio is the ratio of the current densities produced on two specified parts of an electrode in the absence of polarization. It is equal to the reciprocal of the ratio of the effective resistances from the anode to the two specified parts of the cathode.

Addition Agent   60.21.035

An addition agent is a substance which, when added to an electrolyte, produces a desired change in the structure or properties of an electrodeposit, without producing any appreciable change in the conductivity of the electrolyte, or in the activity of the metal ions or hydrogen ions.

Brightener   60.21.040

A brightener is an addition agent used for the purpose of producing bright deposits.

Dip   60.21.045

A dip is a solution used for the purpose of producing a chemical reaction upon the surface of a metal.

Bright Dip   60.21.050

A bright dip is a dip used to produce a bright surface on a metal.

Matte Dip   60.21.055

A matte dip is a dip used to produce a matte surface on a metal.

Blue Dip   60.21.060

A blue dip is a solution containing a mercury compound, and used to deposit mercury by immersion upon a metal, usually prior to silver plating.

Pickle   60.21.065

A pickle is an acid dip used to remove oxides or other compounds from the surface of a metal by chemical action.

Pickling   60.21.070

Pickling is the removal of oxides or other compounds from a metal surface by means of an acid solution which acts chemically upon the compounds.

Electrolytic Pickling   60.21.075

Electrolytic pickling is pickling during which a current is passed through the metal and the pickling solution.

Anode Pickling   60.21.080

Anode pickling is electrolytic pickling in which the metal to be treated is made the anode.

Cathode Pickling   60.21.085

Cathode pickling is electrolytic pickling in which the metal to be treated is made the cathode.

Inhibitor   60.21.090

An inhibitor is a substance added to a pickle for the purpose of reducing the rate of solution of the metal during the removal from it of oxides or other compounds.

Strike (bath)   60.21.095

A strike is an electrolyte used to deposit a thin initial film of metal.

Strike (deposit)   60.21.096

A strike is a thin initial film of metal to be followed by other coatings.

Striking   60.21.100

Striking is the electrodeposition of a thin initial film of metal, usually at a high current density.

Flash Plate   60.21.105

A flash plate is a thin electrodeposited coating, produced in a short time.

Strip   60.21.110

A strip is a solution used for the removal of a metal coating from the base metal.

Stripping (chemical)   60.21.115

Chemical stripping is the removal of a metal coating by dissolving it.

Stripping (electrolytic)   60.21.116

Electrolytic stripping is the removal of a metal coat by dissolving it anodically with the aid of a current.

Stripping (mechanical)   60.21.117

Mechanical stripping is the removal of a metal coating by mechanical means.

Immersion Plating   60.21.120

(Dip Plating)

Immersion plating is the deposition, without the application of an external emf, of a thin metal coating upon a base metal by immersing the latter in a solution containing a compound of the metal to be deposited.

Contact Plating   60.21.125

Contact plating is the deposition, without the application of an external emf, of a metal coating upon a base metal, by immersing the latter in contact with another metal in a solution containing a compound of the metal to be deposited.

Burnt Deposit   60.21.130

A burnt deposit is a rough or non-coherent electrodeposit produced by the application of an excessive current density.

Cleaning   60.21.135

Cleaning is the removal of grease or other foreign material from a metal surface, chiefly by physical means.

Solvent Cleaning   60.21.140

Solvent cleaning is cleaning by means of organic solvents.

Alkaline Cleaning   60.21.145

Alkaline cleaning is cleaning by means of alkaline solutions.

Cleaner   60.21.150

(a) A cleaner is a compound or mixture used in the preparation of alkaline cleaning solutions.

(b) A cleaner is an alkaline cleaning solution.

Electrolytic Cleaning   60.21.155

Electrolytic cleaning is alkaline cleaning during which a current is passed through the cleaning solution and the metal to be cleaned.

Cathode Cleaning   60.21.160

Cathode cleaning is electrolytic cleaning in which the metal to be cleaned is the cathode.

NOTE: Unless otherwise specified electrolytic cleaning is cathode cleaning.

Anode Cleaning   60.21.165

(Reverse-Current Cleaning)

Anode cleaning is electrolytic cleaning in which the metal to be cleaned is made the anode.

Spotting Out   60.21.170

Spotting out is the appearance of spots on plated or finished metals.

Stain Spots   60.21.175

Stain spots are spots produced by exudation from pores in the metal, of compounds absorbed from cleaning, pickling or plating solutions.

Crystal Spots   60.21.180

Crystal spots are spots produced by the growth of metal sulphide crystals upon metal surfaces with a sulphide finish and a lacquer coating.

Burnishing   60.21.185

Burnishing is the smoothing of metal surfaces by means of a hard tool or other article.

Hand Burnishing   60.21.190

Hand burnishing is burnishing done by a hand tool, usually of steel or agate.

Ball Burnishing   60.21.195

Ball burnishing is burnishing by means of metal balls.

Grinding   60.21.200

Grinding is the removal of metal by means of rigid wheels containing abrasive distributed throughout them.

Polishing   60.21.205

Polishing is the smoothing of a metal surface by means of abrasive particles attached by adhesive to the surface of wheels or belts.

Cutting Down   60.21.210

Cutting down of a metal or electrodeposit is polishing for the purpose of removing roughness or irregularities.

Buffing   60.21.215

Buffing is the smoothing of a metal surface by means of flexible wheels, to the surface of which fine abrasive particles are applied, usually in the form of a plastic composition or paste.

Coloring (buffing)   60.21.220

Coloring is light buffing of metal surfaces, for the purpose of producing a high luster.

Coloring (chemical)   60.21.221

Coloring is the production of desired colors on metal surfaces by appropriate chemical action.

Oxidizing   60.21.225

Oxidizing is the production by chemical action of a dark colored film (usually a sulphide) on a metal surface.

Pores   60.21.230

Pores are discontinuities in a metal coating which extend through to the base metal or underlying coating.

Free Cyanide   60.21.235

The free cyanide in an electrodepositing solution is the excess of alkali cyanide above the minimum required to give a clear solution.

Total Cyanide   60.21.240

The total cyanide in a solution for metal deposition is the total content of the cyanide radical (CN), whether present as the simple or complex cyanide of an alkali or other metal.

Drag-Out   60.21.245

The drag-out is the quantity of solution that adheres to the cathodes when they are removed from a depositing bath.

Drag-In   60.21.250

The drag-in is the quantity of water or solution that adheres to cathodes when they are introduced into a depositing bath.

Building Up   60.21.255

Building up is electroplating for the purpose of increasing the dimensions of an article.

Relieving   60.21.260

Relieving is the removal of compounds from portions of colored metal surfaces by mechanical means.

Plating Rack 60.21.265

A plating rack is any frame used for suspending and conducting current to one or more cathodes during electrodeposition.

Sponge Plating 60.21.270

Sponge plating is plating in which the anode is surrounded by a sponge or other absorbent article in which the electrolyte is retained, and which is moved over the surface of the cathode.

Resist 60.21.275

A resist is any material applied to part of a cathode or plating rack to render the surface non-conducting.

Stopping Off 60.21.280

Stopping off is the application of a resist to any part of a cathode or plating rack.

Peeling 60.21.285

Peeling is the detachment of a plated metal coating from the base metal.

Mechanical Plating 60.21.290

Mechanical plating is any plating operation in which the cathodes are moved mechanically during the deposition.

Full Automatic Plating 60.21.295

Full automatic plating is mechanical plating in which the cathodes are automatically conveyed through successive cleaning and plating tanks.

Semi-Automatic Plating 60.21.300

Semi-automatic plating is mechanical plating in which the cathodes are conveyed automatically through only one plating tank.

Barrel Plating 60.21.305

Barrel plating is mechanical plating in which the cathodes are held loosely in a container which rotates.

Composite Plate 60.21.310

A composite plate is an electrodeposit consisting of layers of two or more metals.

Alloy Plate 60.21.315

An alloy plate is an electrodeposit which contains two or more metals so intimately mixed or combined as not to be distinguishable to the unaided eye.

Conducting Salts 60.21.320

Conducting salts are salts which when added to a plating solution materially increase its conductivity.

Tank Voltage 60.21.325

The tank voltage of an electroplating tank is the total potential drop between the anode and cathode bus bars during electrodeposition.

See **60.05.230.**

Slinging Wire 60.21.330

A slinging wire is a wire used to suspend and carry current to one or more cathodes in a plating tank.

Parcel Plating 60.21.335

Parcel plating is electroplating upon only a part of the surface of a cathode.

Shadowing 60.21.340

(Shielding)

Shadowing is the interference of any part of an anode, cathode, rack or tank with uniform current distribution upon a cathode.

High Lights 60.21.345

The high lights on any metal article are those portions which are most exposed to buffing or polishing operations, and hence have the highest luster.

Hydrogen Embrittlement 60.21.350

Hydrogen embrittlement is embrittlement of a metal caused by absorption of hydrogen during a cleaning, pickling or plating process.

Gassing

See **60.05.295.**

GROUP 60—ELECTROCHEMISTRY AND ELECTROMETALLURGY

Section 22—Electroforming

Electroforming 60.22.005

Electroforming is the production or reproduction of articles by electrodeposition.

Electrotyping 60.22.010

Electrotyping is the production or reproduction of printing plates by electroforming.

Matrix 60.22.015

A matrix is a form used as a cathode in electroforming.

Negative Matrix 60.22.020

(Negative)

A negative matrix is a matrix the surface of which is the reverse of the surface to be ultimately produced by electroforming.

Positive Matrix 60.22.025

(Positive)

A positive matrix is a matrix with a surface like that which is to be ultimately produced by electroforming.

Mold 60.22.030

A mold is a matrix made by taking an impression in a plastic material.

Wax Mold (electrotyping)   60.22.035

A wax mold is a mold made in wax, which is usually attached to a metal plate.

Lead Mold (electrotyping)   60.22.040

A lead mold is a mold made in thin sheet lead.

Case (electrotyping)   60.22.045

A case is metal plate, to which is attached a layer of wax or a lead mold.

Form   60.22.050

A form is any article such as a printing plate, which is used as a pattern to be reproduced.

Master Form   60.22.055

A master form is an original form from which, directly or indirectly, other forms may be prepared.

Oxidizing (electrotyping)   60.22.060

Oxidizing is the treatment of a graphited wax surface

with copper sulphate and iron filings, to produce a conducting copper coating.

Shell (electrotyping)   60.22.065

A shell is a layer of metal (usually copper or nickel) deposited upon, and separated from, a mold.

Tinning (electrotyping)   60.22.070

Tinning of shells is the melting of lead-tin foil upon the back of shells.

Casting (electrotyping)   60.22.075

Casting is the pouring of molten electrotype metal upon the tinned shells.

Finishing   60.22.080

Finishing of an electrotype is the operation of bringing all parts of the printing surface into the same plane, or, more strictly speaking, into positions having equal printing values.

GROUP 60—ELECTROCHEMISTRY AND ELECTROMETALLURGY

Section 23—Electrorefining

Electrorefining   60.23.005

Electrorefining is the process of electrodissolving a metal from an impure anode and depositing it in a more pure state.

Crude Metal   60.23.010

Crude metal is metal which contains impurities in sufficient quantity to make it unsuitable for specified purposes without refining.

Multiple System   60.23.015

The multiple system is the arrangement in a multi-electrode electrolytic cell whereby in each cell all of the anodes are connected to the positive bus bar and all of the cathodes to the negative bus bar.

Series System   60.23.020

The series system is the arrangement in a multi-electrode electrolytic cell whereby in each cell an anode connected to the positive bus bar is placed at one end and a cathode connected to the negative bus bar is placed at the other end with the intervening electrodes acting as bipolar electrodes.

Bipolar Electrode   60.23.025

A bipolar electrode is an electrode, without metallic connection with the current supply, one face of which acts as an anode surface and the opposite face as a cathode surface when an electric current is passed through the cell.

Anode Slime   60.23.030

Anode slime is the mixture of finely divided insoluble metals and compounds of metals which forms at the surface of a soluble anode in a refining bath.

See 60.20.030.

Foul Electrolyte   60.23.035

Foul electrolyte is an electrolyte in which the amount of impurity is sufficient to cause an undesirable effect on the operation of the electrolytic cell in which it is employed.

Regeneration of Electrolyte   60.23.040

The regeneration of electrolyte is the treatment of foul or spent electrolyte to make it again fit for use in an electrolytic cell.

Starting Sheet   60.23.045

A starting sheet is a thin sheet of metal designed for introduction into an electrolytic cell to act as a cathode and as a foundation for an adherent electrolytic deposit.

Starting-Sheet Blank   60.23.050

A starting-sheet blank is a rigid sheet of conducting material designed for introduction into an electrolytic cell as a cathode to receive a thin cohesive deposit which may be stripped off for use as a starting sheet.

Liberator Tank   60.23.055

A liberator tank is an electrolytic cell equipped with insoluble anodes to effect the decomposition of the electrolyte for the purpose of recovering its metal content in the form of cathode deposit.

Stripper Tank   60.23.060

A stripper tank is an electrolytic cell in which the cathode deposit is received on starting-sheet blanks for the production of starting sheets.

Commercial Tank   60.23.065

A commercial tank is an electrolytic cell in which the cathode deposit is the ultimate electrolytic product.

Stripping (multiple system) 60.23.070

Stripping is the operation of removing the thin deposit mechanically from a starting-sheet blank.

See 60.21.117.

Stripping (series system) 60.23.075

Stripping is the operation of removing mechanically

the remaining undissolved portion of the original anode from the cathode deposit obtained on a bipolar electrode.

See 60.21.117.

Nest or Section (multiple system) 60.23.080

A nest or section is a group of electrolytic cells placed close together and electrically connected in series for convenience and economy of operation.

GROUP 60—ELECTROCHEMISTRY AND ELECTROMETALLURGY

Section 24—Electrowinning

Electrowinning 60.24.005

Electrowinning is the electrodeposition of metals or compounds from solutions derived from ores or other materials using insoluble anodes.

Electroextraction 60.24.010

Electroextraction is the extraction by electrochemical processes of metals or compounds from ores and intermediate compounds.

Hydrometallurgy 60.24.015

Hydrometallurgy deals with the extraction of metals from their ores by the use of aqueous solvents.

Agitator 60.24.020

An agitator in hydrometallurgy is a receptacle in which ore is kept in suspension in a leaching solution.

Anode Mud 60.24.025

The anode mud in the process of electrowinning is the precipitate formed on the insoluble anodes.

Cascade 60.24.030

A cascade is a series of two or more electrolytic cells or tanks so placed that electrolyte from one flows into the next lower in the series, the flow being favored by differences in elevation of the cells, producing a cascade at each point where electrolyte drops from one cell to the next.

Concentrate 60.24.035

The concentrate is the product obtained by concentrating disseminated or lean ores by mechanical or other processes thereby eliminating undesired minerals or constituents.

Extraction Liquor 60.24.040

The extraction liquor is the solvent used in hydrometallurgical processes for extraction of the desired constituents from ores or other products.

Gas Grooves 60.24.045

Gas grooves are the hills and valleys in metallic deposits caused by streams of hydrogen or other gas rising continuously along the surface of the deposit while it is forming.

Leaching 60.24.055

Leaching is the treatment of a solid material with a liquid capable of extracting the soluble portions.

Leach Liquor 60.24.060

(Leach)

Leach liquor is a solution obtained by leaching.

Matte 60.24.065

Matte is a sulphide product obtained by fusion of an ore containing sulphide minerals.

Electrolytic Parting 60.24.070

Electrolytic parting of bullion consists in using the alloy as an anode in an electrolyte capable of taking only one of the metals into solution.

Regenerated Leach Liquor 60.24.075

Regenerated leach liquor is the solution which has regained its ability to dissolve desired constituents from the ore by the removal of those constituents in the process of electrowinning.

Slime 60.24.080

Slime is the finely divided portion of ore which settles very slowly from aqueous suspensions occurring in hydrometallurgy and wet concentration.

See 60.20.030.

Stripping 60.24.085

Stripping is the mechanical removal of electrodeposited metal from a stripping blank of the same or other metal on which it has been deposited.

See 60.21.117.

Stripping Compound 60.24.090

Stripping compound is any suitable material for coating a cathode surface so that the metal electrodeposited on the surface can be conveniently stripped off in sheets.

Tailing 60.24.095

Tailing in hydrometallurgy and in ore concentration is the discarded residue after treatment of an ore to remove desirable minerals.

Thickener 60.24.100

(Tank)

A thickener in hydrometallurgy is a tank in which a suspension of solid material can settle so that the solid material emerges from a suitable opening with only a portion of the liquid while the remainder of the liquid overflows in clear condition at another part of the thickener.

Tops   60.24.105

Tops are the top layers obtained by fusion of a copper-nickel matte with sodium sulphate and carbon.

Bottoms (nickel)   60.24.110

Bottoms (nickel) are the lower molten layers obtained

by fusion of copper-nickel matte with sodium sulphate and carbon.

Bottoms (copper)   60.24.115

Bottoms (copper) are the lower layers resulting from partial conversion of white metal (cuprous sulphide matte) to metal.

GROUP 60—ELECTROCHEMISTRY AND ELECTROMETALLURGY
Section 30—Electrolytic Alkali and Chlorine

Electrolyzer   60.30.005

An electrolyzer is an electrolytic cell for the production of alkali, chlorine, hypochlorites or other allied products.

Brine   60.30.010

Brine is the salt solution which is electrolyzed for producing alkali, chlorine, hypochlorites or other allied products.

Mercury Cells   60.30.015

Mercury cells are electrolytic cells having mercury

cathodes with which the deposited alkali metal forms an amalgam.

Denuder   60.30.020

The denuder is that portion of an electrolytic cell of the mercury type in which the alkali metal is separated from the mercury.

Amalgam   60.30.025

The amalgam is the product formed when alkali metal is deposited upon a cathode of mercury.

GROUP 60—ELECTROCHEMISTRY AND ELECTROMETALLURGY
Section 40—Electrochemical Valves (General)

Electrochemical Valve   60.40.005

An electrochemical valve is an electric valve consisting of a metal in contact with a solution or compound across the boundary of which current flows more readily in one direction than in the other direction and in which the valve action is accompanied by chemical changes.

Electrochemical Valve Metal   60.40.010

An electrochemical valve metal is a metal or alloy having properties suitable for use in an electrochemical valve.

Valve Action (electrochemical)   60.40.015

Valve action is the process involved in the operation of an electrochemical valve.

Valve Ratio   60.40.020

The valve ratio in an electrochemical valve is the ratio of the impedance to current flowing from the valve metal to the compound or solution, to the impedance in the opposite direction.

Forming   60.40.025

Forming is the process which results in a change in impedance at the surface of a valve metal to the passage of current from metal to electrolyte, when the voltage is first applied.

Film   60.40.030

The film in an electrochemical valve is the layer adjacent to the valve metal and in which is located the high-potential drop when current flows in the direction of high impedance.

Formation Voltage   60.40.035

The formation voltage is the final impressed voltage at which the film is formed on the valve metal in an electrochemical valve.

Breakdown Voltage   60.40.040

The breakdown voltage is the lowest voltage at which failure of an electrochemical valve occurs.

GROUP 60—ELECTROCHEMISTRY AND ELECTROMETALLURGY
Section 41—Rectifiers

Rectifier

See **15.50.010.**

Rectification   60.41.005

Rectification is the conversion of alternating current into unidirectional current by means of electric valves.

Half-Wave Rectification   60.41.010

Half-wave rectification is rectification permitting only one-half of the alternating-current cycle to be transmitted as unidirectional current.

Full-Wave Rectification   60.41.015

Full-wave rectification is rectification in which both

halves of the alternating-current cycle are transmitted as unidirectional current.

Electrolytic Rectifier   60.41.020

An electrolytic rectifier is a rectifier in which rectification of an alternating current is accompanied by electrolytic action.

Electronic Rectifier   60.41.025

An electronic rectifier is a rectifier in which rectification of an alternating current is accompanied by the passage of electrons only at the boundary of a valve metal and a compound of that metal.

Vacuum Tube Rectifier   60.41.030

A vacuum tube rectifier is a rectifier in which rectification is accomplished by the unidirectional passage of electrons from a heated electrode within an evacuated space.

Gas-Filled-Tube Rectifier   60.41.035

A gas-filled-tube rectifier is a rectifier in which rectification is accompanied by the ionization of an inert gas caused by a unidirectional flow of electrons from a heated electrode within an enclosed space.

Mechanical Rectifier   60.41.040

A mechanical rectifier is a rectifier in which rectification is accomplished by mechanical action.

Degree of Current Rectification   60.41.045

(DC to AC Ratio)

The degree of rectification is the ratio between the average unidirectional current output and the rms value of the alternating-current input from which it was derived.

Degree of Voltage Rectification   60.41.050

The degree of voltage rectification is the ratio between the average unidirectional voltage and the rms value of the alternating voltage from which it was derived.

D-C Form Factor   60.41.055

The d-c form factor is the ratio of the average unidirectional output current of a rectifier to the rms value of this same current.

Efficiency (of rectification)   60.41.060

The efficiency of rectification is the ratio of the direct-current power output to the alternating-current power input of the rectifier.

Leakage Current   60.41.065

Leakage current is alternating current passing through the rectifier without being rectified.

Leakage Current   60.41.066

Leakage current is a reverse current passing through a rectifier when the alternating-current supply is interrupted.

GROUP 60—ELECTROCHEMISTRY AND ELECTROMETALLURGY

Section 42—Electrolytic Condensers

Electrolytic Condenser   60.42.005

An electrolytic condenser is a combination of two conductors, at least one of which is a valve metal, separated by an electrolyte, and between which a dielectric film is formed adjacent to the surface of one or both of the conductors.

Asymmetrical Cell   60.42.010

An asymmetrical cell is a cell in which the impedance to the flow of current in one direction is greater than in the other direction.

Blocking Condenser   60.42.015

(Check Valve)

A blocking condenser is an asymmetrical cell used to prevent flow of current in a specified direction.

Unit-Area Capacitance   60.42.020

The unit-area capacitance of an electrolytic condenser is the capacitance of a unit area of the anode surface at a specified frequency after formation at a specified voltage.

GROUP 60—ELECTROCHEMISTRY AND ELECTROMETALLURGY

Section 50—Electrothermics

Electrothermics

See 60.05.010.

Pyroconductivity   60.50.005

Pyroconductivity is electric conductivity which develops with rising temperature, and notably upon fusion, in solids that are practically non-conductive at atmospheric temperatures.

Resistance Furnace   60.50.010

A resistance furnace is an electrothermic apparatus the heat energy for which is generated by the flow of electric current against ohmic resistance internal to the furnace.

Resistor Furnace   60.50.015

A resistor furnace is a resistance furnace in which the heat is developed in a resistor which is not a part of the charge.

Charge-Resistance Furnace   60.50.020

A charge-resistance furnace is a resistance furnace in which the heat is developed within the charge acting as the resistor.

Arc Furnace   60.50.025

An arc furnace is an electrothermic apparatus the heat energy for which is generated by the flow of electric current through one or more arcs internal to the furnace.

Direct-Arc Furnace   60.50.030

A direct-arc furnace is an arc furnace in which the arc is formed between the electrodes and the charge.

Indirect-Arc Furnace   60.50.035

An indirect-arc furnace is an arc furnace in which the arc is formed between two or more electrodes.

Smothered-Arc Furnace   60.50.040

A smothered-arc furnace is a furnace in which the arc or arcs is covered by a portion of the charge.

Induction Furnace   60.50.045

An induction furnace is a transformer of electric energy to heat by electromagnetic induction

Low-Frequency Furnace   60.50.050

(Core Type Induction Furnace)

A low-frequency furnace is an induction furnace which includes a primary winding, a core of magnetic material and a secondary winding of one short-circuited turn of the material to be heated.

High-Frequency Furnace   60.50.055

(Coreless Type Induction Furnace)

A high-frequency furnace is an induction furnace in which the heat is generated within the charge, or within the walls of the containing crucible, or in both, by currents induced by high-frequency flux from a surrounding solenoid.

Refractory   60.50.060

A refractory is a non-metallic material highly resistant to fusion and suitable for furnace roofs and linings.

Lining   60.50.065

The lining of a furnace comprises the layer of refractory and heat-insulating material within the enclosing shell.

Charging   60.50.070

Charging is the act of supplying to a furnace the materials to be treated or converted.

Tapping   60.50.075

Tapping is the operation of withdrawing the molten products from a furnace through an aperture.

Flux (in furnaces)   60.50.080

Flux is material capable of forming with gangue or other earthy matter a liquid melt having the fusibility and chemical character suitable to a specified furnace process.

Slag   60.50.085

Slag is the non-metallic fused byproduct of a furnace operation.

Electrode

See **60.05.030.**

Continuous Electrode   60.50.090

A continuous electrode is a furnace electrode which receives successive additions in length at the end remote from the active zone of the furnace to compensate length consumed therein.

Non-Continuous Electrode   60.50.095

A non-continuous electrode is a furnace electrode the residual length of which is discarded when too short for further effective use.

Electrode Economizer   60.50.100

An electrode economizer is a collar which makes a seal between an electrode and the roof of a covered electric furnace with substantial exclusion of air, thereby preventing serious oxidation of the part of the electrode within the furnace.

Radiation Loss   60.50.105

Radiation loss comprises the heat radiated from the entire outer surface of a furnace.

Fuel   60.50.110

Fuel is matter that can be economically burned to supply industrial heat at a temperature suitable to a specified process.

Deoxidation   60.50.115

Deoxidation is the process of abstracting the oxygen content of a dissolved oxide, or of removing dissolved oxygen, with the aid of a suitable reducing agent.

Charge   60.50.120

Charge comprises the collective materials which a furnace receives for treatment or conversion.

Electrothermal Efficiency   60.50.125

Electrothermal efficiency is the ratio of energy usefully employed in a furnace to the total energy supplied.

Pinch Effect   60.50.130

Pinch effect is the result of an electromechanical force that constricts, and sometimes momentarily ruptures, a molten conductor carrying current at high density.

GROUP 60—ELECTROCHEMISTRY AND ELECTROMETALLURGY
Section 55—Electrolysis of Fused Electrolytes

Fused Electrolyte   60.55.005

(Bath) (Fused Salt) (Electrolyte)
A fused electrolyte is a molten anhydrous electrolyte.

Electrolytic Cell

(Pot) (Electrolytic Furnace) (Furnace)
See **60.05.050**.

Anode Butt   60.55.010

An anode butt is a partially consumed anode.

Anode Effect   60.55.015

The anode effect is a phenomenon occurring at the anode, characterized by failure of the electrolyte to wet the anode and resulting in the formation of a more or less continuous gas film separating the electrolyte and anode and increasing the potential difference between them.

Anode Layer   60.55.020

An anode layer is a molten metal or alloy, serving as the anode in an electrolytic cell, which floats on the fused electrolyte, or upon which the fused electrolyte floats.

Cathode Layer   60.55.025

A cathode layer is a molten metal or alloy forming the cathode of an electrolytic cell and which floats on the fused electrolyte, or upon which fused electrolyte floats.

Shell   60.55.030

A shell is the external container in which the electrolysis of fused electrolytes is conducted.

Lining   60.55.035

(Cell Lining)
A cell lining is a protective layer, usually of carbon, used to protect the shell from contact with the fused electrolyte.

Cell Cavity   60.55.040

A cell cavity is the container formed by the cell lining for holding the fused electrolyte.

Metal Fog   60.55.045

(Metal Mist)
A metal fog is a fine dispersion of metal in a fused electrolyte.

Working   60.55.050

Working an electrolytic cell is the process of stirring additional solid electrolyte or constituents of the electrolyte into the fused electrolyte in order to produce a uniform solution thereof.

Collector Plates   60.55.055

Collector plates are metal inserts embedded in the cell lining to minimize the electric resistance between the cell lining and the current leads.

Contact Conductor   60.55.060

(Contact Electrode)
A contact conductor is a device to lead electric current into or out of a molten or solid metal or alloy, which itself serves as the active electrode in the cell.

Crust   60.55.065

A crust is a layer of solidified electrolyte.

Side Crust   60.55.070

A side crust is a layer of electrolyte solidified on the side walls of the cell lining.

Top Crust   60.55.075

A top crust is a layer of solid electrolyte formed above the molten electrolyte.

Internal Heating   60.55.080

Internal heating in the electrolysis of fused electrolytes is the method of maintaining the electrolyte in a molten condition by the heat generated by the passage of current through the electrolyte.

GROUP 65—ELECTROCOMMUNICATION

(Joint report of subcommittees on Wire Communication and Radio Communication)

SECTIONS

10 Transmission—General
11 Transmission—Characteristics
15 Transmission—Instruments for Conversion to and from Electric Waves
20 Transmission—Circuit Elements, Devices and Networks
25 Transmission—Lines
30 Transmission—Antennas
35 Transmission—Radio Transmitters, Radio Receivers and Direction Finders
40 Television
45 Telephone Systems—General
50 Telephone Stations and Sets
55 Telephone Lines and Trunks
60 Telephone Switching Systems and Arrangements
61 Telephone Switching Apparatus

65 Telegraph Systems
70 Two-Way Radio Communication Systems—General
71 Two-Way Point-to-Point Radio Communication Systems
72 Two-Way Mobile Radio Communication Systems
75 Radio Broadcasting Systems—General
76 Radio Program Broadcasting Systems
77 Radio Patrol Systems
80 Other Radio Systems
85 Telecontrol and Telemeter Systems
90 Alarm Systems—General
91 Fire-Alarm Systems
92 Burglar-Alarm Systems
95 Other Forms of Electric Communication

GROUP 65—ELECTROCOMMUNICATION

Section 10—Transmission

General

Frequency

See 05.05.180.

Audio Frequency 65.10.005

An audio frequency is a frequency corresponding to a normally audible sound wave.

NOTE: Audio frequencies range roughly from 20 to 15,000 cycles per second.

Radio Frequency 65.10.010

A radio frequency is a frequency usually higher than those corresponding to normally audible sound waves and lower than those corresponding to heat and light waves.

NOTE: The present practicable limits of radio frequency are roughly 10 kilocycles per second to 2,000 megacycles per second.

Frequency Band 65.10.015

A frequency band is a continuous range of frequencies extending between two limiting frequencies.

Band Width 65.10.020

The band width of a frequency band is the number of cycles per second expressing the difference between its limiting frequencies.

Fundamental Frequency 65.10.025

A fundamental frequency is the lowest component frequency of a periodic quantity.

Harmonic 65.10.030

A harmonic is a component of a periodic quantity which is an integral multiple of the fundamental frequency. For example, a component the frequency of which is twice the fundamental frequency is called the second harmonic.

Subharmonic 65.10.035

A subharmonic is a sinusoidal quantity having a frequency which is an integral submultiple of the frequency of some other sinusoidal phenomenon to which it is referred. For example, a wave the frequency of which is half the fundamental frequency of another wave is called the second subharmonic of that wave.

Cycle

See 05.05.190.

Voice-Frequency Telephony 65.10.100

Voice-frequency telephony is that form of telephony in which the frequencies of the components of the transmitted electric waves are substantially the same as the frequencies of corresponding components of the actuating acoustical waves. This type of electric wave is called a "voice-frequency electric wave".

Carrier Telephony 65.10.105

Carrier telephony is that form of telephony in which carrier transmission is used, the modulating wave being a voice-frequency wave. This term is ordinarily applied only to wire telephony.

Radio Transmission 65.10.110

Radio transmission is the transmission at radio frequencies of signals by means of radiated electromagnetic waves

ELECTRICAL DEFINITIONS

Radio Broadcasting 65.10.115

Radio broadcasting is radio transmission intended for general reception.

Picture Transmission 65.10.120

Picture transmission is the electric transmission of a picture having a gradation of shade values.

Facsimile Transmission 65.10.125

Facsimile transmission is the electric transmission of a graphic record having a limited number of shade values.

Television 65.10.130

Television is the electric transmission and reception of transient visual images, in such a way as to give a substantially continuous and simultaneous reproduction to the eye at a distance.

Telephone Channel 65.10.200

A telephone channel is a path suitable for the transmission of voice-controlled electric waves between two stations.

NOTE: The term "channel" is used to denote either a "one-way channel" providing transmission in one direction only or a "two-way channel" providing transmission in both directions.

Telegraph Channel 65.10.205

A telegraph channel is a path which is suitable for the transmission of telegraph signals between two telegraph stations.

NOTE: The term "channel" is used to denote either a one-way channel providing transmission in one direction only or a two-way channel providing transmission in both directions.
Three basically different kinds of telegraph channels used in providing a number of telegraph channels over a circuit are:
1. One of a number of paths for simultaneous transmission in the same frequency range as in bridge duplex, differential duplex and quadruplex telegraphy.
2. One of a number of paths for simultaneous transmission in different frequency ranges as in carrier telegraphy
3. One of a number of paths for successive transmission as in multiplex printing telegraphy.
Combinations of these three types may be used on the same circuit.

Radio Channel 65.10.210

A radio channel is a band of frequencies of a width sufficient to permit its use for radio communication. The width of a channel depends upon the type of transmission.

Service Band 65.10.215

A service band is a band of frequencies allocated to a given class of radio service.

Frequency Tolerance of a Radio Transmitter 65.10.220

The frequency tolerance of a radio transmitter is the extent to which the frequency of a transmitter may be permitted to vary above or below the frequency assigned.

Interference Guard Bands 65.10.225

The interference guard bands are the two bands of frequencies additional to, and on either side of, the communication band and frequency tolerance, which may be provided in order that there shall be no interference between stations having adjacent frequency assignments.

Radio Circuit 65.10.230

A radio circuit is a radio system for carrying out one communication at a time in either direction between two points.

Frequency Band of Emission 65.10.235

(Communication Band)

The frequency band of emission is the band of frequencies effectively occupied by that emission, for the type of transmission and the speed of signaling used.

Modulation 65.10.300

Modulation is the process whereby the amplitude (or other characteristic) of a wave is varied as a function of the instantaneous value of another wave. The first wave, which is usually a single-frequency wave, is called the "carrier wave"; the second wave is called the "modulating wave".

Double Modulation 65.10.305

Double modulation is the process of modulation in which a carrier wave of one frequency is first modulated by a signal wave and is then made to modulate a second carrier wave of another frequency.

Carrier 65.10.310

Carrier is an abbreviation frequently used to designate carrier wave, carrier current or carrier voltage.

Carrier Current 65.10.315

A carrier current is the current associated with a carrier wave.

Carrier Frequency 65.10.320

The carrier frequency is the frequency of the carrier wave.

Sidebands 65.10.325

Sidebands are the frequency bands on either side of the carrier frequency within which fall the frequencies of the waves produced by the process of modulation. Usually the width of a transmitted sideband is limited to a band width no greater than the band width of the modulating wave.

Demodulation 65.10.330

Demodulation is the process whereby a wave resulting from modulation is so operated upon that a wave is obtained having substantially the characteristics of the original modulating wave.

Detection 65.10.335

Detection is any process of operation on a modulated signal wave whereby the signal imparted to it in the modulation process is obtained.

Linear Detection 65.10.340

Linear detection is that form of detection in which the output voltage under consideration is substantially proportional to the carrier voltage throughout the useful range of the detecting device.

Power Detection 65.10.345

Power detection is that form of detection in which the power output of the detecting device is used to supply a substantial amount of power directly to a device such as a loudspeaker or recorder.

Carrier Transmission 65.10.350

Carrier transmission is that form of electric transmission in which the transmitted electric wave is a wave resulting from the modulation of a single-frequency wave by a modulating wave.

Suppressed Carrier Transmission 65.10.355

Suppressed carrier transmission is that system of transmission in which the carrier component of a modulated wave is suppressed, only the side frequencies being transmitted.

Single Sideband Transmission 65.10.360

Single sideband transmission is that method of operation in which one sideband is transmitted and the other sideband is suppressed. The carrier wave may be either transmitted or suppressed.

Wave

See **05.05.405.**

Wave Front

See **05.05.425.**

Wavelength

See **05.05.435.**

Standing Wave

See **05.05.420.**

Signal Wave

See **05.05.450.**

Carrier Wave

See **05.05.460.**

Damped Wave

See **05.05.465.**

Continuous Waves 65.10.400

Continuous waves are waves the successive oscillations of which are identical under permanent conditions.

Interrupted Continuous Waves 65.10.405

Interrupted continuous waves are waves obtained from continuous waves by interrupting them in a substantially periodic manner.

Tone-Modulated Waves 65.10.410

Tone-modulated waves are waves obtained from continuous waves by modulating them at audio frequency in a substantially periodic manner.

Telegraph-Modulated Waves 65.10.415

Telegraph-modulated waves are continuous waves the amplitude or frequency of which is varied by means of telegraphic keying.

Marking Wave (in telegraphic communication) 65.10.420

The marking wave, in telegraphic communication, is the emission which takes place while the active portions of the code characters are being transmitted.

Spacing Wave (in telegraphic communication) 65.10.425

The spacing wave, in telegraphic communication, is the emission which takes place between the active portions of the code characters or while no code characters are being transmitted.

Spacing Interval 65.10.430

A spacing interval is an interval between successive telegraph signal pulses, during which there either is no current flow or the current is of the polarity opposite to that employed for the signal pulses.

Dot-Cycle 65.10.435

A dot-cycle is one cycle of the periodic wave formed by a succession of dots, each being followed by a spacing interval of the same duration as the dot, and hence consists of one dot and one spacing interval.

Coupling 65.10.500

Coupling is the association of two circuits or systems in such a way that power may be transferred from one to the other.

Capacitive Coupling 65.10.505

Capacitive coupling is the association of one circuit with another by means of mutual capacitance.

Resistive Coupling 65.10.510

Resistive coupling is the association of one circuit with another by means of mutual resistance.

Direct Coupling 65.10.515

Direct coupling is the association of two circuits by means of a self inductance, capacitance, resistance or a combination of them which is common to the circuits.

Inductive Coupling 65.10.520

Inductive coupling is the association of one circuit with another by means of inductance mutual to the circuits.

NOTE: This term, when used without modifying words, is commonly used for coupling by means of mutual inductance, whereas coupling by means of self inductance common to the circuits is called direct inductive coupling.

Tuning 65.10.525

Tuning is the adjustment in relation to frequency of a circuit or system to secure optimum performance; commonly the adjustment of a circuit or circuits to resonance.

Series (Phase) Resonance 65.10.530

Series (phase) resonance is the steady-state condition

which exists in a circuit comprising inductance and capacitance connected in series, when the current in the circuit is in phase with the voltage across the circuit.

Parallel (Phase) Resonance 65.10.535

Parallel (phase) resonance is the steady-state condition which exists in a circuit comprising inductance and capacitance connected in parallel, when the current entering the circuit from the supply line is in phase with the voltage across the circuit.

Beating 65.10.540

Beating is a phenomenon in which two or more periodic quantities of different frequencies add linearly to produce a resultant having pulsations of amplitude.

Beat 65.10.545

A beat is a complete cycle in the phenomenon of beating.

Regeneration 65.10.550

Regeneration is the process by which a part of the power in the output circuit of an amplifying device reacts upon the input circuit in such a manner as to reinforce the initial power, thereby increasing the amplification. (This is sometimes called feed-back or reaction.)

GROUP 65—ELECTROCOMMUNICATION

Section 11—Transmission

Characteristics

Bel 65.11.005

The bel is the fundamental division of a logarithmic scale for expressing the ratio of two amounts of power, the number of bels denoting such a ratio being the logarithm to the base 10 of this ratio.

NOTE: With P_1 and P_2 designating two amounts of power and N the number of bels denoting their ratio:

$$N = \log_{10} (P_1 / P_2) \text{ bels}$$

Decibel 65.11.010

The decibel is one-tenth of a bel, the number of decibels denoting the ratio of two amounts of power being 10 times the logarithm to the base 10 of this ratio. The abbreviation db is commonly used for the term decibel.

NOTE: With P_1 and P_2 designating two amounts of power and n the number of decibels denoting their ratio:

$$n = 10 \log_{10} (P_1 / P_2) \text{ db}$$

When the conditions are such that ratios of currents or ratios of voltages (or analogous quantities in other fields) are the square roots of the corresponding power ratios, the number of decibels by which the corresponding powers differ is expressed by the following formulas:

$$n = 20 \log_{10} (I_1 / I_2) \text{ db}$$
$$n = 20 \log_{10} (V_1 / V_2) \text{ db}$$

where I_1 / I_2 and V_1 / V_2 are the given current and voltage ratios, respectively.

By extension, these relations between numbers of decibels and ratios of currents or voltages are sometimes applied where these ratios are not the square roots of the corresponding power ratios; to avoid confusion, such usage should be accompanied by a specific statement of this application.

Volume 65.11.015

The volume at any point in a telephone circuit is a measure of the power corresponding to a voice-frequency wave at that point.

NOTE: Volume is usually expressed in decibels with respect to an arbitrary standard.

Power Level 65.11.020

Power level is an expression of the power being transmitted past any point in a system.

Overload Level of a Transducer 65.11.025

The overload level of a transducer is that power level at which the transducer ceases to operate satisfactorily as a result of distortion, heating, breakage, etc.

Transmission Level 65.11.030

The transmission level of the signal power at any point in a transmission system is the ratio of the power at that point to some arbitrary amount of power, or to the power at some point in the system chosen as a reference point. This ratio is usually expressed in decibels.

Insertion Loss 65.11.035

The insertion loss at a given frequency caused by the insertion of apparatus in a transmission system is the ratio, expressed in decibels, of the powers at that frequency delivered to that part of the system beyond the point of insertion before and after the insertion.

Reflection Loss 65.11.040

The reflection loss for a given frequency at the junction of a source and an absorber of power is given by the formula

$$20 \log_{10} \frac{Z_A + Z_8}{\sqrt{4 Z_8 Z_A}} \text{ db}$$

where Z_A is the impedance of the absorber and Z_8 is the impedance of the source of power at the given frequency.

Transmission Loss 65.11.045

Transmission loss (frequently abbreviated "loss") is a general term used to denote a decrease in power in transmission from one point to another. Transmission loss is usually expressed in decibels.

The cognate term "transmission gain" (frequently abbreviated "gain") is simply a negative transmission loss if both are expressed on the same logarithmic scale. It is sometimes desirable to measure a decrease or increase in power under different conditions and under specified assumptions so that the terms "transmission loss" and "transmission gain" are used in several ways. Suitable qualification should accompany these terms unless it is clear from the context which specific type of measurement is meant.

NOTE: The following examples indicate uses of the term "transmission loss" when a transducer is considered:
(a) As a synonym for insertion loss, the terminating impedance being specified
(b) As a synonym for the image attenuation constant
(c) As a synonym for other indexes specifying the power transmitting characteristics of a transducer

Standard Cable   65.11.050

The standard cable formerly used for specifying transmission losses had in American practice a linear series resistance and linear shunt capacitance of 88 ohms and 0.054 microfarad, respectively, per loop mile (54.68 ohms and 0.03355 microfarad, respectively, per loop kilometer) with no inductance or shunt conductance.

Attenuation

See 05.05.440.

Voltage Amplification   65.11.055

Voltage amplification is the ratio of the alternating voltage produced at the output terminals of an amplifier, to the voltage impressed at the input terminals.

Current Amplification   65.11.060

Current amplification is the ratio of the alternating current produced in the output circuit of an amplifier, to the signal current supplied to the input circuit.

Power Amplification   65.11.065

Power amplification is the ratio of the power delivered by the output circuit of an amplifier containing a source of local power to the power supplied to its input circuit.

Percentage Modulation   65.11.070

Percentage modulation is the ratio of half the difference between the maximum and minimum amplitudes of a modulated wave to the average amplitude, expressed in percent.

Modulation Factor   65.11.075

The modulation factor is the ratio of the maximum departure (positive or negative) of the envelope of a modulated wave from its unmodulated value to its modulated value.

NOTE: In linear modulation the average amplitude of the envelope is equal to the amplitude of the unmodulated wave provided there is no zero-frequency component in the modulating signal wave. For modulating signal waves having unequal positive and negative peak values both modulation factors must be given separately.

Modulation Capability   65.11.080

Modulation capability is the maximum percentage modulation that is possible without objectionable distortion.

Radio Field Intensity   65.11.085

Radio field intensity is the effective (root-mean-square) value of the electric or magnetic field intensity at a point due to the passage of radio waves of a specified frequency. It is usually expressed in terms of the electric field intensity in microvolts per meter or millivolts per meter. When the direction in which the field intensity is measured is not stated, it is to be taken that it is measured in the direction of maximum field intensity.

Radio Noise Field Intensity   65.11.090

Radio noise field intensity is a measure of the field intensity, at a point (as a radio receiving station) of electromagnetic waves of an interfering character. In practice the quantity measured is not the field intensity of the interfering waves, but some quantity which is proportional to, or bears a known relation to, the field intensity.

Signal–Noise Ratio   65.11.095

Signal–noise ratio is the ratio at a point of the field intensity of a radio wave to the radio noise field intensity. It may also be considered as the ratio, at any point of a circuit, of signal power to total circuit-noise power.

Frequency Range of a Transmission System   65.11.100

The frequency range of a transmission system is the frequency band covering those frequencies at which the system is able to transmit power without attenuating it more than an arbitrarily specified amount.

Filter Transmission Band   65.11.105

(Filter Pass Band)

A filter transmission band is a frequency band of free transmission; that is, a frequency band in which, if the filter is non-dissipative or dissipation is neglected, the attenuation constant is zero.

Filter Attentuation Band   65.11.110

(Filter Stop Band)

A filter attenuation band is a frequency band of attenuation; that is, a frequency band in which, even if the filter is non-dissipative or dissipation is neglected, the attenuation constant is not zero.

Filter Discrimination   65.11.115

The discrimination of a wave filter is the difference between the minimum insertion loss at any frequency in a filter attenuation band and the maximum insertion loss at any frequency in the operating range of a filter transmission band.

NOTE: The insertion loss is determined under the conditions of the filter's normal use.

Critical or Cut-Off Frequency of a Filter   65.11.120

A critical or cut-off frequency of a filter is a frequency at which, disregarding the effects of dissipation, the attenuation constant changes from zero to a positive value or vice versa.

Nominal Cut-Off Frequency of a Loaded Line   65.11.125

The nominal cut-off frequency of a loaded line is the

frequency below which, disregarding the effects of dissipation, the attenuation constant is zero and immediately above which it is positive.

Coupling Coefficient   65.11.130

The coupling coefficient is the ratio of the mutual or common impedance component of two circuits to the square root of the product of the total impedance components of the same kind in the two circuits. (Impedance components may be inductance, capacitance or resistance.)

Condenser Constant   65.11.135

The condenser constant of a condenser at a given frequency is the ratio of its reactance to its effective resistance at that frequency.

Coil Constant   65.11.140

The coil constant of an inductance coil at a given frequency is the ratio of its reactance to its effective resistance at that frequency.

Noise   65.11.200

Noise is any extraneous sound tending to interfere with the proper and easy perception of those sounds which it is desired to receive.

Circuit Noise   65.11.205

Circuit noise is noise which is brought to the receiver electrically from a telephone system, excluding noise picked up acoustically by the telephone transmitters.

Room Noise   65.11.210

Room noise is noise existing in a room, or other location.

Intermodulation   65.11.215

Intermodulation is the modulation of the components of a complex wave by each other, as a result of which are produced waves which have frequencies equal to the sums and differences of those of the components of the original complex wave.

Cross Modulation   65.11.220

Cross modulation is a type of intermodulation due to modulation of the carrier of the desired signal by an undesired signal wave.

Crosstalk   65.11.225

Crosstalk is the sound heard in a receiver associated with a given telephone channel resulting from telephone currents in another telephone channel.

NOTE: In practice, crosstalk may be measured either by the loudness of the overheard sounds or by the magnitude of the coupling between the disturbed and disturbing channels. In the latter case, to specify the loudness of the overheard sounds, the volume in the disturbing channel must also be given.

Near-End Crosstalk   65.11.230

Near-end crosstalk is crosstalk which is propagated in a disturbed channel in the direction opposite to the direction of propagation of the current in the disturbing channel. The terminal of the disturbed channel at which the near-end crosstalk is present is ordinarily near or coincides with the energized terminal of the disturbing channel.

Far-End Crosstalk   65.11.235

Far-end crosstalk is crosstalk which is propagated in a disturbed channel in the same direction as the direction of propagation of the current in the disturbing channel. The terminal of the disturbed channel at which the far-end crosstalk is present and the energized terminal of the disturbing channel are ordinarily remote from each other.

Babble   65.11.240

Babble is the aggregate crosstalk from a large number of disturbing channels.

Thump   65.11.245

Thump is the noise in a receiver, connected to a telephone circuit on which a direct-current telegraph channel is superposed, caused by the telegraph currents.

Flutter   65.11.250

Flutter is the effect of a variation in the transmission characteristics of a telephone circuit caused by the action of superposed direct-current telegraph currents on magnetic materials associated with the circuit.

Ripple Voltage   65.11.255

Ripple voltage is the alternating component of a substantially unidirectional voltage.

Percent Ripple   65.11.260

Percent ripple is the ratio of the effective (root-mean-square) value of the ripple voltage to the average value of the total voltage, expressed in percent.

Interference   65.11.300

Interference in radio communication is disturbance of reception due to strays or undesired signals.

Strays   65.11.305

Strays are electromagnetic disturbances in radio reception other than those produced by radio transmitting systems.

Atmospherics   65.11.310

Atmospherics are strays produced by atmospheric conditions. (In the United States the term "static" has come to be used quite generally as a synonym for atmospherics.)

Absorption   65.11.315

Absorption is the loss of power in transmission of radio waves due to dissipation.

Atmospheric Absorption   65.11.320

Atmospheric absorption is the loss of power in transmission of radio waves due to dissipation in the atmosphere.

Ground Absorption   65.11.325

Ground absorption is the loss of power in transmission of radio waves due to dissipation in the ground.

Fading   65.11.330

Fading is the variation of the signal intensity received at a given location from a radio transmitting station as a result of changes in the transmission media.

Swinging   65.11.335

Swinging is the momentary variation in frequency of a received wave.

Spurious Radiation   65.11.340

Spurious radiation is any emission from a radio transmitter at frequencies outside of its communication band.

Singing   65.11.400

Singing in a transmission system is an undesired self-sustained oscillation existing in the system.

Singing Point   65.11.405

The singing point of a circuit is the limiting efficiency which the circuit can have without singing.

Echo   65.11.410

An echo is a wave which has been reflected from one or more impedance irregularities or otherwise returned with sufficient magnitude and delay to be perceived in some manner as a wave distinct from that directly transmitted.

Talker Echo   65.11.415

Talker echo is echo which reaches the ear of the talker.

Listener Echo   65.11.420

Listener echo is echo which reaches the ear of the listener.

Sidetone   65.11.425

Sidetone is the transmission and reproduction of sounds through a local path from the transmitter to the receiver of the same telephone station.

Distortion   65.11.430

Distortion is a change in wave form.

Frequency Distortion   65.11.435

Frequency distortion is that form of distortion in which the change is in the relative magnitudes of the different frequency components of a wave, provided that the change is not caused by non-linear distortion.

Non-Linear Distortion   65.11.440

Non-linear distortion is that form of distortion which occurs when the ratio of voltage to current, using root-mean-square values (or analogous quantities in other fields), is a function of the magnitude of either.

Delay Distortion   65.11.445

Delay distortion is that form of distortion which occurs when the phase angle of the transfer impedance with respect to two chosen pairs of terminals is not linear with frequency within a desired range, thus making the time of transmission or delay vary with frequency in that range.

Fidelity   65.11.450

Fidelity is the degree to which a system, or a portion of a system, accurately reproduces at its output the form of the signal which is impressed upon its input.

Self Impedance   65.11.500

The self impedance at any pair of terminals of a network is the ratio of an applied potential difference to the resultant current at these terminals, all other terminals being open.

NOTE: The terms and definitions in this section covering line and network parameters, whether electrical, acoustical or mechanical, pertain to currents and potentials, or the analogous quantities in acoustical and mechanical lines and networks, which have a single frequency and are in the steady state. The lines and networks are assumed to have electrical, acoustical or mechanical properties which are independent of the magnitudes of these currents and potentials. The quantities defined are complex numbers independent of time.

According to the usual alternating-current theory currents and potentials (and analogous quantities) are represented mathematically by complex exponential functions of time. Under these conditions the factors involving the time cancel out in the ratios called for in the definitions, leaving complex numbers independent of time. Solutions based on complex exponential functions under these conditions give the solution for real sinusoidal oscillations.

Mutual Impedance†   65.11.505

The mutual impedance between any two pairs of terminals of a network is the ratio of the open-circuit potential difference between either pair of terminals to the current applied at the other pair of terminals, all other terminals being open.

NOTE: Mutual impedance may have either of two signs depending upon the assumed directions of input current and output voltage; the negative of the above ratio is usually used. As ordinarily used, mutual impedance is additive if two coils of a transformer are connected in series or in parallel aiding and is subtractive if two coils of a transformer are in series or in parallel opposing.

Driving-Point Impedance†   65.11.510

The driving-point impedance at any pair of terminals of a network is the ratio of an applied potential difference to the resultant current at these terminals, all terminals being terminated in any specified manner.

Transfer Impedance†   65.11.515

The transfer impedance between any two pairs of terminals of a network is the ratio of a potential difference applied at one pair of terminals to the resultant current at the other pair of terminals, all terminals being terminated in any specified manner.

Sending-End Impedance†   65.11.520

The sending-end impedance of a line is the ratio of an applied potential difference to the resultant current at the point where the potential difference is applied. The sending-end impedance of a line is synonymous with the driving-point impedance of the line.

NOTE: For an infinite uniform line the sending-end impedance and the characteristic impedance are the same; and for an infinite periodic line the sending-end impedance and the iterative impedance are the same.

† See Note under 65.11.500.

Characteristic Impedance†   65.11.525

The characteristic impedance of a uniform line is the ratio of an applied potential difference to the resultant current at the point where the potential difference is applied, when the line is of infinite length.

NOTE: It is recommended that this term be applied only to a uniform line. For lines or structures which are not uniform, the recommended corresponding term is "iterative impedance".

Iterative Impedance†   65.11.530

The iterative impedance at a pair of terminals of a four-terminal transducer is the impedance which will terminate the other pair of terminals in such a way that the impedance measured at the first pair of terminals is equal to this terminating impedance.

NOTE: (a) It follows that the iterative impedance of a transducer is the same as the impedance measured at the input terminals when an infinite number of identically similar transducers are formed into an iterative or recurrent structure of infinite length by connecting the output terminals of the first transducer to the input terminals of the second, the output terminals of the second to the input terminals of the third, etc.

(b) The iterative impedances of a four-terminal transducer are, in general, not equal to each other but for any symmetrical transducer the iterative impedances are equal and are the same as the image impedances. The iterative impedance of a uniform line is the same as its characteristic impedance.

Image Impedances†   65.11.535

The image impedances of a transducer are the impedances which will simultaneously terminate each pair of terminals of the transducer in such a way that at each pair of terminals the impedances in both directions are equal.

NOTE: The image impedances of a four-terminal transducer are in general not equal to each other, but for any symmetrical transducer the image impedances are equal, and are the same as the iterative impedances.

Conjugate Impedances†   65.11.540

Conjugate impedances are impedances which have equal resistance components and reactance components equal in magnitude but opposite in sign; that is, conjugate impedances are expressible by conjugate complex quantities.

Propagation Constant†   65.11.550

1. The propagation constant per unit length of a uniform line is the natural logarithm of the ratio of the current at a point of the line to the current at a second point, at unit distance from the first point along the line in the direction of transmission, when the line is infinite in length, or is terminated in its characteristic impedance.

2. The propagation constant per section of a periodic line is the natural logarithm of the ratio of the current entering a section to the current leaving the same section, when the periodic line is infinite in length, or is terminated in its iterative impedances.

3. The propagation constant of an electric transducer is the natural logarithm of the ratio of the current entering the transducer to the current leaving the

transducer, when the transducer is terminated in its iterative impedances.

Attenuation Constant†   65.11.555

The attenuation constant is the real part of the propagation constant.

Phase Constant†   65.11.560

(Wavelength Constant)

The phase constant is the imaginary part of the propagation constant.

Transfer Constant†   65.11.565

The transfer constant of an electric transducer is the arithmetic mean of the natural logarithm of the ratio of input to output voltages and the natural logarithm of the ratio of input to output currents when the transducer is terminated in its image impedances.

NOTE: For a symmetrical transducer the transfer constant is the same as the propagation constant.

Image Attenuation Constant†   65.11.570

The image attenuation constant is the real part of the transfer constant.

Image Phase Constant†   65.11.575

The image phase constant is the imaginary part of the transfer constant.

Reflection Coefficient†   65.11.580

The reflection coefficient at the junction of a source of power and an absorber of power is unity minus the ratio of the current which is actually received to the current which would be received if the impedance of the absorber of power were equal to the impedance of the source of power. The reflection coefficient is given by the formula $(Z_A - Z_S)(Z_A + Z_S)$, where Z_S is the impedance of the source and Z_A is the impedance of the absorber of power.

Blocked Impedance† (of an electroacoustic transducer)   65.11.600

(Damped Impedance)

The blocked impedance of an electroacoustic transducer is the measured terminal impedance of its electric system with the attached mechanical system impedance infinite.

Normal Impedance† (of an electroacoustic transducer)   65.11.605

The normal impedance of an electroacoustic transducer is the measured terminal impedance of its electric system when the mechanical system is connected to its normal load.

Motional Impedance† (of an electroacoustic transducer)   65.11.610

The motional impedance of an electroacoustic transducer is the vector difference between the normal and blocked impedance.

---

† See Note under **65.11.500.**

† See Note under **65.11.500.**

Compliance of a Mechanical Element†   **65.11.615**

The compliance of a mechanical element is its displacement per unit of force. This is the reciprocal of its stiffness. Compliance in a mechanical system is expressed in centimeters per dyne. Negative compliance (reciprocal of negative stiffness) occurs in a case of unstable equilibrium where a small displacement results in a force tending to give a further displacement in the same direction.

Mechanical Impedance†   **65.11.620**

The mechanical impedance of a mechanical system is the complex quotient of the alternating force applied to the system by the resulting alternating linear velocity in the direction of the force at its point of application.

Mechanical Resistance†   **65.11.625**

The mechanical resistance is the real component of the mechanical impedance.

Mechanical Reactance†   **65.11.630**

The mechanical reactance is the magnitude of the imaginary component of the mechanical impedance.

Acoustic Impedance of a Sound Medium†   **65.11.635**

The acoustic impedance of a sound medium, on a given surface, is the complex quotient of the pressure (force per unit area) on the surface by the flux (volume velocity, or linear velocity multiplied by the area) through that surface. The acoustic impedance may be expressed in terms of mechanical impedance, acoustic impedance being equal to the mechanical impedance divided by the square of the area of the surface considered.

Acoustic Resistance of a Sound Medium†   **65.11.640**

The acoustic resistance of a sound medium is the real component of the acoustic impedance.

Acoustic Reactance of a Sound Medium†   **65.11.645**

The acoustic reactance of a sound medium is the magnitude of the imaginary component of the acoustic impedance.

Force Factor†   **65.11.650**

The force factor of an electroacoustic transducer is the measure of the coupling between its electric and mechanical systems. It is a ratio of the open-circuit force or voltage in the secondary system to the current or velocity in the primary system.

GROUP 65—ELECTROCOMMUNICATION
Section 15—Transmission

Instruments for Conversion to and from Electric Waves

Electroacoustic Transducer   **65.15.005**

An electroacoustic transducer is a transducer by which power may flow from an electric system to an acoustic system or *vice versa*.

Telephone Receiver   **65.15.010**

A telephone receiver is a device whereby electric waves produce substantially equivalent sound waves.

Thermal Telephone Receiver   **65.15.015**

(Thermophone)

A thermal telephone receiver is a telephone receiver in which the temperature of a conductor is caused to vary in response to the current input, thereby producing sound waves as a result of the expansion and contraction of the adjacent air.

Hand Receiver   **65.15.020**

A hand receiver is a telephone receiver designed to be held to the ear by the hand.

Head Receiver   **65.15.025**

A head receiver is a telephone receiver designed to be held to the ear by a headband.

Loudspeaker   **65.15.030**

A loudspeaker is a telephone receiver designed to effectively radiate acoustic power for reception at a distance.

Acoustic Radiator   **65.15.035**

An acoustic radiator is that portion of an electroacoustic transducer which initiates the radiation of sound vibrations.

Motor Element   **65.15.040**

The motor element is that portion of a telephone receiver which receives power from the electric system and converts it into mechanical power.

Baffle   **65.15.045**

A baffle is a partition which may be used with an acoustic radiator to impede circulation between front and back.

Magnetic Loudspeaker   **65.15.050**

A magnetic loudspeaker is a loudspeaker in which the mechanical forces result from magnetic reactions.

Induction Loudspeaker   **65.15.055**

An induction loudspeaker is a loudspeaker in which mechanical forces result from inductive reactions.

Condenser Loudspeaker   **65.15.060**

A condenser loudspeaker is a loudspeaker in which the mechanical forces result from electrostatic reactions.

† See Note under **65.11.500**.

    † See Note under **65.11.500**.

Pneumatic Loudspeaker　　　　　　　65.15.065

A pneumatic loudspeaker is a loudspeaker in which the acoustic output results from controlled variation of an air stream.

Moving-Conductor Loudspeaker　　　　65.15.070

A moving-conductor loudspeaker is a loudspeaker in which the mechanical forces are developed by the interaction of the field set up by the currents in the conductor and the polarizing field surrounding it.

Magnetic-Armature Loudspeaker　　　　65.15.075

A magnetic-armature loudspeaker is a loudspeaker the operation of which involves vibration in a ferromagnetic circuit. (This is sometimes called an electromagnetic or magnetic speaker.)

Moving-Coil Loudspeaker　　　　　　　65.15.080

(Dynamic Loudspeaker)

A moving-coil loudspeaker is a moving-conductor loudspeaker in which the movable conductor is given the form of a coil.

Magnetostriction Loudspeaker　　　　　65.15.085

A magnetostriction loudspeaker is a magnetic loudspeaker in which the mechanical forces are obtained by magnetostriction.

Piezoelectric Loudspeaker　　　　　　　65.15.090

A piezoelectric loudspeaker is one in which the mechanical forces are obtained by the use of a piezoelectric element.

Horn　　　　　　　　　　　　　　　　　65.15.100

A horn is an acoustic transducer consisting of a tube of varying sectional area.

Throat of a Horn　　　　　　　　　　　65.15.105

The throat of a horn is the end with the smaller cross-sectional area.

Mouth of a Horn　　　　　　　　　　　65.15.110

The mouth of a horn is the end with the larger cross-sectional area.

Exponential Horn　　　　　　　　　　　65.15.115

An exponential horn is a horn whose sectional area varies exponentially with its length. It is defined by the following relation:

$$\frac{S}{S_0} = e^{Tx}$$

where

S is the area of plane section of the horn normal to the axis at a distance x from the throat of the horn

S_0 is the area of plane section of the horn normal to the axis at the throat

T is a constant which determines the rate of taper of the horn

Conical Horn　　　　　　　　　　　　　65.15.120

A conical horn is a horn the equivalent sectional

radius $(\sqrt{S/\pi})$ of which has a constant rate of increase, where S is the cross-section of the horn.

Telephone Transmitter　　　　　　　　　65.15.200

A telephone transmitter is a device whereby sound waves produce substantially equivalent electric waves.

Microphone　　　　　　　　　　　　　　65.15.205

Microphone is a term frequently used as a synonym for telephone transmitter, particularly in radio and sound picture fields.

Carbon Microphone　　　　　　　　　　65.15.210

A carbon microphone is a microphone which depends for its operation upon the variation in resistance of carbon contacts.

Condenser Microphone　　　　　　　　　65.15.215

A condenser microphone is a microphone whose electric output results from variation in electrostatic capacity.

Push-Pull Microphone　　　　　　　　　65.15.220

A push-pull microphone is a microphone which makes use of two microphone elements operating 180 degrees out of phase.

Magnetic Microphone　　　　　　　　　　65.15.225

A magnetic microphone is a microphone the electric output of which is generated by the relative motion of a magnetic field and a coil or conductor located within the magnetic field.

Moving-Conductor Microphone　　　　　65.15.230

A moving-conductor microphone is a magnetic microphone in which the electric output results from the motion of a conductor in a magnetic field.

NOTE: The conductor may be given the form of a coil or a ribbon.

Moving-Coil Microphone　　　　　　　　65.15.235

A moving-coil microphone is a moving-conductor microphone in which the movable conductor is given the form of a coil. (This is sometimes called a dynamic microphone.)

Telegraph Transmitter　　　　　　　　　65.15.300

A telegraph transmitter is a device for controlling a source of electric power so as to form telegraph signals.

Telegraph Key　　　　　　　　　　　　　65.15.305

A telegraph key is a hand operated telegraph transmitter.

Telegraph Sounder　　　　　　　　　　　65.15.310

A telegraph sounder is a telegraph receiving instrument by means of which Morse signals are interpreted aurally, or "read", by noting the intervals of time between two diverse sounds.

Phonograph Pickup　　　　　　　　　　　65.15.400

A phonograph pickup is an electromechanical transducer actuated by a phonograph record and delivering power to an electric system, the electric currents having a wave form substantially identical with the waves in the phonograph record grooves.

Magnetic Pickup   65.15.405

A magnetic pickup is a phonograph pickup the electric output of which is generated by the relative motion of a magnetic field and a coil or conductor located within the magnetic field.

Carbon Contact Pickup   65.15.410

A carbon contact pickup is a phonograph pickup which depends for its operation upon the variation in resistance of carbon contacts.

Condenser Pickup   65.15.415

A condenser pickup is a phonograph pickup the electric output of which is generated by a mechanical variation of its capacitance.

Electric Phonograph Recorder   65.15.420

An electric phonograph recorder is an electromechanical transducer actuated by power in an electric system and supplying power to a recording mechanical system, the recorded waves produced by the mechanical system having a wave form corresponding to that in the electric system.

GROUP 65—ELECTROCOMMUNICATION
Section 20—Transmission
Circuit Elements, Devices and Networks

Modulator   65.20.005

A modulator is a device to effect the process of modulation. It may be operated by virtue of some non-linear characteristics or by a controlled variation of some circuit quantity.

Magnetic Modulator   65.20.010

A magnetic modulator is a modulator employing a magnetic circuit as the modulating element.

Vacuum Tube Modulator   65.20.015

A vacuum tube modulator is a modulator employing a vacuum tube as the modulating element.

Detector   65.20.020

A detector is a device having an asymmetrical conduction characteristic which is used for operation on a frequency or combination of frequencies to produce certain desired frequencies or changes in current.

Rectifier

See 15.50.010.

Full-Wave Rectifier   65.20.025

A full-wave rectifier is a double element rectifier which allows unidirectional current to pass to the load circuit during each half cycle of the alternating-current supply, one element functioning during positive half cycles and the other during negative half cycles.

Half-Wave Rectifier   65.20.030

A half-wave rectifier is a rectifier which changes alternating current into pulsating current, utilizing only one-half of each cycle.

Linear Rectifier   65.20.035

A linear rectifier is a rectifier the output current or voltage of which contains a wave having a form identical with that of the envelope of an impressed signal wave.

Transrectifier   65.20.040

A transrectifier is a device, ordinarily a vacuum tube, in which rectification occurs in one electrode circuit when an alternating voltage is applied to another electrode.

Oscillator

See 05.45.160.

Master Oscillator   65.20.045

A master oscillator is an oscillator of comparatively low power so arranged as to establish the carrier frequency of the output of an amplifier.

Oscillatory Circuit   65.20.050

An oscillatory circuit is a circuit containing inductance and/or capacitance and resistance, so arranged or connected that a voltage impulse will produce a current which periodically reverses.

Amplifier   65.20.100

An amplifier is a device which, by enabling a received wave to control a local source of power, is capable of delivering an enlarged copy of the wave.

Class A Amplifier

See 70.30.010.

Class AB Amplifier

See 70.30.015.

Class B Amplifier

See 70.30.020.

Class C Amplifier

See 70.30.025.

Filament Power Supply   65.20.120

The filament power supply for a thermionic vacuum tube is the means for supplying and delivering power with proper regulation to the filament for the heating of the filament.

NOTE: This term is also applied to the means for supplying power to the heaters of tubes of the unipotential cathode type.

Plate Power Supply   65.20.125

The plate power supply of a thermionic vacuum tube is the means for supplying power to the plate of the vacuum tube at a properly regulated voltage which is usually positive with respect to the cathode.

Grid Voltage Supply   65.20.130

The grid voltage supply of a thermionic vacuum tube is the means for supplying and applying with proper regulation a potential to the grid of the vacuum tube, which is usually negative with respect to the cathode.

Reflex Circuit Arrangement   65.20.135

A reflex circuit arrangement is a circuit arrangement in which the signal is amplified, both before and after detection, in the same amplifier tube or tubes.

Automatic Volume Control   65.20.140

An automatic volume control is a self-acting device which maintains the output of a radio receiver or amplifier substantially constant within relatively narrow limits while the input voltage varies over a wide range.

Telephone Repeater   65.20.200

A telephone repeater is a combination of one or more amplifiers together with their associated equipment for use in a telephone circuit.

Two-Wire Repeater   65.20.205

A two-wire repeater is a telephone repeater which provides for transmission in both directions over a two-wire telephone circuit.

NOTE: In practice this may be either a 21 type repeater or a 22 type repeater.

21 Type Repeater   65.20.210

A 21 type repeater is a two-wire telephone repeater in which there is one amplifier serving to amplify the telephone currents in both directions, the circuit being arranged so that the input and output terminals of the amplifier are in one pair of conjugate branches, while the lines in the two directions are in another pair of conjugate branches.

22 Type Repeater   65.20.215

A 22 type repeater is a two-wire telephone repeater in which there are two amplifiers, one serving to amplify the telephone currents being transmitted in one direction and the other serving to amplify the telephone currents being transmitted in the other direction.

Four-Wire Repeater   65.20.220

A four-wire repeater is a telephone repeater for use in a four-wire circuit and in which there are two amplifiers, one serving to amplify the telephone currents in one side of the four-wire circuit and the other serving to amplify the telephone currents in the other side of the four-wire circuit.

Carrier Repeater   65.20.225

A carrier repeater is a repeater for use in carrier transmission.

Terminal Repeater   65.20.230

A terminal repeater is a repeater for use at the end of a trunk or line.

Intermediate Repeater   65.20.235

An intermediate repeater is a repeater for use in a trunk or line at a point other than an end.

Cord Circuit Repeater   65.20.240

A cord circuit repeater is a telephone repeater associated with a cord circuit so that it may be inserted in a telephone circuit by an operator.

Telegraph Repeater   65.20.300

A telegraph repeater is an arrangement of apparatus and circuits for receiving telegraph signals from one line and retransmitting corresponding signals into another line.

Direct-Point Repeater   65.20.305

A direct-point repeater is a telegraph repeater in which the receiving relay controlled by the signals received over a line repeats corresponding signals directly into another line or lines without the interposition of any other repeating or transmitting apparatus.

Regenerative Repeater   65.20.310

A regenerative repeater is a telegraph repeater which receives mechanically sent, electrically transmitted signals and resends them in substantially perfect form.

Half-Duplex Repeater   65.20.315

A half-duplex repeater is a duplex telegraph repeater provided with interlocking arrangements which restrict the transmission of signals to one direction at a time.

Radio-Frequency Transformer   65.20.400

A radio-frequency transformer is a transformer for use with radio-frequency currents.

Audio-Frequency Transformer   65.20.405

An audio-frequency transformer is a transformer for use with audio-frequency currents.

Tuned Transformer   65.20.410

A tuned transformer is a transformer the associated circuit elements of which are adjusted as a whole to be resonant at the frequency of the alternating current supplied to the primary, thereby causing the secondary voltage to build up to higher values than would otherwise be obtained.

Banked Winding   65.20.415

A banked winding is a compact multilayer form of coil winding, for the purpose of reducing distributed capacitance, in which single turns are wound successively in each of two or more layers, the entire winding proceeding from one end of the coil to the other, without return.

Induction Coil   65.20.420

An induction coil is a transformer used in a telephone set for the interconnection of the transmitter, receiver and line terminals.

Choke Coil 65.20.425

A choke coil is an inductor inserted in a circuit to offer relatively large impedance to alternating current.

Hybrid Set 65.20.430

A hybrid set is comprised of two or more transformers interconnected to form a network having four pairs of accessible terminals to which may be connected four impedances so that the branches containing them may be made conjugate in pairs.

NOTE: This term is commonly applied to an arrangement for interconnecting a four-wire and a two-wire circuit. This arrangement is sometimes called a "four-wire terminating set".

Hybrid Coil 65.20.435

A hybrid coil is a single transformer having effectively three windings which, within certain limitations as to the impedances to which it is connected, performs the function of a hybrid set.

Loading Coil (in radio) 65.20.440

A loading coil, in radio usage, is an inductor inserted in a circuit to increase its inductance but not to provide coupling with any other circuit.

Loading Coil (in wire communication) 65.20.445

A loading coil, in wire communication, is an inductance coil for use in coil loading.

Phantom-Circuit Loading Coil 65.20.450

A phantom-circuit loading coil is a loading coil for introducing a desired amount of inductance in a phantom circuit and a minimum amount of inductance in the constituent side circuits.

Side-Circuit Loading Coil 65.20.455

A side-circuit loading coil is a loading coil for introducing a desired amount of inductance in a side circuit and a minimum amount of inductance in the associated phantom circuit.

Repeating Coil 65.20.460

Repeating coil is a term frequently used in telephone practice to designate a transformer.

Phantom Repeating Coil 65.20.465

A phantom repeating coil is a term which initially was used to designate a side-circuit repeating coil but which has come to be used to refer to either a side-circuit repeating coil or a phantom-circuit repeating coil, when discrimination between these two types is not necessary.

Side-Circuit Repeating Coil 65.20.470

A side-circuit repeating coil is a repeating coil which functions simultaneously as a transformer at a terminal of a side circuit and as a device for superposing one side of a phantom circuit on that side circuit.

Phantom-Circuit Repeating Coil 65.20.475

A phantom-circuit repeating coil is a repeating coil used at a terminal of a phantom circuit, in the non-superposed terminal circuit extending from the associated side-circuit repeating coils.

Retardation Coil 65.20.480

A retardation coil is an inductance coil for use in a circuit to discriminate against the flow of alternating current in favor of direct current or to offer an impedance to a varying current.

By-Pass Condenser 65.20.485

A by-pass condenser is a condenser which will provide an alternating-current path of comparatively low impedance around some circuit element.

Stopping Condenser 65.20.490

(Blocking Condenser)

A stopping condenser is a condenser connected in series which introduces a comparatively high impedance for limiting the current flow of low-frequency alternating current or direct current without materially affecting the flow of high-frequency alternating current.

Relay 65.20.500

A relay is an electromechanical device by means of which a change of current or potential in one circuit can be made to produce a change in the electrical condition of another circuit.

Electromagnetic Type Relay 65.20.505

An electromagnetic type relay is an electromagnetically operated switch ordinarily composed of one or more coils which control an armature, the movement of which actuates directly one or more sets of contacts.

Polarized Relay 65.20.510

A polarized relay is a relay in which the movement of the armature depends upon the direction of the current in the circuit controlling the armature.

Neutral Relay 65.20.515

A neutral relay (sometimes called "non-polarized relay") is a relay in which the movement of the armature does not depend upon the direction of the current in the circuit controlling the armature.

Vacuum Tube Voltmeter 65.20.540

A vacuum tube voltmeter is a device utilizing the characteristics of a vacuum tube for measuring voltages.

Volume Indicator 65.20.545

A volume indicator is a type of high-impedance voltmeter, usually of the vacuum tube type, designed to measure volume in a telephone circuit.

Decremeter 65.20.550

A decremeter is an instrument for measuring the logarithmic decrement of a train of waves.

Voltage Divider 65.20.555

A voltage divider is a resistor provided with fixed or movable contacts and with two fixed terminal contacts; current is passed between the terminal contacts, and a desired voltage is obtained across a portion of the resistor. (The term potentiometer is often erroneously used for this device.)

Expansion Type Hot-Wire Ammeter

See 30.20.215.

Thermocouple Ammeter

See 30.20.220.

Thermoelement   65.20.560

A thermoelement is a device consisting of a thermocouple and a heating element arranged for measuring small currents.

Frequency Meter

See 30.40.045.

Pilot Wire Regulator   65.20.570

A pilot wire regulator is an automatic device for controlling adjustable gains or losses associated with transmission circuits to compensate for transmission changes caused by temperature variations, the control usually depending upon the resistance of a conductor or "pilot wire" having substantially the same temperature conditions as the conductors of the circuits being regulated.

Echo Suppressor   65.20.575

An echo suppressor is a device which is operated by telephone currents so as to attenuate or eliminate echoes.

Heat Coil   65.20.580

A heat coil is a protective device which grounds or opens a circuit, or does both, by means of a mechanical element which is allowed to move when the fusible substance which holds it in place is heated above a predetermined temperature by current in the circuit.

Duplex Artificial Line   65.20.590

A duplex artificial line is a balancing network, simulating the impedance of the real line and distant terminal apparatus, which is employed in a duplex circuit for the purpose of making the receiving device unresponsive to outgoing signal currents.

Transducer   65.20.600

A transducer is a device by means of which energy may flow from one or more transmission systems to one or more other transmission systems.

NOTE: The energy transmitted by these systems may be of any form (for example, it may be electric, mechanical or acoustical), and it may be of the same form or different forms in the various input and output systems.

Passive Transducer   65.20.605

A passive transducer is a transducer containing no source of power.

Active Transducer   65.20.610

An active transducer is a transducer containing one or more sources of power.

Electric Transducer   65.20.615

An electric transducer is an electric network by means of which energy may flow from one or more trans-

mission systems to one or more other transmission systems.

NOTE: In the cases generally considered, an electric transducer has four terminals, two taken as input and two as output terminals.

Symmetrical Transducer   65.20.620

A symmetrical transducer is a transducer of which the image impedances are equal.

Electric Network   65.20.625

An electric network is a combination of any number of electric elements, the impedances of which may be either lumped or distributed or both, which are connected in any manner, conductively, inductively or capacitatively.

NOTE: An electric network is understood to be passive unless the contrary is stated.

Active Electric Network   65.20.630

An active electric network is an electric network containing one or more sources of energy.

Passive Electric Network   65.20.635

A passive electric network is an electric network containing no source of energy.

Conjugate Branches of a Network   65.20.640

Conjugate branches of a network are any two branches such that an electromotive force inserted in one branch produces no current in the other branch.

L Network   65.20.645

An L network is a network composed of two impedance branches in series, the free ends being connected to one pair of terminals and the junction point and one free end being connected to another pair of terminals.

C Network   65.20.650

A C network is a network composed of three impedance branches in series, the free ends being connected to one pair of terminals and the junction points being connected to another pair of terminals.

T Network   65.20.655

A T network is a network composed of three impedance branches connected in star, that is, one end of each branch is connected to a common point, while the three remaining ends are connected to an input terminal, an output terminal, and a common input and output terminal, respectively.

H Network   65.20.660

An H network is a network composed of five impedance branches, two connected in series between an input terminal and an output terminal, two connected in series between another input terminal and another output terminal, and the fifth connected from the junction point of the first two branches to the junction point of the second two branches.

π Network   65.20.665

A π network is a network composed of three impedance

branches connected in delta, that is, connected in series with each other to form a closed circuit, the three junction points forming an input terminal, an output terminal, and a common input and output terminal, respectively.

O Network   65.20.670

An O network is a network composed of four impedance branches connected in series to form a closed circuit, two adjacent junction points serving as input terminals, while the remaining two junction points serve as output terminals.

Lattice Network   65.20.675

A lattice network is a network composed of four impedance branches connected in series to form a closed circuit, two non-adjacent junction points serving as input terminals, while the remaining two junction points serve as output terminals.

Equivalent Network   65.20.680

An equivalent network is a network which, under certain conditions of use, may replace another network.

NOTE: If one network can replace another network in any system whatsoever without altering in any way the electrical operation of that portion of the system external to the networks, the networks are said to be "networks of general equivalence."

If one network can replace another network only in some particular system without altering in any way the electrical operation of that portion of the system external to the networks, the networks are said to be "networks of limited equivalence." Examples of the latter are networks which are equivalent only at a single frequency, over a single band, in one direction only, or only with certain terminal conditions (such as H and T networks).

Artificial Line   65.20.685

An artificial line is apparatus which simulates a line in its electrical characteristics.

NOTE: Although the term basically is applied to the case of simulation of an actual line, by extension it is used to refer to all periodic lines which may be used for laboratory purposes in place of actual lines, but which may represent no physically realizable line—for example, an artificial line may be composed of pure resistances.

Attenuator   65.20.690

An attenuator is an adjustable transducer for reducing the amplitude of a wave without introducing appreciable distortion.

Pad   65.20.695

A pad is a non-adjustable transducer for reducing the amplitude of a wave without introducing appreciable distortion.

Resonant Circuit

See 05.05.401.

Selective Network   65.20.700

A selective network is a transducer which, when inserted in a circuit for which it is designed, causes in this circuit an insertion loss, or a phase shift, or both, varying with frequency in some desired way.

Electric Wave Filter   65.20.705

An electric wave filter is a selective network which transmits freely electric waves having frequencies within one or more frequency bands and which attenuates substantially electric waves having other frequencies.

Low-Pass Filter   65.20.710

A low-pass filter is a wave filter having a single transmission band extending from zero frequency up to some critical or cut-off frequency, not infinite.

High-Pass Filter   65.20.715

A high-pass filter is a wave filter having a single transmission band extending from some critical or cut-off frequency, not zero, up to infinite frequency.

Band-Pass Filter   65.20.720

A band-pass filter is a wave filter which has a single transmission band, neither of the critical or cut-off frequencies being zero or infinite.

Band-Elimination Filter   65.20.725

(Low- and High-Pass Filter)

A band-elimination filter is a wave filter which has a single attenuation band, neither of the critical or cut-off frequencies being zero or infinite.

Ripple Filter   65.20.730

A ripple filter is a low-pass filter designed to reduce the ripple current, while freely passing the direct current, from a rectifier or generator.

Corrective Network   65.20.735

A corrective network is an electric network designed to be inserted in a circuit to improve its transmission properties, its impedance properties, or both.

Attenuation Equalizer   65.20.740

An attenuation equalizer is a corrective network which is designed to make the absolute value of the transfer impedance, with respect to two chosen pairs of terminals, substantially constant for all frequencies within a desired range.

Delay Equalizer   65.20.745

(Phase Corrector)

A delay equalizer is a corrective network which is designed to make the phase angle of the transfer impedance, with respect to two chosen pairs of terminals, substantially linear with the frequency within a desired range, thus making the time of transmission or delay substantially constant in that frequency range.

Impedance Compensator   65.20.750

An impedance compensator is an electric network designed to be associated with another network or a line with the purpose of giving the impedance of the combination a desired characteristic with frequency over a desired frequency range.

Filter Impedance Compensator   65.20.755

A filter impedance compensator is an impedance compensator which is connected across the common terminals of electric wave filters when the latter are used in parallel in order to compensate for the effects of the filters on each other.

Balancing Network 65.20.760

A balancing network is an electric network designed for use in a circuit in such a way that two branches of the circuit are made substantially conjugate.

Basic Network 65.20.765

A basic network is an electric network designed to simulate the iterative impedance, neglecting dissipation, of a line at a particular termination.

Building-Out Network 65.20.770

A building-out network is an electric network designed to be connected to a basic network so that the combination will simulate the sending-end impedance, neglecting dissipation, of a line having a termination other than that for which the basic network was designed.

Low-Frequency Impedance Corrector 65.20.775

A low-frequency impedance corrector is an electric network designed to be connected to a basic network, or to a basic network and a building-out network, so that the combination will simulate at low frequencies the sending-end impedance, including dissipation, of a line.

Telegraph Distributor 65.20.800

A telegraph distributor is a device which effectively associates one direct-current or carrier telegraph channel in rapid succession with the elements of one or more signal sending or receiving devices.

Vibrating Circuit 65.20.805

A vibrating circuit is an auxiliary local timing circuit associated with the main line receiving relay of a telegraph circuit for the purpose of assisting the operation of the relay when the definition of the incoming signals is indistinct.

Signal Shaping Network 65.20.810

A signal shaping network is an electric network inserted in a telegraph circuit, usually at the receiving end, for improving the wave shape of the signals.

Noise Killer 65.20.815

A noise killer is an electric network inserted in a telegraph circuit, usually at the sending end, for the purpose of reducing interference with other communication circuits.

Spark Killer 65.20.820

(Spark Condenser)

A spark killer is an electric network, usually consisting of a condenser and resistance in series, connected across a pair of instrument contact points for the purpose of diminishing sparking at these points.

Spark Gap

See 05.45.115.

GROUP 65—ELECTROCOMMUNICATION

Section 25—Transmission

Lines

Uniform Line 65.25.005

A uniform line is a line which has identical electrical properties throughout its length.

Linear Electrical Constants of a Uniform Line 65.25.010

The linear electrical constants of a uniform line are the series resistance, series inductance, shunt conductance and shunt capacitance per unit length of line.

Periodic Line 65.25.015

A periodic line is a line consisting of successive identically similar sections, similarly oriented, the electrical properties of each section not being uniform throughout.

NOTE: The periodicity is in space and not in time. An example of a periodic line is the loaded line with loading coils uniformly spaced.

Equivalent Uniform Line 65.25.020

The equivalent uniform line of a periodic line is a uniform line having the same electrical behavior as the periodic line, at a given frequency, when measured at its terminals or at corresponding section junctions.

Equivalent Periodic Line 65.25.025

The equivalent periodic line of a uniform line is a periodic line having the same electrical behavior, at a given frequency, as the uniform line when measured at its terminals or at corresponding section junctions.

Metallic Circuit 65.25.100

A metallic circuit is a circuit of which the ground or earth forms no part.

Ground-Return Circuit 65.25.105

A ground-return circuit is a circuit which has a conductor (or two or more in parallel) between two points and which is completed through the ground or earth.

Two-Wire Circuit 65.25.110

A two-wire circuit is a metallic circuit formed by two conductors insulated from each other.

NOTE: The term is also used in contrast with "four-wire circuit" to indicate a circuit using one line or channel for transmission of electric waves in both directions.

Four-Wire Circuit 65.25.115

A four-wire circuit is a circuit using two lines or channels so arranged that the electric waves are transmitted in one direction only by one line or channel and in the other direction only by the other line or channel.

Superposed Circuit 65.25.120

A superposed circuit is an additional channel obtained from one or more circuits, normally provided for other channels, in such a manner that all the channels can be used simultaneously without mutual interference.

Phantom Circuit 65.25.125

A phantom circuit is a superposed circuit, derived usually from either two two-wire or two four-wire circuits, all the circuits being suitable for the simultaneous transmission of currents in the same frequency range.

Side Circuit 65.25.130

A side circuit is a circuit arranged for deriving a phantom circuit.

NOTE: In the case of two-wire side circuits, the conductors of each side circuit are placed in parallel to form a side of the phantom circuit.

In the case of four-wire side circuits, the lines of the two side circuits which are arranged for transmission in the same direction provide a one-way phantom channel for transmission in that same direction, the two conductors of each line being placed in parallel to provide a side for that phantom channel. Similarly the conductors of the other two lines provide a phantom channel for transmission in the opposite direction.

Non-Phantom Circuit 65.25.135

A non-phantom circuit is a two-wire or four-wire circuit which is not arranged for deriving a phantom circuit.

Simplexed Circuit 65.25.140

A simplexed circuit is a circuit which can be used simultaneously for telephony and direct-current telegraphy or signaling, separation between the two being accomplished by using the sides of the circuit in parallel for telegraph operation or signaling.

Composited Circuit 65.25.145

A composited circuit is a circuit which can be used simultaneously for telephony and direct-current telegraphy or signaling, separation between the two being accomplished by frequency discrimination.

Loading 65.25.200

Loading is the alteration of the linear reactance of a line for the purpose of improving its transmission characteristics throughout a given frequency band.

Loaded Line 65.25.205

A loaded line is a line to which loading has been applied.

Series Loading 65.25.210

Series loading is loading in which reactances are inserted in series with the conductors.

Shunt Loading 65.25.215

Shunt loading is loading in which reactances are applied in shunt across the conductors.

Continuous Loading 65.25.220

Continuous loading is loading in which added inductance is distributed continuously along the conductors.

Coil Loading 65.25.225

Coil loading is loading in which inductance coils, commonly called loading coils, are inserted in the line at intervals.

NOTE: The loading coils may be inserted either in series or in shunt. As commonly understood, coil loading is a series loading in which the loading coils are inserted at uniformly spaced recurring intervals.

Loading Coil Spacing 65.25.230

The loading coil spacing is the line distance between the successive loading coils of a coil-loaded line.

Cable 65.25.300

A cable is an assembly of conductors within an enveloping protective sheath in such structural arrangement of the individual conductors as will permit of their use separately or in groups.

Quad 65.25.305

A quad is a structural unit employed in cable, consisting of four separately insulated conductors twisted together.

NOTE: Two kinds of quads are now in use: (a) The multiple twin quad in which the four conductors are arranged in two twisted pairs, and the two pairs twisted together.

(b) The spiral quad (or spiral four) in which the four conductors are twisted about a common axis.

Quadded Cable 65.25.310

A quadded cable is a cable in which at least some of the conductors are arranged in the form of quads.

Paired Cable 65.25.315

(Non-Quadded Cable)

A paired cable is a cable in which all of the conductors are arranged in the form of twisted pairs, none of which is arranged with others to form quads.

Underground Cable 65.25.320

An underground cable is a cable installed below the surface of the ground.

NOTE: Due to the extensive use of ducts in the placing of underground cable, this term has frequently been employed to cover cables installed under conditions where they can readily be placed or withdrawn without disturbing the surrounding ground and it is, therefore, desirable that underground cable installed under other conditions always be referred to with some qualifying terms such as "buried."

Buried Cable 65.25.325

A buried cable is a cable installed under the surface of the ground in such a manner that it cannot be removed without disturbing the soil.

Aerial Cable 65.25.330

An aerial cable is a cable installed on a pole line, or similar overhead structure.

Cable Splice 65.25.335

A cable splice is a connection between two or more separate lengths of cable with the conductors in one length individually connected to conductors in the other lengths, and with the protecting sheaths so connected as to extend protection over the joint.

See Note under **35.70.206.**

Cable Terminal 65.25.340

A cable terminal is a structure adapted to be associated with a cable, by means of which electric connection is made available for any predetermined group of cable conductors in such a manner as to permit of their individual selection and extension by conductors outside of the cable.

Duct (*35.70.130*)

A duct is a single enclosed runway for conductors or cables.

Conduit (*35.70.124*)

A conduit is a structure containing one or more ducts.

NOTE: Conduit may be designated as iron pipe conduit, tile conduit, etc. If it contains one duct only, it is called "single-duct conduit;" if it contains more than one duct, it is called "multiple-duct conduit", usually with the number of ducts as a prefix, as "two-duct multiple conduit".

Conduit Run (*35.70.140*)

A conduit run is an arrangement of conduit providing one or more continuous ducts between two points.

NOTE: An underground runway for conductors or cables, large enough for workmen to pass through, is termed a gallery or tunnel.

Manhole (*35.70.220*)

A manhole is a subsurface chamber, large enough for a man to enter, in the route of one or more conduit runs, and affording facilities for placing and maintaining in the runs, conductors, cables and any associated apparatus.

Handhole (*35.70.195*)

A handhole is a subsurface chamber, not large enough for a man to enter, in the route of one or more conduit runs, and affording facilities for placing and maintaining in the runs, conductors, cables and any associated apparatus.

Subsidiary Conduit 65.25.425

(Lateral)

A subsidiary conduit is a terminating branch of an underground conduit run extending from a manhole or handhole to a nearby building, handhole or pole.

Pole Line 65.25.430

A pole line is a series of poles arranged to support conductors above the surface of the ground; and the structures and conductors supported thereon.

Open Wire 65.25.435

An open wire is a conductor separately supported above the surface of the ground.

NOTE: An open wire is usually a conductor of a pole line.

Open-Wire Circuit 65.25.440

An open-wire circuit is a circuit made up of conductors separately supported on insulators.

NOTE: The conductors are usually bare wire, but they may be insulated by some form of continuous insulation. The insulators are usually supported by crossarms or brackets on poles.

Open-Wire Pole Line 65.25.445

An open-wire pole line (sometimes abbreviated to "open-wire line") is a pole line whose conductors are principally in the form of open wire.

Cable Pole Line 65.25.450

(Aerial Cable Line)

A cable pole line is a pole line whose conductors are principally in cable.

Span 65.25.455

A span is that part of any conductor, cable or suspension strand between two consecutive points of support or the space between two such consecutive points of support.

Section of a Pole Line 65.25.460

A section of a pole line is that part of the line more than one span in length which is included between any two designated points in the line.

Suspension Strand 65.25.465

(Messenger)

A suspension strand is a stranded group of wires supported above the ground at intervals by poles or other structures and employed to furnish within these intervals frequent points of support for conductors or cables.

Guy

See **35.60.145.**

Telephone Drop 65.25.500

A telephone drop is a pair of conductors serving to extend a circuit from a pole line to the terminals of the interior wiring of a telephone station.

Cord 65.25.505

A cord is one or a group of flexible insulated conductors, enclosed in a flexible insulating covering and equipped with terminals.

GROUP 65—ELECTROCOMMUNICATION

Section 30—Transmission

Antennas

Antenna   65.30.005

An antenna is a conductor or a system of conductors for radiating or receiving radio waves exclusive of the connecting wires between its main portion and the apparatus associated with it.

Loop Antenna   65.30.010

(Coil Antenna)

A loop antenna is an antenna consisting essentially of one or more complete turns of wire.

Condenser Antenna   65.30.015

A condenser antenna is an antenna consisting of two conductors or systems of conductors, the essential characteristic of which is its capacitance.

Directional Antenna   65.30.020

A directional antenna is an antenna having the property of radiating or receiving radio waves in larger proportion along some directions than others. (An antenna of this type used for transmitting is often called a directive antenna.)

Multiple Tuned Antenna   65.30.025

A multiple tuned antenna is an antenna with connections to ground or counterpoise through tuning reactances at more than one point, these being so determined that their reactances in parallel present a total reactance equal to that necessary to give the antenna the desired frequency.

Wave Antenna   65.30.030

A wave antenna is a horizontal conductor having a length of an order of magnitude which is the same as or greater than that of the radio wave received, which operates to receive energy by virtue of the tilt of the radio waves while passing along the ground, and is so used as to be strongly directional.

Artificial Antenna   65.30.035

An artificial antenna is a device having all the necessary characteristics of an antenna with the exception that it dissipates in the form of heat instead of in the form of radio waves substantially all the power fed to it.

Doublet Antenna   65.30.040

A doublet antenna is an antenna consisting of two elevated conductors substantially in the same straight line of substantially equal length, with the power delivered at the center.

Antenna Reflector   65.30.045

An antenna reflector is that portion of a directional antenna array, frequently indirectly excited, which tends to reduce the field intensity behind the array and increase it in the forward direction.

Antenna Array   65.30.050

An antenna array is a system of elemental antennas, usually similar, excited by the same source, for the purpose of obtaining directional effects.

Broadside Directional Antenna   65.30.055

A broadside directional antenna is an antenna array directional substantially at a right angle to the line along which its elements are arrayed.

Antenna Resistance   65.30.060

Antenna resistance is the quotient of the power supplied to the entire antenna circuit by the square of the effective antenna current measured at the point where the power is supplied to the antenna.

NOTE: Antenna resistance includes radiation resistance, ground resistance, radio-frequency resistance of conductors in antenna circuit, equivalent resistance due to corona, eddy currents, insulator leakage, dielectric power loss, etc.

Radiation Resistance (of an antenna)   65.30.065

Radiation resistance of an antenna is the quotient of the power radiated by an antenna by the square of the effective antenna current measured at the point where the power is supplied to the antenna.

Radiation Efficiency (of an antenna)   65.30.070

The radiation efficiency of an antenna is the ratio of the power radiated to the total power supplied to the antenna at a given frequency.

Natural Frequency (of an antenna)   65.30.075

The natural frequency of an antenna is its lowest resonant frequency without added inductance or capacitance.

Lead-In   65.30.080

A lead-in of an antenna is that element which completes the electric connection between the instruments or disconnecting switches and the antenna.

Counterpoise   65.30.100

A counterpoise is a system of wires or other conductors, elevated above and insulated from the ground, forming the lower system of conductors of an antenna.

Ground System of an Antenna   65.30.105

The ground system of an antenna is that portion of the antenna, below the antenna loading devices or generating apparatus, most closely associated with the ground, and including the ground itself.

Ground Wire   65.30.110

A ground wire is a conductor leading to an electric connection with the ground.

End-On Directional Antenna   65.30.200

An end-on directional antenna is an antenna array directional substantially along the line in which its elements are arrayed.

Aerial   65.30.205

An aerial is the elevated conductor portion of a condenser antenna.

GROUP 65—ELECTROCOMMUNICATION
Section 35—Transmission
Radio Transmitters, Radio Receivers and Direction Finders

Radio Transmitter   65.35.005

A radio transmitter is a device for producing radio-frequency power, with means for producing a signal.

Vacuum Tube Transmitter   65.35.010

A vacuum tube transmitter is a radio transmitter in which vacuum tubes are utilized to convert the applied electric power into radio-frequency power.

Radio-Frequency Alternator   65.35.015

A radio-frequency alternator is a rotating type generator for producing radio-frequency power.

Alternator Transmitter   65.35.020

An alternator transmitter is a radio transmitter which utilizes radio-frequency power generated by a radio-frequency alternator.

Arc Converter   65.35.025

An arc converter is a form of oscillator utilizing an electric arc for the generation of alternating or pulsating current.

Spark Transmitter   65.35.030

A spark transmitter is a radio transmitter which utilizes the oscillatory discharge of a condenser through an inductor and a spark gap as the source of its radio-frequency power.

Impulse Excitation   65.35.035

Impulse excitation is a method of producing oscillatory current in a circuit in which the duration of the impressed voltage is relatively short compared with the duration of the current produced.

Radio Receiver   65.35.100

A radio receiver is a device for converting radio waves into perceptible signals.

Monitoring Radio Receiver   65.35.105

A monitoring radio receiver is a radio receiver arranged to permit a check to be made on the operation of a transmitting station.

Heterodyne Reception   65.35.110

(Beat Reception)

Heterodyne reception is the process of receiving radio waves by combining in a non-linear circuit element a received radio-frequency voltage (or a group of voltages resulting from modulation) with a locally generated alternating voltage, with the result that in the output there are frequencies equal to the sum and difference of the combining frequencies. If the received waves are continuous waves of constant amplitude, as in telegraphy, it is customary to adjust the locally generated frequency so that the difference frequency is audible. If the received waves are modulated the locally generated frequency is generally such that the difference frequency is superaudible and an additional operation is necessary if the original signal wave is to be reproduced.

See 65.35.130.

Intermediate Frequency (in superheterodyne reception)   65.35.115

Intermediate frequency, in superheterodyne reception, is a frequency resulting from the combination of the received frequency and the locally generated frequency and is usually equal to their difference.

Autodyne Reception   65.35.120

Autodyne reception is a system of heterodyne reception through the use of a device which is both an oscillator and a detector.

Homodyne Reception   65.35.125

Homodyne reception is a system of reception by the aid of a locally generated voltage of carrier frequency. (Homodyne reception is sometimes called zero-beat reception.)

Superheterodyne Reception   65.35.130

Superheterodyne reception is a method of receiving radio waves in which the process of heterodyne reception is used to convert the voltage of the received wave into a voltage of an intermediate, but usually superaudible, frequency, which at the intermediate frequency is then detected with or without amplification.

Direction Finder   65.35.200

A direction finder is a radio receiving device which permits determination of the line of travel of radio waves as received.

Radio Compass   65.35.205

A radio compass is a direction finder used for navigational purposes.

Sense Finder   65.35.210

A sense finder is that portion of a direction finder which permits determination of direction without 180-degree ambiguity.

Radio Beacon   65.35.215

A radio beacon is a radio transmitting station in a fixed geographic location which emits a distinctive or characteristic signal for enabling mobile stations to determine bearings or courses.

Radio Range Beacon   65.35.220

A radio range beacon is a radio beacon which transmits directed waves by means of which deviations from a given course may be observed.

Equisignal Radio Range Beacon   65.35.225

An equisignal radio range beacon is a radio range beacon which transmits two distinctive signals which may be received with equal intensity only in a certain direction.

Balancer   65.35.300

A balancer is that portion of a direction finder which

is used for the purpose of improving the sharpness of the direction indication.

Compensator   65.35.305

A compensator is that portion of a direction finder which automatically applies to the direction indication all or a part of the correction for the deviation.

GROUP 65—ELECTROCOMMUNICATION
Section 40—Television

Frame   65.40.005

A frame is a single complete picture.

Framing   65.40.010

Framing is the adjustment of the picture to a desired position with respect to the field of view, generally a central position.

Synchronizing of Images   65.40.015

Synchronizing of images is the maintaining of the time and thus space relations between part of the transmitted and reproduced pictures.

Scanning   65.40.020

Scanning is the process of successively analyzing, according to a predetermined method, the light values of picture elements constituting the total picture area.

Rectilinear Scanning   65.40.025

Rectilinear scanning is the process of scanning an area in a predetermined sequence of narrow parallel strips.

Scanning Line   65.40.030

A scanning line is a single continuous narrow strip which is determined by the process of scanning.

Picture Element   65.40.035

A picture element is the smallest subdivision of a television image arbitrarily defined by assuming equal vertical and horizontal resolution, the resulting elemental

square having a dimension equal to the width of one scanning line.

Frame Frequency   65.40.040

Frame frequency is the number of times per second that the picture area is completely scanned.

Line Frequency (in rectilinear scanning)   65.40.045

Line frequency, in rectilinear scanning, is the number of scanning lines traced in one second.

Aspect Ratio   65.40.050

The aspect ratio of a frame is the ratio of the frame width to the frame height.

Progressive Scanning   65.40.055

Progressive scanning is that in which scanning lines trace one dimension substantially parallel to the side of the frame and in which successively traced lines are adjacent.

Positive Light Modulation   65.40.060

Positive light modulation occurs when an increase in initial light intensity causes an increase in the transmitted power.

Negative Light Modulation   65.40.065

Negative light modulation occurs when a decrease in initial light intensity causes an increase in the transmitted power.

GROUP 65—ELECTROCOMMUNICATION
Section 45—Telephone Systems
General

Telephone System   65.45.005

A telephone system is an assemblage of telephone stations, lines, channels and switching arrangements for their interconnection, together with all the accessories for providing telephone communication.

Telephone Exchange   65.45.010

A telephone exchange is a telephone system for providing telephone communication within a particular local area, usually within or embracing a city, town or village, and environs.

Single-Office Exchange   65.45.015

A single-office exchange is an exchange served by a single central office.

Multioffice Exchange   65.45.020

A multioffice exchange is an exchange served by more than one local central office.

Private Exchange   65.45.025

A private exchange is a telephone system which serves one business organization or individual, and is not connected to a central office.

Private Branch Exchange   65.45.030

A private branch exchange (abbreviated PBX) is a telephone system, usually installed on the premises of a subscriber, having centralized switching equipment for interconnecting the stations of the subscriber and for connecting these stations to lines to a central office.

Central Office 65.45.100

A central office is an office in a telephone system providing service to the general public where orders for or signals controlling telephone connections are received and connections established.

NOTE: The term "central office" as applied to either manual or dial equipment used in switching subscriber lines includes any unit of equipment having a separate office name or code and in addition having independent incoming trunks and switching equipment for switching subscriber lines. A central office may serve some subscribers on a theoretical office basis with additional names or codes. In this case for special reasons some separate incoming trunk groups may be provided for the traffic to the theoretical offices. There may be one or more central offices in a central office building.

Local Central Office 65.45.105

A local central office is a central office arranged for terminating subscriber lines and provided with trunks for establishing connections to and from other central offices.

Toll Office 65.45.110

A toll office is a central office primarily arranged for terminating toll lines, toll switching trunks, recording trunks and recording-completing trunks and for their interconnection with each other as necessary for the purpose of establishing connections over toll lines.

Tandem Office 65.45.115

A tandem office is a central office used exclusively for interconnection of other central offices within the same exchange and nearby exchanges.

Common Battery Central Office 65.45.120

A common battery central office is a central office which supplies transmitter and signaling currents for its associated stations and current for the central office equipment from batteries located in the central office.

Magneto Central Office 65.45.125

A magneto central office is a central office serving stations each of which is provided with a local battery for talking and a magneto for signaling.

Manual Central Office 65.45.130

A manual central office is a central office of a manual telephone system.

Dial Central Office 65.45.135

A dial central office is a central office of a dial telephone system.

Operating Room 65.45.140

An operating room is a room in which operators handle calls by means of a switchboard.

Terminal Room 65.45.145

A terminal room is a room, associated with a central office, private branch exchange or private exchange, which contains distributing frames, relays and similar apparatus except that mounted in the switchboard sections.

Switch Room 65.45.150

A switch room is that part of a central office building which contains an assemblage of switching mechanisms and the associated apparatus of the dial central office, group of dial central offices, dial private branch exchange or private automatic exchange.

Telephone Subscriber 65.45.200

A telephone subscriber is a customer of a telephone system who is served by the system under a specific agreement or contract.

Telephone Operator 65.45.205

A telephone operator is a person who handles switching and signaling operations needed to establish telephone connections between stations or who performs various auxiliary functions associated therewith.

NOTE: An operator at a private branch exchange is called an "attendant".

"A" Operator 65.45.210

An "A" operator is an operator assigned to an "A" switchboard.

"B" Operator 65.45.215

A "B" operator is an operator assigned to a "B" switchboard.

Telephone Connection 65.45.300

A telephone connection is a two-way telephone channel completed between two points by means of suitable switching apparatus and arranged for the transmission of telephone currents, together with the associated arrangements for its functioning with the other parts of a telephone system in switching and signaling operations.

NOTE: The term is also sometimes used to mean a two-way telephone channel permanently established between two telephone stations.

Telephone Current 65.45.305

A telephone current is an electric current produced or controlled by the operation of a telephone transmitter.

To Release, To Disconnect or To Clear 65.45.310

To release, to disconnect or to clear is to disengage the apparatus used in a telephone connection and to restore it to its condition when not in use.

Busy Test 65.45.315

A busy test is a test made to find out whether or not certain facilities which may be desired, such as a subscriber line or trunk, are available for use.

GROUP 65—ELECTROCOMMUNICATION
Section 50—Telephone Stations and Sets

Telephone Station   65.50.005

A telephone station is an installed telephone set and associated wiring and apparatus, in service for telephone communication.

NOTE: As generally applied, this term does not include the telephone sets employed by central office operators and by certain other personnel in the operation and maintenance of a telephone system.

Main Station   65.50.010

A main station is a telephone station with a distinct call number designation, directly connected to a central office.

Extension Station   65.50.015

An extension station is a telephone station associated with a main station through connection to the same subscriber line and having the same call number designation as the associated main station.

Public Telephone Station   65.50.020

A public telephone station (often referred to as a "pay station") is a station available for use by the public generally on the payment of a fee which is deposited in a coin collector or is paid to an attendant.

Telephone Set   65.50.100

A telephone set (often abbreviated "telephone") is an assemblage of apparatus including a telephone transmitter, a telephone receiver, and usually a switch, and the immediately associated wiring and signaling arrangements for the use of these instruments in telephony

Common Battery Telephone Set   65.50.105

A common battery telephone set is a telephone set for which both the telephone transmitter and the signaling currents are supplied from a central office, private branch exchange or other centralized power source

Local Battery Telephone Set   65.50.110

A local battery telephone set is a telephone set for which the transmitter current is supplied from a battery, or other current supply circuit, individual to the telephone set. The signaling current may be supplied from a local hand generator or from a centralized power source.

Magneto Telephone Set   65.50.115

A magneto telephone set is a local battery telephone set provided with a hand generator, or magneto, for supplying signaling current.

Dial Telephone Set   65.50.120

A dial telephone set is a telephone set equipped with a dial.

Manual Telephone Set   65.50.125

A manual telephone set is a telephone set not equipped with a dial.

Deskstand Telephone Set   65.50.130

A deskstand telephone set is a telephone set having a deskstand.

Deskstand   65.50.135

A deskstand is a movable pedestal or stand (adapted to rest on a desk or table) which serves as a mounting for the transmitter of a telephone set and which ordinarily includes a hook for supporting the associated receiver when not in use.

Hand Telephone Set   65.50.140

A hand telephone set is a telephone set having a handset and a mounting which serves to support the handset when the latter is not in use.

NOTE: The prefix "desk", "wall", "drawer", etc., may be applied to the term hand telephone set to indicate the type of mounting.

Handset   65.50.145

A handset is a combination of a telephone transmitter and a telephone receiver mounted on a handle.

Wall Telephone Set   65.50.150

A wall telephone set is a telephone set arranged for wall mounting.

Operator's Telephone Set   65.50.155

An operator's telephone set is a telephone set which consists of a head receiver, a telephone transmitter usually supported on a breastplate, and the associated cord and plug.

Anti-Sidetone Telephone Set   65.50.160

An anti-sidetone telephone set is a telephone set which includes a balancing network for the purpose of reducing sidetone.

Sidetone Telephone Set   65.50.165

A sidetone telephone set is a telephone set which does not include a balancing network for the purpose of reducing sidetone.

Station Ringer   65.50.200

A station ringer is an alternating-current electric bell or similar device associated with a telephone station for indicating a telephone call to the station.

GROUP 65—ELECTROCOMMUNICATION

Section 55—Telephone Lines and Trunks

Telephone Line   65.55.005

Telephone line is a general term used in communication practice in several different senses, the more important of which are:

(a) The conductor or conductors and supporting or containing structures extending between subscriber stations and central offices or between central offices whether they be in the same or different communities.

(b) The conductors and circuit apparatus associated with a particular communication channel.

Subscriber Line   65.55.010

A subscriber line (sometimes called a "subscriber loop" or "central office line") is a telephone line between a central office and a station, private branch exchange or other subscriber switching equipment.

Individual Line   65.55.015

An individual line is a subscriber line arranged to serve only one main station although additional stations may be connected to the line as extensions.

An individual line is not arranged for discriminatory ringing with respect to the stations on that line.

Party Line   65.55.020

A party line is a subscriber line arranged to serve more than one main station. Provision is made for discriminatory ringing with respect to the stations of each subscriber on that line.

Tie Trunk   65.55.025

A tie trunk is a telephone line or channel directly connecting two private branch exchanges.

Trunk   65.55.100

A trunk is a telephone line or channel between two central offices or switching devices, which is used in providing telephone connections between subscribers generally.

Interoffice Trunk   65.55.105

An interoffice trunk is a direct trunk between local central offices in the same exchange.

Toll Switching Trunk   65.55.110

A toll switching trunk is a trunk extending from a toll office to a local central office for connecting toll lines to subscriber lines.

Recording Trunk   65.55.115

A recording trunk is a trunk, extending from a local central office or private branch exchange to a toll office, which is used for passing the instructions regarding a desired toll connection from the calling station to an operator in the toll office, but not for completing the connection.

Recording-Completing Trunk   65.55.120

A recording-completing trunk is a trunk, extending from a local central office or private branch exchange to a toll office, which is used for passing the instructions regarding a desired toll connection from the calling station to an operator in the toll office and also for connecting the calling station to the desired toll line.

NOTE: This term may be preceded by "operator" or "subscriber" to differentiate between the two types whereby:

(a) Connection to the recording-completing trunk is made by an operator in the local central office and

(b) Connection is made mechanically when the calling party dials the proper code.

Tandem Trunk   65.55.125

A tandem trunk is a trunk, extending from a central office to a tandem office, used as part of a telephone connection between stations.

Tandem-Completing Trunk   65.55.130

A tandem-completing trunk is a trunk, extending from a tandem office to a central office, used as part of a telephone connection between stations.

Toll Line   65.55.200

A toll line is a telephone line or channel between two central offices in different exchanges.

GROUP 65—ELECTROCOMMUNICATION

Section 60—Telephone Switching Systems and Arrangements

Manual Telephone System   65.60.005

A manual telephone system is a telephone system in which telephone connections between customers are ordinarily established manually by telephone operators in accordance with orders given verbally by the calling parties.

Dial Telephone System   65.60.010

A dial telephone system is a telephone system in which telephone connections between customers are ordinarily established by electric and mechanical apparatus controlled by manipulations of dials operated by the calling parties.

Panel Dial System   65.60.015

A panel dial system is a type of dial telephone system in which the switching apparatus is generally characterized by the following features.

1. The contacts of the multiple banks over which selection occurs are mounted vertically in flat rectangular panels.

2. The brushes of the selecting mechanisms are raised and lowered by motor-driven apparatus.

3. The dial pulses are received and stored by controlling mechanisms which govern the subsequent operations necessary in establishing a telephone connection.

Step-by-Step Dial System   65.60.020

A step-by-step dial system is a type of dial telephone

system in which the switching apparatus is generally characterized by the following features:

1. The wipers of the selecting mechanisms are moved both vertically and in horizontal circular arcs.
2. The selecting mechanisms are individually driven by a combination of electromagnet and ratchet mechanisms.
3. The dial pulses may either actuate the successive selecting mechanisms directly or may be received and stored by controlling mechanisms, which, in turn, actuate the selecting mechanisms by pulses similar to dial pulses.

Rotary Dial System 65.60.025

A rotary dial system is a type of dial telephone system in which the switching apparatus is generally characterized by the following features:

1. The brushes of the selecting mechanisms are moved in a circular arc by a rotating member.
2. The selecting mechanisms are driven by power apparatus.
3. The dial pulses are received and stored by controlling mechanisms which govern the subsequent operations necessary in establishing a telephone connection.

Ringing 65.60.100

Ringing is the production of an audible or visual signal at a station or switchboard by means of an alternating or pulsating current.

Manual Ringing 65.60.105

Manual ringing is ringing which is effected by the manual operation of a key, and continues only during the time the key is held operated.

Machine Ringing 65.60.110

Machine ringing is ringing which is started either mechanically or by an operator, after which it continues automatically until a response to the signal has been obtained or until stopped by disconnection upon abandoning the call.

Keyless Ringing 65.60.115

Keyless ringing is a form of machine ringing used in manual central offices which does not require that an operator press a key in order to select the desired station but the ringing is automatically started by the insertion of the plug of the completing cord into the jack of the called party's line.

A-C-D-C Ringing 65.60.120

A-c-d-c ringing is ringing in which a combination of alternating and direct currents is utilized, the direct current being provided to facilitate the functioning of the relay which stops the ringing.

Superposed Ringing 65.60.125

Superposed ringing is party-line ringing in which a combination of alternating and direct currents is utilized, the direct currents, of both polarities, being provided for selective ringing.

Selective Ringing 65.60.130

Selective ringing is party-line ringing wherein the

ringer of the called subscriber's station (or stations) only is rung.

Harmonic Selective Ringing 65.60.135

Harmonic selective ringing is selective ringing which employs currents of several frequencies and ringers, each tuned mechanically or electrically to the frequency of one of the ringing currents, so that only the desired ringer may be actuated.

Semi-Selective Ringing 65.60.140

Semi-selective ringing is party-line ringing wherein the ringers of two subscribers' stations are rung, differentiation between subscribers being by a one-ring, two-ring code.

Code Ringing 65.60.145

Code ringing is party-line ringing wherein the number of rings, or their duration, or both, indicate which subscriber is being called.

NOTE: The term code ringing is not used to cover semi-selective ringing, although the latter employs a form of code ringing.

Audible Ringing Signal 65.60.200

An audible ringing signal is a signal audible to the calling party to indicate that the called station is being rung.

Supervisory Signal 65.60.205

A supervisory signal is a device for attracting attention of an attendant to a duty in connection with the switching apparatus or its accessories.

Alarm Signal 65.60.210

An alarm signal is a device for attracting attention to some abnormal condition.

Supervisory Relay 65.60.215

A supervisory relay is a relay which, during a call, is generally controlled by the transmitter current supplied to a subscriber line in order to receive from the associated station directing signals which control the actions of operators or switching mechanisms with regard to the connection.

Audible Busy Signal 65.60.220

An audible busy signal is a signal audible to the calling party, indicating that the called party's line is in use.

Dial Tone 65.60.300

Dial tone is a tone employed in dial telephone systems to indicate that the equipment is ready for the dialing operation.

Pulse (for relay operation) 65.60.305

(Impulse)*

A pulse is a sudden change of brief duration, produced in the current or voltage of a circuit in order to actuate or control a switch or relay.

---

* Deprecated.

GROUP 65—ELECTROCOMMUNICATION
Section 61—Telephone Switching Apparatus

Distributing Frame   65.61.005

A distributing frame is a structure for terminating permanent wires of a central office, private branch exchange or private exchange and for permitting the easy change of connections between them by means of cross-connecting wires.

Main Distributing Frame   65.61.010

A main distributing frame (abbreviated MDF) is a distributing frame, on one part of which terminate the permanent outside lines entering the central office building and on another part of which terminate the subscriber line multiple cabling, trunk multiple cabling, etc., used for associating any outside line with any desired terminal in such a multiple or with any other outside line. It usually carries the central office protective devices and functions as a test point between line and office. In a private exchange the main distributing frame is for similar purposes.

Intermediate Distributing Frame   65.61.015

An intermediate distributing frame (abbreviated IDF) in a local central office is a distributing frame, the primary purpose of which is to cross-connect the subscriber line multiple to the subscriber line circuit. In a private exchange the intermediate distributing frame is for similar purposes.

Telephone Switchboard   65.61.100

A telephone switchboard is a switchboard for interconnecting telephone lines and associated circuits.

Switchboard Section   65.61.105

A switchboard section is a structural unit, providing for one or more operator positions. A complete switchboard may consist of one or more sections.

Switchboard Position   65.61.110

A switchboard position is that part of a switchboard designed for the use of one operator.

Switchboard Lamp   65.61.115

A switchboard lamp is a small electric lamp associated with the wiring of a switchboard in such a way as to give a visual indication of the status of a call, or to give information concerning the condition of trunks, subscriber lines, apparatus, etc.

Cord Circuit   65.61.120

A cord circuit is a connecting circuit terminating in a plug at one or both ends and used at switchboard positions in establishing telephone connections

Multiple   65.61.125

(a) (Noun) A multiple is a group of terminals arranged to make a circuit or group of circuits accessible at a number of points at any one of which connection can be made.

(b) (Verb) To multiple is to render a circuit accessible at a number of points at any one of which connection can be made.

Key   65.61.130

A key is a hand operated switching device ordinarily formed of concealed spring contacts with an exposed handle or push button, capable of switching one or more parts of a circuit.

Talking Key   65.61.135

A talking key is a key which when operated makes it possible for the person operating the key to converse on the circuit with which the contacts of the key are associated.

Monitoring Key   65.61.140

A monitoring key is a key which when operated makes it possible for an attendant or operator to "monitor" or to listen on a telephone circuit without appreciably impairing transmission on the circuit.

Switchboard Cord   65.61.145

A switchboard cord is a cord which is used in conjunction with switchboard apparatus to complete or build up a telephone connection.

Plug   65.61.150

A plug is a device to which may be attached the conductors of a cord and which, by insertion in a jack, establishes contact between the conductors of the attached cord and the conductors connected permanently to the jack. The plug most generally used has three separate contacting parts: the tip, the ring and the sleeve.

Tip   65.61.155

The tip of a plug is the contacting part at the end of the plug.

Ring   65.61.160

The ring of a plug is the ring-shaped contacting part of the plug immediately back of the tip.

Sleeve   65.61.165

The sleeve of a plug is the cylindrical contacting part of the plug immediately back of the ring.

Jack   65.61.170

A jack is a connecting device to which the wires of a circuit may be attached and which is arranged for the insertion of a plug. The jacks most generally used have three separate contacting parts: the tip spring, the ring spring and the sleeve, which make contact with the corresponding parts of the plug.

Tip Side   65.61.175

(Tip Wire)

The tip side, or tip wire, is that conductor of a circuit

which is associated with the tip of a plug, or the tip ring spring of a jack.

NOTE: By extension, it is common practice to designate by these terms the conductors having similar functions or arrangements in circuits where plugs or jacks may not be involved.

Ring Side 65.61.180

(Ring Wire)

The ring side, or ring wire, is that conductor of a circuit which is associated with the ring of a plug or the ring spring of a jack.

NOTE: By extension, it is common practice to designate by these terms the conductors having similar functions or arrangements in circuits where plugs or jacks may not be involved.

Sleeve Wire 65.61.185

The sleeve wire is that conductor of the circuit which is associated with the sleeve of a plug or jack.

NOTE: By extension, it is common practice to designate by this term the conductors having similar functions or arrangements in circuits where plugs or jacks may not be involved.

Manual Switchboard 65.61.200

A manual switchboard is a switchboard in a manual telephone system.

"A" Switchboard 65.61.205

An "A" switchboard is a switchboard in a local central office arranged primarily for receiving from subscribers orders for telephone connections, for the completion of these connections, either at the same switchboard or by way of trunks to other switching equipment, and for their supervision.

"B" Switchboard 65.61.210

A "B" switchboard is a switchboard in a local central office arranged primarily for receiving and completing to subscriber lines telephone connections which have been routed over trunks from other switchboards or dial switching equipment.

Toll Board 65.61.215

A toll board is a switchboard used primarily for establishing connections over toll lines.

Test Board 65.61.220

A test board is a switchboard equipped with testing apparatus, so arranged that connections can be made from it to telephone lines or central office equipment for testing purposes.

Finder Switch 65.61.300

A finder switch is a switching mechanism, associated with a circuit, designed to move over a number of terminals to which are connected circuits, over any one of which a signal to start the switch may be transmitted, in order to find the specific circuit from which the starting signal has come and connect it to the circuit associated with this finder switch.

Selector 65.61.305

(Selector Switch)

A selector is a switching mechanism, associated with a circuit, designed to move over a number of terminals to which are connected groups of circuits in order to select a particular group of circuits in accordance with signals received over the circuit associated with this selector, and then to choose from the group an idle circuit and connect to it the circuit associated with this selector.

Connector 65.61.310

A connector is a switching mechanism designed to connect a trunk to a desired subscriber line or PBX extension and often having facilities to hunt for an idle terminal when the terminals are grouped.

Sender, Register or Director 65.61.315

A sender, register or director is a part of a dial telephone system which receives pulses from a dial or other source and, in accordance with them, controls the further operations necessary in establishing a telephone connection.

Translator 65.61.320

A translator is a mechanism, usually permanently associated with a sender, which receives from the sender an indication of the destination of the connection and returns to the sender signals which are recorded by the sender and which serve to control the routing of the connection. Cross-connecting facilities associated with the translator permit changing such controlling signals at will.

Decoder 65.61.325

A decoder is a mechanism performing the functions of a translator although differing from the translator in its equipment arrangement and in the fact that one or more decoders may be used in common by a number of senders.

Trunk Hunting 65.61.330

Trunk hunting is the operation of a selector, or other similar device, in moving its wipers or brushes to a terminal or contact associated with an idle circuit of a chosen group. This is usually accomplished by successively testing terminals associated with this group until a terminal is found which has an electrical condition indicating it to be idle.

Bank 65.61.335

A bank is an assemblage of fixed contacts formed into a single rigid unit to which permanent electric connections may be made and over which, or assigned sections of which, may move the wipers or brushes of a selector or switch capable of making electric connections with the contacts.

Wiper 65.61.340

(Brush)

A wiper or brush is that portion of the moving member of a selector, or other similar device, which makes contact with the terminals of a bank.

Pulse Repeater 65.61.345

A pulse repeater is an arrangement of apparatus used

in dial telephone systems for receiving pulses from one circuit and retransmitting corresponding pulses into another circuit. It may also correct the wave form of the pulses and perform other functions such as supplying transmitter current to stations.

Calling Device   65.61.400

A calling device is an apparatus which generates the

pulses required for establishing connections in a dial system.

Dial   65.61.405

A dial is a type of calling device, which, when wound up and released, generates pulses required for establishing connections in a dial system.

GROUP 65—ELECTROCOMMUNICATION
Section 65—Telegraph Systems

Morse Telegraphy   65.65.005

Morse telegraphy is that method of telegraph operation in which the signals are formed in accordance either with the American or with the Continental (also called the International) Morse code.

Wheatstone Automatic Telegraphy   65.65.010

Wheatstone automatic telegraphy is that form of Morse telegraphy in which telegraph signals are transmitted mechanically from a perforated tape and recorded automatically in dots and dashes on a tape.

Printing Telegraphy   65.65.015

Printing telegraphy is that method of telegraph operation in which the received signals are automatically recorded in printed characters.

Start-Stop Printing Telegraphy   65.65.020

Start-stop printing telegraphy is that form of printing telegraphy in which the signal receiving mechanisms, normally at rest, are started in operation at the beginning and stopped at the end of each character transmitted over the channel.

Multiplex Printing Telegraphy   65.65.025

Multiplex printing telegraphy is that form of printing telegraphy in which the line circuit is employed to transmit in turn one character (or one or more impulses of a character) for each of two or more independent channels.

Duplex System   65.65.100

A duplex system is a telegraph system which affords simultaneous independent operation in opposite directions over the same channel.

Bridge Duplex System   65.65.105

A bridge duplex system is a duplex system based on the Wheatstone bridge principle in which a substantial neutrality of the receiving apparatus to the sent currents is obtained by an impedance balance. Received currents pass through the receiving relay which is bridged between the points which are equipotential for the sent currents.

Differential Duplex System   65.65.110

A differential duplex system is a duplex system in which the sent currents divide through two mutually

inductive sections of the receiving apparatus, connected respectively, to the line and to a balancing artificial line, in opposite directions so that there is substantially no net effect on the receiving apparatus, whereas the received currents pass mainly through one section, or through the two sections in the same direction, and operate the apparatus.

Single Operation   65.65.115

(Simplex Operation)

Single operation, or simplex operation, of a telegraph system is operation in only one direction at a time.

NOTE: A distinction is sometimes made between single operation and simplex operation in applying single operation to Morse telegraphy and simplex operation to printing telegraphy. Another distinction is sometimes made in applying single operation to the operation of channels which may be worked in either direction at the will of the operators, and simplex operation to the operation of channels which are set up to carry signals in one direction only.

Duplex Operation   65.65.120

Duplex operation is the operation of associated transmitting and receiving apparatus at one location in conjunction with associated transmitting and receiving equipment at another location, in which the processes of transmission and reception are simultaneous.

Full-Duplex Operation   65.65.125

Full-duplex operation of a telegraph system is simultaneous operation in opposite directions.

Half-Duplex Operation   65.65.130

Half-duplex operation of a telegraph system is operation of a duplex system arranged to permit operation in either direction at a time but not in both directions simultaneously.

Multiplex Operation   65.65.135

Multiplex operation of a telegraph system is simultaneous transmission of two or more messages in either or both directions over the same transmission path.

Diplex Operation   65.65.140

Diplex operation is the simultaneous transmission or reception of two signals using a specified common feature, such as a single antenna or a single carrier.

Direct-Current Telegraphy   65.65.200

Direct-current telegraphy is that form of telegraphy in which, in order to form the transmitted signals, direct current is supplied to the line under the control of the transmitting apparatus.

Neutral Direct-Current Telegraph System   65.65.205
(Single Morse System)

A neutral direct-current telegraph system, or single Morse system, is a telegraph system employing impulses of either polarity and zero-current spacing intervals for transmission of signals over the line.

Polar Direct-Current Telegraph System   65.65.210

A polar direct-current telegraph system is a telegraph system employing positive and negative impulses for transmission of signals over the line.

Direct-Current Quadruplex System   65.65.215

A direct-current quadruplex system is a direct-current telegraph system which affords simultaneous transmission of two messages in each direction over the same line, operation being obtained by superposing neutral telegraph upon polar telegraph.

Carrier Telegraphy   65.65.300

Carrier telegraphy is that form of telegraphy in which, in order to form the transmitted signals, alternating current is supplied to the line after being modulated under the control of the transmitting apparatus.

Voice-Frequency Carrier Telegraphy   65.65.305

Voice-frequency carrier telegraphy is that form of carrier telegraphy in which the carrier currents have frequencies such that the modulated currents may be transmitted over a voice-frequency telephone channel.

High-Frequency Carrier Telegraphy   65.65.310

High-frequency carrier telegraphy is that form of carrier telegraphy in which the carrier currents have their frequencies above the range transmitted over a voice-frequency telephone channel.

Telegraph Concentrator   65.65.400

A telegraph concentrator is a switching system by means of which a large number of branch lines, used for the transmission of telegraph messages, may be connected to a limited number of telegraph or telephone instruments, concentrated at a central traffic distribution point, to facilitate the reception of messages from and the transmission of messages to the branch stations.

Telegraph Selector   65.65.405

A telegraph selector is a device which performs a switching operation in response to a definite signal or group of successive signals received over a controlling circuit.

Telegraph Transmission Speed   65.65.500

Telegraph transmission speed is the rate at which signals are transmitted, and may be measured by the equivalent number of dot-cycles per second or by the average number of letters or words transmitted and received per minute.

NOTE: A given number of dot-cycles per second (often abbreviated to dots per second) may be expressed as twice that number of "bauds" which is the unit of signal transmission speed recommended by the International Consultative Committee on Telegraph Communication. Where words per minute are used as a measure of transmission speed, five letters and a space per word are assumed.

Lag   65.65.505

Lag in a telegraph system is the time elapsing between the operation of the transmitting device and the response of the receiving device.

Telegraph Signal Distortion   65.65.510

Telegraph signal distortion is the deviation of signals from a facsimile reproduction of the impressed signals as regards the time of beginning and the time of ending of the corresponding individual components, aside from the average lag of the signals.

Crossfire   65.65.600

Crossfire is interfering current in one telegraph or signaling channel resulting from telegraph or signaling currents in another channel.

Current Margin   65.65.700

Current margin is, in a neutral direct-current telegraph system, the difference between the steady-state currents flowing through a receiving instrument corresponding, respectively, to the two positions of the telegraph transmitter.

To Break   65.65.705

To break, in the operation of a telegraph system, is to interrupt the sending operator so as to take from him the control of the circuit.

GROUP 65—ELECTROCOMMUNICATION

Section 70—Two-Way Radio Communication Systems—General

* * *

Section 71—Two-Way Point-to-Point Radio Communication Systems

* * *

Section 72—Two-Way Mobile Radio Communication Systems

* * *

Section 75—Radio Broadcasting Systems—General

* * *

Section 76—Radio Program Broadcasting Systems

* * *

Section 77—Radio Patrol Systems

* * *

Section 80—Other Radio Systems

* * *

Section 85—Telecontrol and Telemeter Systems

* * *

Section 90—Alarm Systems—General

* * *

Section 91—Fire-Alarm Systems

* * *

Section 92—Burglar-Alarm Systems

* * *

Section 95—Other Forms of Electric Communication

* * *

*** No terms in the present edition.

GROUP 70—ELECTRONICS

SECTIONS

05	General	35	Gas Tubes
10	Vacuum Tubes	40	Phototubes
15	Vacuum Tube Electrodes	45	Cathode-Ray Oscillograph Tubes
20	Electrode Voltage, Current and Power	50	X-Ray Tubes
25	Electrode Impedances and Admittances	95	Not Otherwise Classified
30	Amplifiers		

Section 05—General

Electronics   70.05.005

Electronics is that branch of science and technology which relates to the conduction of electricity through gases or in vacuo.

Electron

See 05.10.040.

Ion

See 05.10.050.

Electrode

See 60.05.030.

Electron Emission   70.05.025

Electron emission is the liberation of electrons from an electrode into the surrounding space. Quantitatively, it is the rate at which electrons are emitted from an electrode.

Thermionic Emission   70.05.030

Thermionic emission is electron or ion emission due directly to the temperature of the emitter.
See 05.40.070.

Secondary Emission   70.05.035

Secondary emission is electron emission due directly to the impact of electrons or ions.

Ionization

See 05.10.055.

Ionization Current

See 75.05.080.

Gas Current   70.05.050

Gas current is a current flowing to an electrode and composed of positive ions which have been produced as a result of gas ionization by an electron current flowing between other electrodes.

GROUP 70—ELECTRONICS

Section 10—Vacuum Tubes

Vacuum Tube   70.10.005

A vacuum tube is a device consisting of an evacuated enclosure containing a number of electrodes between two or more of which conduction of electricity through the vacuum or contained gas may take place.

High-Vacuum Tube   70.10.010

(Electron Tube)

A high-vacuum tube is a vacuum tube evacuated to such a degree that its electrical characteristics are essentially unaffected by gaseous ionization.

Thermionic Tube   70.10.015

A thermionic tube is a vacuum tube in which one of the electrodes is heated for the purpose of causing electron or ion emission from that electrode.

Gas Tube   70.10.020

A gas tube is a vacuum tube in which the pressure of the contained gas or vapor is such as to affect substantially the electrical characteristics of the tube.

Mercury-Vapor Tube   70.10.025

A mercury-vapor tube is a gas tube in which the active contained gas is mercury vapor.

Phototube   70.10.030

(Photoelectric Tube)

A phototube is a vacuum tube in which one of the electrodes is irradiated for the purpose of causing electron emission from that electrode.

Cathode-Ray Oscillograph Tube   70.10.035

A cathode-ray oscillograph tube is a vacuum tube in which the deflection of an electron beam, effected by means of applied electric and/or magnetic fields, indicates the instantaneous values of the actuating voltages and/or currents.

Diode   70.10.040

A diode is a two-electrode vacuum tube containing an anode and a cathode.

Triode   70.10.045

A triode is a three-electrode vacuum tube containing an anode, a cathode and a control electrode.

Tetrode   70.10.050

A tetrode is a four-electrode vacuum tube containing an anode, a cathode, a control electrode and one additional electrode ordinarily in the nature of a grid.

Pentode   70.10.055

A pentode is a five-electrode vacuum tube containing an anode, a cathode, a control electrode and two additional electrodes ordinarily in the nature of grids.

Hexode   70.10.060

A hexode is a six-electrode vacuum tube containing an anode, a cathode, a control electrode and three additional electrodes ordinarily in the nature of grids.

Heptode   70.10.065

A heptode is a seven-electrode vacuum tube containing an anode, a cathode, a control electrode and four additional electrodes ordinarily in the nature of grids.

Octode   70.10.070

An octode is an eight-electrode vacuum tube containing an anode, a cathode, a control electrode and five additional electrodes ordinarily in the nature of grids.

Multiple-Unit Tube   70.10.075

A multiple-unit tube is a vacuum tube containing within one envelope two or more groups of electrodes associated with independent electron streams.

NOTE: A multiple-unit tube may be so indicated, as, for example: duodiode, duotriode, diode-pentode, duodiode-triode, duodiode-pentode and triode-pentode.

GROUP 70—ELECTRONICS

Section 15—Vacuum Tube Electrodes

Anode (of a vacuum tube)   70.15.005

(Plate)
An anode of a vacuum tube is an electrode to which a principal electron stream flows.

Plate   70.15.010

Plate is a common name for the principal anode in a vacuum tube.

Cathode (of a vacuum tube)   70.15.015

A cathode of a vacuum tube is an electrode which is the primary source of an electron stream.

Indirectly Heated Cathode   70.15.020

(Equipotential Cathode) (Unipotential Cathode)
An indirectly heated cathode is a cathode of a thermionic tube to which heat is supplied by an independent heater element.

Heater   70.15.025

A heater is an electric heating element for supplying heat to an indirectly heated cathode.

Filament   70.15.030

A filament is a cathode of a thermionic tube, usually in the form of a wire or ribbon, to which heat may be supplied by passing current through it.

Control Electrode   70.15.035

A control electrode is an electrode on which a voltage is impressed to vary the current flowing between two or more other electrodes.

Grid   70.15.040

A grid is an electrode having one or more openings for the passage of electrons or ions.

Control Grid   70.15.045

A control grid is a grid, ordinarily placed between the cathode and an anode, for use as a control electrode.

Screen Grid   70.15.050

A screen grid is a grid placed between a control grid and an anode, and usually maintained at a fixed positive potential, for the purpose of reducing the electrostatic influence of the anode in the space between the screen grid and the cathode.

Space-Charge Grid   70.15.055

A space-charge grid is a grid which is placed adjacent to the cathode and positively biased so as to reduce the limiting effect of space charge on the current through the tube.

Suppressor Grid   70.15.060

A suppressor grid is a grid which is interposed between two electrodes (usually the screen grid and plate), both positive with respect to the cathode, in order to prevent the passing of secondary electrons from one to the other.

GROUP 70—ELECTRONICS

Section 20—Electrode Voltage, Current and Power

Electrode Voltage   70.20.005

Electrode voltage is the voltage between an electrode and a specified point of the cathode.

Anode Voltage

See 70.20.005.

Peak (or Crest) Forward Anode Voltage   70.20.015

Peak (or crest) forward anode voltage is the maximum instantaneous anode voltage in the direction in which the tube is designed to pass current.

Peak (or Crest) Inverse Anode Voltage   70.20.020

Peak (or crest) inverse anode voltage is the maximum instantaneous anode voltage in the direction opposite to that in which the tube is designed to pass current.

Heater Voltage   70.20.025

Heater voltage is the voltage between the terminals of a heater.

Filament Voltage   70.20.030

Filament voltage is the voltage between the terminals of a filament.

Grid Voltage

See **70.20.005**.

Direct Grid Bias   70.20.040

Direct grid bias is the direct component of grid voltage.

NOTE: This is commonly called grid bias.

Electrode Current   70.20.045

Electrode current is the current passing to or from an electrode through the vacuous space.

Anode Current

See **70.20.045**.

Cathode Current   70.20.055

Cathode current is the total current passing to or from the cathode through the vacuous space.

Heater Current   70.20.060

Heater current is the current flowing through a heater.

Filament Current   70.20.065

Filament current is the current supplied to a filament to heat it.

Grid Current

See **70.20.045**.

Grid Emission   70.20.075

Grid emission is electron or ion emission from a grid.

Leakage Current   70.20.080

Leakage current is a conductive current which flows between two or more electrodes by any path other than across the vacuous space.

Electrode Characteristic   70.20.085

An electrode characteristic is a relation, usually shown by a graph, between an electrode voltage and current, other electrode voltages being maintained constant.

Transfer Characteristic   70.20.090

A transfer characteristic is a relation, usually shown by a graph, between the voltage of one electrode and the current to another electrode, all other voltages being maintained constant.

Emission Characteristic   70.20.095

An emission characteristic is a relation, usually shown by a graph, between the emission and a factor controlling the emission (as temperature, voltage or current of the filament or heater).

Electrode Dissipation   70.20.100

Electrode dissipation is the power dissipated in the form of heat by an electrode as a result of electron and/or ion bombardment.

Grid Driving Power   70.20.105

Grid driving power is the average product of the instantaneous value of the grid current and the alternating component of the grid voltage over a complete cycle.

NOTE: This comprises the power supplied to the biasing device and the grid dissipation.

GROUP 70—ELECTRONICS

Section 25—Electrode Impedances and Admittances

Mu Factor   70.25:005

Mu factor is the ratio of the change in one electrode voltage to the change in another electrode voltage, under the conditions that a specified current remains unchanged and that all other electrode voltages are maintained constant. It is a measure of the relative effect of the voltages on two electrodes upon the current in the circuit of any specified electrode.

NOTE: As most precisely used, the term refers to infinitesimal changes.

Amplification Factor   70.25.010

Amplification factor is the ratio of the change in plate voltage to a change in control electrode voltage, under the conditions that the plate current remains unchanged and that all other electrode voltages are maintained constant. It is a measure of the effectiveness of the control-electrode voltage relative to that of the plate voltage upon the plate current. The sense is usually taken as positive when the voltages are changed in opposite directions.

NOTE: As most precisely used, the term refers to infinitesimal changes. Amplification factor is a special case of mu factor.

Electrode Admittance   70.25.015

Electrode admittance is the quotient of the alternating component of the electrode current by the alternating component of the electrode voltage, all other electrode voltages being maintained constant.

NOTE: As most precisely used, the term refers to infinitesimal amplitudes.

Transadmittance   70.25.020

Transadmittance from one electrode to another is the quotient of the alternating component of the current of the second electrode by the alternating component of the voltage of the first electrode, all other electrode voltages being maintained constant.

NOTE: As most precisely used, the term refers to infinitesimal amplitudes.

Electrode Impedance   70.25.025

Electrode impedance is the reciprocal of the electrode admittance.

Electrode Conductance   70.25.030

Electrode conductance is the quotient of the in-phase component of the electrode alternating current by the electrode alternating voltage, all other electrode voltages being maintained constant.

NOTE: This is a variational and not a total conductance. As most precisely used, the term refers to infinitesimal amplitudes.

Plate Conductance

See **70.25.030.**

Grid Conductance

See **70.25.030.**

Transconductance   70.25.045

Transconductance from one electrode to another is the quotient of the in-phase component of the alternating current of the second electrode by the alternating voltage of the first electrode, all other electrode voltages being maintained constant.

NOTE: As most precisely used, the term refers to infinitesimal amplitudes.
See **70.25.050.**

Control-Grid—Plate Transconductance   70.25.050

(Transconductance) (Mutual Conductance)

Control-grid—plate transconductance is the name for the plate current to control-grid voltage transconductance.

NOTE: This is ordinarily the most important transconductance and is commonly understood when the term transconductance or mutual conductance is used.

Mutual Conductance

See **70.25.050.**

Electrode Resistance   70.25.060

Electrode resistance is the reciprocal of the electrode conductance.

NOTE: This is the effective parallel resistance and is not the real component of the electrode impedance.

Plate Resistance

See **70.25.070.**

Capacitance   70.25.070

The various capacitances of any system of conductors are defined in definitions **05.15.060** to **05.15.092**, inclusive, which are directly applicable to the case of the vacuum tube.

Interelectrode Capacitance   70.25.075

Interelectrode capacitance is the direct capacitance between two electrodes.

Electrode Capacitance   70.25.080

Electrode capacitance is the capacitance of one electrode to all other electrodes connected together.

Input Capacitance   70.25.085

The input capacitance of a vacuum tube is the sum of the direct capacitances between the control grid and the cathode and such other electrodes as are operated at the alternating potential of the cathode.

NOTE: This is not the effective capacitance, which is a function of the impedances of the associated circuits.

Output Capacitance   70.25.090

The output capacitance of a vacuum tube is the sum of the direct capacitances between the output electrode (usually the plate) and the cathode and such other electrodes as are operated at the alternating potential of the cathode.

NOTE: This is not the effective capacitance, which is a function of the impedances of the associated circuits.

GROUP 70—ELECTRONICS

Section 30—Amplifiers

Amplifier

See **05.45.155.**

Class A Amplifier   70.30.010

A class A amplifier is an amplifier in which the grid bias and alternating grid voltages are such that plate current in a specific tube flows at all times.

NOTE: To denote that grid current does not flow during any part of the input cycle, the suffix 1 may be added to the letter or letters of the class identification. The suffix 2 may be used to denote that grid current flows during some part of the cycle.

Class AB Amplifier   70.30.015

A class AB amplifier is an amplifier in which the grid bias and alternating grid voltages are such that plate current in a specific tube flows for appreciably more than half but less than the entire electrical cycle.

NOTE: See Note under **70.30.010.**

Class B Amplifier   70.30.020

A class B amplifier is an amplifier in which the grid bias is approximately equal to the cut-off value so that the plate current is approximately zero when no exciting grid voltage is applied, and so that plate current in a specific tube flows for approximately one-half of each cycle when an alternating grid voltage is applied.

NOTE: See Note under **70.30.010.**

Class C Amplifier   70.30.025

A class C amplifier is an amplifier in which the grid bias is appreciably greater than the cut-off value so that the plate current in each tube is zero when no alternating grid voltage is applied, and so that plate current flows in a specific tube for appreciably less than one-half of each cycle when an alternating grid voltage is applied.

NOTE: See Note under **70.30.010.**

GROUP 70—ELECTRONICS

Section 35—Gas Tubes

Tube Voltage Drop   70.35.005

Tube voltage drop in a gas tube is the anode voltage during the conducting period.

Critical Grid Voltage   70.35.010

Critical grid voltage in a gas tube is the instantaneous value of grid voltage when the anode current starts to flow.

Critical Grid Current   70.35.015

Critical grid current in a gas tube is the instantaneous value of grid current when the anode current starts to flow.

Control Characteristic   70.35.020

The control characteristic of a gas tube is a relation, usually shown by a graph, between critical grid voltage and anode voltage.

Cathode Heating Time   70.35.025

Cathode heating time is the time required for the cathode to attain operating temperature with normal voltage applied to the heating element.

Tube Heating Time   70.35.030

Tube heating time in a mercury-vapor tube is the time required for the coolest portion of the tube to attain operating temperature.

GROUP 70—ELECTRONICS

Section 40—Phototubes

Static Sensitivity (of a phototube)   70.40.005

Static sensitivity of a phototube is the quotient of the direct anode current by the incident radiant flux of constant value.

Dynamic Sensitivity (of a phototube)   70.40.010

Dynamic sensitivity of a phototube is the quotient of the alternating component of anode current by the alternating component of incident radiant flux.

NOTE: This is a variational and not a total sensitivity. As most precisely used, the term refers to infinitesimal amplitudes.

Luminous Sensitivity (of a phototube)   70.40.015

Luminous sensitivity of a phototube is the quotient of the anode current by the incident luminous flux.

2870 Tungsten Sensitivity (of a phototube)   70.40.020

2870 tungsten sensitivity of a phototube is the quotient of the anode current by the total incident luminous flux

in lumens from a tungsten filament lamp at a color temperature of 2870 degrees Kelvin.

Gas Amplification Factor (of a phototube)   70.40.025

Gas amplification factor of a phototube is the factor of increase in the sensitivity of a gas phototube due solely to the ionization of the contained gas.

NOTE: For a gas phototube having a structure such as to permit saturation to occur at a voltage less than that causing appreciable ionization, the gas amplification factor at a specified operating voltage is the ratio of the sensitivity measured at that voltage to the sensitivity measured at the saturation voltage.

Current–Wavelength Characteristic (of a phototube)   70.40.030

Current–wavelength characteristic of a phototube is a relation, usually shown by a graph, between the direct anode current per unit energy of the incident radiant flux and the wavelength of the flux.

GROUP 70—ELECTRONICS

Section 45—Cathode-Ray Oscillograph Tubes

Gas Focusing   70.45.005

Gas focusing is a method of focusing an electron stream in which focus is produced through the action of ionized gas.

Electrostatic Focusing   70.45.010

Electrostatic focusing is a method of focusing an electron stream in which focus is produced through the action of an electric field.

Magnetic Focusing   70.45.015

Magnetic focusing is a method of focusing an electron stream in which focus is produced through the action of a magnetic field.

Deflection Sensitivity (of a cathode-ray oscillograph tube)   70.45.020

The deflection sensitivity of a cathode-ray oscillograph tube is the quotient of the displacement of the electron beam at the place of impact by the change in the deflecting field.

NOTE: It is usually expressed in millimeters per volt applied between the deflection electrodes, or in millimeters per gauss of the deflecting magnetic field.

Deflection Factor (of a cathode-ray oscillograph tube)   70.45.025

The deflection factor of a cathode-ray oscillograph tube is the reciprocal of the deflection sensitivity.

GROUP 70—ELECTRONICS
Section 50—X-Ray Tubes

X-Rays

See **75.10.005.**

X-Ray Tube   **70.50.010**

An x-ray tube is a vacuum tube designed for producing x-rays by accelerating electrons to a high velocity by means of an electrostatic field and then suddenly stopping them by collision with a target.

Gas X-Ray Tube   **70.50.015**

A gas x-ray tube is an x-ray tube in which the emission of electrons from the cathode is produced by positive ion bombardment.

Hot-Cathode X-Ray Tube   **70.50.020**

A hot-cathode x-ray tube is a high-vacuum x-ray tube in which the cathode is heated in order to produce the emission of electrons.

Target   **70.50.025**

(Anode) (Anti-Cathode)*

A target is an electrode, or part of an electrode, on which cathode rays are focused and from which x-rays are emitted.

GROUP 70—ELECTRONICS
Section 95—Not Otherwise Classified

Rectifier

See **15.50.010.**

Mercury-Arc Rectifier

See **15.50.020.**

Metal-Tank Mercury-Arc Rectifier

See **15.50.030.**

Controlled Mercury-Arc Rectifier

See **15.50.035.**

Discharge Tube   **70.95.025**

A discharge tube is an evacuated enclosure containing a gas at low pressure which permits the passage of electricity through the gas upon application of sufficient voltage.

NOTE: The tube is usually provided with metal electrodes, but one form permits an electrodeless discharge with induced voltage.

Geissler Tube   **70.95.030**

A Geissler tube is a special form of discharge tube for showing the luminous effects of discharges through rarefied gases.

NOTE: The density of gas is roughly one-thousandth of that of the atmosphere.

Cathode Glow   **70.95.035**

The cathode glow is the luminous glow which covers the surface of the cathode in a discharge tube, between the cathode and the cathode dark space.

Cathode Dark Space   **70.95.040**

(Crookes Dark Space)

The cathode dark space is the relatively non-luminous region in a discharge tube between the cathode glow and the negative glow.

Negative Glow   **70.95.045**

The negative glow is the luminous glow in a discharge tube between the cathode dark space and the Faraday dark space.

Faraday Dark Space   **70.95.050**

The Faraday dark space is the relatively non-luminous region in a discharge tube between the negative glow and the positive column.

Positive Column   **70.95.055**

The positive column is the luminous glow, often striated, in a discharge tube between the Faraday dark space and the anode.

---

* Deprecated.

GROUP 75—RADIOLOGY

SECTIONS

05 General
10 Kinds of Rays
20 Physical Properties

40 Tubes
45 Other Apparatus

Section 05—General

Radiology   75.05.005

Radiology is that branch of science which relates to roentgen rays and radium rays.

Radiologist   75.05.010

A radiologist is a medical specialist in employing roentgen rays and/or radioactive substances.

Roentgenology   75.05.015

Roentgenology is that branch of science which relates to the application of roentgen rays for diagnostic or therapeutic purposes.

Roentgenography   75.05.020

Roentgenography is the art of producing roentgenograms.

Radiography   75.05.025

Radiography is the art of producing radiographs.

Radiation   75.05.030

Radiation is the radiant energy emitted by an x-ray tube, by radioactive substances, or by other sources.

Roentgenogram   75.05.035

(Skiagraph)* (Skiagram)*
A roentgenogram is a photographic record of the relative transparency of the various parts of an object to roentgen rays.

Fluoroscopy   75.05.045

(Roentgenoscopy)
Fluoroscopy is the use in diagnosis, testing, etc., of a fluorescent screen which is activated by roentgen rays.

Radiometallography   75.05.050

Radiometallography is the radiography of metals.

X-Ray Crystallography   75.05.055

X-ray crystallography is the study of the arrangement of the atoms in a crystal by the use of roentgen rays.

Radiotherapy   75.05.060

Radiotherapy is the treatment of disease by the application of roentgen rays or the rays from radioactive substances.

Roentgentherapy   75.05.065

Roentgentherapy is the treatment of disease by roentgen rays.

Radiumtherapy   75.05.070

Radiumtherapy is the treatment of disease by the use of radioactive substances.

Ionization   75.05.075

Ionization is the process by which neutral atoms or molecules become charged, either positively or negatively.

Ionization Current   75.05.080

Ionization current is the electric current resulting from the movement of electric charges in an ionized medium, under the influence of an applied electric field.

Irradiation   75.05.085

(Raying)*
Irradiation is the application of roentgen rays, radium rays or other radiation to a patient or other object.

GROUP 75—RADIOLOGY

Section 10—Kinds of Rays

Roentgen Rays   75.10.005

(X-Rays) (Röntgen Rays)
Roentgen rays are penetrating radiations similar to light, having wavelengths of the order of a thousandth to a millionth of those of light in the visible spectrum (10^{-7} to 10^{-10} cm). In practice they are usually generated by allowing a stream of high-speed electrons to impinge on a metal target.

NOTE: "Roentgen rays" is preferred by medical authorities, but "x-rays" is in more general use by physicists.

Secondary Roentgen Rays   75.10.010

Secondary roentgen rays are the roentgen rays emitted by any matter irradiated with roentgen rays.

Scattered Roentgen Rays   75.10.015

Scattered roentgen rays are roentgen rays which during their passage through a substance, have been deviated in direction and also may have been modified by an increase in wavelength.

* Deprecated.

* Deprecated.

Characteristic Roentgen Rays — 75.10.020

(Characteristic Spectra)

Characteristic roentgen rays are roentgen rays having wavelengths determined by the atomic constitution of the object which emits them.

Fluorescent Roentgen Rays — 75.10.025

Fluorescent roentgen rays are secondary rays whose wavelengths are characteristic of the substance which emits them.

Cathode Rays — 75.10.030

Cathode rays are streams of electrons emitted from the cathode of an evacuated tube or from the ionized region in proximity thereto, under the influence of an applied voltage.

Lenard Rays — 75.10.035

Lenard rays are cathode rays which have passed outside the discharge tube.

Positive Rays — 75.10.040

(Canal Rays)

Positive rays are streams of positive ions which are started in motion in an evacuated tube in a direction from the anode to the cathode.

NOTE: These rays are commonly observed in space beyond the cathode after passing through openings or "canals" in the electrode.

GROUP 75—RADIOLOGY

Section 20—Physical Properties

Hardness (of roentgen rays) — 75.20.005

[Quality (of roentgen rays)]

Hardness is the attribute which determines the penetrating ability of roentgen rays. The shorter the wavelength, the harder the rays and the greater their penetrating ability.

Hardness (of a gas tube) — 75.20.010

Hardness is the degree of rarefaction of the residual gas.

NOTE: The higher the vacuum, the higher the voltage required to cause a discharge with a cold cathode, and hence the shorter the wavelength of the resulting roentgen rays.

Filtration (of roentgen rays) — 75.20.015

Filtration of roentgen rays is the process of absorption of some of the rays (usually the longer wavelengths) by placing in the path of the beam a selectively absorbing medium such as copper or aluminum.

X-Ray Spectrum — 75.20.020

X-ray spectrum is the orderly arrangement according to wavelength of a heterogeneous beam of roentgen rays.

Minimum Wavelength — 75.20.025

(Quantum Limit)

Minimum wavelength is the shortest wavelength in an x-ray spectrum. It is definitely related to the maximum voltage applied to the x-ray tube in accordance with the Planck-Einstein quantum equation.

Absorption Coefficient — 75.20.030

Absorption coefficient is the ratio of the linear rate of change of intensity of roentgen rays in a given homogeneous material to the intensity at a given point.

Mass Absorption Coefficient — 75.20.031

The mass absorption coefficient of a substance is the ratio of its absorption coefficient to its density.

Half-Value Thickness — 75.20.035

(Half-Value Layer)

Half-value thickness is the thickness of a given substance which, when introduced in the path of a given beam of rays, will reduce its intensity to one-half of the initial value.

Intensity (of roengten rays) — 75.20.040

Intensity is the attribute of a beam of roentgen rays which determines the rate of ionization of air at a given point, under the conditions stipulated in the definition of roentgen. (See 75.20.050.) It is expressed in roentgens per unit of time.

Quantity (of roentgen rays) — 75.20.045

Quantity is the product of intensity and time.

NOTE: It should be clearly understood that quantity is used here in a sense different from that customary in other fields, such as radiant energy in general. It is not proportional to energy, but rather to the product of energy density and a coefficient expressing the ability to cause ionization.

Roentgen — 75.20.050

Roentgen is the international unit of quantity of roentgen rays adopted by the Second International Congress of Radiology at Stockholm in 1928. It is the quantity of x-radiation which, when the secondary electrons are fully utilized and the wall effect of the chamber is avoided, produces in one cubic centimeter of atmospheric air at zero degree centigrade and 760 mm of mercury pressure, such a degree of conductivity that one electrostatic unit of charge is measured at saturation current.

GROUP 75—RADIOLOGY
Section 40—Tubes

Cathode-Ray Tube   75.40.025

(Lenard Tube)

A cathode-ray tube is a discharge tube with a thin window at the end opposite the cathode to allow the cathode rays to pass outside.

Crookes Tube   75.40.035

Crookes tube is an early form of discharge tube devised by Sir William Crookes and used by him for the study of cathode rays.

NOTE: The density of gas is roughly one-millionth that of the atmosphere.

Hot-Cathode Tube   75.40.040

Hot-cathode tube is a vacuum tube in which the cathode is electrically heated (usually to incandescence) in order to increase the emission of electrons.

Valve Tube   75.40.050

A valve tube is an electric valve consisting of a vacuum tube having for one electrode a hot filament.

GROUP 75—RADIOLOGY
Section 45—Other Apparatus

X-Ray Machine   75.45.005

An x-ray machine is an assembly of electric devices necessary to activate an x-ray tube and control its operation.

X-Ray Apparatus   75.45.010

X-ray apparatus is an x-ray tube and its accompanying accessories, including the x-ray machine.

Electrostatic Generator   75.45.015

(Influence Machine) (Static Machine) (Wimshurst Machine)

An electrostatic generator is a device for the production of electric charges by electrostatic action.

Induction Coil   75.45.020

(Coil) (Spark Coil) (Ruhmkorff Coil)

An induction coil is a transformer with open magnetic circuit which is excited by an interrupted or variable current.

Interrupter   75.45.025

[Break (of an induction coil)]

An interrupter is a device for interrupting the primary current mechanically or otherwise.

Fluorescent Screen   75.45.030

A fluorescent screen is a sheet of suitable material coated with a substance which fluoresces visibly when roentgen rays, radium rays or electrons impinge upon it.

Fluoroscope   75.45.035

(Roentgenoscope)

A fluoroscope is a device consisting of a fluorescent screen suitably mounted, either separately or in conjunction with an x-ray tube, by means of which x-ray shadows of objects interposed between the tube and the screen are made visible.

Intensifying Screen   75.45.040

An intensifying screen is a thin screen, coated with a finely divided substance which fluoresces under the influence of roentgen rays, and intended to be used in close contact with the emulsion of a photographic plate or film for the purpose of increasing the effect on the film.

X-Ray Spectrometer   75.45.045

An x-ray spectrometer is an instrument for producing an x-ray spectrum and measuring the wavelengths of its components.

Ionization Chamber   75.45.050

An ionization chamber is an enclosure containing two or more electrodes between which an electric current may be passed when the enclosed gas is ionized. It is commonly used for determining the intensity of roentgen rays and other ionizing rays.

Penetrometer   75.45.055

(Qualimeter) (Radiosclerometer)*

A penetrometer is an instrument for indicating the hardness of roentgen rays.

Dosage Meter   75.45.060

(Dosimeter) (Intensimeter)

A dosage meter is an instrument designed to estimate the quantity of radiation, so as to determine the duration of exposure when using roentgen rays for therapy.

Roentgenometer   75.45.065

(Roentgen Meter) (Ionometer)

A roentgenometer is an instrument for measuring the quantity or intensity of roentgen rays.

Oscilloscope   75.45.070

An oscilloscope is an instrument for making visible the presence and/or the nature and form of oscillations or irregularities of an electric current.

NOTE: There are several different types of instrument serving this general purpose which have been designated by this name.

---

* Deprecated.

GROUP 80—ELECTROBIOLOGY INCLUDING ELECTROTHERAPEUTICS

SECTIONS

05 General	25 Kinds of Current
10 Biological	30 Kinds of Discharge
20 Electrotherapeutic	40 Apparatus

Section 05—General

Electroculture   80.05.005

Electroculture is the stimulation of growth, flowering or seeding by electrical means.

Electrodiagnosis   80.05.010

Electrodiagnosis is the determination of the functional states of various organs and tissues by the study of their response to electric stimulation.

Electrocution   80.05.015

Electrocution is the destruction of life by means of electric current.

GROUP 80—ELECTROBIOLOGY INCLUDING ELECTROTHERAPEUTICS

Section 10—Biological

Electrocardiogram   80.10.005

An electrocardiogram is a graphic trace of the variation with time of the electric current or voltage associated with action of the heart muscles.

Galvanotaxis   80.10.010

Galvanotaxis is the tendency of a living organism to arrange itself in a medium so that its axis bears a certain relation to the direction of the current in the medium.

Galvanotropism   80.10.015

Galvanotropism is the tendency of an organism to grow, turn or move into a certain relation with an electric current.

Electrotonus   80.10.020

Electrotonus is the change in the irritability of a nerve or muscle during the passage of an electric current.

Anelectrotonus   80.10.025

Anelectrotonus is the state of diminished excitability of a nerve or muscle produced in the region near the anode during the passage of an electric current.

Catelectrotonus   80.10.030

Catelectrotonus is the state of increased excitability produced in a nerve or muscle in the region near the cathode during the passage of an electric current.

Neuroelectricity   80.10.035

Neuroelectricity is electric current generated in the nervous system.

GROUP 80—ELECTROBIOLOGY INCLUDING ELECTROTHERAPEUTICS

Section 20—Electrotherapeutic

Electrotherapy   80.20.005

Electrotherapy is the art of treating disease by means of electricity.

Electrotherapist   80.20.010

An electrotherapist is a medical specialist in employing electricity for the treatment of disease.

Electric Sleep   80.20.015

Electric sleep is anesthesia produced by means of Leduc currents.

Electrocoagulation   80.20.020

Electrocoagulation is coagulation of tissue by means of a high-frequency electric current.

NOTE: The heat producing the coagulation is generated within the tissue to be destroyed.

Diathermy   80.20.025

Diathermy is the therapeutic use of a high-frequency current to generate heat within some part of the body.

NOTE: The frequency is greater than the maximum frequency for neuromuscular response, and ranges from several hundred thousand to millions of cycles per second.

Autocondensation   80.20.030

Autocondensation is a method of applying high-frequency currents for therapeutic purposes, in which the patient constitutes one plate of a capacitor.

Autoconduction   80.20.035

Autoconduction is a method of applying high-frequency currents for therapeutic purposes by electromagnetic induction, the patient being placed inside a large solenoid and constituting the secondary of a transformer.

High-Frequency Treatment   80.20.040

(D'Arsonvalism)*

High-frequency treatment is the therapeutic use of intermittent and isolated trains of heavily damped oscillations of high frequency, high voltage and relatively low current.

---

* Deprecated.

Faradism   80.20.045

Faradism is the therapeutic use of an interrupted electric current to stimulate muscles and nerves. Such a current is derived from an induction coil, usually from the secondary though occasionally from the primary.

Galvanism   80.20.050

Galvanism is the therapeutic use of direct current.

Phoresis   80.20.055

Phoresis is the migration of ions through a membrane by the action of an electric current.

NOTE: The direction of migration is sometimes distinguished by the use of the terms "cataphoresis" and "anaphoresis" for migrations toward cathode and anode respectively.

Medical Ionization   80.20.070

(Ionic Medication)

Medical ionization is the therapeutic use of an electric current for the purpose of introducing ions of soluble salts into the tissues.

See 80.20.055.

Electrodesiccation   80.20.075

(Fulguration)*

Electrodesiccation is the destruction of animal tissue by high-frequency electric sparks whose action is controlled by a movable electrode.

Faradization   80.20.080

Faradization is the treatment of nerves or muscles with faradic current.

GROUP 80—ELECTROBIOLOGY INCLUDING ELECTROTHERAPEUTICS

Section 25—Kinds of Current

Static Induced Current   80.25.005

A static induced current is the charging and discharging current of a pair of Leyden jars or other capacitors, which current is passed through a patient.

Static Wave Current   80.25.010

A static wave current is the current resulting from the sudden periodic discharging of a patient who has been raised to a high potential by means of an electrostatic generator.

Galvanic Current   80.25.015

A galvanic current is a steady unidirectional current.

Leduc Current   80.25.020

A Leduc current is an interrupted direct current, each pulse of which is approximately of the same current strength and same duration.

Faradic Current   80.25.025

A faradic current is an intermittent asymmetric alternating current obtained from the secondary winding of an induction coil.

D'Arsonval Current   80.25.030

A D'Arsonval current is a high-frequency, low-voltage current of comparatively high amperage.

Oudin Current   80.25.035

An Oudin current is a high-frequency current of very high voltage.

Tesla Current   80.25.040

A Tesla current is a high-frequency current having a voltage which is high, but intermediate between an Oudin current and a D'Arsonval current.

Morton Wave Current   80.25.045

A Morton wave current is an interrupted current obtained from a static machine by applying to the part to be treated a flexible metal electrode connected to the positive terminal of the machine, the negative terminal being grounded and a suitable spark gap being employed between the terminals.

Direct Vacuum Tube Current   80.25.050

A direct vacuum tube current is a current obtained from a direct-current source by applying to the part to be treated a vacuum electrode connected to one terminal of the source, the other terminal being grounded.

GROUP 80—ELECTROBIOLOGY INCLUDING ELECTROTHERAPEUTICS

Section 30—Kinds of Discharge

Brush Discharge   80.30.005

A brush discharge is the discharge from a static machine (or less commonly from a high-frequency apparatus) having a disruptoconvective character.

Convective Discharge   80.30.010

A convective discharge is the discharge through the air from a high-voltage source in the form of visible or invisible streams of charged particles.

Disruptive Discharge   80.30.015

A disruptive discharge is the passage of current through an insulating medium due to the breakdown of the medium under the electrostatic stress.

Effluve   80.30.020

An effluve is the convective discharge of high current through a dielectric.

Static Breeze   80.30.025

(Static Brush)

A static breeze is the brush discharge as used in therapy.

---

* Deprecated.

GROUP 80—ELECTROBIOLOGY INCLUDING ELECTROTHERAPEUTICS
Section 40—Apparatus

Electrophorus 80.40.005

An electrophorus is a non-rotating apparatus for obtaining static electricity by means of induction.

Oudin Resonator 80.40.010

An Oudin resonator is a coil of wire with an adjustable number of turns, designed to be connected to a source of high-frequency current, such as a spark gap and induction coil, for the purpose of applying an effluve to a patient.

Spark Ball 80.40.015

A spark ball is a metallic ball at the end of an insulating handle; it is used in applying electric sparks.

Point Electrode 80.40.020

A point electrode is an electrode with an insulating handle at one end and a metallic point at the other for use in applying electric sparks.

Detonating Chamber 80.40.025

A detonating chamber is a muffler surrounding the discharge balls of a static machine or resonator to deaden the sound of a spark discharge.

Electrocautery 80.40.030

An electrocautery is an apparatus for cauterizing tissue, consisting of a holder supporting a wire, which may be heated to a red or white heat by a current of electricity.

Hook-Up 80.40.035

A hook-up is the arrangement of circuits, electrodes and apparatus used in giving any particular treatment.

Electrolyzer 80.40.040

An electrolyzer is a device for reducing urethral stricture with the aid of electricity.

GROUP 95—MISCELLANEOUS

SECTIONS

05 General
10 Interior Wiring
15 Accessories to Interior Wiring
25 Insulation
30 Thermoelectricity
35 Appliances (Including Portable)

50 Signaling Equipment
55 Miscellaneous Equipment
70 Lightning and Lightning Rods
90 Qualifying Terms
95 Not Otherwise Classified

Section 05—General

Distinctive Features   95.05.020

Distinctive features are exclusive elements of a design which are characteristic or which are not common to other designs.

Reconstruction   95.05.025

Reconstruction is the replacement or rearrangement of any portion of an existing installation by new equipment or construction. It does not include ordinary maintenance replacements.

Utilization Equipment   95.05.030

Utilization equipment is equipment, devices and connected wiring which utilize electric energy for mechanical, chemical, heating, lighting, testing or similar purposes and which are not a part of supply equipment, supply lines or communication lines.

Voltage (of a circuit)   95.05.035

Voltage is the greatest effective difference of potential between any two conductors of the circuit concerned.

Voltage to Ground

See **35.15.025**.

GROUP 95—MISCELLANEOUS

Section 10—Interior Wiring

Master Service   95.10.015

Master service is a service supplying the service equipment which supplies a group of buildings under one management.

Mains (in interior wiring)   95.10.020

Mains are the conductors extending from the service switch, generator bus or converter bus to the main distribution center.

Feeder (in interior wiring)   95.10.025

A feeder is a set of conductors originating at a main distribution center, and supplying one or more secondary distribution centers, one or more branch-circuit distribution centers, or any combination of these two types of equipment.

Lighting Feeder   95.10.030

A lighting feeder is a feeder supplying principally a lighting load.

Power Feeder   95.10.035

A power feeder is a feeder supplying principally a power or heating load.

Sub-Feeder   95.10.040

A sub-feeder is a set of conductors originating at a distribution center other than the main distribution center, and supplying one or more branch-circuit distribution centers.

Branch Circuit   95.10.045

A branch circuit is that portion of a wiring system extending beyond the final automatic overload protective device of the circuit.

Lighting Branch Circuits   95.10.050

Lighting branch circuits are circuits supplying energy to lighting outlets only.

Appliance Branch Circuits   95.10.055

Appliance branch circuits are circuits supplying energy either to permanently wired appliances or to attachment-plug receptacles, that is, appliance or convenience outlets or to a combination of permanently wired appliances and additional attachment-plug outlets on the same circuit; such circuits to have no permanently connected lighting fixtures.

Combination Lighting and Appliance Branch Circuits   95.10.060

Combination lighting and appliance branch circuits are circuits supplying energy to both lighting outlets and appliance outlets.

Motor Branch Circuit   95.10.065

A motor branch circuit is a branch circuit supplying energy only to motors.

Distribution Center   95.10.070

A distribution center is a point at which is located

equipment consisting generally of automatic overload protective devices connected to buses, the principal functions of which are subdivision of supply and the control and protection of feeders, sub-feeders or branch circuits, or any combination of feeders, sub-feeders or branch circuits.

Main Distribution Center 95.10.075

A main distribution center is a distribution center supplied directly by mains.

Feeder Distribution Center 95.10.080

A feeder distribution center is a distribution center at which feeders or sub-feeders are supplied.

Branch-Circuit Distribution Center 95.10.085

A branch-circuit distribution center is a distribution center at which branch circuits are supplied.

Outlet 95.10.090

An outlet is a point on the wiring system at which current is taken to supply fixtures, lamps, heaters, motors or current-consuming equipment generally.

NOTE: The use of the term outlet for a point in the wiring system where a switch is located is deprecated, unless qualified to make the meaning clear.

Lighting Outlet 95.10.095

A lighting outlet is an outlet intended for the direct connection of a lampholder, a lighting fixture or a pendant cord terminating in a lampholder.

Receptacle Outlet 95.10.100

A receptacle outlet is an outlet intended to be equipped with one or more receptacles, not of the screw-shell type; or to be provided with one or more points of attachment within one foot intended to receive attachment-plug caps.

Raceway 95.10.105

(Conduit)*

A raceway is any channel for holding wires or cables, which is designed expressly and used solely for this purpose.

NOTE: Raceways may be of metal, wood or insulating material, and the term includes a rigid metal conduit, flexible metal conduit, electrical metal tubing, cast-in-place raceways, under-floor raceways, surface metal raceways, surface wooden raceways, wireways, busways and auxiliary gutters.

Rigid Steel Conduit 95.10.115

A rigid steel conduit is a raceway specially constructed for the purpose of pulling in or withdrawing of wires or of cables after the conduit is in place and made of mild steel pipe of standard weight and thickness permitting cutting standard threads, that has been cleaned of scale and rust, and has enamel and/or metallic corrosion-resistant coatings.

Flexible Metal Conduit 95.10.120

A flexible metal conduit is a flexible raceway of circular cross-section specially constructed for the purpose

* Deprecated.

of permitting drawing in or withdrawing of wires and cables after the conduit and its fittings are in place, and is made of metal strip, usually of steel with metallic corrosion-resistant coating, helically wound and with interlocking edges.

Electrical Metal Tubing 95.10.125

Electrical metal tubing is a thin-walled steel raceway of circular cross-section, constructed for the purpose of pulling in or withdrawing wires after it is installed in place, coated inside and out to be corrosion-resistant and connected by means of threadless fittings.

Surface Metal Raceway 95.10.130

(Metal Molding)

A surface metal raceway is an assembly of backing and capping made of metal suitably coated to be corrosion-resistant, and having an interior finish designed to avoid abrasion of the insulation of the electric conductors which it contains.

Surface Wooden Raceway 95.10.135

(Wood Molding)

A surface wooden raceway is an assembly of backing and capping made of wood which has been coated with waterproofing or impregnated with a moisture repellent, and in which the channels for individual wires are separated by a barrier.

Armored Cable (in interior wiring) 95.10.140

An armored cable is a fabricated assembly of rubber-covered conductors and a flexible metallic corrosion-resistant covering.

NOTE: Armored cable for interior wiring has its flexible outer sheath or armor formed of metal strip, helically wound and with interlocking edges. Armored cable is usually circular in cross-section but may be oval or flat and may have a thin lead sheath between the armor and the conductors to exclude moisture, oil, etc., where such protection is needed.

Non-Metallic Sheathed Cable 95.10.145

A non-metallic sheathed cable is an assembly of two or more rubber-covered conductors in an outer sheath of non-conducting fibrous material which has been treated to make it flame-resistant and moisture-repellent.

Flexible Tubing 95.10.150

(Loom)

A flexible tubing is a mechanical protection for electric conductors which consists of a flexible circular tube having a smooth interior and a single or double wall of non-conducting fibrous material treated to make it flame-resistant and moisture-repellent.

Cleat 95.10.205

A cleat is an assembly of two pieces of insulating material provided with grooves for holding one or more conductors at a definite spacing from the surface wired over and from each other, and with screw holes for fastening in position.

Knob 95.10.210

A knob is an insulator, in one or two pieces, having a

central hole for a nail or screw, and one or more peripheral grooves for wire, used for supporting conductors at a definite spacing from the surface wired over.

Tube 95.10.215

A tube is a hollow cylindrical piece of porcelain, usually unglazed, having a head or shoulder at one end, through which an electric conductor is threaded where passing through a wall, floor, ceiling, joist, stud, etc.

Coupling 95.10.225

A coupling is a short piece of raceway intended to connect two lengths of rigid metal conduit or other metal raceway or perform a similar function.

Nipple 95.10.230

A nipple is a straight piece of rigid metal conduit not more than two feet in length and threaded on each end.

Bend 95.10.235

A bend is a short curved piece of rigid conduit or other metal raceway which serves to connect the ends of two adjacent lengths of conduit which are at an angle to one another or perform a similar function.

Elbow 95.10.240

(Sharp Bend)

An elbow is a bend of comparatively short radius.

NOTE: This term is usually applied when the angle is 90 degrees but may be applied for angles as small as 15 degrees.

Fitting 95.10.244

A fitting is an accessory (such as a locknut or bushing) to a wiring system which is intended primarily to perform a mechanical rather than an electrical function.

Conduit Fittings 95.10.245

Conduit fittings are the accessories necessary for the completion of a conduit system, such as boxes, bushings and access fittings.

Split Fitting 95.10.250

A split fitting is a conduit fitting split longitudinally so that it can be placed in position after the wires have been drawn into the conduit, the two parts being held together by screws or other device.

Access Fitting 95.10.255

An access fitting is a fitting permitting access to the conductors in a concealed or enclosed type of wiring elsewhere than at an outlet.

Cabinet 95.10.260

A cabinet is an enclosure designed either for surface or flush mounting, and provided with a frame, mat or trim in which swinging doors are hung.

See 95.10.265.

Cutout Box 95.10.265

A cutout box is an enclosure designed for surface mounting and having swinging doors or covers secured directly to and telescoping with the walls of the box proper.

See 95.10.260.

Conduit Box 95.10.270

A conduit box is a metal box adapted for connection to conduit for the purpose of facilitating wiring, making connections, mounting devices, etc.

Pull Box 95.10.275

A pull box is a metal box with a blank cover which is inserted in a run of conduit, raceway or tubing to facilitate pulling in the conductors, or which is installed at the termination of one or more runs of conduit, raceway, tubing or wireway for the purpose of distributing the conductors.

Junction Box 95.10.280

A junction box is a metal box with a blank cover which serves the purpose of joining different runs of conduit, tubing, wireway or other raceway, and provides space for the connection and branching of the enclosed conductors.

See 35.70.050.

Conductor Support Box 95.10.285

A conductor support box is a metal box which is inserted in a vertical run of conduit, raceway, tubing or wireway to give access to the conductors for the purpose of providing supports for them.

Equipment Box 95.10.290

An equipment box is a metal box designed for housing electric equipment and provided with one or more doors attached directly to the box, or attached to a trim or cover which does not surround the door or doors.

Knockout 95.10.295

A knockout is a portion of the wall of a box or cabinet so fashioned that it may be removed readily by the blow of a hammer at the time of installation in order to provide a hole, usually circular in shape, for the entrance of wires or the attachment of conduit, cable, etc.

Splice 95.10.305

(Straight-Through Joint)

A splice is a joint used for connecting in series two lengths of conductor or cable.

Tee Joint

(Tap)

See 35.70.200.

Looping-In (in interior wiring) 95.10.315

Looping-in is a method of avoiding tee joints by carrying the conductor to and from the point to be supplied.

Friction Tape 95.10.405

Friction tape is a cotton tape impregnated with a sticky, moisture-repellent compound.

Insulating Joint 95.10.410

An insulating joint is a coupling or joint used to insulate electrically adjacent pieces of conduit, pipes, rods, lighting fixtures, etc., from each other while mechanically connecting them.

Rosette   95.10.415

A rosette is an enclosure of porcelain or other insulating material, fitted with terminals and intended for connecting the flexible cord carrying a pendant to the permanent wiring.

Lampholder   95.10.420

(Socket) (Lamp Receptacle)

A lampholder is a device intended to support an electric lamp mechanically and connect it electrically to circuit wires.

Receptacle   95.10.425

(Convenience Receptacle)

A receptacle is a contact device installed at an outlet for the connection of a portable lamp or appliance by means of a plug and flexible cord.

Fuse Holder   95.10.430

(Cutout Base)

A fuse holder is the supporting device which is mounted in an electric circuit for the purpose of carrying a fuse and providing connections for its terminals.

Sealable Equipment   95.10.450

Sealable equipment is equipment so arranged or enclosed that it may be sealed or locked to prevent operation and/or access to live parts.

NOTE: Enclosed equipment may or may not be operable without opening the enclosure.

GROUP 95—MISCELLANEOUS

Section 15—Accessories to Interior Wiring

Plug   95.15.005

(Plug Adaptor)*

A plug is a device, which, by insertion in a receptacle, establishes connection between the conductors of the attached cord and the conductors connected permanently to the receptacle.

Current Tap   95.15.010

(Plug Cluster)*

A current tap is an assembly in one device of a plug and two or more sockets and/or receptacles electrically connected, usually in parallel.

Hickey   95.15.015

A hickey is a fitting used to mount a lighting fixture in an outlet box or on a pipe or stud. It has openings through which fixture wires may be brought out of the fixture stem.

Snake   95.15.020

(Fishing Wire)

A snake is a tempered steel wire, usually of rectangular cross-section, which is pushed through a run of conduit, or through an inaccessible space, such as a partition, and used for drawing in the wires.

Binding Screw   95.15.025

(Binding Post) (Terminal Screw) (Clamping Screw)

A binding screw is a screw for holding a conductor to the terminal of a switch, rosette, lampholder or other electric apparatus.

Insulated Screw Eye   95.15.030

An insulated screw eye is a screw terminating in an insulated eye through which flexible cords or wires for signaling purposes may be run and supported.

Insulated Clip   95.15.035

An insulated clip is a clip terminating in an insulated

eye through which flexible cords or wires for signaling purposes may be run and supported.

Insulated Hook   95.15.040

An insulated hook is a hook terminating in an insulated eye through which flexible cords or wires for signaling purposes may be run and supported.

Pendant   95.15.045

A pendant is a fitting which is suspended from overhead either by means of the flexible cord carrying the current or otherwise.

Rise-and-Fall Pendant   95.15.050

A rise-and-fall pendant is a pendant the height of which can be regulated by means of a cord adjuster.

Cord Adjuster   95.15.055

A cord adjuster is a device for altering the pendant length of the flexible cord of a pendant.

NOTE: This device may be a ratchet reel, a pulley and counterweight, a tent-rope stick, etc.

Cord Grip   95.15.060

A cord grip is a device by means of which the flexible cord entering a lampholder or other accessory is gripped in order to relieve the terminals from tension in the cord.

Fixture Stud   95.15.065

(Stud)

A fixture stud is a fitting used to mount a lighting fixture in an outlet box. The stud is fastened to the box and the fixture is fastened to the stud by a hickey.

Crowfoot   95.15.070

A crowfoot is a fitting used to mount a lighting fixture. It has female threads mounted away from the supporting surface, and openings through which fixture wires may be brought out.

NOTE: The use of outlet boxes at all outlets has resulted in obsolescence of the crowfoot.

---

* Deprecated.

GROUP 95—MISCELLANEOUS
Section 25—Insulation

Hevea Rubber   95.25.005

Hevea rubber is rubber from the Hevea Brasiliensis tree.

NOTE: Compounds containing 30 to 40 percent of Hevea rubber have electrical and mechanical properties superior to compounds insulated in accordance with the requirements of the National Electrical Code.

Class A Insulation   95.25.010

Class A insulation consists of: (1) cotton, silk, paper and similar organic materials when either impregnated† or immersed in a liquid dielectric; (2) molded and laminated materials with cellulose filler, phenolic resins and other resins of similar properties; (3) films and sheets of cellulose acetate and other cellulose derivatives of similar properties; and (4) varnishes (enamel) as applied to conductors.

Class B Insulation   95.25.015

Class B insulation consists of mica, asbestos, fiber glass and similar inorganic materials in built-up form with organic binding substances. A small proportion of Class A materials may be used for structural purposes only.††

Class C Insulation   95.25.020

Class C insulation consists entirely of mica, porcelain, glass, quartz and similar inorganic materials.

Class O Insulation   95.25.025

Class O insulation consists of cotton, silk, paper and similar organic materials when neither impregnated† nor immersed in a liquid dielectric.

GROUP 95—MISCELLANEOUS
Section 30—Thermoelectricity

Thermocouple   95.30.005

A thermocouple is a pair of dissimilar conductors so joined as to produce a thermoelectric effect.
See 05.50.080.

Thermojunction   95.30.010

A thermojunction is the point of contact of a pair of conductors forming a thermocouple.

Thermopile   95.30.015

A thermopile is a group of thermocouples assembled so as to act jointly as a source of electric energy.

GROUP 95—MISCELLANEOUS
Section 35—Appliances (Including Portable)

Appliance   95.35.005

Appliance is a current-consuming equipment, fixed or portable, such as heating or motor-operated equipment.

Portable Appliance   95.35.010

A portable appliance is an appliance which can be carried readily from place to place and which can be served by means of a flexible extension cord and attachment plug.

Hot Plate   95.35.015

A hot plate is an appliance fitted with heating elements and arranged to support a flat-bottomed utensil containing the material to be heated.

Space Heater   95.35.020

A space heater is a heater without reflector or other means of directing its output of heat, which is dissipated mainly by convection and conduction.

† An insulation is considered to be "impregnated" when a suitable substance replaces the air between its fibers, even if this substance does not completely fill the spaces between the insulated conductors. The impregnating substances in order to be considered suitable, must have good insulating properties; must entirely cover the fibers and render them adherent to each other and to the conductor; must not produce interstices within itself as a consequence of evaporation of the solvent or through any other cause; must not flow during the operation of the machine at full working load or at the temperature limit specified; and must not unduly deteriorate under prolonged action of heat.

†† The electrical and mechanical properties of the insulated winding must not be impaired by application of the temperature permitted for Class B material. (The word "impair" is here used in the sense of causing any change which could disqualify the insulating material for continuous service.) The temperature endurance of different Class B insulation assemblies varies over a considerable range, in accordance with the percentage of Class A materials employed, and the degree of dependence placed on the organic binder for maintaining the structural integrity of the insulation.

Radiant Heater   95.35.025

A radiant heater is an electric heating appliance having an exposed incandescent heating element.

Reflector (of a heating appliance)   95.35.030

A reflector is a device, generally constructed of bright metal, so fitted to electric heating apparatus as to direct the radiant heat from the elements in any given direction.

Heating Element   95.35.035

(Heating Unit)

A heating element is the complete resistor, including the element carrier on which the wire is wound, as used in ovens, electric fires, radiators, etc.

Electric Sign   95.35.040

An electric sign is a fixed or portable self-contained electrically illuminated appliance with words or symbols designed to convey information or attract attention.

GROUP 95—MISCELLANEOUS

Section 50—Signaling Equipment

Electric Bell   95.50.005

(Bell)

An electric bell is a signaling apparatus in which a hammer is actuated electromagnetically so as to strike a gong or bell.

Buzzer   95.50.010

A buzzer is a signaling apparatus similar to an electric bell, but without hammer or gong, and serving to produce sound by the vibration of an armature.

Annunciator   95.50.015

An annunciator is a signaling apparatus operated electromagnetically, and serving to indicate whether a current is flowing or has flowed in one or more circuits. It is usually employed in connection with electric bells or buzzers.

Burglar Alarm   95.50.020

A burglar alarm is an automatic electric signaling device intended to indicate attempted access to the protected premises.

Fire-Alarm Box   95.50.105

A fire-alarm box is a box or cabinet containing the equipment necessary to transmit over an electric circuit to some central point a signal intended to give an alarm of fire.

Municipal Street Fire-Alarm Box   95.50.110

A municipal street fire-alarm box is a fire-alarm box provided for the use of the public.

Master Fire-Alarm Box   95.50.115

(Auxiliarized Fire-Alarm Box)

A master fire-alarm box is a fire-alarm box included in the circuit of municipal street fire-alarm boxes, which can be tripped from a remote point by manual or automatic means.

Auxiliary Fire-Alarm Box   95.50.120

An auxiliary fire-alarm box is a fire-alarm box containing the apparatus necessary to trip a master fire-alarm box from a remote point.

GROUP 95—MISCELLANEOUS

Section 55—Miscellaneous Equipment

Flasher   95.55.010

A flasher is a device for rapidly and automatically lighting and extinguishing electric lamps.

Choke Coil   95.55.015

A choke coil is a coil of low resistance and sufficient inductance to impede definitely alternating or transient currents as distinguished from direct currents or currents of normal frequency.

GROUP 95—MISCELLANEOUS

Section 70—Lightning and Lightning Rods

Lightning

See 20.30.005.

Conductor (for lightning protection)   95.70.010

A conductor is the portion of a protective system designed to carry the current of a lightning discharge from air terminal to ground.

Branch Conductor   95.70.015

A branch conductor is a conductor which branches off at an angle from a continuous run of conductor.

Down Conductor   95.70.020

A down conductor is the vertical portion of a run of conductor which ends at the ground.

Roof Conductor   95.70.025

A roof conductor is the portion of the conductor above the eaves running along the ridge, parapet or other portion of the roof.

Cable (for lightning protection)   95.70.030

A cable is a number of wires twisted or braided to form a conductor.

Elevation Rod (for lightning protection)   95.70.035

An elevation rod is the vertical portion of conductor in an air terminal by means of which it is elevated above the object to be protected.

Air Terminal (for lightning protection)   95.70.040

An air terminal is the combination of elevation rod and brace, or footing placed on upper portions of structures, together with tip or point if used.

Point (for lightning protection)   95.70.045

A point is the pointed piece of metal used at the upper end of the elevation rod to receive a lightning discharge.

Fastener   95.70.050

A fastener is a device used to secure the conductor to the structure which supports it.

Metal-Roofed Building   95.70.060

A metal-roofed building is a building with a roof made of or covered with metal.

Metal-Clad Building   95.70.065

A metal-clad building is a building with sides made of or covered with metal.

Cone of Protection   95.70.070

The cone of protection is the space enclosed by a cone formed with its apex at the highest point of a lightning rod or protecting tower, the diameter of the base of the cone having a definite relation to the height of the rod or tower which has been determined experimentally.

NOTE: This relation depends on the height of the rod and the height of the cloud above the earth. The higher the cloud, the larger the radius of the base of the protecting cone. The ratio of radius of base to height varies approximately from two to four.

Cage   95.70.075

(Faraday Cage)

A cage is a system of non-corrodible wires or cables, forming an enclosing cage, especially over the roof of the tank, and forming an essentially continuous mesh or network over the tank and the protecting roof, this cage including the necessary conductors, which are connected to the tank and to an adequate ground.

Spark Gap

See 05.45.115.

Copper-Clad Steel   95.70.085

Copper-clad steel is steel with a coating of copper welded to it as distinguished from copper-plated or copper-sheathed material.

GROUP 95—MISCELLANEOUS

Section 90—Qualifying Terms

Air (used as a prefix)   95.90.005

The prefix "air" applied to a device which interrupts an electric circuit indicates that the interruption occurs in air.

Oil (used as a prefix)   95.90.010

The prefix "oil" applied to a device which interrupts an electric circuit indicates that the interruption occurs in oil.

Proof (used as a suffix)   95.90.015

Apparatus is designated as splashproof, dustproof, etc., when so constructed, protected or treated that its successful operation is not interfered with when subjected to the specified material or condition.

Resistant (used as a suffix)   95.90.020

Apparatus is designated as moisture-resistant, fume-resistant, etc., when so constructed, protected or treated that it will not be injured readily when subjected to the specified material or condition.

Tight (used as a suffix)   95.90.025

Apparatus is designated as watertight, dust-tight, etc., when so constructed that the enclosing case will exclude the specified material.

Electric†   95.90.030

Electric means containing, producing, arising from, actuated by, or carrying electricity, or designed to carry electricity and capable of so doing.

Examples: Electric eel, energy, motor, vehicle, wave.

Electrical†   95.90.035

Electrical means related to, pertaining to, or associated with electricity, but not having its properties or characteristics.

Examples: Electrical engineer, handbook, insulator, rating, school, unit.

Gasproof   95.90.105

Gasproof means so constructed or protected that the specified gas will not interfere with its successful operation.

Gastight   95.90.110

Gastight means so constructed that the specified gas will not enter the enclosing case under specified conditions of pressure.

† Some dictionaries indicate these terms as synonymous but usage in the electrical engineering field has in general been restricted to the meaning given in the definitions above. It is recognized that there are borderline cases wherein the usage determines the selection.

Fume-Resistant 95.90.115

Fume-resistant means so constructed that it will not be injured readily by the specified fumes.

Vaportight 95.90.120

Vaportight means so enclosed that vapor will not enter the enclosure.

Dustproof 95.90.125

Dustproof means so constructed or protected that the accumulation of dust will not interfere with its successful operation.

Dust-Tight 95.90.130

Dust-tight means so constructed that dust will not enter the enclosing case.

Moisture-Repellent 95.90.135

Moisture-repellent means so constructed or treated that moisture will not penetrate.

Moisture-Resistant 95.90.140

Moisture-resistant means so constructed or treated that it will not be injured readily by exposure to a moist atmosphere.

Watertight 95.90.145

Watertight means provided with an enclosing case which will exclude water applied in the form of a hose stream for a specified time.

NOTE: A common form of specification for "watertight" is: "so constructed that a stream of water from a hose (1 inch in diameter) under a head of about 35 feet and from a distance of 10 feet can be played on the apparatus for five minutes without penetration of water into the interior".

Drip-Proof 95.90.150

Drip-proof means so constructed or protected that its successful operation is not interfered with when subjected to falling moisture or dirt.

Driptight 95.90.155

Driptight means so constructed or protected as to exclude falling moisture or dirt.

Splashproof 95.90.160

Splashproof means so constructed and protected that external splashing will not interfere with its successful operation.

Acid-Resistant 95.90.165

Acid-resistant means so constructed that it will not be injured readily by exposure to acid fumes.

Sleetproof 95.90.170

Sleetproof means so constructed or protected that the accumulation of sleet will not interfere with its successful operation.

Raintight 95.90.175

(Weathertight)

Raintight means so constructed or protected that exposure to a beating rain will not result in the entrance of water.

Weatherproof (applied to conductor covering) 95.90.180

Weatherproof means made up of braids of fibrous material, which are thoroughly impregnated with a dense moistureproof compound after they have been placed on the conductor, or an equivalent protective covering designed to withstand weather conditions.

Weatherproof 95.90.185

(Outdoor)

Weatherproof means so constructed or protected that exposure to the weather will not interfere with its successful operation.

Indoor (used as a prefix) 95.90.190

The prefix "indoor" means not suitable for exposure to the weather.

Outdoor (used as a prefix) 95.90.192

The prefix "outdoor" means designed for outdoor service.

Submersible 95.90.195

(Immersible) *

Submersible means so constructed that it will operate successfully when submerged in water under specified conditions of pressure and time.

Metal-Clad 95.90.205

Metal-clad means that the conducting parts are entirely enclosed in a metal casing.

Enclosed 95.90.210

(Inclosed)

Enclosed means surrounded by a case which will prevent accidental contact of a person with live parts.

Semi-Enclosed 95.90.215

(a) Semi-enclosed means having the ventilating openings in the frame protected with wire screen, expanded metal, or perforated covers.

(b) Semi-enclosed means having a solid enclosure except for a slot for an operating handle or small openings for ventilation, or both.

Totally Enclosed 95.90.220

Totally enclosed means so enclosed as to prevent circulation of air between the inside and the outside of the case, but not necessarily sufficiently to be termed airtight.

Ventilated 95.90.225

Ventilated means provided with a means to permit circulation of the air sufficiently to remove an excess of heat, fumes or vapors.

Enclosed Ventilated Apparatus 95.90.230

Enclosed ventilated apparatus is apparatus totally enclosed except that openings are provided for the admission and discharge of the cooling air.

NOTE: These openings may be so arranged that inlet and outlet ducts or pipes may be connected to them.

An enclosed ventilated apparatus or machine may be separately ventilated or self-ventilated.

Explosion-Proof Apparatus 95.90.235

Explosion-proof apparatus is apparatus capable of

* Deprecated.

withstanding an internal explosion of a specified mixture without emission of flame.

Flameproof Apparatus   95.90.240

Flameproof apparatus is apparatus so treated that it will not maintain a flame or will not be injured readily when subjected to flame.

Fire-Resistant   95.90.245

(Fire-Resistive)

Fire-resistant means so constructed or treated that it will not be injured readily by exposure to fire.

Accessible (as applied to wiring methods)   95.90.305

Accessible means not permanently closed in by the structure or finish of the building; capable of being removed without disturbing the building structure or finish.

Accessible (as applied to equipment)   95.90.310

Accessible means admitting close approach because not guarded by locked doors, elevation or other effective means.

See **95.90.315**.

Readily Accessible   95.90.315

Readily accessible means capable of being reached quickly, for operation, renewal or inspection, without requiring those to whom ready access is requisite to climb over or remove obstacles or to resort to portable ladders, chairs, etc.

Exposed (as applied to equipment)   95.90.320

Exposed means that an object or device can be inadvertently touched or approached nearer than a safe distance by any person. It is applied to objects not suitably guarded or isolated.

Exposed (as applied to wiring methods)   95.90.325

Exposed means accessible; not concealed.

Isolated   95.90.330

Isolated means that an object is not readily accessible to persons unless special means for access are used.

Isolated by Elevation   95.90.335

Isolated by elevation means elevated sufficiently so that persons may walk safely underneath.

Guarded   95.90.340

Guarded means covered, shielded, fenced, enclosed, or otherwise protected, by means of suitable covers or casings, barrier rails or screens, mats or platforms, to remove the likelihood of dangerous contact or approach by persons or objects to a point of danger.

Concealed   95.90.345

Concealed means rendered inaccessible by the structure or finish of the building. Wires in concealed raceways are considered concealed, even though they may become accessible by withdrawing them.

Impregnated (as applied to fibrous insulation)   95.90.350

Impregnated means that a suitable substance replaces the air between its fibers, even though this substance does not fill completely the spaces between the insulated conductors.

NOTE: To be considered suitable, the impregnating substance must have good insulating properties, must cover the fibers and render them adherent to each other and to the conductor.

Insulated   95.90.355

Insulated means separated from other conducting surfaces by a dielectric permanently offering a high resistance to the passage of current and to disruptive discharge.

NOTE: When any object is said to be insulated, it is understood to be insulated in suitable manner for the conditions to which it is subjected.

Insulating   95.90.360

Insulating means (where applied to the covering of a conductor, or to clothing, guards, rods and other safety devices) that a device, when interposed between a person and current-carrying parts, protects the person making use of it against electric shock from the current-carrying parts with which the device is intended to be used; the opposite of conducting.

Externally Operable   95.90.365

Externally operable means capable of being operated without exposing the operator to contact with live parts.

NOTE: This term is applied to equipment, such as a switch, that is enclosed in a case or cabinet.

Alive   95.90.405

(Live)

Alive means electrically connected to a source of potential difference, or electrically charged so as to have a potential different from that of the earth.

NOTE: The term "live" is sometimes used in place of the term "current-carrying", where the intent is clear, to avoid repetitions of the longer term.

Dead   95.90.410

Dead means free from any electric connection to a source of potential difference and from electric charge; not having a potential different from that of the earth. The term is used only with reference to current-carrying parts which are sometimes alive.

Manual   95.90.415

Manual means capable of being operated by personal intervention only.

Automatic   95.90.420

Automatic means self-acting, operating by its own mechanism when actuated by some impersonal influence, as, for example, a change in current strength; not manual, without personal intervention.

NOTE: Remote control that requires personal intervention is not automatic, but manual.

Substantial   95.90.425

Substantial means so constructed and arranged as to be of adequate strength and durability for the service to be performed under the prevailing conditions.

Qualified   95.90.430

Qualified means familiar with the construction and operation of the apparatus and the hazards involved.

GROUP 95—MISCELLANEOUS

Section 95—Not Otherwise Classified

Loop Test   95.95.005

Loop test is a method of testing employed to locate a fault in the insulation of a conductor when the conductor can be arranged to form part of a closed circuit or loop.

Insulated Bolt   95.95.015

Insulated bolt is a bolt provided with insulation.

Isolated Plant   95.95.020

An isolated plant is an electric installation deriving energy from its own generator driven by a prime mover, and not serving the purpose of a public utility.

Qualified Person   95.95.025

A qualified person is one familiar with the construction and operation of the apparatus and the hazards involved.

Solid Enclosure   95.95.030

A solid enclosure is one which will neither admit accumulations of flyings or dust nor transmit sparks or flying particles to the accumulations outside.

INDEX

A

H

INDEX